GW00578341

Politics and People
in Revolutionary England

Politics and People
in Revolutionary England

ESSAYS IN HONOUR OF
IVAN ROOTS

EDITED BY
Colin Jones, Malyn Newitt
and Stephen Roberts

BASIL BLACKWELL

© Basil Blackwell Ltd 1986

First published 1986

Basil Blackwell Ltd
108 Cowley Road, Oxford OX4 1JF, UK

Basil Blackwell Inc.
432 Park Avenue South, Suite 1503,
New York, NY 10016, USA

British Library Cataloguing in Publication Data

Politics and people in revolutionary
    England : essays in honour of Ivan Roots.
    1. Great Britain—Politics and
    government—1603–1714
    I. Jones, Colin   II. Newitt, Malyn
    III. Roberts, Stephen   IV. Roots, Ivan
    320.942   JN191
    ISBN 0–631–14613–X

Library of Congress Cataloging in Publication Data

Politics and people in revolutionary England.

    Includes index.
    1. Great Britain—History—Puritan Revolution,
    1642–1660.   2. Great Britain—Politics and government—1642–1660.
    3. Roots, Ivan Alan.   I. Roots, Ivan Alan.
    II. Jones, Colin, 1947–   III. Newitt, M. D. D.
    IV. Roberts, Stephen, 1950–
    DA405.P59   1986   941.06   86–6801
    ISBN 0–631–14613–X

Typeset by Freeman Graphic, Tonbridge, Kent
Printed in Great Britain by The Bath Press, Avon

Contents

Acknowledgements

The editors would like to acknowledge the help of the following whose advice proved of great value in the preparation of this book: Jonathan Barry, Bob Helps, Ann Hughes and Sarah Jones. The map was drawn by Seàn Goddard in the Department of History and Archaeology at Exeter University.

Abbreviations

A & O	*Acts and Ordinances of the Interregnum, 1642–1660*, ed. C. H. Firth and R. S. Rait (3 vols, London, 1911)
Add.	Additional
BL	British Library
Bodl.	Bodleian Library
CJ	*Commons Journals*
Clarendon State Papers	Edward Hyde, Earl of Clarendon, *State Papers* (3 vols, Oxford, 1767–86)
DNB	*Dictionary of National Biography*
HMC	*Historical Manuscripts Commission Reports*
Rushworth, *Historical Collections*	John Rushworth, *Historical Collections of Private Passages of State* . . . (London, 1659–1701)
LJ	*Lords Journals*
NLW	National Library of Wales
PH	*Parliamentary or Constitutional History of England . . . collected by several hands* (London, 1751–62)

Pléiade	Cardinal de Retz, *Oeuvres*, Pléiade edn, ed. M. T. Hipp and M. Pernot (Paris, 1984)
PRO	Public Record Office
RO	Record Office
Thurloe State Papers	*A Collection of the State Papers of John Thurloe*, ed. T. Birch (7 vols, Oxford, 1742)
TRHS	*Transactions of the Royal Historical Society*

Ivan Roots

DONALD PENNINGTON

Ivan Alan Roots was born in 1921 at Maidstone, Kent. I am not sure that the place was well chosen; for though his native town and his family were always dear to him, he seemed by nature to belong to the provinces rather than to the Home Counties. When he arrived at Balliol in 1938, an Exhibitioner in History from Maidstone Grammar School, he was drawn at once to those outside the circles of rich descendants and future cabinet ministers who abounded in the college at the time. It was the year in which Christopher Hill returned to Balliol as a fellow; and round him radical historians gathered. Ivan was, like most enemies of conservatism and tepid liberalism in those days, a marxist or semi-marxist, though he preferred discussion of the works of Lenin to demonstrations with the workers of Cowley. He hated claims to intellectual certainty. Most of all he hated pomposity, moral superiority and the vaunted tolerance that broke down in the face of real disagreement. But one of Ivan's outstanding qualities was soon evident: he could be on friendly terms with almost everyone.

No-one doubted that Ivan was on the top academic level. He had no liking for rowing or rugger. Indeed, he has always claimed that where physical exertion is threatened he is thoroughly lazy. It was not, however, that history occupied all his time. Literature, and especially poetry was to him an essential part of life. So was the cinema. As Schools approached, he could find it hard to keep on with the boredom of the *Clarendon State Papers* instead of seeing *The Grapes of Wrath* yet again. By that time Christopher Hill had gone to the wars and we studied the Protectorate and Restoration together under the benign but less inspiring tutorship of Mary Coate. (Typically, Ivan remained her friend until her death and long afterwards shared some of her enthusiasm for the south-west.) That Special Subject established his fascination with Cromwell; but it was from Christopher Hill that we first heard of Gerrard Winstanley. The rebel whose lyrical prose called upon the counsellors and powers of the earth to restore the birthright of the poor and oppressed, who denounced the empty promises of men of power and riches – including the 'traditional parrot-like speaking from the universities' – and whose hope was in universal love and reason had for Ivan a powerful appeal. Eleven years later he named his son Gerrard.

In 1941 the first-class degree was duly awarded, and immediately came the army service that took Ivan to India, Burma and the Arakan campaigns. The cramped microfilm letters he was able to send back showed how even from the army he was able to gain an experience of the east that roused new compassions. No-one would have expected him to rise to the top ranks of military power: he would have hated it. But he became a captain and presumably saw something of administration. When the war ended he returned to Balliol for two terms; but in 1946 he gave up the prospect of a higher degree to take an Assistant Lectureship at Cardiff. Within a year he had met and married Tegwyn Williams, who has shared his life and career ever since.

Assistant lecturers in those days were insecure, impoverished and excluded from almost all participation in the running of departments. Ivan bore the frustrations without malice and managed to see the virtues of at least some of the professorial ogres. Exeter in the 1970s must have benefited greatly from the sins of Cardiff in the 1940s. The city, like the college, had its deficiencies in the cultural sphere. He did something to improve matters by his help to the film society, producing brilliant programme-notes that might be ranked as his first published work. And Wales had one unexpected benefit to offer: it was from book sales and auctions around the principality – visited in his monstrous eight-cylinder Wolseley – that he started his collection of historical and literary works. Gradually he became known. His reviewing, begun in the *Western Mail*, spread to a greater variety of periodicals than could now be traced. (What was that 'obscure Irish subversive sheet' for which he admitted to doing a little work?) He became a regular contributor to the *Daily Telegraph* and the *Observer* as well as to the journals of the history trade. His reading for publishers must have helped the careers of many writers and the deserved suppression of a few. He established a position in academic life that has suited him perfectly. He has not aspired to a vast learned output, nor to the scholarship that finds greater truth in even longer footnotes. Least of all would he join an aristocracy of historians preserved by putting down the newcomers. He has preferred to divide his time between expert articles on Cromwellian topics and work that in one way or another has made high-grade history more widely accessible. *The Great Rebellion*, published twenty years ago and now in its fifth edition, became generally recognized as the best one-volume survey of the subject. In form it is narrative rather than analytical, making chaotic events comprehensible partly by the hidden skill of its selection but perhaps mainly by entering so perceptively and sympathetically into the muddled heads of the participants. Ivan revels in writing vividly and choosing in abundance equally vivid quotations; and through this human treatment many of the arguments of more arid social and economic studies somehow emerge. Some of his best work, in early and in later years, has survived obscurely or not at all. There was his dramatic reconstruction of the Battle of Dunbar for the BBC Third Programme in its experimental days; and I wish I could find the text of his broadcast talk on 'Serendipity', revealing his delight in the unexpected recurrence of names and places throughout his vast reading. How many talks he has given to Historical Association meetings and organizations of many kinds is hard to guess: he was soon in wide demand and tried never to refuse a request. But university teaching was always his real vocation. He knew how dismal some old-style courses could be, and contrived to improve them. On the subjects he enjoys, and with the ever-growing number of his postgraduate students, he is obviously an immense success as an unassertive but powerful teacher.

None of this means that he lacks any of the qualities of the scholar. Having shared with him the tedium and the occasional excitement of scrutinizing the trivial and blundering proceedings of the Staffordshire County Committee, I can vouch for his ability to extract the scraps of significance from the verbiage of a manuscript. Mistranscribing a word or even omitting to look up the last conceivable source for identifying a name do not reduce him to despair. Percentages and prices do not inspire him; but what others write in quantitative or sociological terms he takes due note of. The extent of his bibliographical knowledge has been demonstrated in his contributions to the *Annual Bulletin of Historical Literature*, which leave the ignorant wondering how he got so much information.

Gradually Ivan became a distinguished member of the Cardiff faculty. He represented the non-professorial staff on senate and council, observing the unscrupulous manoeuvres of some departmental heads and evidently exercising now and then an effective reforming influence. In 1960–1 he spent a year as visiting professor at Lafayette College, Pennsylvania. Then, in 1967, he was appointed to the chair at Exeter from which he now retires. Cardiff, slowly, had won his affection: he was sad to leave it and goes back when he can. After watching the follies of academic power from the fringes, he was now, inescapably, a man of power himself. He became Dean of Arts, with the consequent membership of a multitude of committees. In what became with his guidance the Department of History and Archaeology he has brought about the changes that would have been expected of him. His liberating influence after the old authoritarian regimes has been appreciated most of all by the younger members, whose careers are one of his prime concerns. The post of Public Orator seemed an unlikely one for such an enemy of formality; but reading some of his tributes to the recipients of honorary degrees shows how successfully he applied his wit and ingenuity to the task. They achieve the required blend of urbane praise with occasional gentle teasing and avoid all the pitfalls of triteness and facetiousness. And the job gave him the chance to meet many of the truly great. The Publications Committee is one that he has found truly worthwhile. The development of Exeter University Publications, including the inauguration of *Exeter Studies in History*, is one large achievement. Exciting too is The Rota, the society he founded with Maurice Goldsmith in 1971, which has made available a superb variety of seventeenth-century writing in edited facsimiles. Never widely advertised, and moderately erratic in its production and distribution arrangements, it has done more than any commercial or academic publisher in enabling the unmonied enthusiast to acquire a collection of known and almost unknown pamphlets.

I suspect Ivan of holding other offices and titles that I do not know about. But there is one that must have pleased him greatly: in 1978 the Cromwell Association chose him as its chairman. Its council, composed of eminent and highly respectable devotees of the great commander and Lord Protector, may not have shared unanimously his vision of their hero. But he had made that vision clear in his address to the society's annual commemoration service in 1971, in terms that say much about Ivan himself. It was not Cromwell's boldness and confidence he admired but his capacity for honest doubt, his indefatigability, his compassion, his true humanity. 'It is for these things above all', he ended, 'that I honour him today.' Much the same could well be said of Ivan Roots.

I

Introduction

STEPHEN ROBERTS

'In history there are many mansions.' Ivan Roots's irenic judgement to a young researcher on a notorious academic bloodletting might serve as a motto on his own career. He belongs to no sect of historians, and no 'ism' could claim him as its own. Colleagues and friends might well feel envious of the ease with which Ivan Roots moves among the historical tabernacles: not to overthrow the tables of the social scientists or to smite hip and thigh, but to encourage, to nurture and to enthuse. Sixth-formers and adult education students have probably seen more of Ivan over the years than have the solemnly ambitious participants in research seminars, and so it is fitting that on the occasion of his retirement he should be presented with a volume of essays which together reflect the diversity of writing on his beloved seventeenth century. No particular view of the period prevails in these pages. The aim of the volume is to highlight current debate rather than to weigh in on any side in current controversy. The chronological focus is firmly on the 1640s and 1650s, and the emphasis is largely, though not exclusively, on British history. This is home ground for Ivan Roots and where he has taught and written for forty years.

Controversy cannot be completely eschewed, however, and like the English Revolution in another characterization, 'revisionism' is the Cheshire Cat here, leaving behind it its 'persistent grin'. Revisionism – the term is defined and assessed in Barry Coward's opening chapter in this collection – is not like the celebrated controversy over the 'rise of the gentry': at least not yet, for revisionists may only now be getting into their stride. So far it seems to be more diffuse and less vital than its precursor of forty years ago, when Ivan Roots's career was beginning. Revisionism is slower and more pervasive, clinging to the edifice of the seventeenth century like wisteria (if you like it) or creeping almost imperceptibly through its structure like dry rot (if you do not). The main timbers so adorned or affected are the significance of parliament, the outbreak of the Civil War, the meaning of the war itself and, most recently, the consequences of the conflict. Recent revisionist writing on the survival of Anglicanism in the late 1640s takes the revision to its latest frontier Finland station. One of its characteristic features – perhaps an inevitable one in any root-and-branch reassessment – is that each new inroad of revisionism leaves the country beyond it more puzzling and difficult to explain than it was before. If the groundswell of conservatism in the late 1640s was so profound, then not only the events of late 1648 and of 1649, but also most recent work on the importance of the Interregnum, are made to seem very puzzling indeed. Most historians who have written recently on the 1650s seem to agree, for example, that the major-generals won more assent than was once thought, and that the House of Cromwell was built on firmer foundations than its critics would have wished. It is not easy to see how these views can be squared with interpretations of the 'Late Troubles' which stress continuity, conservatism, 'normalcy' and the accidents of high politics.

Revisionism does not carry all before it, in fact: the work of Bernard Capp, William Lamont, Barry Reay and J. F. McGregor[1] shows that radical religion is still a fertile Beulah land for historians of the English Revolution. Revisionism is preoccupied with the political history of national elites, with the vagaries of patronage and clientage. Reay has shown how the recipients and dispensers of patronage, the local bosses, were plagued by Quakers and how the Friends came within shouting distance of their political objectives by infiltrating the army in the late 1650s. The eventual result was disaster: fear of Quakers proved more potent than the Quakers themselves, and their 1659 came to look like the Levellers' 1647. Both these dates have come to be seen not as a revolutionary dawn, but as the start of a Thermidorian reaction. In the event, Putney gave the army officers a solidarity they might otherwise have lacked, and in 1659 fear of Quakers hastened a regrouping of the ruling class and thus indirectly led to the Restoration of 1660. Work on radical

[1] For a sample cf. J. F. McGregor and B. Reay (eds), *Radical Religion in the English Revolution* (Oxford, 1984) and C. Hill, B. Reay and W. Lamont (eds), *The World of the Muggletonians* (London, 1983).

religion owes much – in fact, an incalculable amount – to Christopher Hill. What it continues to confirm is how important radical thought was among the 'middling sort', and how crucial was its contribution to the complexion of life in mid-seventeenth-century Britain. This is surely beyond any revisionist challenge.

The significance of the revolution in the development of the British state continues to be reappraised, and one of the contributions to this volume is an attempt to show how the middling sort in at least one county in Wales could come to have a vested interest in the new legislation of the Interregnum. Elsewhere, David Underdown's work on popular culture and political behaviour is a most interesting and ambitious exploration of two areas, and a relationship, not hitherto given the attention they deserve. The result is not encouraging to revisionists: 'The Civil War occurred at the end of a long period of social, political and religious instability . . . Contrasts in popular allegiance had a regional basis and were related to local differences in social structure, economic development and culture.'[2] We have much to learn from economic history.

Another dimension of conflict in seventeenth-century England which deserves more attention than it has so far received is the role of language in political debate. Christopher Hill here shows that how people spoke or formulated their ideas was as important as the ideas and causes fought over, and contributed to the development of those ideas. Revisionist history is 'archivally-sensitive' history, and rightly so. Its practitioners tend to pride themselves on their methodology. An unlooked for by-product of record office rectitude is that some historians seem to believe that a document in the record office is superior to a pamphlet or a book or a poem or a play. Imaginative writing of the century has long been an important vein in Ivan Roots's attempts to discover 'the heart of the matter'. As one would expect from so elegant a stylist, Andrew Marvell and John Dryden, not to mention Gerrard Winstanley and Lady Eleanor Davies, have over the years proved more useful to Roots than has PRO SP 28.

Revisionists have also rightly emphasized the importance of institutions – parliament, the Privy Council, the Church of England – and their role in shaping or reflecting political change, but an important theme addressed by several of our contributors is that of the effectiveness of the state in governing the three (or four) nations.

[2] D. Underdown, *Revel, Riot and Rebellion: Popular politics and culture in England 1603–60* (Oxford, 1985).

How did the government extend its sway over the individual in society? Hugh Trevor-Roper long ago diagnosed a 'general crisis' of relations between European states and the societies they governed. Historians are divided on the significance of the rigours of the 1640s and 1650s. Robert Ashton, and elsewhere J. S. Morrill, have both stressed the 'tyranny' of the parliamentary regime, which on their reckonings established an absolutism more oppressive than that which it came into being to roll back. The acts and ordinances of parliament, occupying 1,500 pages of Firth and Rait's fat edition of them, are a monument to the extension of state powers. Magna Carta broken, juries abolished, popular culture stamped out under the cavalry boot – the images suggest an historically unconscious, brutal regime. Much remains to be said on the other side, however. The provisions of Magna Carta were violated 'at every turn . . . . debarring men from their legal rights of sueing those who had wronged them'.[3] And yet, as Ann Hughes states,[4] the adherents of parliament were very conscious of the conflict between the law and what Cromwell might have called 'cruel necessity'. Moreover, juries and private individuals in the provinces would have formed their views of indemnity cases according to their opinions on the legitimacy of the Civil War itself.

The 1650s saw a great expansion of activity by the state and an extension of its influence into areas of national life. The localities were interfered with more vigorously, and the government acquired finer apparatus for monitoring the behaviour of the population. Administration undoubtedly improved. Nor was this extension of state activity confined to domestic policy. Abroad, trading interests were being extended and developed, as Derek Massarella shows, under the aegis of the Commonwealth and Protectorate governments. In the face of a relentless expansion of government activity, individuals were forced into new relationships with the state. Maurice Goldsmith stresses the common values of Levellers, Diggers and Ranters, but in the cases of the last two at least, historians can only discuss with certainty the views of individuals rather than of collective groups. When we say Diggers we mean Winstanley, and when we say Ranters we mean Coppe and Clarkson. The reactive nature of radical egalitarianism, as of the British radical tradition in general, needs to be emphasized. Levellers, Diggers and Ranters

[3] Robert Ashton, ch. 7 below.
[4] Ann Hughes, 'Parliamentary tyranny? Indemnity proceedings and the impact of the Civil War: a case study from Warwickshire', *Midland History* (forthcoming).

were responding to changes in the state and in the distribution of political power, as were the proponents of ideas about parliamentary tyranny during the reaction against county committees in the late 1640s.

Individuals had to respond to change of bewildering speed and complexity – Jim Sharpe's essay on 'malignant priests' is a valuable example of this in the religious sphere – but there were plenty of developments of a more plainly collective kind during the Revolution too. The armies of parliament and the king were social strata in arms, and as commentators observed at the time, enabled ideas to be disseminated and developed. The existence of royalist armies challenges interpretations of the Civil War which highlight the affinity between the middling sort and the parliamentary armies. Some middling sorts, and in some unlikely places, were undoubtedly royalist. The current debate on the significance of elites in the royalist armies to which Peter Newman's chapter here contributes should be viewed as proof that military history is more than the chronicles of battles and tactics. Ronald Hutton's work on the royalist war effort is a counterpart to J. S. Morrill's findings in *The Revolt of the Provinces*. On the other side, revisionism resurfaces at Putney: a recent view of the New Model Army is that its radicalism was not inherent but was 'only an incidental precondition to the Army's ideology'.[5] Austin Woolrych's essay is a corrective to a full-frontal assault on the concept of the 'Saints in Arms'.

An important concern of Ivan Roots's own work has been parliament, and particularly the parliaments of the 1650s, a decade unwarrantably neglected twenty years ago but now happily much less so. He has, in a number of essays, developed a view of 'Oliver Cromwell and his parliaments' which has been sympathetic to the problems faced by the Lord Protector. The spur to this reappraisal was Hugh Trevor-Roper's rather 'brusque' (Ivan's description) treatment of the theme in the mid-1960s. We now have – from Peter Gaunt – a complementary survey of the First Protectorate Parliament. Some themes will be familiar to readers of Ivan Roots's work. Both authors find much that was positive in the work of the legislature during the 1650s and both feel the verdict of earlier historians to have been carelessly dismissive. One difference between them perhaps is that Gaunt's Cromwell seems more culpable, more responsible both for the breakdown and for the unattractive reputation

[5] M. Kishlansky, *The Rise of the New Model Army* (Cambridge, 1979).

the parliament has acquired. Ivan Roots has tended to view sections of the membership of Interregnum parliaments as bent on their own destruction; in 1659 the Commonwealthsmen were 'their own executioners'. Whoever was responsible for the breakdown of successive parliaments from the dissolution of the Rump onwards, *au fond* there was a chronic and persistent weakness in relations between governments and representative institutions in the Interregnum, which the Civil War had exacerbated, not improved. To explain it, we have to look beyond the mechanics of parliaments themselves and into the sectarian divisions infecting political life, at election time, in the jury chamber or in the courtroom. Parliament did not sit in a vacuum: MPs 'tended . . . to mirror what was going on elsewhere'.[6] And what was going on was divisive and tended to faction. To try to implement the ordinances of governments or the acts of parliaments, to be an agent or a subject of an ordinance, one of the thousands who 'post o'er land and Ocean without rest' was to court unpopularity, abuse and isolation. Equally, to be the victim of a local purge was no less uncomfortable.

To reach new understanding of events in parliaments, historians have opened up what is usually called the 'local dimension' of the seventeenth century. Two persuasive essays by Ivan Roots, with Andrew Marvell brought in to testify, were early contributions to what has since become the 'county community' debate.[7] Ten years ago, the importance of local studies would have needed to be stressed in a volume such as this; by now, the work of local historians has been fully integrated into research on the 'high politics' of the period. Recently, attacks have been launched on the notion of the 'county community', a shorthand term for a view of the English and Welsh provinces which stresses the primacy of the idea of the county in the deliberations of local elites. The county community historians are alleged to have held that each county was ruled by peers and gentry who identified their interests with those of the county, reified as an object of cultural as well as political allegiance. Their county was their 'country', and their loyalties lay there first, to the monarchy or the nation second. It may seem now that to modify the idea of the county community,

---

[6] C. Russell, *Parliaments and English Politics 1621–9* (Oxford, 1979).
[7] I. Roots, 'The central government and the local community', in E. W. Ives (ed.), *The English Revolution 1600–60* (London, 1968), pp. 434–47, and 'Swordsmen and decimators: Cromwell's major-generals', in R. H. Parry (ed.), *The English Civil War and After 1642–58* (London, 1970), pp. 78–92.

the critics have set up a straw man to knock down; what has been under fire has been almost a parody of the original thesis. Conceptual weaknesses in some early contributions to the genre do nothing to diminish the vitality of the work of Alan Everitt and other county historians. County studies are still being written, now with a great deal more sophistication than was open to the pioneers. There are no county community studies in this volume, but several case studies of politics in the localities.

In local studies of the 1650s the problem of consent – as Anthony Fletcher demonstrates in his chapter here – is a predominant theme. On the one hand there is the view of the 1650s regimes as doomed by their failure to win the consent of the local elites or to create enough support to develop beyond a pattern of partisan adherence only. An alternative view also advanced in this volume is that at least in some specific regions and in cases of specific legislation, governments were not only capable of wooing the middling sort but may even have succeeded in winning them, too, and not necessarily with the gentry 'wedded or glued' to them. Most of the evidence and writing so far available supports the former rather than the latter view, it must be admitted, if the focus is on the most notorious points of tension. Elections were one such point. The major-generals' strivings in Suffolk were mirrored elsewhere; and in other places, too, the contests were complicated and difficult to unravel. Elections defy simple analysis at least partly because they challenge the vocabulary of historians. The political manoeuvrings which preceded and accompanied elections, and the alliances and schisms between 1647 and 1656, were numerous and their permutations bewildering. We tend to run out of labels. Paul Pinckney's chapter complements his own earlier pioneering work on Cheshire.

There remain the British perspective and the continental dimension. Ivan Roots has been a localist, but never a parochial one. His interest in seventeenth-century attempts to reshape the British state may have been awakened during his time at University College, Cardiff. He has been concerned to modify the anglocentricity of what should be called the British Revolution, and the success of his Exeter Studies in History volume testifies to the need for an accessible treatment of this theme. He remains, nevertheless, a sceptic on the 'general crisis of the seventeenth century'. Over thirty years ago, Eric Hobsbawm first developed the idea that the monarchies of Europe were disturbed by the same force, and

that upheavals of different scales and with different efficient causes
were still symptoms of the transition from feudalism to capitalism
or proto-capitalism. There followed a highly fruitful debate in the
pages of *Past and Present* beginning with Trevor-Roper's non-
marxist view of a general crisis in the relations between the state
and society, and proceeding to dissect the crisis in many European
countries and socio-economic contexts. Like the 'rise of the gentry'
debate, the small change of the discussion has proved as stimulating as the 'broad sweep' theories being contested. No-one now sees
the history of England as being 'special' or incapable of being
illuminated by comparisons with other European countries. Similarly with the role of actors in the crisis: our understanding of
Oliver Cromwell, 'God's Englishman', as Colin Jones shows, as
well as of French mid-century politics, is enhanced by a study of the
Cardinal de Retz.

This volume celebrates the diversity of writing on the seventeenth century, as well as the breadth of Ivan Roots's scholarly
interests. If the concept of 'total history' ever had any meaning, the
various approaches and persuasions of our contributors suggest
that in the field of seventeenth-century studies, it is as far off as
ever. Ivan Roots's contribution to scholarship has been to explore
that diversity; for him the fascination of a man like Oliver Cromwell lies in the failure of historians to be able to sum him up in a
neat phrase or sobriquet; so let it be with the seventeenth century
itself.

2

Was there an English Revolution in the Middle of the Seventeenth Century?

BARRY COWARD

Since Ivan Roots's antipathy to describing the history of England in the middle of the seventeenth century as 'the English Revolution' is well known,[1] it would be wise to make it clear at the outset that this chapter is not designed to give him apoplexy by maintaining that what happened in England between 1640 and 1660 fits any theoretical model of revolutions. Indeed one of my two main aims is to underline the value of the work of Roots and others warning against exaggerating the revolutionary character of what happened in England in the 1640s and 1650s. The titles of many major books on this period written since the publication of *The Great Rebellion* reflect the new recognition by historians of the contemporary importance of consensus politics, conservatives and conservatism in early seventeenth-century England.[2] One of the major legacies of this corpus of writing has been to show that England underwent no permanent 'revolutionary' changes in the period and that attempts to force explanations of the events that took place between 1640 and 1660 and their consequences into any model of revolutions in general will produce a distorted analysis. However, there is a danger that the trend may be carried too far, so that it too produces an unbalanced interpretation. Reading some recent accounts of the period before 1640 one might be excused for forgetting (at least

---

[1] I. Roots, *The Late Troubles in England*, inaugural lecture (Exeter, 1969), pp. 6–10.

[2] For example, J. S. Morrill, *The Revolt of the Provinces: conservatives and radicals in the English Civil War 1630–50*, 2nd edn (London, 1980), and Robert Ashton, *The English Civil War: conservatives and revolution 1603–49* (London, 1978).

temporarily) that the constitutional crisis of 1640 was only one among other periods of political tension between the crown and the political nation which punctuate the history of late sixteenth- and early seventeenth-century England. Moreover, emphasis on the strength of political and religious conservatism in the 1640s has made it more difficult than before to explain the radical escalation from a constitutional crisis in 1640–1 to civil war in 1642, and thence via army revolt in 1647 to the execution of Charles I and the abolition of monarchy in 1649. There is also a danger of suggesting that the consequences of what happened between 1640 and 1660 were either totally negative or irrelevant in explaining many later developments in England. Therefore, my second main aim here is to suggest that both conservative *and* radical, negative *and* positive, strands ought to be integrated in explanations of the causes, course and consequences of the events of the 1640s and 1650s.

In the rest of this chapter I will use the phrase 'the English Revolution' to describe those events. Although, as I set out to show, there was much about the period that was not revolutionary, other labels are equally one-sided, like 'the Puritan Revolution' and 'the Great Rebellion', or are ambiguous in that they only cover part of the period like 'the Civil War' and 'the Interregnum', or are neutral but cumbersome phrases like the one I have used so far: 'what happened between 1640 and 1660'. My case for keeping the phrase 'the English Revolution' is not so much that the period did see some undeniably revolutionary events, especially in the winter of 1648–9, but that it is the one that is now most widely used by historians writing on the 1640s and 1650s. Those who use it are not necessarily waving an ideological banner, and it need not be a bar to well-rounded and objective historical reappraisals.

THE CAUSES OF THE ENGLISH REVOLUTION

During the last ten years a sustained 'revisionist' offensive has been mounted against existing, well-established explanations of the outbreak of the English Revolution which have maintained that it came about as the inevitable result of long-term changes taking place in the century before 1640. Ironically, the pioneer of this new attack, G. R. Elton, had previously been so aligned with the ortho- dox explanation of the causes of the English Revolution that in his general book *England under the Tudors* he endorsed the views of those like J. E. Neale who claimed that the trends which culminated in the English Revolution originated in the sixteenth century.[3] Elton's conversion to 'revisionism' coincided with his period as president of the Royal Historical Society in the mid-1970s, when he produced a series of presidential addresses which set out a fundamentally different view of sixteenth-century parliamentary history from that developed by Neale. Typically, however, Elton's most forthright attack on Neale's interpretation of Tudor parliaments was reserved for a lecture in December 1978, the J. E. Neale Memorial Lecture, funded by Neale's publishers, delivered in Neale's old college, University College London, and with Lady Neale present in the audience.[4] While Elton was mounting this attack on the traditional view of Tudor parliaments, the main thrust against the orthodox account of early seventeenth-century political history was being developed by Conrad Russell. In a series of articles and especially in his book *Parliaments and English Politics 1612–29* (1979), Russell presents a picture of early Stuart parliaments that is as different from that described by Wallace Notestein as is Elton's character-ization of Tudor parliaments from Neale's.[5]

To Neale and the many historians who were influenced by him, the decision taken by Henry VIII to carry out the dissolution of the monasteries and the break with Rome in the 1530s by parliamen-tary statutes ensured that the Reformation Parliament marked a turning point in the history of parliament's place in the constitu-tion, because it was thought to have awakened among MPs a demand that they and parliament should have a more important permanent place in the government of the country. It was therefore seen to be natural that during the reign of Elizabeth I this 'rise of parliament' should continue, and Neale in his books on Eliza-

---

[3] In his *England under the Tudors* (London, 1955), p. 479, Professor Elton wrote that J. E. Neale's *Elizabeth and her Parliaments* is 'likely to be the last word on the subject'.

[4] G. R. Elton, 'Tudor government: points of contact: I parliament', *TRHS*, 5th ser. 24 (1974); 'Parliament in the sixteenth century: functions and fortunes', *Historical Journal*, 22 (1979).

[5] Conrad Russell, 'Perspectives in parliamentary history 1604–29', *History*, 41 (1976); *Parliaments and English Politics 1621–9* (Oxford, 1979); 'The parliamentary career of John Pym 1621–9', in *The English Commonwealth 1547–1640: Essays presented to Joel Hurstfield*, ed. P. Clark, A. G. R. Smith and N. Tyacke (Leicester, 1979); 'Monarchies, wars and estates in England, France and Spain c.1580–1640', *Legislative Studies Quarterly*, 7 (1982); 'The nature of parliament in early Stuart England', in *Before the English Civil War: Essays on early Stuart politics and government*, ed. H. Tomlinson (London, 1983).

bethan parliaments described the ways in which it seemed to do so, especially as the House of Commons secured important procedural innovations and established parliamentary privileges.[6] All this seemed to reflect what Neale called the attainment by parliament of 'institutional maturity'. Indeed Neale once wrote that by 1597 'parliament's adolescence was over.'[7] This view seemed eminently acceptable because it neatly complemented the view already current of early seventeenth-century parliamentary history which was associated with the work of Wallace Notestein, whose influential lecture in 1924 had seemed to show conclusively that the House of Commons in the reigns of James I and Charles I was aiming to free itself from royal control and was claiming the right to be consulted in the initiation of government policy, and that it persevered in this in the face of determined resistance from both early Stuart kings.[8]

The 'revisionism' of Elton and Russell has highlighted three persuasive reasons for believing that there was no 'rise of parliament' in the century before 1640. Firstly, such an idea makes the false assumption that parliaments before the 1530s were mere cyphers of the crown, which some patently were not.[9] Secondly, those who have argued for 'the rise of parliament' have often based their argument on the questionable assumption sometimes made by historians, that records are an accurate reflection of contemporary power and influence. Late sixteenth- and early seventeenth-century parliaments have left more records than late medieval parliaments, but a plausible logical deduction is that what this indicates is not a rise of parliament so much as a fall in the price of paper and the rapid spread of printing.[10] Nor is it necessarily useful to assume that institutions develop like people. Just as writers of childrens' books give animals human characteristics, so historians

[6] J. E. Neale, *Elizabeth and her Parliaments* (2 vols, London, 1953, 1957); *The Elizabethan House of Commons* (London, 1949; rev. edn 1963).

[7] Neale, *Elizabethan House of Commons*, p. 376.

[8] Wallace Notestein, *The Winning of the Initiative by the House of Commons* (London, 1924). See also D. H. Willson, *The Privy Councillors in the House of the Commons* (Minneapolis, 1940).

[9] J. S. Roskell, 'Perspectives in English parliamentary history', in *Historical Studies of the English Parliament* ed. E. B. Fryde and E. Miller, (Cambridge, 1970), II, pp. 296–323; G. L. Harriss, 'Medieval doctrines in the debate on supply', in *Faction and Parliament: Essays on early Stuart history*, ed. K. Sharpe (Oxford, 1978).

[10] I first saw the point about the price of paper in Conrad Russell, *The Crisis of Parliaments* (London, 1971), p. 219, where Professor Russell, in turn, acknowledges his thanks to a former pupil.

of parliament often anthropomorphize that institution. But did parliament develop in a linear way from infancy through adolescence to maturity? Quite clearly the active early fifteenth-century parliaments do not fit this model and, if the model is accepted, where does one fit late parliamentary history into it? Have later parliaments been going through a prolonged period of senility? Above all, however, the most unconvincing assumption behind the notion of a rise of parliament is that MPs wanted to enhance the constitutional powers of parliaments. It is true that they wanted certain privileges for parliament and its members, but few of them wanted to initiate government policy or usurp the crown's right to do that. They saw parliaments as an essential part of the constitution, but their ambitions for parliaments were essentially limited and conservative.

Parallel with and reinforcing this revisionist view of Tudor and early Stuart parliaments, the last decade has also seen the formulation of doubts that the 'rise of Puritanism' in the late sixteenth and early seventeenth centuries is any more adequate an explanation for the growing tensions that culminated in this English Revolution than is the 'rise of parliament'. It used to be argued that Puritans were people who were not only dissatisfied with the conservative nature of the church established in 1559, but also had religious views that ensured that they would inevitably take a lead in challenging the *status quo* in society and state as well as in the church. This was a view that was shared by such different historians as Christopher Hill and J. E. Neale. Puritans, according to Hill, had 'a doctrine which gave men courage to fight tenaciously, if necessarily alone. Puritanism supplied a superb fighting morale. It appealed to men with social consciences, to those who felt that the times were out of joint . . . and that they could, and therefore must, help to set them right.'[11] Similarly, in his books on Elizabethan parliaments Neale usually labels critics of royal policy as 'Puritans', and in one typical passage Neale describes 'those remarkable pioneers in political tactics, the Puritans, whose precocious modernity came from the organising genius of Calvinism. The Puritans had a parliamentary programme; and their electioneering was truly modern in its purpose.'[12] The recent work of Nicholas Tyacke, Peter Lake and (more prolifically) Patrick Collinson has done

[11] Christopher Hill, *The Century of Revolution 1603–1714*, 2nd edn (Walton-on-Thames, 1980), p. 69.
[12] Neale, *Elizabethan House of Commons*, pp. 230–1.

much to cause that view of Puritanism as a revolutionary ideology
to be discredited.[13] Their work has shown that in the period before
1625 those people who are often said to have been Puritans do not
appear to have been basically different from those categorized as
Anglicans. Indeed before 1625 the distinction between Puritans
and Anglicans is a very misleading one, simply because most of the
characteristics often described as 'Puritan' were in fact shared by
most English protestants. All of them were bound together in an
ecclesiastical consensus that consisted of a broadly Calvinist predestinarian theology, the primacy of the Bible and its exposition by
preaching and sermons, and a general acceptance of episcopal
government in the church; above all, protestant unity was maintained by a deeply ingrained anti-catholicism. It is true that before
1625 there was a minority of protestants whom one may call
Puritans (though they themselves would have preferred to be called
'the godly'), whose lives were much more influenced by these
shared protestant principles than the majority and who were much
less tolerant of aspects of the reformed church that had not been
removed at the Reformation, like the wearing of vestments by
church ministers. Such people did feel themselves to be different
and set apart from other protestants, and occasionally their beliefs
did produce some political tension in the reign of James I, as will be
seen. But it is of overriding importance to recognize that before
1625 this did not amount to a major fracture in the English church.
Even the most extreme Puritans during the reign of James I did not
attempt to separate from the church. The vast majority of protestants were willing conformists of the church, had no intention of
challenging the structure of church government, and were in the
main conservative upholders of the *status quo* in society.

As the two ideas – the rise of parliament and of Puritanism –
around which late sixteenth- and early seventeenth-century history

[13] N. Tyacke, 'Puritanism, Arminianism and counter-revolution', in *Origins of
the English Civil War*, ed. Conrad Russell (London, 1973), an article which makes
one eagerly await Dr Tyacke's book on Arminianism; Patrick Collinson, *The
Elizabethan Puritan Movement* (London, 1967); *The Religion of Protestants: the church in
English society 1559–1625* (Oxford, 1982). Many of Professor Collinson's articles
have been conveniently collected together in P. Collinson (ed.) *Godly People: Essays
on English Protestantism and Puritanism* (London, 1983). See also Peter Lake, *Moderate
Puritans and the Elizabethan Church* (Cambridge, 1982), and his articles cited in notes
19 and 26 below.

[14] J. E. Neale, *Queen Elizabeth* (London, 1934), and D. H. Willson, *James VI and I*
(London, 1956), are the classic statements of the traditional views of these
monarchs.

has often been written have crumbled, so too have orthodox assessments of the characters and achievements of Elizabeth I and James I. In meeting the twin attack from parliament and Puritanism, it used to be said that the Tudor regime survived much better than its successor because it produced a powerful personality, Elizabeth I, whose political skill and judgement allowed it to weather the storm of parliamentary and Puritan opposition. In contrast, James I, the first Stuart monarch, was a pompous buffoon, at best an intellectual out of his depth in the real world of politics, and consequently a personality not suited to withstand the rise of parliament and of Puritanism. The 'wisest fool in Christendom' label was consequently hung round his neck. In the case of Elizabeth I historical revisionism has only just begun, resisted by a huge barrier of uncritical praise, what Neale called 'the recognition of her greatness by the consensus of the centuries'.[15] Only a few historians have begun to batter down that barrier and to develop a case that Elizabeth I's genius was flawed. There is a case for suggesting that Elizabeth I carried parsimoniousness, vindictiveness and indecision to a point way beyond the demands of political necessity, and that 'she quietly allowed England to become ungovernable.'[16] More historians have turned to the defence of James I than have dared to criticize Elizabeth I, and it is now clear that, despite his patent defects, the extent to which James was disliked by his English subjects has been grossly exaggerated in the past, especially by those who have made too much of religious differences between the king and opinion in the country.[17] It is true that some found it impossible to make the nice distinction James made between good and bad catholics,[18] and in this context it was difficult for them to understand James's policy of negotiating with catholic Spain, especially after 1618 when Europe was embroiled in the Thirty Years War, which was interpreted by some as a major

[15] J. E. Neale, 'The Elizabethan Age', in Neale, Essays in Elizabethan History (London, 1958), p. 22.
[16] John Guy, 'The Tudor Age', in The Oxford Illustrated History of Britain, ed. K. O. Morgan (Oxford, 1984), p. 264. See also the essays in Christopher Haigh (ed.), The Reign of Elizabeth I (Basingstoke, 1984).
[17] M. L. Schwarz, 'James I and the historians: a revaluation', Journal of British Studies, 13 (1973); R. C. Munden, 'James I and the "growth of mutual distrust": King, Commons and reform 1603–47', in Sharpe, Faction and Parliament; J. Wormald, 'James VI and I: two kings or one?', History, 68 (1983).
[18] J. R. Tanner (ed.), Constitutional Documents of the Reign of James I 1603–25 (Cambridge, 1961), p. 29.

episode in the continuing struggle between the forces of Christ and Antichrist.[19] Yet it is now more difficult to argue that the Hampton Court Conference in 1604 was the prelude to a major religious controversy. Generally, James I's religious views were in the mainstream post-Reformation protestant tradition. With one or two exceptions Jacobean promotions in the church were of conservative bishops, and local studies show that during James's reign there was a large measure of toleration of all kinds of protestant diversity under the umbrella of the Jacobean church.[20] Religion was not a major divisive issue during the reign of James I, and few people took the drastic course of breaking with the court during his reign.

Indeed, in looking at the history of England before 1640 historians have been too willing to assume that contemporaries, like themselves, knew of the impending constitutional crisis of 1640–1 and that they were preparing for it for many years beforehand. Of course, this is not true. When writing about the 1620s and 1630s, for example, it is highly misleading to describe someone as 'a future parliamentarian' or 'future royalist', referring to their activities in the later Civil War. Everyone was a royalist before 1642. The biggest salutary lesson of recent revisionism has been that there is more to the period between 1580 and 1640 than the growth of conflict between crown and parliament and that often the monarchy and the political nation worked harmoniously together. Moreover, even when there was political conflict, it does not always fit easily into a crown versus parliament model. Many of the political quarrels in the parliaments of the 1620s are explicable as inter-court differences of opinion and not as reflections of king-parliament confrontations.[21] Nor is it certain that political conflict was continuous. One of the mistakes of analysing historical development is to assume that events proceed evenly along an unbroken line. That there is abundant evidence of opposition to

[19] Peter Lake, 'Constitutional consensus and puritan opposition in the 1620s: Thomas Scott and the Spanish match', *Historical Journal*, 25 (1982); Simon Adams, 'Spain or the Netherlands? The dilemma of early Stuart foreign policy', in Tomlinson, *Before the Civil War*.

[20] P. Collinson, 'The Jacobean religious settlement: the Hampton Court Conference', in Tomlinson, *Before the Civil War*; Collinson, *Religion of Protestants*, especially chs. 2, 4, and 6; Tyacke, 'Puritanism, Arminianism and counter-revolution'; P. S. Seaver, *The Puritan Lectureships: the Politics of religious Dissent 1560–1662* (Stanford, 1970); R. A. Marchant, *The Puritans and the Church Courts in the Diocese of York 1560–1642* (London, 1960).

[21] Russell, *Parliaments and English Politics*, passim.

Charles I in 1628, when the Petition of Right was produced, does not necessarily mean that that level of opposition was maintained – let alone that it grew greater – in the 1630s.[22]

There is, then, much of value in the revisionist case. However, it is possible that its most valuable lessons have been negative ones. So anxious have some of the revisionists been to emphasize consensus politics that they have diverted attention away from the constitutional conflicts that did take place in the later parliaments of Elizabeth I's reign, in the parliaments of James I's and Charles I's reigns and in 1640, all occasions when there were long debates about the royal prerogative and constitutional issues. There is evidently, then, a problem that still needs solving, but it is of the utmost importance to make a clear distinction between the problem of explaining the reasons for the political conflicts of the late sixteenth and early seventeenth centuries down to the meeting of the Long Parliament on 3 November 1640 and that of explaining why the latter crisis of 1640 developed and escalated in a radical direction. Some historians[23] have been guilty of confusing and conflating these two separate problems. They are not the same problem; they are different problems that require different answers. How, then, can one explain the constitutional conflicts that periodically erupted between 1580 and 1640 in terms other than a rising parliament, the rise of Puritanism or the rise of an inept personality in the shape of James I?

Since that is currently the most puzzling question facing early Stuart historians any answer to it must be presented in the full recognition that it can be at best tentative in the present state of historical knowledge of the period. However, it is perhaps not straining the known facts too much to suggest that there were two features inherent in the religious and political structure of England in the late sixteenth and early seventeenth century which made periodic political conflicts, if not inevitable, then highly probable in the period down to 1640 and especially after the accession to the

[22] K. Sharpe, 'The personal rule of Charles I', in Tomlinson, *Before the Civil War*. Dr Sharpe may underestimate the degree of opposition to the court in the 1630s, but he (and J. S. Morrill, 'What was the English Revolution?', *History Today*, 34 [March 1984], pp. 11–12) makes out a good case for believing that the political tension of the later 1620s was defused in the 1630s. William Hunt, *The Puritan Moment. The Coming of Revolution in an English County* (Boston, 1983) is a timely warning not to carry this argument to extremes.

[23] For example, Lawrence Stone, *The Causes of the English Revolution 1529–1642* (London, 1972).

throne of Charles I. Moreover, the way that conflict came about as a result of these two features is the antithesis of the traditional 'rise of parliament' explanation.

The first of these two features is the development from the 1580s of a militant protestant (Puritan) view of the world, which tended to cause political conflict, but in a way markedly different from the traditional 'rise of Puritanism' theory. The central belief of this militant protestant world-view was that the world was involved in a great international struggle between the forces of Christ (who some identified with all the reformed protestant churches of Europe and others merely with England, the Elect Nation) and the forces of Antichrist (which were identified with catholicism and with catholic states like Spain).[24] Moreover, it was believed that this struggle, which had been taking place since the beginning of time, was currently in its decisive phase and that very soon it would reach its moment of climax in the victory of Christ over Antichrist and that the outcome would be the Millennium, which some interpreted literally as the Second Coming of Christ to earth. The great temptation is to treat such views as so fantastic that they must have been held by a minority. It is a temptation to be resisted, however, because there is mounting evidence that such ideas were held by many respectable and responsible people in the early seventeenth century, and indeed that they were part and parcel of mainstream protestant thought.[25] This being so, then what was the danger posed by these ideas as far as the English crown was concerned? It needs to be said that they did not necessarily pose any danger whatsoever. Many people who held this view, in fact, identified English monarchs as the heirs of the first Christian emperor, Constantine, in the sense that they were in the vanguard of the fight against the Antichrist and must therefore be supported. Sir Richard Grosvenor, a Cheshire gentleman, whom Richard Cust and Peter Lake have recently studied, was led by his intense fear of popery to exalt the royal prerogative: 'It hath beene an unspeakable blessinge and mercie upon this land', he wrote 'that our princes have thoroughly understood theire owne due and have

---

[24] For these critical differences of view see Peter Lake, 'The significance of the Elizabethan identification of the Antichrist', *Journal of Ecclesiastical History*, 31 (1980), and *Moderate Puritans*.

[25] P. Christianson, *Reformers and Babylon: English apocalyptic visions from the Reformation to the eve of the Civil War* (Toronto and London, 1978), brings together recent work on this subject.

vindicated theire own right forth out of the usurpinge hands of forraine prieste.'[26] However, the danger for English monarchs of views like this, held by militant protestants like Grosvenor, was that their actions were inevitably judged in the context of this world-view and political criticism could easily be inflated into the serious charge of association with the Antichrist. That this could be a danger is illustrated by the political storm raised by James I's apparently pro-Spanish foreign policy. Nevertheless, this fear of popery did not become serious for the English crown until 1625, when England acquired a monarch who had adopted a form of religion, a theology and liturgy, that was so close to catholicism that most people failed to see the difference. Recent attempts to question the extent to which Charles's adoption of Arminianism was hated have been signally unsuccessful, flying in the face of overwhelming evidence of the disaffection it caused.[27] Arminianism was hated because it represented – or was seen to represent, which is probably more important – a direct challenge to the English church as it had existed since 1559, that is, for sixty or seventy years.[28] It was seen as a challenge to many basic fundamentals of the protestant post-Reformation tradition that were now deeply entrenched: to the belief that church and churchmen were subordinate to the state; to the belief that preaching and sermons were central to religious activity and secondary to church ceremonial; and to the tradition that given obedience to certain fundamentals there was room in the church for those who differed on minor, less fundamental matters. By challenging these central tenets of the Elizabethan-Jacobean church, Charles I and his Arminian advisers came to be seen as revolutionary innovators moving along the road to catholicism. The obsessive anti-popery, and especially the fear of popery at court which was a principal driving force behind the

[26] R. Cust and P. Lake, 'Sir Richard Grosvenor and the rhetoric of magistracy', *Bulletin of the Institute of Historical Research*, 54 (1981), pp. 42–3.
[27] K. Sharpe, 'Archbishop Laud', *History Today*, 33 (August 1983), pp. 26–30; Peter White, 'The rise of Arminianism reconsidered', *Past and Present*, no. 101 (1983), raises doubts about how sharply the Arminians differed from other English protestants on theology, but this does not weaken the central point that many protestants *thought* that Arminianism represented a totally alien theological viewpoint.
[28] Tyacke, 'Puritanism, Arminianism and counter-revolution', passim. For examples of reactions to attempts to impose Arminianism on the localities see Anthony Fletcher, *A County Community in Peace and War: Sussex 1600–60* (London, 1975), pp. 76–93.

leaders of the parliamentary opposition, was given great credence
by Charles's religion.[29] With the advent of Arminianism it *is*
possible to see a clear divide between Anglicans and Puritans,
because the Church of England under Charles I departed from the
religious mainstream followed by most of Charles's subjects. In this
respect Charles's personality and policies are much more important than his father's in explaining the growth of political tension in
the early seventeenth century. Charles I and his advisers came to
be seen, rightly, as a threat to the church as it had developed since
1559: in other words, they came to be seen as dangerous innovators.

A second long-term determinant of political tension before 1640
brought about the same result. This was the administrative
machinery of the English crown, that is, of the government. The
key features of this administrative machinery are well known: its
shortage of money, its lack of a police force or a standing army or a
paid dependent bureaucracy. What is not generally appreciated
about these features – these apparent weaknesses – is that they did
not by themselves undermine the monarchy. Indeed, many of these
apparent weaknesses strengthened rather than weakened the
attachment to the crown of powerful people, who valued advantages the system gave them, such as massive under-assessment for
taxation purposes and a large degree of control over local government. These were powerful reasons for people to support the
regime, not to oppose the system. Unfortunately for the cause of
political order and harmony, it was the crown not the political
nation that found the existing financial and administrative system
inadequate, most notably because it did not produce sufficient
income to meet escalating government costs in times of inflation
and war. As a result the crown was forced to bring about financial
and administrative changes, like the introduction of non-
parliamentary taxation and the use of administrative patents in the
1590s and 1620s, and by so doing it again laid itself open to the
damaging charge that it was an innovator.[30]

What is interesting and significant is that some MPs should have
been so sensitive to the introduction of new financial and adminis-

[29] Russell, 'John Pym'; Anthony Fletcher, *The Outbreak of the English Civil War*
(London, 1981); Caroline Hibbard, *Charles I and the Popish Plot* (North Carolina,
1983).
[30] For an account of these measures, see Ashton, *English Civil War*, pp. 45–9, and
Barry Coward, *The Stuart Age. A History of England 1603–1714* (London, 1980),
pp. 136–42.

trative procedures. There were at least three reasons why this was so. The first is that people in the early seventeenth century were brought up to believe that the constitution that existed was perfect. It was 'the ancient constitution', hallowed by age and tradition. In order to appreciate this one has to make a great mental leap from the prevalent current assumption that new ideas and ways are better than old, to an age in which old ideas and ways were automatically thought to be better than new ones. In this situation, any attempt to alter the 'ancient constitution' was distrusted. There is no evidence that James I or Charles I ever envisaged destroying that constitution, but that in a sense does not matter. What does matter is that MPs came to see the crown's extra-parliamentary measures as confirmation of their fear that one day the royal prerogative might destroy parliament. Secondly, this fear was heightened by Charles's utter failure to communicate his views to his people, so that his actions were even more misunderstood than they might otherwise have been. Lastly, the situation was made still more alarming by the fact that on the continent representative assemblies were being stripped of their powers by absolutist monarchs. The outcome was that early seventeenth-century MPs were primarily anxious, not that parliaments should have greater powers, but merely that parliaments should survive.

This explanation for the political tensions of the late sixteenth and early seventeenth centuries rests finally on the argument that by its innovations in religion and in administrative and financial procedures the crown (especially after 1625) brought about an increasing national political awareness among sections of provincial local opinion, so that when the Scottish wars at the very end of the 1630s brought about another intensive bout of extraordinary demands for men and money by the crown, the crisis of 1640 erupted.[31] There are two points here that need underlining. Firstly, this is an argument primarily intended to explain the outbreak of political crises up to and including that of 1640, not the origins of the Civil War. Secondly, it is an argument that (in great contrast to the traditional explanations) maintains that the political tensions of the period up to and including 1640 came about because of the innovations of the crown. There is a lot of truth in what the parliamentarians of 1640 said. In speeches in the early weeks of the Long Parliament, they maintained that it was they who were the

---

[31] Suggestive remarks on this theme are made by Anthony Fletcher in 'National and local awareness in the county communities', in Tomlinson, *Before the Civil War*.

conservatives and Charles I and the court who were the revolutionaries. However, almost from their own time down to ours few
have believed them. Their protestations of conservatism have been
discounted as being a cloak disguising their true aims, and they
have traditionally been seen as revolutionaries at the vanguard of a
rising, progressive, Puritan parliament that was challenging a
conservative, reactionary regime. It may be that the historical truth
is the reverse of this: that the crisis of 1640 came about, as the
parliamentary leaders said, because the crown and its advisers, not
the parliamentary classes, were the revolutionaries, and that the
parliamentary classes, not the crown, were the conservatives trying
to defend the old ways.

THE COURSE OF THE ENGLISH REVOLUTION

The pronounced trend in recent writing emphasizing consensus
and conservatism among the political nation in the period before
the English Revolution has been paralleled by a similar stress on
the importance of religious and political conservatism during the
Revolution. The best major historian now working on radicals and
radical ideas in the period is still Christopher Hill.[32] More typical
of the character of recent work on the English Revolution – indeed
perhaps the most influential force in shaping it – are Conrad
Russell's seminal articles on John Pym, in which Pym and his allies
in the early years of the English Revolution are persuasively
portrayed as men with extremely limited, conservative aims, who
believed that Charles I was being manipulated by a group of evil
councillors which caused him to adopt disruptive, radical measures
during the first fifteen years of his reign.[33] Consequently, their
principal aim was to rescue Charles from this malign influence and
to restore the 'ancient constitution'. Their original proposal to
achieve this was to try to persuade Charles to appoint themselves to
key offices around him – the so-called 'bridge appointments'
scheme – so that they could ensure that royal government would be
restored to its normal channels.[34] They also aimed to improve the

[32] Christopher Hill, *The World Turned Upside Down: Radical ideas during the English
Revolution* (London, 1972); *Milton and the English Revolution* (London, 1977).
[33] Conrad Russell, 'Parliament and the king's finances', in Russell (ed.), *Origins
of the English Civil War*; 'John Pym'.
[34] Earl of Clarendon, *The History of the Rebellions and Civil Wars in England*, ed.

efficiency of government by carrying out the reform of royal finances which had been shirked by Elizabeth I and prevented by opponents after 1603. That was the limit of their ambitions in 1640–1. They had no intentions of making incursions into the royal prerogative, let alone of instituting a civil war, and certainly not of bringing about a republic. That anti-monarchical sentiments are absent in this period is shown by the lack of any discussion in England of theoretical justifications for resistance to established authority of the kind that was taking place on the continent. 'The Great Rebellion', writes Austin Woolrych, 'was not the outcome of radical political ideologies; it generated them.'[35] One consequence of this sort of interpretation of the early years of the English Revolution has been to stress that the Civil War was a 'surprising and unintended catastrophe'.[36]

Another consequence, however, has been to make it more difficult than before to explain the radical escalation of events in the 1640s. Why, since no-one (with the possible exception of Henry Marten[37]) during the first session of the Long Parliament gave any indication that they had radical aims, did succeeding regimes in the 1640s adopt increasingly radical policies? The most common answers to this question in recent years have been expressed in terms of 'functional radicalism': that the king's opponents throughout the 1640s were forced by the pressure of events to adopt radical measures that they had previously not even considered. Time after time during the 1640s fear of what might happen – of a possible 'counter-revolution' – drove the king's opponents to adopt defensive but 'revolutionary' measures; these in turn provoked conservative fears and so stimulated another twist of the 'revolutionary/ counter-revolutionary' spiral.

Three phases of the English Revolution in the 1640s can be identified in which the radical escalation of events can be explained in terms of functional radicalism. In the first, the period from the

---

W. D. Macray (6 vols, Oxford, 1888), I, pp. 280–2; Clayton Roberts, 'The Earl of Bedford and the coming of the English Revolution', *Journal of Modern History*, 49 (1979).

[35] Austin Woolrych, 'Political theory and political practice', in *The Age of Milton: Background to seventeenth-century literature*, ed. C. A. Patrides and R. B. Waddington (Manchester, 1980), p. 34.

[36] Fletcher, 'National and local awareness', in Tomlinson, *Before the Civil War*, p. 174.

[37] C. Durston, 'Henry Marten and the High Shoon of Berkshire: the Levellers in Berkshire in 1648', *Berkshire Archaeological Journal*, 70 (1979–80), p. 89.

24 BARRY COWARD

first meeting of the Long Parliament in November 1640 to the outbreak of the Civil War in August 1642, a central theme is the way the parliamentary leaders were driven by practical considerations to adopt more and more radical policies. It was not only the cogency of Strafford's defence at his trial which forced them to support a bill of attainder against the king's minister. As important a consideration was the knowledge that, if Strafford were allowed to live, then their own lives would be endangered. Essex's 'stone dead hath no fellow' was a powerful pragmatic incentive to adopt a measure that some conservative gentlemen considered illegal and as great a threat to the ancient constitution as anything Charles I had countenanced before 1640.[38] Similar pressing matters – this time the failure of the 'bridge appointments' scheme and the burgeoning evidence of Charles's untrustworthiness in 1641 – lay behind the formulation of the Additional Instructions and the Grand Remonstrance in November, which embodied radical proposals for parliamentary approval of the king's ministers and parliamentary control of the militia, as well as being an appeal to the people normally outside the political nation. The ways in which measures like this prompted the emergence of a group of 'constitutional royalists' who broke away from the parliamentary cause in the winter of 1641–2 to support the king has recently been well studied and understood.[39] It has also become clear that it was not only these influential conservatives like Hyde, Falkland and Colepepper who wanted a quick resolution of the crisis in 1642. Probably more numerous were those people who tried to remain neutral as other sections of opinion polarized for and against the king. One of the many new themes of J. S. Morrill's *Revolt of the Provinces* is a highly successful account of the reasons for the prevalance of neutralism in many English counties in the months immediately preceding and succeeding the outbreak of the Civil War.

Yet despite the broad band of conservatism that such studies have shown existed in England in 1642, from outright royalism to conservative neutralism and a desire to return to political normality as soon as possible, the country did slide into a civil war which

[38] Clarendon, *History*, I, pp. 320–1.
[39] B. H. G. Wormald, *Clarendon: Politics, history and religion 1640–60* (Cambridge, 1951); C. C. Weston, 'The theory of mixed monarchy under Charles I and after', *English Historical Review*, 75 (1960); C. C. Weston and J. R. Greenberg, *Subjects and Sovereigns* (Cambridge, 1981).

(certainly after the first few months) was fought with much bitterness and ferocity. Why then, did the strength of conservative sentiment in 1642 have little impact on the course of events and fail to bring about the eagerly desired settlement between parliament and king? During this second phase of the English Revolution functional radicalism again supplies a persuasive answer: the continuing mistrust some felt for the king and his evil councillors, together with the fear of the consequences of a total royalist military victory that seemed possible in the spring of 1643,[40] decided the influential middle group among the parliamentarians to reform radically the financial and administrative system of central government so as to make it efficient and wealthy enough to mount a military threat to the king. The royalists, too, were only slightly less slow in introducing a similar package of war measures, including direct, realistic taxation and central government direction of local affairs. The pressure of events consequently had an ironic outcome, as John Morrill points out: 'In the course of 1643 almost every clause of the Petition of Right was ignored: imprisonment without trial or appeal; the suspension of courts of law; the imposition of arbitrary taxes and the subordination of private rights were all endorsed by parliamentary ordinance.'[41] In addition, contrary to the opinion of some earlier commentators, the English Civil War, like other civil wars, had a major impact on the economic and social life of the country.[42] It is therefore not surprising that the war provoked another bout of intense 'counter-revolutionary' conservatism. During the last months of the war both in London and in the provinces opinion snowballed in favour of an end to the war and a speedy settlement between king and parliament.

[40] This is one of the many examples when contemporary perceptions of what happened are more important than what actually did happen. There was no 'three-pronged' military offensive by the armies of Newcastle, Hopton and the king on London co-ordinated from Oxford as some contemporaries and historians believed.

[41] Morrill, *Revolt of the Provinces*, p. 42. For the royalist war measures see Ian Roy, 'The royalist council of war 1642–6', *Bulletin of the Institute of Historical Research*, 31 (1962), and Ronald Hutton, *The Royalist War Effort* and 'The structure of the royalist party 1642–6', *Historical Journal*, 24 (1981).

[42] Ian Roy, 'The English Civil War and English society', in *War and Society: a yearbook of military history*, ed. B. Bond and I. Roy (London, 1975), and 'England turned Germany? The aftermath of the Civil War in its European context', *TRHS*, 5th ser. 28 (1978).

As has long been emphasized, explanations of the failure of the post-war 'quest for settlement' which had such strong support in the country lie mainly in the radicalization of the parliamentary New Model Army in the first months of peace. This process and the subsequent assertion of radical demands for political and religious liberties by the Army is one of the best known (apparently) 'revolutionary' features of the 1640s. The way in which this came about as a result of the infiltration into the ranks of the army of the radical ideology of the Levellers has been a central plank of the orthodox explanation for the slide towards the revolutionary events of 1648–9. Yet even this 'revolutionary' aspect of the period has now been questioned. Mark Kishlansky's spirited 'revisionist' view of the origins and politicization of the New Model Army is well in line with the prevailing emphasis on 'functional' explanations for any radicalization that occurred in the 1640s.[43] To Kishlansky, the Levellers were peripheral to that process in the army. In his view the origins of its politicization are to be found *inside* the army as the *esprit de corps* built up during the war was affronted by the callous way parliament treated the army in 1646–7. It was parliament's refusal to pay the army's arrears before demobilizing the bulk of the soldiers, and its failure to give any guarantees of indemnity to soldiers for their wartime activities, that impelled the army to formulate radical political demands that began with the right to petition parliament and culminated in the conversion of the army leaders – especially Ireton, the conservative spokesman for a prop-ertied franchise at the army debates at Putney in October 1647 – only twelve months later to the idea that Charles Stuart was 'a man of blood' who must be brought to trial and executed. To Kishlans-ky, neither the ideology of the Levellers nor that of religion played a central role in this politicization. 'Whatever its impact,' he writes, 'religion does not appear to have held pride of place with the three fundamental components of the Army's belief . . . .'[44]

Just as it has been shown that the radical drift of events in the 1640s occurred in spite of the conservative aspirations of most of the leaders of the king's opponents, so parallel work has done much

---

[43] Mark Kishlansky, *The Rise of the New Model Army* (Cambridge, 1979); 'The case of the army truly stated: the creation of the New Model Army', *Past and Present*, no. 81 (1979); 'The army and the Levellers: the road to Putney', *Historical Journal*, 22 (1979).

[44] Mark Kishlansky, 'Ideology and politics in the parliamentary armies', in *Reactions to the English Civil War*, ed. J. S. Morrill (London, 1982), p. 182.

to undermine the belief that there was a great deal of support for radical causes during the English Revolution. The most recent restatement of the contrary view – that radical ideas were popular during the English Revolution and that people normally outside the political nation (especially the 'middling sort') tended to support parliament – can be found in the works of Christopher Hill and Brian Manning.[45] However, detailed work on patterns of allegiances gives little support to their views, or indeed to any analyses of divisions along simple geographical or 'ecological' lines.[46] Few historians would probably now agree with Hill's assertion that 'support for Parliament came from the commercially advanced south and east of England, the King's support from the commercially backward areas of the north and west'.[47] Even 'parliamentary-Puritan' East Anglia had its royalist supporters,[48] and by no means all towns were as solidly parliamentarian as was once thought.[49] Moreover, David Underdown's investigation of allegiances using the 'wood-pasture' and 'fielden' distinction that has proved valuable in recent economic and social history studies has been inconclusive, apart from pointing to the 'generally traditionalist and socially conservative' attitudes of the mass of people, as well as of the landed and urban elites.[50] In all parts of the country, in both 'wood-pasture' and 'fielden' areas, and at all social levels, there is at least as much evidence of conservatism as of radicalism in the 1640s. At the beginning of the war it was reflected in peace petitions from grand juries and neutrality pacts, and as the war progressed it became more pronounced. It is true that contemporary accounts of popular riots and disorders against the existing social and political hierarchy are numerous, but the work of John

[45] Hill, *World Turned Upside Down*; B. Manning, *The English People and the English Revolution* (London, 1976). See also J. Malcolm, 'A king in search of soldiers: Charles I in 1642', *Historical Journal*, 21 (1978), and *Caesar's Due: Loyalty and King Charles 1642–6* (London, 1983).

[46] The most recent survey of the complex pattern of allegiances during the early stages of the war is Anthony Fletcher, 'The coming of the war', in Morrill, *Reactions*.

[47] Hill, *Century of Revolution*, p. 103.

[48] Clive Holmes, *The Eastern Association in the English Civil War* (Cambridge, 1974), pp. 16–30.

[49] Robert Howell, 'Neutralism, conservatism and political alignment in the English Revolution: the case of the towns 1642–9', in Morrill, *Reactions*; Morrill, 'Introduction', in ibid., p. 14.

[50] David Underdown, 'The problem of popular allegiance in the English Civil War', *TRHS*, 5th ser. 31 (1981), p. 13.

Morrill and John Walter suggest that such accounts reflect the exaggerated fear of propertied society rather than the reality.[51] In London militant popular conservatism surfaced in the form of the 'counter-revolution' led by Denzil Holles in 1646.[52] The Clubmen movement in counties in southern England and south Wales in 1645–6 was a provincial manifestation of the same trend. The ambiguity of the evidence for reconstructing the history of the Clubmen and the diverse nature of Clubmen activities in various areas leaves room for divergent interpretations of the movement;[53] but a study of Clubmen manifestoes indicates that it was part of a general current of opinion that wanted to end the war and reach a settlement with the king that would restore the pre-war social and political order and the old church and prayer book.

The loyalty of the Clubmen to the church as it had developed under Elizabeth I and James I points towards another theme of the period that has recently been emphasized: that there was as strong a groundswell of religious conservatism as political conservatism in England during the English Revolution. John Morrill's evidence drawn from parish sources, especially churchwardens' books, indicates that the 'godly reformation' being planned in the House of Commons and Westminster Assembly of Divines, and which was set out in a series of parliamentary ordinances from 1643 to 1649, received minimal support at the grass-roots parochial level, where traditional church festivals like Christmas and Easter survived along with the Book of Common Prayer, which had been officially outlawed in 1646.[54] Nor did the English Revolution seriously disrupt the continuity of personnel in English parishes. Ian Green's calculation[55] that only a small proportion of all parish clergy was ejected in the 1640s underlines the point that radical protestant aspirations for a 'godly reformation' and 'reformation of manners'

[51] J. S. Morrill and J. Walter, 'Order and disorder in the English Revolution' in *Order and Disobedience in Early Modern England*, ed. A. Fletcher and J. Stevenson (Cambridge, 1986).

[52] V. Pearl, 'London's counter-revolution', in *The Interregnum: the quest for Settlement 1646–60*, ed. G. E. Aylmer (London, 1972).

[53] Compare the different approaches of D. Underdown, 'The chalk and the cheese: contrasts among English Clubmen', *Past and Present*, no. 85 (1979); Morrill, *Revolt of the Provinces*, pp. 98–111; and Ronald Hutton, 'The Worcestershire Clubmen in the English Civil War', *Midland History*, 5 (1979–80), and *Royalist War Effort*.

[54] J. S. Morrill, 'The church in England 1642–9', in Morrill, *Reactions*.

[55] Ian Green, 'The persecution of "scandalous" and "malignant" clergy during the English Civil War', *English Historical Review*, 94 (1979), p. 525.

were expressed only by a few vociferous Puritans during the English Revolution and were realized only in exceptional areas.[56]

A great deal of recent work, then, has established that political and religious conservatism, ranging from neutralism to militant royalism and Anglicanism, was at least as important a feature of the English Revolution as radical ideas and aspirations. Yet this work, like 'revisionist' writing on the period before 1640, has raised as many historical problems as it has solved. There was a 'revolution' in the winter of 1648–9; Charles I was executed on 30 January 1649 and monarchy and other parts of the ancient constitution were formally abolished soon afterwards. One wonders if explanations couched in terms of functional radicalism are sufficient to account for the drift of events that culminated in this dramatic climax of the English Revolution. It is heartening, therefore, that the very latest work on the Revolution amounts to a welcome reassertion of a 'revolutionary' strand: the importance of religion as an ideological force that helped to impel events in a radical direction in the 1640s. Research by both Anthony Fletcher and John Morrill[57] indicates that the common feature of those who committed themselves, whether to the king or parliament, in 1642 was not social class, geographical origins or divergent attitudes to the constitution (there were 'constitutional parliamentarians' as well as 'constitutional royalists' in 1642).[58] What set the two sides apart was religious commitment: in the case of the royalists, commitment to the kind of church that had developed between 1559 and 1625 and, in the case of the parliamentarians, commitment to the cause of a Puritan 'godly reformation'. Fear of religious radicalism was what helped to drive some men into the arms of the king, while fear of a Popish Plot fired the political zeal and activism of Pym and his allies in the early years of the English Revolution. Commitment to the pre-Arminian church led avowed 'neutrals' like Thomas Knyvett[59] to reveal their true royalist allegiance during the Civil War, while it was aspirations for a 'godly reforma-

[56] Serious attempts to establish Presbyterianism were made only in some London and Lancashire parishes.
[57] Fletcher, *Outbreak of the Civil War*, pp. 405–6; J. S. Morrill, 'The religious context of the English Civil War', *TRHS* 5th ser. 34 (1984), and *England's Wars of Religion* (forthcoming).
[58] Richard Tuck, '"The ancient law of freedom": John Selden and the Civil War', in Morrill, *Reactions*.
[59] Fletcher, *Outbreak of the Civil War*, p. 403.

tion' that maintained Simonds D'Ewes's support for parliament
and overcame his deep-seated fears that events were heading for
political and social anarchy. From 1642 onwards loyalty to the
church was less apparent and has had to be patiently uncovered by
historians, but the dwindling minority that remained committed to
opposition to the king in the 1640s made no secret of their radical
religious zeal. It was this which the 'honest radicals' in English
towns and counties shared in the post-war years.[60] In the army,
too, surely religious fervour was at least one element which (*pace*
Kishlansky) converted some rank and file soldiers and army 'grandees' in the autumn of 1648 to a programme designed to purge
parliament and to try and execute the king. It was this which
determined Henry Ireton and, more reluctantly and belatedly,
Oliver Cromwell, the spokesman for the propertied in the Putney
debates on the franchise, to lead the English Revolution into the
climacteric events of December 1648 and January 1649.

The English Revolution in 1648–9 was led by men who were
conservatives in social and political attitudes but who were religious radicals. Oliver Cromwell is an embodiment of these diverse,
ambivalent trends within the English Revolution, which is perhaps
one key which helps to explain his complex career, his fairly
successful rule as Protector, and his eventual failure to make
republican rule permanent in England.[61] Everyone who has written
about Cromwell has commented on the puzzling fact that his career
provides examples of apparently cynical pragmatism as well as
apparently unbridled religious enthusiasm. Some, beginning with
the Levellers in 1649, have explained this in terms of Cromwell's
hypocrisy, arguing that he used radical ideas and allies as a cloak
for his selfish ambitious ends. Others have explained his ambiguities in terms of a man whose youthful 'backbench' idealism was
jettisoned and replaced by pragmatism when he came to grips with
the problems of running the country. Yet Cromwell's career fits
neither of these simple patterns. Indeed the prime feature of it is the
way that Cromwell oscillates rapidly and frequently from what
looks like genuine radicalism to conservatism and *vice versa*, which
may have been brought about by the tensions inherent in his

[60] D. Underdown, ' "Honest" radicals in the counties', in *Puritans and Revolutionaries: Essays in seventeenth-century history presented to Christopher Hill*, ed. D. H. Pennington
and K. V. Thomas (Oxford, 1978), pp. 186–205.
[61] There are illuminating (if brief) assessments of Cromwell's character in
A. B. Worden, *The Rump Parliament 1648–53* (Cambridge, 1974), p. 56, 69, 209–10.

character, as in the English Revolution, between political conservatism and religious radicalism. There were many times when Cromwell's aspirations for a godly reformation conflicted with his ambitions to uphold the social and political status quo.

Cromwell was not alone in facing this dilemma; it was central to the English Revolution. Other Puritan gentlemen in 1640 had inherited the desire for a godly reformation which had been gaining ground since at least the 1580s.[62] Up to 1640, however, few saw any conflict between this aim and the traditional social and political order. After 1640 the conflicts became glaringly obvious, so that many propertied gentlemen who had shared Cromwell's vision of a godly reformation drew back from it when they saw the alarming drift of events towards a major political and ecclesiastical revolution and, what was perhaps worse, the prospect that a social revolution might take place as well. What set Cromwell apart from many of his contemporaries is that he remained committed to the aim of bringing about a godly reformation within a society organized on traditional lines. It is that which helps to explain Cromwell's apparently inconsistent behaviour during the English Revolution. What lay behind it were the tensions implicit in his desire to find policies that would satisfy his hopes and those of others in the army and the sects for reforms in the church, the law and universities, and at the same time measures that would satisfy the concern he shared with many propertied people in England to re-establish stability and normality in government. At times, for example during the last weeks of 1648, after the battle of Worcester in 1651 and during the debates on the Humble Petition and Advice, such tensions were especially pronounced and emphasize the immensity of the task he faced in trying to resolve the dilemma.

Amid the many uncertainties about Cromwell, it is clear that it was only he who had any chance of resolving the conflicting strands of the English Revolution. After his death no-one emerged who was able to straddle the two: the conservative demand for a settlement and the radical pressure for further reform. Consequently, the Republic collapsed into anarchy and the Stuarts were restored as the guarantors of social and political order. It was the failure of post-Oliverian republican regimes to offer this guarantee, not any

---

[62] J. T. Cliffe, *The Puritan Gentry: the great Puritan families of early Stuart England* (1984), is a good recent assessment of these kinds of aspirations by Puritan gentlemen before 1640.

strong groundswell of support for the Stuarts, that was the major reason for the restoration of the monarchy in 1660. The English Revolution was halted by its own internal contradictions.

THE CONSEQUENCES OF THE ENGLISH REVOLUTION

Since, as has been seen, a predominant recent historiographical tendency has been to argue that the English Revolution was not brought about by fundamental, long-term causes and that the radical events came about in spite of the prevailing conservative prejudices of the vast majority of people, it is not surprising that one effect of historical writing on the period after 1660 has been to minimize the consequences of the English Revolution. Although the volume of recent work on Restoration England has been much less than on the period before 1660, it is possible to see an historical consensus emerging that 1660 is not a major dividing line either in the development of English government or the constitution or in economic, social and intellectual matters, and that the English Revolution did not bring about irrevocable changes in any of these spheres of English life. The value of this new emphasis cannot be exaggerated, since before it began 1660 had replaced 1485 as the major watershed in post-medieval history, a situation reflected in the organization of many history courses and history books which either end or begin in 1660.[63] Indeed a system of historical apartheid has traditionally operated, so that the list of historians who have written on the period before 1660 has few names in common with that of historians who specialize in the history of England after 1660. During the last few years there has been an attempt, though less coherent and sustained than pre-1660 revisionism, to break through the 1660 barrier and to deny that the English Revolution had any major long-term impact on constitutional, economic, social and intellectual developments in England.

One of the most misleading effects that the '1660 barrier' has had on seventeenth-century English history has been to entrench the assumption that after 1660 the constitutional structure of the

---

[63] Even the most recent series of general books on the history of England, the Longman Foundation of Modern Britain series, ignores 1485 but takes 1660 as a major dividing line: A. G. R. Smith, *The Emergence of a Nation State: the Commonwealth of England 1529–1660* (London, 1984), and G. Holmes, *The Making of a Great Power: Preindustrial Britain 1660–1783* (forthcoming).

country could never be the same again. It is often argued that so powerful and deep-rooted were the historical processes that led to the English Revolution and so revolutionary were its consequences that inevitably the restored monarchy was fundamentally and permanently changed, so that English constitutional development diverged permanently from the general European trend towards absolutism, and that it was thus irrevocably set on the road which eventually led to constitutional monarchy. 'The sixteen-forties and 'fifties', writes Christopher Hill, 'marked the end of medieval and Tudor England.'[64] However, it may be that this view makes too stark a contrast between government under the restored monarchy and that by medieval, Tudor and early Stuart monarchs. There is no denying, of course, that some events during the English Revolution did put constraints on the power of the restored monarchy. Some of the legislation of 1641 remained in force in 1660, the royal financial expedients of the 1630s remained illegal and the royal prerogative courts remained abolished. Moreover, the Revolution produced a hatred of standing armies which rebounded against the monarchy and, as has been emphasized many times, the memory of 30 January 1649 must have been a salutary lesson to later Stuart kings that there were limits to what they could do. Yet what has not been so frequently emphasized is that these kinds of limitations that were underlined in 1660 were not new. English monarchs before 1640 had had to rule with the co-operation of their leading subjects. In this respect Charles II's position was not all that different from that of Elizabeth I, James I or Charles I, or from that of medieval monarchs before them. They had to maintain, in K. B. McFarlane's phrase, 'the community of interests between crown and baronage',[65] if they wanted to maintain strong effective government, and that principle still stood in 1660. Moreover, far from weakening the crown, the English Revolution may have strengthened it by bringing about a conservative backlash in its favour, so that the Cavalier Parliament left most of its powers untouched. The attempts which parliament had made in the winter of 1641–2 and later to control the king's right both to appoint his own officials and advisers and to control the militia were abandoned at the Restora-

---

[64] Christopher Hill, *Reformation to Industrial Revolution: a social and economic history of Britain 1530–1780* (London, 1967).

[65] K. B. McFarlane, 'Service, maintenance and politics', in *The Nobility of Later Medieval England* (Oxford, 1973), p. 121.

tion. Moreover, their fear and hatred of regicide and republicanism drove MPs in the Cavalier Parliament to pass legislation outlawing other claims made by parliament during the Revolution, including the right to legislate without the king and to call parliament without the king's consent. What is more, the Cavalier Parliament gave Charles II massive powers of censorship and left untouched many of the crown's prerogative powers. Above all, as C. D. Chandaman's work has made clear, from the early 1670s the royal government's financial problems were considerably eased.[66] The potential strength of the restored monarchy was great.

That this potential strength was not fully realized in Restoration England is partly explained by Charles II's and James II's failure to maintain that 'community of interests' between the crown and its leading subjects which successful medieval monarchs had done. In fact they adopted policies of religious comprehension and toleration which horrified militant Anglicans. By the 1660s a policy of reconstructing a comprehensive church of the type that had developed before 1625 was doomed to failure. Charles I's attempt to impose Arminianism on the English church after 1625 had begun a process which splintered the protestant consensus which had been maintained for eighty years since 1558. The collapse of the hierarchy and discipline of the church and of censorship in the 1640s merely escalated a process in which many varied forms of protestant emerged, including Presbyterians, Baptists and Quakers. In the 1650s Oliver Cromwell attempted to reconstruct a church which, like the Elizabethan-Jacobean church, was broad enough to encompass all these groups within it, and in 1660–1 Charles II and Clarendon backed another attempt to bring about such a church at the Worcester House and Savoy House conferences.

By that stage, however, religious nonconformity and political sedition had become too closely identified in the minds of many influential people to be accepted. Any move towards including protestant Dissenters within a comprehensive church came to be seen as countenancing the political revolution that had taken place, and the social revolution that it was feared had just been about to

[66] C. D. Chandaman, *The English Public Revenue 1660–88* (Oxford, 1975).
[67] J. R. Western, *Monarchy and Revolution: the English state in the 1680s* (London, 1972); J. Miller, 'The later Stuart monarchy', in *The Restored Monarchy 1660–88*, ed. J. R. Jones (London, 1979); J. Miller, 'The potential for "absolutism" in later Stuart England', *History*, 65 (1984); A. McInnes, 'When was the English Revolution?', *History*, 67 (1982).

take place, during the English Revolution. 'Dissent is sedition'
became a powerful political slogan and in that spirit some gentlemen, while they themselves were restored to militia commissions
and commissions of the peace, restored an intolerant church,
ejecting ministers whose views were not acceptable to them. Ian
Green has recently shown that, even before the Cavalier Parliament put the savage, repressive Clarendon Code on the statute
book, the Anglican church was being restored spontaneously from
the grass-roots.[68] In a great euphoric wave of militant Anglicanism
some local gentlemen suppressed conventicles and ejected church
ministers. This was all part of a great and violent reaction to
everything that was associated with the Good Old Cause that is
everywhere apparent in the 1660s. Moreover, these vindictive
sentiments of the 1660s were long-lived. They were there beneath
the surface of later-Stuart society like embers waiting to be fanned
into life, as occasionally they were, principally in the 1690s and
1700s by demagogic preachers like Frances Atterbury and Dr
Henry Sacheverell, who used the slogan 'the Church in Danger' to
rally Tories to protect their political hegemony, which was still seen
as being inextricably bound up with an intolerant church. In the
light of this Anglican-Tory tradition, of which Sacheverell was an
extreme exponent, the decisions of Charles II and James II to
follow policies aimed at tolerating Dissenters were obviously unwise. Just how strong an alliance between restored monarchy and
church could be was seen when Charles II adopted it during the
last years of his life. In these circumstances it is difficult to see the
English Revolution as bringing about a decisive shift in English
constitutional development towards greatly enhancing the power of
parliament and weakening that of the crown. Such a development
had taken place by the early eighteenth century, but it came about
not because of the English Revolution but partly because of the
unwise religious policies of Charles II and James II and primarily
because of the impact of the long wars against France between 1689
and 1713. The development of constitutional parliamentary
monarchy in England was in large measure a long-term consequence of these later wars and not of the mid-seventeenth-century
Civil War.

Recent work on economic, social and intellectual history has
suggested that similar conclusions might be made about long-term

[68] Ian Green, *The Re-establishment of the Church of England 1660-3* (Oxford, 1978).

developments in these areas as well: that the English Revolution is
largely irrelevant to the task of explaining the course such developments took in the late seventeenth and early eighteenth centuries.[69]
This, of course, flies in the face of common assumptions that the
English Revolution, amongst other things, produced an economy
that was capitalistic and individualistic and that there was a close
link   between   the   Scientific   Revolution   and   the   English
Revolution.[70] Recent studies suggest that the effects of the English
Revolution were largely negative. For example, the economic recovery from the 'decay of trade' that contemporaries had complained of intermittently for a century before 1640 was possibly
delayed by the depredations (both direct and indirect) of warfare
during the English Revolution. One instance of this from many has
just been revealed by Dr Stephen Porter, whose study of urban
destruction during the Civil War makes clear that some towns were
still struggling in the 1660s and 1670s to repair damage to buildings
that had occurred during the Civil War.[71] In the history of ideas,
too, it has become clear that the English Revolution hindered
rather than advanced the course of the Scientific Revolution by
causing science and reform generally to be open to the charge of
radicalism. It is significant, for example, that many late
seventeenth-century scientists, like Robert Boyle, had to spend
time and money defending their work against the charge of religious and social radicalism. The drift of recent work suggests that
the fertility of Restoration science can only be partially explained
by what took place during the English Revolution.[72] This is no less
true of economic and social developments. Although it is now clear
that a point roughly in the middle of the seventeenth century marks
the beginning of crucial changes in the structure of the English
economy and society, the major determinants of these seem not to
have been events during the English Revolution but long-term
movements in the levels of populations and prices.[73]

[69] Unfortunately there is insufficient space to expand on this theme here.

[70] As reflected for example in Hill, *Reformation to Industrial Revolution*.

[71] S. Porter, 'The destruction of urban property in the English Civil War 1642–
52', PhD thesis, University of London (1983), pp. 186ff.

[72] M. Hunter, *Science and Society in Restoration England* (1981), pp. 21–9.

[73] D. C. Coleman, *The Economy of England 1450–1750* (London, 1977), describes
economic developments after 1660 as a 'new context' but makes clear that this did
not arise as a result of the English Revolution. See also C. Wilson, *England's
Apprenticeship 1603–1763* (London, 1965), pp. 108–38. The work of H. J. Habbakuk,
J. Thirsk and others has demolished the view that the English Revolution fun-

Valuable as these new approaches to the consequences of the English Revolution are, it is possible to take them too far. Just as the causes and course of the English Revolution cannot be fully explained without taking account of diverse, contrasting strands in the history of England before 1660, so there needs to be a recognition that the consequences of the Revolution were not totally negative but were many and ambivalent. In some respects the English Revolution did speed up, rather than hold back, economic, social and intellectual changes. For example, knowledge among English farmers and landlords of advanced agricultural techniques and new crops used by farmers in the Low Countries became much more widespread as a result of the enforced continental travels of royalist *émigrés* like Richard Weston, who wrote *A Discourse on Husbandry in Brabant and Flanders* in the 1640s, and, more importantly, by the publication of agricultural treatises which, like printed books and pamphlets of all kinds, underwent a publication boom during the English Revolution. Moreover, the conditions of lax censorship during much of the Revolution which made this possible and the consequent intellectual ferment of the period provided a congenial intellectual climate in which to pursue scientific research. John Aubrey exaggerated when he said that 'the searching into Natural Knowledge began but since or about the death of King Charles the first',[74] but his comment is a reminder that the effects of the English Revolution were not simply reactionary.

However, it is in religious and political history that there is perhaps the greatest danger of historians failing to recognize that the English Revolution had diverse, contrasting effects. The more one reads about the religious and political history of Restoration England, the more one is able to detect a positive, as well as negative, reaction to what had happened before 1660. It is a less obvious response because it was often expressed quietly, unlike

---

damentally changed the structure of English society: J. Thirsk, 'The sale of royalist lands during the Interregnum', *Economic History Review*, 5 (1952–3); idem, 'The Restoration Land Settlement', *Journal of Modern History*, 26 (1954); H. J. Habbakuk, 'Landowners and the Civil War', *Economic History Review*, 16 (1965); idem, 'Public finance and the sale of confiscated lands during the interregnum', ibid., 15 (1962); idem, 'The land settlement at the Restoration of Charles II', *TRHS*, 5th ser. 28 (1978); P. G. Holiday, 'Land sales and repurchases in Yorkshire after the Civil Wars 1650–70', *Northern History*, 5 (1970); B. Coward, *The Stanleys, Lords Stanley, Earls of Derby 1385–1672* (Manchester, 1983), pp. 68–79.

[74] Quoted in M. Hunter, *John Aubrey and the Realm of Learning* (London, 1975), p. 42.

strident militant Anglicanism. It is to be seen, not in public parliamentary speeches, but in private diaries,[75] and above all in the activities (or rather the inactivities) and the beliefs of some Anglican gentlemen, divines and academics. The more work that is done on the local history of Restoration England, the more it becomes apparent that historians have been blinded by those who have written about protestant Dissent after 1660 in terms of 'the period of the Great Persecution'. While the Clarendon Code was enacted and put into effect in the early 1660s against some Dissenters, notably Quakers and Baptists, it is clear if one takes a longer perspective that the Code was enforced in a far from systematic and extensive manner.[76] Why were not all Anglican JPs infected by the vindictive mood of militant Anglicanism? When more work on Restoration England has been done it may be found that they were more sympathetic to the long post-Reformation tradition of a comprehensive church, broken by Charles I and Laud in the 1620s and 1630s and revived by Cromwell in the 1650s, than they were to the narrow church erected in the 1660s. What lends support to this idea is the emergence after the Restoration of ideological support for a comprehensive church by the Latitudinarians, including John Tillotson, Isaac Barrow and Simon Patrick. Like many others, they reacted against 'the enthusiasm' of the Quakers, Ranters and others, but, unlike High Church divines, they reacted not negatively by urging repression of Dissent but positively by stressing the importance in religion of rational arguments rather than faith and revelation. Moreover, they turned away from the intolerance of the High Church-Tory party to advocate a widening of toleration, a position which became associated in the party politics of later Stuart England with the Whigs.

Both features of later Stuart politics – the more tolerant attitudes of the Whigs as well as the bigotry of the Tories – were rooted in the English Revolution. In the present state of knowledge of Restora-

[75] See, for example, *The Diary of Samuel Pepys*, III (London, 1970), ed. R. Latham and W. Matthews, p. 294; IV (London, 1971), p. 35; VIII (London, 1974), pp. 50, 332, 382.

[76] M. R. Watts, *The Dissenters* (Oxford, 1978), ch. 3; J. J. Hurwich, '"A fanatical town": the political influence of Dissenters in Coventry 1660–72', *Midland History*, 4 (1977); R. M. Dunn (ed.), *The Norfolk Lieutenancy Journal 1660–76*, Norfolk Record Society, 45 (1977), p. 10; G. F. T. Jones, *Saw-pit Wharton* (Sydney, 1967), pp. 212–13; A. Fletcher, 'The enforcement of the Conventicle Acts 1664–79', in *Persecution and Toleration*, ed. W. Sheils, Studies in Church History, 21 (Oxford, 1984), pp. 235–46.

tion England this division and its connections with the English Revolution are more apparent in the Westminster political scene. This is reflected, for example, in the fact that during the reigns of William III and Queen Anne accounts of the English Revolution were published to buttress the party political propaganda of Whigs and Tories. It is no coincidence that Edmund Ludlow's *Memoirs* of the Revolution were first published in 1696, suitably edited by John Toland to help the Whig cause,[77] while Clarendon's *History of the Rebellion* was first published in 1702 as a Tory counterblast. Nevertheless, there are a few indications that in the localities, as well as at Westminster, the struggle between factions over the question of toleration of protestant Dissenters was a central feature of political life that persisted in a major 'church-chapel' divide in English society.[78]

In this and in many other ways the consequences of the English Revolution were diverse. It set in motion contradictory trends: negative forces of reaction and suppression alongside more positive responses to what had happened. As a result the legacy of the English Revolution was neither what seventeenth-century or present-day admirers of the Good Old Cause wanted, nor was it a complete restoration of the state of affairs before the Revolution. Although his terminology differs from mine, Ivan Roots neatly expressed the same substantive point when he wrote that 'the Great Rebellion had permanent consequences. Like some many-lived Cheshire cat it left a persistent grin behind.'[79]

[77] *A Voyce from the Watch Tower*, ed. A. B. Worden, Camden Society, 4th ser., 21 (London, 1978).
[78] Fletcher, 'Enforcement of Conventicle Acts', pp. 245–54; P. Jenkins, *The Making of a Ruling Class: the Glamorgan gentry 1640–1790* (Cambridge, 1983), p. 124; B. Coward, 'The social and political position of the Earls of Derby in seventeenth-century Lancashire', in *Seventeenth-Century Lancashire: Essays presented to J. J. Bagley*, ed. J. Kermode and C. B. Phillips, *Transactions of the Historic Society of Lancashire and Cheshire*, 1.32 (1983), pp. 138–50.
[79] I. Roots, *The Great Rebellion 1642–60* (1960), p. 257.

3

Political Discourse in Early
Seventeenth-Century England

CHRISTOPHER HILL

Critics of scholasticism in seventeenth-century England emphasized strongly that things are more important than the words which
describe them. Words must be related to actions if we are to
understand them. The point needs stressing in relation to current
controversies about seventeenth-century English history, since it is
easy for inexperienced historians, or historians approaching the
seventeenth from the sixteenth century, or those who limit themselves to political and administrative matters, to take parliamentary discourse at its face value; and to believe that because the
gentry spoke of themselves as 'the county community', therefore
nobody else in the county mattered. This is to fall for what Marx
called 'the illusion of the epoch'.

In every society subject to censorship we should be wary of
resting on the surface of what politicians say. Kremlinologists
understand this, even if their interpretations are sometimes a little
fanciful. Every Conservative MP today knows that a special language of codes and symbols must be used if the leader is to be
criticized: she cannot be attacked directly. Anyone who during the
Second World War was in the army – that last survival of the
hierarchical society – knows what venom and contempt could be
put into the correctly deferential words 'Yes – sir!' The printed
page cannot convey the different significances which context and
emphasis may give to accepted forms of discourse. I want to discuss
some confusions which historians risk falling into by failing to allow
for seventeenth-century conventions of political discourse.

Members of parliament constantly professed boundless respect
for the king, and horror of any suggestion of opposition to the
government. Even in 1643, after parliament had been fighting the

king for a year, Henry Marten was sent to the Tower for suggesting that the kingdom might be more important than the royal family.[1] If we look only at official sources – parliamentary debates, state papers – the case for believing that the Civil War happened by accident seems strong. But formal documents are not the only evidence available. Side by side with Sir Simonds D'Ewes's subserviently monarchical speeches in the House of Commons, his hope in 1625 that 'the affection of prince and people would be settled in a firm concord and correspondence',[2] we have his diary, which he wrote in cypher 'that I might write more freely, as of the public occurrrents, so of mine own private occasions'. With this safeguard D'Ewes referred to James I's sin of sodomy, his 'base and cowardly nature', for which he was 'laughed at by the vulgar'. God justly punished James's 'self-conceit of his wisdom in the carriage of his Spanish match'.[3]

When Prince Charles left for Spain D'Ewes prayed that 'God would preserve him from damned apostacy.' James 'showed small policy in giving credence to base informers against his lower House of Commons'. D'Ewes recorded portents which reminded him of 'Richard II's time'. 'God forbid the like consequents as succeeded them.' (But earlier riots of the unemployed in Wiltshire had 'raised a rumour of a hoped-for rebellion'.) After describing public dissatisfaction with the king's reasons for the dissolution of parliament in 1622, D'Ewes continued with heavy irony: 'To-day also went his worthy Majesty out of town towards his pleasure, leaving all his good subjects much perplexed.' D'Ewes's conclusion was 'to pray . . . and to arm myself for preparation against worser times should come, which without God's admirable and infinite mercy towards us, we could not but shortly expect'. He thought that Thomas Scott's illegal but vastly popular *Vox Populi* (1620) was 'generally approved of not only by the meaner sort that were zealous for the cause of religion but also by all men of judgement'.[4]

D'Ewes was a convinced Puritan. Can he really have respected a

---

[1] S. R. Gardiner, *History of the Great Civil War, 1642–9* (4 vols, London, 1901), I, p. 202.

[2] *The Autobiography and Correspondence of Sir Simonds D'Ewes*, ed. J. O. Halliwell (2 vols, London, 1845), I, p. 279; cf. p. 241.

[3] *The Diary of Sir Simonds D'Ewes 1622–4*, ed. E. Bourcier (Paris, 1974), pp. 55, 92–3, 113, 135.

[4] Ibid., pp. 58–60, 65, 121, 130; cf. pp. 85, 145, 158; D'Ewes, *Autobiography*, ed. Halliwell, I, p. 159.

king guilty of the sin of sodomy? Or one capable of 'damned apostacy'? The contrast between D'Ewes's public speeches and his private words gives food for thought. Drummond of Hawthornden is another example. When James came to Scotland in 1617 Drummond published *Forth Feasting: A Panegyric to the Kings most Excellent Majesty*, whose extravagance in praise startled his biographer, David Masson.[5] Drummond left unpublished *The Five Senses*, an extremely critical poem about James in which he prayed, with much detail, that:

> Thou wilt be pleased, great God, to save
> My sovereign from a Ganymede,
> Whose whorish breath hath power to lead
> His excellence which way it list.[6]

Prynne, Burton and Bastwick, the three most inveterate opponents of the Laudian regime who in 1637 were condemned to severe corporal penalties and perpetual imprisonment, never failed to express their reverence for and confidence in the king.

Another example is John Preston, whose court sermons use Aesopian language to press home political recommendations – in his case a change of foreign policy – without actually saying so. The Bible showed that God had stirred up rebels against wicked princes: Preston quoted Mordecai to Esther: 'If thou holdest thy tongue at this time, deliverance shall appear to the Jews from another place, but thou and thy house shall perish.' God 'doth not need princes', said Preston in a Cambridge sermon.[7]

Even better documented is Fulke Greville, a life-long aspirant to royal office, who ultimately became Chancellor of the Exchequer. His public persona throughout his life was that of devoted servant to Elizabeth, James I and Charles I. But in his *Life of Sidney* and his poems and plays, all written long before his death in 1628, Greville deals with problems which did not surface till after 1640. He warns continually of the dangers of the drift towards absolutism, arguing

---

[5] D. Masson, *Drummond of Hawthornden: the story of his life and writings* (London, 1873), pp. 55–9.

[6] *The Poems of William Drummond of Hawthornden*, ed. W. C. Ward (2 vols, London and New York, 1894), II, pp. 185–7.

[7] John Preston, *A Sermon of Spirituall Life and Death* (1630), p. 27; *Life Eternall*, 4th edn (1634), sermon 7, p. 126; cf. *A Sermon . . . preached before the Commons-House* (July 1625), printed with *The Saints Qualification*, 2nd edn (1634), pp. 261–2. See C. Hill, *Puritanism and Revolution*, Panther edn (London, 1969), 'The political sermons of John Preston', esp. pp. 245–50, 259–60.

consistently for parliamentary control over taxation and for a forward commercial-colonial policy in alliance with the Dutch. Assuming that absolutism corrupts, his interest is in analysing those who sell themselves to power, those who sit on the fence (especially prelates), and those who try inadequately to maintain their integrity (presumably Greville himself). Well before the Laudian ascendancy he had profound contempt for most churchmen.

It may well be that compilers of parliamentary diaries – aware that their papers might be seized – omitted direct attacks on the king. We find few remarks like Rudyerd's in 1624: 'let us not lay all the blame on the King . . . . We have had our own heats'; or Sir William Herbert's, à propos a financial grant: 'the people would be satisfied', it 'being given to the war, and not to the King'.[8] The Venetian ambassador was amazed at some of the direct attacks on James in the Commons in 1610. We need not believe his story that one member called the king a traitor and was defended by the House; but certainly men were already distinguishing between the king and the commonwealth. The French ambassador was talking of a general insurrection.[9] Why did James I make such a song and dance about monarchy being the divinest thing on earth? Surely because men were now denying what Henry VIII and Elizabeth had never needed to emphasize.

John Selden was a trained lawyer and parliamentary politician, whose propaganda services Charles I used. Selden's cool sceptical intelligence is revealed in his *Table Talk*, probably to be dated from the 1640s. However, it is unlikely that the jovial irreverence with which Selden treated sacred cows had been acquired only after 1640.

A king is a thing men have made for their own sakes, for quietness' sake. Just as in a family one man is appointed to buy the meat . . . A king that claims privileges in his own country because they have them in another, is just as a cook that claims fees in one lord's house because they are allowed in another. If the master of the house will yield them, well and good. . . . The king's oath is not security enough for our property, for he swears to govern according to law; now the judges they interpret the law, and what judges can be made to do we know.[10]

[8] *The Holles Account of Proccedings in the House of Commons in 1624*, ed. Christopher Thompson (Orsett, Essex, 1985), pp. 29, 49.

[9] *Proceedings in Parliament, 1610*, ed. E. R. Foster (2 vols, Newhaven, Conn., 1966), I, p. xii; II, p. 142; cf. pp. 241, 332.

[10] John Selden, *The Table Talk of John Selden Esq* (London, 1847), pp. 97–8, 103–4.

It was easier to express such sentiments after 1640. But good Calvinists could hardly at any time have disagreed with what John Harington was free to say in January 1641–2. The king can do no wrong, but 'all kings, even the best that ever were . . . are extremely full of infirmities and commit innumerable sins. It is needless to cite examples of that that is so common and apparent.' The meaning of the phrase 'the king can do no wrong' is 'to preserve the affections of all the English to their prince', since they will 'lay the blame wholly upon the councillors of the king'.[11]

Long before the Civil War many had accepted the merely conventional nature of the king's incapacity of doing wrong. Buchanan in 1570, writing of earlier Scottish aristocrats, said 'lest they should . . . appear to be violators of their oath and fidelity promised to the King, they proclaimed [that they] were not against him but against his wicked councillors.'[12] The Dutch sixteenth-century rebels professed loyalty to their king whilst attacking his ministers: so did French Huguenots, D'Avila records in 'Mr Hamden's *vade mecum*'; so too did Czech rebels in 1618.[13] In *The Birth of Merlin*, a play probably dating from James's reign, King Aurelius denounces his natural councillors as traitors, and allies with Saxon invaders to revenge himself on them. Clearly he must be opposed. But how can such opposition be justified? The answer anticipates the Parliamentarian position in the Civil War: we must 'with all the speed we can / Preserve the person of the King and kingdom' against the 'traitorous Saxons . . . / That with advantage thus have won the King'.[14] Sir Roger Cholmley in *Sir Thomas More* said 'his majesty / Is not informed of this base abuse . . .; / For if he were, I know his gracious wisdom / Would soon redress it.'[15]

[11] *The Diary of John Harington MP 1646–53*, ed. Margaret F. Stieg, Somerset Record Society (Yeovil, 1972), p. 103.

[12] H. R. Trevor-Roper, 'George Buchanan and the ancient Scottish constitution', *English Historical Review*, suppl. no. 3 (1966), p. 43.

[13] J. L. Motley, *The Rise of the Dutch Republic* (3 vols, London, 1892), II, pp. 178–9, 240–2, 358, 566; H. C. D'Avila, *The History of the Civil Wars of France*, 2nd imp. (London, 1678), p. 271; Geoffrey Parker, *Europe in Crisis 1590–1648* (Brighton, 1980), p. 159. In Marlowe's *The Massacre at Paris*, the Guises called the Huguenots 'Puritans'. So did Richard Bancroft.

[14] In *The Shakespeare Apocrypha*, ed. C. F. Tucker Brooke (Oxford, 1967), p. 372; cf. p. 390. The play was not published until 1662, but it is most improbable that such a passage would have been interpolated then.

[15] *The Book of Sir Thomas More*, ed. V. Gabrieli and G. Melchiori (Bari, 1981), p. 121.

MPs regularly used 'the king can do no wrong' in this sense, not that his actions are above criticism (as some councillors argued) but that where wrong was done it must be attributed to ministers. During the Civil War this came to mean that the king had somehow been kidnapped by evil councillors who were fraudulently issuing orders in his name. Somewhere along the line the doctrine that the king is literally incapable of wrong-doing had been replaced by the later constitutional doctrine. It is worth pondering the logic of Sir John Strangeways's remark: 'By how much we extol the goodness of the King, by so much we must think worse of those who counsel these courses.'[16] Already Fuller in 1610 and Coke in 1628 interpreted the maxim to mean that in certain circumstances the king could not legally do what he wanted to do. 'Nothing that is against the good of the King and his people' could be part of the prerogative, Coke declared: 'the common law hath so admeasured the King's prerogative as he cannot prejudice any man in his inheritance', including his person.[17] If the property rights of subjects and their personal liberty are always to be respected, the doctrine that the king can do no wrong falls far short of meaning what it appears to mean.

MPs never forgot the threat to property posed by unparliamentary taxation. Liberty and property were the same thing: the liberties of Englishmen meant the property rights of well-to-do Englishmen. This issue would not go away, because the crown's ever-increasing financial problems continually forced it to seek for new sources of revenue. Conflict over taxation was a fact of life, only secondarily of constitutional theory. It also seemed to many MPs a religious issue. God's law, the Ten Commandments, defended property. Almost the only theoretical defenders of arbitrary taxation were the high-flying 'Arminians'. Selden said of 'our property, I never heard it denied but in the pulpit.'[18]

That blaming 'evil councillors' was often a fiction is apparent. In a private letter to Sir Ralph Winwood, John Pory asked in 1610 'with what cords we shall bind Samson's hands, that is to say his Majesty's prerogative?'[19] Pym in 1621 was much praised for 'a neat

---

[16] *Commons Debates, 1628*, ed. R. C. Johnson and M. J. Cole (3 vols, Newhaven, Conn., 1977), III, p. 196; cf. p. 212 – Wentworth.

[17] *1610 Parliament*, II, p. 187; S. D. White, *Sir Edward Coke and 'The Grievances of the Commonwealth', 1621–28* (North Carolina, 1979), pp. 122, 232, 241, 247.

[18] *Commons Debates, 1628*, III, p. 96.

[19] *1610 Parliament*, II, p. 284.

speech' in which 'he laboured to show that the King's piety, clemency, justice, bounty, facility, peaceable disposition and other his natural virtues were by the adverse party perverted and turned to a quite contrary course.'[20] Would not this line of argument lead men to ask how 'the adverse party' won such powerful positions in the king's confidence? 'Adversary politics' was not an invention of the 1640s. Pym filled in a delicate pause in negotiations about the Petition of Right by raising the question of Mainwaring. 'Great is the love and piety of his Majesty to his subjects, and *therefore* [my italics] it may be easily judged, his abhorring this man that would draw him from justice and piety.'[21] Can his tongue really have been entirely out of his cheek when he said that? How did he feel when Charles made Mainwaring a bishop?

The king called the bluff of the Commons in 1628 by ordering them to cease distinguishing between him and his ministers. 'It is not vox regis', cried Coke. 'It is not King Charles that advised himself', added Phelips, 'but King Charles advised by others,'[22] Desperate attempts were made to contradict the king without contradicting him, in order to recover 'liberties and privileges which have been seized upon by some of the king's ministers', by 'the enemies of the kingdom.' The only way out was suggested by Coke. 'We must name the Duke [of Buckingham] lest the aspersion lie on his Majesty.' 'It is certain the King has the same ends that we have', Pym explained. 'How far particular persons do mislead him let us show.' 'We know the King cannot have knowledge himself of these things', Wentworth agreed; it was 'a lewd and hateful speech' when Auditor Sawyer pleaded the king's command for actions questioned in the House.[23]

Similarly in 1640, when Lord Keeper Finch pleaded the king's commands in defence of his actions, Stroud was 'much troubled'. He hoped 'no more of that kind will be spoken of his Majesty.'[24] It was not long before Charles's attempted arrest of the Five Mem-

---

[20] *The Letters of John Chamberlain*, ed. N. E. McClure (2 vols, Philadelphia, 1939), II, p. 412.

[21] *Commons Debates, 1628*, IV, p. 103.

[22] Ibid., IV, pp. 115, 139.

[23] C. Hill, 'Parliament and people in seventeenth-century England', *Past and Present*, no. 92 (1981), pp. 106–7, 110, 116–17; *Commons Debates, 1628*, III, pp. 212, 238, 272, 278–82, 553, 560, 569–70, 584; IV, pp. 49, 64, 115–16, 123–4, 139, 191–6, 211, 244–8, 258, 292–5.

[24] *Notebook of Sir J. Northcote*, ed. A. H. A. Hamilton (1877) pp. 94–6.

bers was described as a 'traitorous design against *the King* and Parliament' [my italics]. Pretences were collapsing. A clause deleted from the Grand Remonstrance at the instance of the moderates declared roundly that 'the King has not bread to put in his head . . . but by the bounty of his people.' 'If this King will join with us', said Pym, 'we shall set him up on as great grounds of honour and greatness in that all the world shall not be able to move him.'[25] Does the unusual phrase, 'this king' imply the possibility of another king? Chillingworth in December 1641 was speculating about whether MPs would have a right to protest against legislation to depose the king.[26]

Sir Thomas Barrington had no doubt that in 1628 it was the king, not his ministers, who had been pressurized. 'Princes', he told his wife, 'should in policy have some time and way left to evade when the point of honour is in competition; if they acknowledge their actions past illegal and their ministers confess it and plead ignorance', we should leave it at that – as had been done in the Petition of Right.[27]

Lord Chancellor Ellesmere indeed had seen a high road to civil war opening up as early as 1610. 'The popular state', he wrote, 'hath swelled more and more.' He accused the Commons of 'a new invented and supposed privilege and liberty'. 'Some particular persons . . . used very audacious and contemptuous speeches against the King's royal prerogative . . . . This hath passed with applause of many others there, and with little or no reprehension at all.'[28]

Ellesmere saw aggression only from the Commons. Chamberlain, writing to Sir Ralph Winwood in the same year, thought that the aggression came from the Crown. 'If the practice should follow the positions, we are not like to leave our successors that freedom we received from our forefathers.'[29] The practice did not follow the positions, on either side. The positions had been taken up not

---

[25] *The Journal of Sir Simonds D'Ewes, from the first recess of the Long Parliament to the withdrawal of King Charles from London*, ed. W. H. Coates (Newhaven, Conn., 1942), pp. 394, 185–6; *The Journal of Sir Simonds D'Ewes, from the beginning of the Long Parliament to the opening of the Trial of the Earl of Strafford*, ed. W. Notestein (Newhaven, Conn., 1923), pp. 233–4.

[26] D'Ewes, *Journal*, ed. Coates, pp. 232–4.

[27] *Barrington Letters, 1628–32*, ed. A. Searle, Camden Society Fourth Series 28 (1983), p. 59.

[28] *1610 Parliament*, I, pp. 276–8; cf. pp. 278–83.

[29] Chamberlain, *Letters*, ed. McClure, I, p. 301.

because of the wicked ambition of leaders of the Commons or the petulant ignorance of a foreign king, but because continuing inflation was undermining royal finance. That is why the 'undertaking' of 1614 turned the House of Commons against those who had appeared to be its leaders and spokesmen in the preceding parliament: the conflicts were not between 'ins' and 'outs' but reflected slowly diverging interests between which mediation became impossible.[30] 'The most popular men', wrote Arthur Wilson, 'as soon as they wore the court livery, lost the love of the people; but those that suffered for them, were the more beloved and admired by them.'[31] This does not fit very easily into the picture of a House of Commons whose members' main wish was to co-operate with the government.

In 1626 the Venetian ambassador reported that the kingdom was divided into two: the king, Buckingham and a few lucky individuals against the rest of the country.[32] Rejection of 'courtiers' in elections, even when they had the king's backing, would seem to support this. In the elections of 1624 and 1625 the word 'royalist' was used disparagingly of court candidates.[33] In 1628 Joseph Mede referred to opponents of the court as 'patriots' – a phrase which anticipates the French Revolution.[34] But there was no more a continuous 'court' interest than there was a continuing opposition in parliament. There was much disaffection among courtiers and government servants. The diarist Robert Bowyer was secretary to Lord Buckhurst and clerk to the House of Lords; but his sympathies were with the Puritans.[35] Many courtiers opposed dissolu-

---

[30] Cf. D. H. Willson, *The Privy Councillors in the House of Commons, 1604–29* (Minneapolis, 1940), p. 144.

[31] A. Wilson, *The History of Great Britain* (1653), p. 192.; Willson, *The Privy Councillors*, pp. 70–9, 158, 203, 212; cf. C. Thomspon, *The Holles Account*, p. 59 – against court papists.

[32] Willson, *The Privy Councillors*, pp. 189, 200; R. E. Ruigh, *The Parliament of 1624* (Boston, 1971), pp. 44, 57, 148.

[33] D. Hirst, *The Representative of the People? Voters and Voting in England under the Early Stuarts* (Cambridge, 1975), p. 144; *Calendar of State Papers, Venetian, 1625–6*, p. 63; Chamberlain, *Letters*, ed. McClure, II, p. 540; Fulke Greville had used the phrase in his *Life of Sir Philip Sidney*, not published until 1652 (1907 edn, p. 187). So did Bacon in 1612: *Works*, ed. J. Spedding, R. L. Ellis and D. D. Heath (1857–72), IV, pp. 279–80.

[34] T. Birch (ed.), *The Court and Times of Charles I* (2 vols, London, 1848), I, p. 327.

[35] *The Parliamentary Diary of Robert Bowyer, 1606–7*, ed. D. H. Willson (Minneapolis, 1931), p. xiii.

tions of parliament. It is as naive to think that divisions within
parliament were stirred up by dissident courtiers as to think that
agitators cause strikes. We should assume rather that divisions in
parliament, court and privy council reflected divisions in the
country.

So we should be prepared to use evidence from outside the House
of Commons to assess the nuances of what was said there in highly
stylized and conventional language. It is important in such matters
not to try to be wiser than S. R. Gardiner, Wallace Notestein and
R. H. Tawney, who were not only great historians of parliamentary
politics but were also soaked in the literature and culture of the
times they studied. Fortunately literary historians can help us here,
notably Margot Heinemann, Jonathan Dollimore, Simon Shepherd,
David Norbrook and Martin Butler.[36]

From about the beginning of the century dramatists clearly
assume that courts and courtiers are corrupt. Wicked favourites
deceive and abuse their masters, sometimes ultimately attempting
to supplant them. The nature and duties of kingship were under
continual discussion in plays from Marlowe and Shakespeare onwards. There are repeated contrasts between the God-given nature
of the office and the all too human individuals who fill it.[37] One
critic has identified a series of plays just after 1610 which he
believes relate to the parliamentary crisis that terminated with the
dissolution of that year.[38] Another has studied a series of 'preten-
der' plays from the 1630s. They do not offer evidence of proposed
alternatives to Charles I but they allow freedom to speculate about
a 'good' if illegitimate monarch.[39] Middleton's A Game of Chess
shows what sort of plays audiences would have flocked to see if they
had more often been given the chance.[40]

There were other influences moulding public opinion. Sir Walter
Ralegh's provocatively entitled The Prerogative of Parliaments could

[36] M. Heinemann, Puritanism and Theatre: Thomas Middleton and opposition drama
under the Early Stuarts (Cambridge, 1980); J. Dollimore, Radical Tragedy: Religion,
ideology and power in the drama of Shakespeare and his contemporaries (Brighton, 1984);
S. Shepherd, Amazons and Warrior Women: Varieties of feminism in seventeenth-century
drama (Brighton, 1981), esp. chs. 9 and 13; David Norbrook, Poetry and Politics in the
English Renaissance (1984); M. Butler, Theatre and Crisis, 1632-42 (Cambridge, 1984).
[37] Dollimore, Radical Tragedy, pp. 3-4.
[38] Shepherd, Amazons and Warrior Women, p. 120.
[39] Philip Edwards, 'The royal Pretenders in Massinger and Ford', Essays and
Studies (1974), pp. 34-5; cf. Butler, Theatre and Crisis, passim.
[40] Heinemann, Puritanism and Theatre, esp. ch. 10.

not be published in England before 1640, but it circulated exten-
sively in manuscript; three illegal editions appeared in the critical
year 1628. It was written in dialogue form – a convenient way of
avoiding responsibility for dangerous views. Ralegh's Justice put
forward a programme for action based on the proto-Harringtonian
assumption that parliament represents forces which cannot be
wished out of existence: the king must accept historical necessity.[41]
'A prince by racking his sovereign authority to the utmost extent',
Ralegh observed in his best-selling *History of the World*, only brings
evil consequences on his successors.[42] Ralegh's remark was topical:
Chamberlain in 1610 said that James's speeches 'bred generally
much discomfort to see our monarchical power and royal prerogative stretched so high and made so transcendent every way.'[43]

Historians too easily forget the censorship, on published and
unpublished material. In 1626 a man was twice racked for writing a
private letter which contained 'words and insinuations against His
Majesty'.[44] The Barringtons feared lest their private correspondence should be opened and read.[45] D'Ewes kept his diary in cypher;
Selden employed anagrams in his correspondence.

The views which could be expressed were not the only views
which were held. Men like Thomas Hobbes, Joseph Mede,
D'Ewes, Fulke Greville and Sir Henry Spelman deliberately refrained
from publishing (or from writing) through fear of censorship.
Others (like Coke) were forcibly prevented from publishing. It is
difficult even to guess how many writers said less than they
thought, for prudential reasons. For 'public opinion' expressed in
works published in the 1620s and 1630s is so different from what
surfaced after the collapse of the censorship that it would be foolish
not to suppose that many men previously held views which could
be printed only after the liberation of the press. Any other assumption would have to postulate a remarkable revolution in opinion.[46]

Nevertheless, there were ways in which, whilst maintaining

---

[41] *The Prerogative of Parliaments*, in *The Works of Sir Walter Ralegh Kt.*, ed. T. Birch
(2 vols, London, 1751), I, pp. 242–7; cf. II, p. 318.
[42] Sir Walter Ralegh, *History of the World* (6 vols, Edinburgh, 1820), VI, p. 35;
see R. H. Tawney, *Harrington's Interpretation of his Age*, Raleigh Lecture (1941), for
Ralegh's anticipation of Harrington's version of English history.
[43] Chamberlain, *Letters*, ed. McClure, I, p. 301.
[44] Birch, *Court and Times of Charles I*, I, p. 99.
[45] *Barrington Letters*, ed. Searle, pp. 53, 100.
[46] I have argued this case at some length in *Writing and Revolution in 17th Century
England* (Brighton, 1985), ch. 2.

decorum of discourse, criticism of the monarchy could be implied.
MPs might call for a fast, in order to propitiate God for the nation's
sins. Governments could hardly resist this, for no accusations were
made. But among the sins to be forgiven there were always some for
which it was difficult to exonerate the government – the prevalence
of popery, failure to support our protestant brethren on the continent, and so on. The plagues of 1625 and 1635 seemed additional
evidence of God's anger with England's sins. The neatest example
was when in 1640 the Commons called for a fast on 17 November –
Queen Elizabeth's accession day.

The poems of Drayton, Browne and Wither are full of political
criticism in the form of pastoral and allegory: Sidney and Spenser
had indeed recommended these genres for this very purpose. The
golden age existed before monarchy was invented. 'Had all been
virtuous men', wrote Chapman, 'There never had been prince
upon the earth.'[47] History was useful too, especially in the House of
Commons. Sherland in 1625 prudently chose an example from the
reign of Henry V, when 'the Commons did desire the King he would
keep his promise for execution of the laws better than heretofore.
This did anger the King, but the blame rested upon them that had
given him ill counsel.'[48] In the same year Sir Robert Phelips
described Henry VI's Duke of Suffolk who 'made a marriage for the
King, wholly possessed the government, caused an alteration of
lands, did encroach upon the honour and dignity of the kingdom,
etc.'; there was no need to name Buckingham. The conclusion
followed: 'when he was laid by, the reformation followed.' Coke
came even nearer home when he said 'the office of Lord Admiral is
a place of greatest trust. . . . It will be well when offices are restored
to men of sufficiency. If an office be granted to an unexperienced
man, it is void.' The Master of Ordnance had normally been a
tradesman until 20 Henry VIII; 'and since it was possessed by the
nobility, was never well executed'. 'Our story mentioneth no levies
against law,' mused Sherland, 'which have not bred tumults and
commotions.' To cite a precedent was a polite way of saying No.[49]
Pym in 1628 was unspecific when he said 'some times have
produced such kings as, if they had had the whole kingdom to

[47] George Chapman, *The Gentleman Usher*, in *Comedies and Tragedies* (3 vols,
London, 1873), I, p. 331.
[48] S. R. Gardiner (ed.) *Debates in the House of Commons in 1625*, Camden Society
New Series, 6 (London, 1873), p. 124.
[49] Ibid., pp. 85, 109, 125, 130–1; cf. pp. 146, 148.

dispense, it had not been unlike to have been spent.'[50] In the Short Parliament he was more precise: 'we know how unfortunate Henry III of France and other princes have been by occasion of such breaking their laws [as those which he had just listed in England]. I pray God we never see such times.'[51]

The most obvious historical example was Queen Elizabeth I, who could be praised to the skies for virtues which her successors conspicuously lacked. Ellesmere referred to the House of Commons 'seditiously looking back', and implying that 'the times past were golden days.'[52] Phelips drew the contrast in 1625: 'It was not wont to be so when God and we held together; witness that glorious Queen.'[53] Eliot returned to 'that never-to-be-forgotten excellent Queen Elizabeth' at the crisis of the debate on the Petition of Right.[54] Conrad Russell just missed the point when he said that 'for Eliot, saying something was a cornerstone of Elizabethan policy was normally synonymous with saying he agreed with it.'[55] Eliot was not merely agreeing with it; he was passionately advocating it in conditions of discourse which made it difficult to do so directly. Adulation of Prince Henry, before and especially after his death, had a similar function.[56]

The ever-present fear that 'we are the last monarchy in Christendom that retain our original rights and constitutions'[57] was repeated in every parliament from 1604 onwards, and by many outside parliament.[58] Since Charles and his ministers rubbed the point home by threatening to discontinue parliaments, the eleven years of personal rule took no one by surprise: it looked like the culmination of a deliberate policy.[59]

[50] *Commons Debates, 1628*, IV, p. 104.
[51] E. S. Cope and W. H. Coates (eds), *Proceedings of the Short Parliament of 1640*, Camden Society Fourth Series, 19 (London, 1977), p. 259.
[52] *1610 Parliament*, I, p. 278.
[53] *Commons Debates, 1625*, p. 31.
[54] *Commons Debates, 1628*, IV, pp. 144, 62.
[55] C. Russell, *Parliaments and English Politics, 1621-9* (Oxford, 1979), p. 80.
[56] Cf. E. K. Wilson, *Prince Henry and English Literature* (Cornell, 1946), and C. Hill, *Intellectual Origins of the English Revolution* (Oxford, 1965), pp. 213-19.
[57] *Commons Debates, 1625*, p. 110.
[58] Timothy Turner of Gray's Inn feared in 1616 that no more parliaments would be held 'et tunc valeat antiqua libertas Angliae'. Quoted by W. R. Prest in his forthcoming *Professors of the Law: a social history of the English Bar, 1590-1640*, which he kindly allowed me to read in advance of publication. Cf. *Diary of John Rous*, ed. M. A. E. Green, Camden Society First Series, 66 (London, 1856), pp. 2-3.
[59] Chamberlain, *Letters*, ed. McClure, II, p. 321.

We do not perhaps sufficiently emphasize the sense of imminent catastrophe which many Englishmen felt in the 1620s and 1630s. To take random phrases from the Barrington correspondence in 1628–9: 'God's heavy judgment most like to befall us'; 'God can bring upon us a worse scourge' even than Buckingham; 'we never had such need [to cry to the Lord] as now; . . . we have no other refuge to fly to'; 'these storms which in the eye of reason this sinful nation is likely to endure'. Sir William and Lady Masham besought 'the Lord to prepare us with comfort to brave what he may lay upon us'.[60] Such fears drove the Pilgrim Fathers and the Massachusetts Bay settlers to risk the horrors of the Atlantic crossing and life in the wilderness.

The Spanish marriage negotiations of the early 1620s led to intensified public interest in questions of foreign policy, stimulated by Puritan preachers, and to 'an attempt to marshal public opinion in opposition to the foreign policy of a government' for the first time in English history.[61] In 1623 Thomas Scott in exile was calling on ministers and freeholders to get godly men elected to parliament.[62]

Historians should take very seriously the evidence for Charles I's Popish Plot collected by Caroline Hibbard.[63] Many contemporaries were decisively influenced by belief in the existence of a plot against England's religion and national independence. During the Civil War even royalists were alarmed.[64] On the other side Stephen Marshall was soon to refer to 'many of the nobles, magistrates, knights and gentlemen' as 'arrant traitors and rebels against God' – words even stronger than those of the Grand Remonstrance.[65] We cannot ignore the feeling behind such language, given the belief that a life-and-death struggle was going on between Christ and Antichrist. Frustrations had long been accumulating in the 'beleaguered isle'.[66] Under Grindal and Abbot there had been hope; under Whitgift, Bancroft and Laud, growing despair and despera-

[60] *Barrington Letters*, ed. Searle, pp. 29, 36–7, 56, 60, 77, 90.
[61] G. Davies, 'English political sermons', *Huntingdon Library Quarterly*, 3 (1939), pp. 4–13; cf. Hill, *Society and Puritanism*, Panther edn, pp. 41–2.
[62] T. Scott, *The High-waies of the King* (1623), p. 86.
[63] C. Hibbard, *Charles I and the Popish Plot* (North Carolina, 1983), passim.
[64] Lord Henry Spencer and Captain John Fenwick, quoted in John Adair, *By the Sword Divided: Eyewitnesses of the English Civil War* (London, 1983), pp. 37–8, 131.
[65] Stephen Marshall, *Reformation and Desolation* (1642), p. 45; cf. Hibbard, *Charles I and the Popish Plot*, pp. 246–7.
[66] Carol Z. Wiener, 'The Beleaguered Isle: a study of Elizabethan and early Jacobean anti-catholicism', *Past and Present*, no. 51 (1971).

tion. The fact that Laud rejected the traditional protestant equa-
tion of Antichrist with the Pope seemed evidence of his own
antichristianity.

This may help to resolve the paradox that the enemies of bishops
seem to have been motivated mainly by religion, their defenders
mainly by social considerations:[67] if bishops went, the attack might
turn against peers and landlords. Conservatives were more aware
of the revolutionary implications of Puritan ideology than the
radicals: this had been true since the days of Martin Marprelate.
The Marprelate Tracts offer a last example of irreverent plebeian
discourse, referring to the Archbishop of Canterbury as 'nunckle
Canterbury', 'that Caiaphas of Cant.,' 'that miserable and desperate caitiff'; to Bishop Aylmer as 'dumb dunsical John of good
London'.[68] When it became impossible to publish such tracts in
England, Thomas Scott and others carried on the tradition from
the Netherlands. The Marprelate Tracts were reprinted as soon as
the censorship collapsed in 1640. Richard Overton echoed Marprelate; Levellers, Diggers, Ranters and early Quakers continued and
developed this rival tradition of irreverent prose.

Until the government collapsed, all members of the propertied
class were interested in preserving the king as the keystone of the
social arch. For most of the time most of the people seem, so far as
we can tell, to have accepted unquestioningly the necessity of a
hierarchical society. But we must emphasize 'so far as we can tell'.
I have been dealing throughout with respectable opinions. We get
occasional glimpses of a different world among the lower classes.
'By God I do not care a turd neither for the King nor his laws', said
an Essex man at the beginning of James I's reign; and Mr Emmison found much subversive talk attacking king, Council, officers
and the church among the lower classes of this county.[69] How
much significance should be attached to such letting off of steam is
hard to assess. But the poverty, wars and misgovernment of the
1620s and 1630s, and the knowledge that their betters were dissa-

[67] Joyce Malcolm, *Caesar's Due: Loyalty and King Charles I, 1642–6* (London, 1983), p. 163.
[68] Martin Marprelate, *The Epistle* (1588), p. 20; *Hay any worke for Cooper?* (1589), p. 43; *Theses Martinianae* (1589), Sig. C iiv; *The just censure and reproofe* (1589), Sig. A iiv, B iiiv – C ii.
[69] F. G. Emmison, *Elizabethan Life: Disorder, mainly from Essex sessions and assize records* (Chelmsford, 1976), pp. viii, 39; cf. J. Sharpe, 'The people and the law', in *Popular Culture in Seventeenth-Century England*, ed. B. Reay (London, 1985), p. 249.

tisfied, unleashed a rebelliousness which Brian Manning has documented. A country ballad singer, we are told in 1629, would have his songs 'interlarded with anything against the state, they are main helps to him and he will adventure to sing them though they cost him a whipping.'[70] Popular opinion in London was shown in the matter of bonfires. Ordered to celebrate Prince Charles's landing in Spain in 1623, they were 'thin and poor'; on his return, unmarried, they were spontaneous, 'many and great'.[71] Unofficial bonfires lit for the passing of the Petition of Right were 'such as were never seen but upon his Majesty's return from Spain'.[72]

'The whole land murmured' at the dissolution of 1622, D'Ewes told his diary; the king's reasons for it 'gave little satisfaction to any, and therefore, if the English had not altogether lost their spirits, some rebellion was expected.'[73] The twenty-year-old D'Ewes no doubt exaggerated; but fear (or hope) of popular rebellion was not unique to him. Fulke Greville in 1593 had reminded MPs that 'if the feet knew their strength as we know their oppression, they would not bear as they do'.[74] In 1626 the Suffolk parson John Rous found that 'men be disposed to speak the worst of state business and to nourish discontent, as if there were a false carriage in all these things.' He thought that 'these men prepare' the way to 'an insurrection'. 'Our King's proceedings have caused men's minds to be incensed, to rove and project . . . looking towards the Lady Elizabeth' which 'is fearful to be thought of'. Rous believed this last idea could be dismissed as 'merely the conceit of the multitude', in itself a remarkable admission.[75] The French and Venetian ambassadors were aware of new tensions which might break out into rebellion once authority at the centre collapsed. So was an observer like Bacon, who said 'civil wars . . . seem to me apt to spread through many countries – because of certain ways of life not long since introduced'.[76] Fear that breakdown of ruling class consensus might lead to social revolt was widespread. Keith Thomas collected

[70] B. Manning, *The English People and the English Revolution* (London, 1976), passim; B. Capp, 'Popular literature', in Reay, *Popular Culture*, pp. 227–8.

[71] D'Ewes, *Diary*, ed. Bourcier, p. 162.

[72] *Commons Debates, 1628*, IV, p. 183.

[73] D'Ewes, *Diary*, ed. Bourcier, p. 58; cf. pp. 64–5, 83, 130, 145.

[74] D'Ewes, *A Complete Journal of the . . . House of Commons* (1693), p. 490.

[75] Rous, *Diary*, ed. Green, pp. 11–12, 19. 'The Lady Elizabeth' is of course the Queen of Bohemia.

[76] F. H. Anderson, *The Philosophy of Francis Bacon* (Chicago, 1948), p. 11.

a list of people alleged to have predicted the Civil War; they included Richard Hooker, Lancelot Andrewes, archbishops Abbot and Ussher, Nicholas Ferrar and others.[77]

Given this background, it might have been dangerous to allow even mildly critical speeches by MPs to be circulated to the general public. After the dissolution of 1614 notes and papers of suspect members were seized and burnt; and again in 1629.[78] In 1628 Sir Dudley Digges would 'rather cover the power the subjects have than let it be openly spoke abroad, that mean men may not know it, which perhaps if they did should be inconvenient.' Sir Nathaniel Rich thought 'the meaner sort of people [were] in danger to join with [soldiers] and to fall into mutiny and rebellion.' The point was incorporated into a petition against billeting: 'the meaner sort . . . being exceeding poor . . . are not easily ruled' and were ready to cast off the reins of government [79] Such considerations were in the minds of MPs when they instructed Sir Henry Marten to remind the peers how undesirable it would be to refer to the limits on royal sovereignty in a document which would be printed and so made accessible to the vulgar.[80] A breach between the Commons on the one hand and the king and Lords on the other would be no less disastrous. 'Consider the consequences if we join not with the Commons,' said the Earl of Clare.[81] The popularity of Felton, Buckingham's assassin, with the lower classes must have given their betters food for thought.

The fiercest quarrel in the House of Commons before the Civil War arose over the proposal to appeal outside parliament by printing the Grand Remonstrance in November 1641. Sir Edward Dering was shocked by 'this descension from a Parliament to a people . . . . The better sort think best of us . . . I did not dream that we should remonstrate downwards, tell stories to the people.'[82] In the Short Parliament, Lord Keeper Finch referred to those who would be prepared to adopt 'Kett's and Cade's principles, which is to ruin the nobility, to ruin the gentry, to ruin learning and devour and eat up one another.'[83] In his Declaration in answer to the

[77] Keith Thomas, *Religion and the Decline of Magic* (London, 1971), p. 132.
[78] Chamberlain, *Letters*, ed. McClure, I, p. 539.
[79] *Commons Debates, 1628*, II, pp. 287, 391, 452.
[80] C. Hill, 'Parliament and people', pp. 116–18.
[81] F. H. Relf (ed.), *Notes of the Debates of the House of Lords* Camden Society Third Series, 42 (London, 1929), p. 203.
[82] Rushworth, *Historical Collections*, IV, p. 425.
[83] *Proceedings of the Short Parliament*, p. 131–2.

Grand Remonstrance, Charles I referred to the spate of 'seditious' pamphlets and sermons: 'We are many times amazed to consider by what eyes these things are seen, and by what ears they are heard.'[84] Answering the Nineteen Propositions Charles predicted that 'at last the common people' will 'set up for themselves, and destroy all rights and properties'; government would 'end in a dark, equal chaos of confusion . . . in a Jack Cade or a Wat Tyler'.[85] The king exaggerated for effect, but the repeated warnings would have been pointless if there were no basis for them. Contemporaries were not as surprised as some historians at what happened when revolution broke out.

If we think then of the ideas current in the world in which MPs lived, there were plenty which might make them sceptical of royal claims. Thomas Beard, Oliver Cromwell's schoolmaster, wrote a very popular book describing God's judgements on (among others) wicked princes. 'If you be mighty, puissant and fearful, know that the Lord is greater than you; . . . in what place soever you are, he is always above you, ready to hurl you down.'[86] Archbishop Grindal had used similar words to Queen Elizabeth on a famous occasion. 'It is as easy with the Almighty to destroy the mightiest king as the poorest babe,' said John Harington in the spirit of Beard.[87] Wallace MacCaffrey emphasizes the tension between protestant loyalty to the sovereign and loyalty to what Puritans believed to the the Word of God. Unfortunately the two did not always coincide.[88] This was one reason for not wanting the finer points of the dispute between Calvinists and Arminians to be 'talked of openly by the vulgar'.[89]

James I thought Ralegh's *History of the World* was 'too saucy in censuring princes'.[90] Hobbes believed that translations of the republican classics had been a significant contributory cause of the

[84] J. Nalson, *An Impartial Collection of the Great Affairs of State* (2 vols, London, 1683), II, p. 747.

[85] Rushworth, *Historical Collections*, V, p. 732.

[86] Beard, *The Theatre of Gods Judgments*, 4th edn (1648), title-page. First published 1597.

[87] Harington, *Diary*, ed. Stieg, p. 106.

[88] W. T. MacCaffrey, *Queen Elizabeth and the Making of Policy 1572–88* (Princeton, 1981), p. 492.

[89] John Young to Samuel Ward, quoted by Peter White, 'The rise of Arminianism reconsidered', *Past and Present*, no. 101 (1983), p. 13 and passim.

[90] Ralegh, *History of the World*, I, pp. viii–xv, xxviii–xxxviii.

Civil War.[91] There were many books on Venice, which Bacon among others admired as 'the wisest state of Europe'.[92] Above all there was the successful example of the United Provinces. Elizabethan government propaganda had stressed the 'perpetual unions of the . . . hearts together' of the peoples of England and the Netherlands.[93] Ralegh had drawn attention to the confiscation of aristocratic property in the Netherlands, and to the prosperity which resulted from merchants' control of the republic.[94] From 1604 onwards many MPs, including Coke, praised what they took to be the economic and social consequences of the Dutch revolt from Spain.[95] Hobbes indeed thought that London citizens 'were inclined to think that the like change of government would to them produce the like prosperity'. He was echoing what Nashe had said eighty-seven years earlier.[96]

The early Christian church could be held up as a model, without actually questioning the legitimacy of episcopacy. The liberty of the Anglo-Saxons before the introduction of Norman tyranny could be extolled, without specifying what if any elements of the Norman Yoke still remained. At the opposite pole of human history there was a widespread belief that the end of the world was approaching. Christ was the 'shortly-expected King' for many besides Milton. The evils which men saw around them could be attributed to 'these dead and declining times'[97] which would imediately precede the Second Coming. The fasts which the Commons called for to expiate the sins of the land were more than a formality. But speculations about the millennium could not circulate in print before 1640: they

[91] Thomas Hobbes, *Leviathan*, Everyman edn (London, 1914), p. 174; *Behemoth*, in *English Works of Thomas Hobbes*, ed. Sir W. Molesworth (1839–48), VI, pp. 190–1.

[92] Anon, *Cabala, Mysteries of State* (London, 1654), I, p. 8.

[93] MacCaffrey, *Queen Elizabeth and the Making of Policy*, pp. 340–1, 487.

Ralegh, *Works*, II, pp. 15, 112–36; cf. pp. 89–90, 17–20.

[95] S. R. Gardiner (ed.) *Parliamentary Debates in 1610*, Camden Society First Series 81 (London, 1862), p. 114; W. Notestein, F. H. Relf and H. Simpson, *Commons Debates in 1621* (7 vols, Newhaven, Conn., 1935), V, p. 93; J. Forster, *Sir J. Eliot: a biography* (2 vols, London, 1865), I, p. 169.

[96] Hobbes, *Behemoth*, ed. Molesworth, p. 168; Thomas Nashe, *Pierce Penilesse his Supplication to the Divell* (1592), in *Works*, ed. R. B. McKerrow (5 vols, Oxford, 1958), I, pp. 212–13.

[97] *Barrington Letters*, ed. Searle, p. 77; cf. Ralegh, *History of the World*, I, p. 20; cf. II, p. 650.

were thought to be dangerous and divisive. The seminal writings of Thomas Brightman were not allowed to be published in England, and Joseph Mede's scholarly work remained in Latin until a committee of the Long Parliament ordered its translation.

The logic of Puritanism called social hierarchy into question. Lords Brooke and Saye and Sele were astonished when the Massachusetts colonists politely but firmly refused to promise them the privileges of peers if they emigrated to New England. If they became church members they would enjoy the political rights of other church members; but no more.[98] That was an extreme position: but Beard's principles must have influenced many of the godly. 'In this Parliament', noted Yonge in 1624, 'there was not any one public bill sent to the lower house by them [the peers]. See what care they have for the commonwealth.'[99] 'I fear few lords have the main,' Lady Elizabeth Masham wrote to her mother in January 1630, 'the true fear of God which I prefer before all the honour in the world.'[100] She was discussing a marriage proposal, but there are wider implications. Henry Oxinden wrote in 1642: 'If I see a man of what low degree or quality soever that is virtuous, rich, wise or powerful, him will I prefer before the greatest lord in the kingdom that comes short of him in these.'[101] (The words 'rich' and 'powerful' show that this is social rather than moral comment.)

Full hostility to the peerage was developed only by the radicals in the 1640s, attacking all distinction of ranks. But members of the lower house which could buy the lords up three times over must often have reflected on this disparity. Some historians tend to exaggerate the importance of the peerage in this period, because peers, like the king, were still addressed with conventional respect. In that deferential society, a gentleman would ask a peer for a favour with proper humility. It does not prove that a Hampden, a Harrington or an Eliot was not equal in effective standing with

---

[98] Avihu Zakai, 'Exile and kingdom: reformation, separation and the millenial quest in the formation of Massachusetts and its relationship with England, 1628–60', DPhil. thesis, Johns Hopkins University, 1982, p. 309. I am grateful to Dr Zakai for sending me a copy of this thesis.

[99] Diary of Walter Yonge, ed. G. Roberts, Camden Society First Series, 41 (1848), p. 76. Cf. D'Ewes, Journal, ed. Coates, p. 224: 'I hope the citizens will be careful never to trust lord again, but to make them pay ready money.'

[100] Barrington Letters, ed. Searle, p. 123.

[101] D. Gardiner, The Oxinden Letters, 1607–42 (London, 1933), p. 279.

many peers,[102] nor even that a lesser gentleman like Pym would take orders from the Earl of Bedford.[103]

It was Oliver Cromwell who was said to have wished to see the Earl of Manchester but Mr Montagu again: the Montagus were parvenus even more recent than the Cromwells. It was Cromwell who pushed through the Self-Denying Ordinance which deprived peers of their traditional right of military command; it was Cromwell who 'had rather have a plain russet-coated captain than that which you call "a gentleman" and is nothing else.'[104] Beard's and Cromwell's principles had perhaps a more decisive influence on the outcome of the Civil War than is always recognized. The royalist armies suffered from what Monk called 'a rabble of gentility', who were expensive and bad for discipline. Parliament's shortage of officers helped to get Cromwell's principle of the career open to talents enforced despite the reluctance of some commanding officers.[105]

In retrospect perhaps the most important fact about Cromwell was his irreverence, his subversion of degree. ' "The man is an Anabaptist?" What of it?' Provided he has the root of the matter in him his private opinions are as irrelevant as the colour of his blood. At Naseby, Oliver reported, 'God would by things that are not bring to nought things that are.'[106] That looks forward to the world of revolutionary democracy; but it also looks back to Foxe's conception of the godly English common people. It was Cromwell who in November 1641 proposed what was to become the militia ordinance of March 1642, the first direct challenge to the king's sovereignty.[107] He was reported as saying that if he met the king on the battlefield he would shoot him as he would any other enemy. 'We will cut off his head with the crown on it.' His irreverence was directed not only against social rank and the divinity hedging kings but also against all the formality of authority. 'Take away that bauble.' Whether or not Oliver did refer to 'Magna farta' the

[102] J. H. Hexter, 'Power struggle, parliament and liberty in early Stuart England', *Journal of Modern History*, 50 (1978), p. 70.

[103] Hill, 'Parliament and people', pp. 106–7.

[104] W. C. Abbot (ed.), *Writings and Speeches of Oliver Cromwell* (4 vols, Cambridge, Mass., 1937–47), I, pp. 256, 262.

[105] J. Malcolm, *Caesar's Due* (London, 1983), ch. 4, which contains much useful information on this question.

[106] Abbott, *Writings and Speeches of Oliver Cromwell*, I, pp. 278, 365.

[107] D'Ewes, *Journal*, ed. Coates, pp. 97–8.

attribution is *ben trovato*. Such remarks would go down well with the troops.

The seventeenth century saw a turning-point in English and world history, from a deference society dominated by an aristocracy of the armigerous, whose weapons made them traditionally immune, to something beginning to look more like the modern world, a society of relative equality, of social mobility, of promotion by merit. Bacon had envisaged such a society and ineffectually recommended it to the young Sir George Villiers as 'that which I think was never done since I was born'.[108]

But the break came with revolution: Cromwell had the appropriate sentiments for leading it. Oliver was no intellectual: it is difficult to think of him as the ideologist of the English Revolution. But he gave colourful expression to ideas which motivated its most enthusiastic supporters. His irreverence dates back to his co-operation with the freemen of Huntingdon and with the Fenmen. It relates to the social changes so carefully demonstrated by Stone, Manning, Hirst, Wrightson and Hunt – decline of the aristocracy, growing class tensions, new importance of parish elites who found Puritanism sociologically as well as theologically attractive, growing importance of rank-and-file electors to parliament. As early as 1610 an MP said, à propos taxation and control of ale-houses, 'If we bring not ease in these things home with us to our neighbours, we shall hardly be welcome.'[109]

Historians who have failed to find long-term causes of the English Revolution, as well as those who have failed to notice that there was a revolution at all, have perhaps been looking for the wrong things in the wrong places. There were no revolutionaries who willed what happened, no Lenin: there were virtually no republicans in the Long Parliament. But there were tensions in the society, slowly building up in the decades before 1640: and there was an ideology, popularized by Foxe and Beard, which in appropriate circumstances could become revolutionary, as it did in Cromwell. Men remembered Marprelate in 1641. Scholars have spoken of a 'polarization of taste'.[110] There were also those un-

[108] *Cabala*, II, p. 71.
[109] *1610 Debates*, II, p. 95.
[110] Capp, 'Popular literature', pp. 231–2; P. W. Thomas, 'Two Cultures? Court and Country under Charles I', in *The Origins of the English Civil War*, ed. C. Russell (London, 1975).

speakable lower classes, some of whom expressed opinions far removed from those approved in respectable discourse.

The problem of those who wanted change was not to foment rebellion, but to prevent social revolt from below breaking out. Sir Robert Cotton in 1628 argued that although parliament must do all it could to get rid of the Duke of Buckingham, still in the last resort intransigence must not be pushed too far lest it open the gates to popular insurrection.[111] In Harrington's famous words, 'the dissolution of this government caused the [civil] war, not the war the dissolution of the government'.[112] Charles I had lost his crown already, Cardinal Barberini informed Henrietta Maria in February 1642.[113] It is surely more plausible to see continuities than to assume that the startling shifts in opinion between 1640 and 1649 had no antecedent causes.

Take an analogous case where contemporary modes of discourse can mislead. Some historians have argued that the passion of love was non-existent before the eighteenth century, because few talked about it and the preachers preached against it. The fact that it was not talked about was a convention of discourse: passion was not regarded as morally desirable. But the preachers would not have warned so regularly and so strongly against something that did not exist. The same is true of love for children. It too was not an invention of the eighteenth century, as a reaction of demand to an increase in supply. The preachers here too warned against excessive displays of emotion which became fashionable only with the rise of romanticism.

The restoration of 1660 was followed by a reinforcement of censorship and tacit agreement on conventions of responsible political discourse, including condemnation of anything that savoured of 'enthusiasm'. But the emphasis had subtly shifted. The king was once more immune from criticism; but now England had a 'mixed monarchy'. Royal power was indissolubly linked with that of parliament, with liberty, property and the protestant religion, all of which the king was now deemed to support.[114] It was as treason-

---

[111] R. Cotton, *The Dangers Wherein the Kingdome now Standeth* (1628). I owe this reference to Simon Adams.
[112] Harrington, *Political Works*, ed. J. G. A. Pocock (Cambridge, 1977), p. 198.
[113] D'Ewes, *Journal*, ed. Notestein, p. 321.
[114] See the valuable study by S. N. Zwicker, *Politics and Language in Dryden's Poetry* (Princeton, 1984); J. Miller, 'Charles II and his parliaments', *TRHS*, 5th ser., 32 (1982), p. 17.

able, Marvell argued in 1677, to make monarchy absolute as to 'alter our monarchy into a commonwealth'.[115] Political revolution necessitated a change in the accepted terms of discourse.

There is, it seems to me, far more to explain if we abandon some such concept as the Great Rebellion, the Puritan Revolution or the English Revolution. To say it was an accident leaves army democracy, Levellers and the execution of Charles I totally inexplicable. The leaders' compulsion to act came from religion: when the breakdown of government could no longer be prevented, revolutionary Puritanism took over, first leading to revolt, then suppressing the radicals. But the breakdown was no accident: it was foreseen by the articulate few who crossed the Atlantic because 'God is leaving England.' The religious perspective, the sense of God's continuing watchfulness over England, explained in retrospect what Cromwell called 'the revolutions of Christ'. God called the Long Parliament, God created the New Model Army. Oliver Cromwell was 'the force of angry heaven's flame' [which] 'cast the kingdom old/Into another mould'.[116]

---

[115] Andrew Marvell, *An Account of the Growth of Popery and Arbitrary Government in England* (Amsterdam, 1677), in *Complete Works in Verse and Prose*, ed. A. B. Grosart (4 vols, London, 1872–5), IV, p. 261.

[116] I read Susan Staves's 'Where is history but in texts? Reading the history of marriage', in *The Golden and the Brazen World: Papers in Literature and History 1650–1800*, ed. J. M. Wallace (Berkeley, 1985), after this article was written. What she has to say is very relevant to my argument.

4
Levelling by Sword, Spade and Word: Radical Egalitarianism in the English Revolution

MAURICE GOLDSMITH

Despite, or because of, much recent work on the radicals of the English Revolution, there are many disagreements about the meaning of their views and proposals. The prevailing orthodoxy tends to emphasize the distinctions among various sorts of radicals, spreading them out along a spectrum from left to right. On this view, the Levellers, or some of them, turn out to be petit bourgeois, not-quite democrats, and their clash with the Grandees at Putney in 1647 a squabble over the enfranchisement of a few thousand voters.[1] However, notwithstanding differences in style and programme,

[1] C. B. Macpherson, *The Political Theory of Possessive Individualism: Hobbes to Locke* (Oxford, 1962), pp. 107–59, holds that 'the Levellers consistently excluded from their franchise proposals two substantial categories of men, namely servants or wage earners, and those in receipt of alms or beggars' (p. 107, n. 4). Thus they proposed to enfranchise only c. 205,000 additional electors, a mere 42,000 more than the Grandees. Christopher Hill in *The World Turned Upside Down: radical ideas during the English Revolution* (London, 1972), pp. 46–58, 86–103, apparently wishes to retain Macphersons's rejection of the Levellers as democrats while linking them to True Levellers and Diggers. He postulates differences between the Leveller leaders and distinctions between a moderate, civilian official leadership and several types of more radical Levellers. But although they may have been a heterogenous party, the Levellers' unity is impressive: the principal Levellers continued to co-operate with each other until the movement was crushed. Moreover, to support the theory, *The Moderate*, which treated the Diggers with sympathy, must be regarded as 'unofficial'.

Macpherson's views, although widely accepted, have been subjected to considerable critical scrutiny; see Peter Laslett, 'Market society and political theory', *Historical Journal*, 7 (1964); Keith Thomas, 'The Levellers and the franchise', in *The Interregnum: the quest for Settlement 1646–60*, ed. G. E. Aylmer (London, 1972); J. C. Davis, 'The Levellers and Christianity', in *Politics, Religion and the Civil War*

Levellers, Diggers and Ranters shared a core of basic values and spoke a common language.

All these radicals agree that men are by nature equal and free. One of the clearest statements of this principle is in Richard Overton's *An Arrow Against All Tyrants*:

For by naturall birth, all men are equally and alike born to the like propriety, liberty and freedome, and as we are delivered of God by the hand of nature into this world, every one with a naturall innate freedome and propriety (as it were writ in the table of every mans heart, never to be obliterated) even so are we to live, every one equally and alike to enjoy his Birth-right and priviledge; even all whereby God by nature hath made him free.[2]

Overton takes this principle to imply substantively equal treatment, for he enjoins Henry Marten and the Commons' committee to be impartial and to 'be no respector of persons, let not the *greatest peers* in the Land, be more respected with you, than so many *old Bellowesmenders, Broom men, Coblers, Tinkers or Chimneysweepers, who are all equally Free borne*, with the *hudgest men*, and *loftiest Anachims* in the Land'.[3]

That the Levellers, and not just Overton, generally adhered to this principle is easily illustrated. In *The Case of the Armie Truly Stated*, probably mainly by John Wildman, the rights and liberties of the free-born commoners to be insisted on include that, in the elections for the annual parliaments, 'all the free born at the age of

---

(London, 1973); Iain Hampsher-Monk, 'The political theory of the Levellers: Putney, property and Professor Macpherson', *Political Studies*, 24 (1976), who shows that the Grandees, who were willing to go well beyond the existing franchise, consistently supposed the Levellers to be advocating manhood suffrage at Putney and that the arguments cannot be read as a debate, especially about whether four out of five were to be mere hewers of wood and drawers of water, on Macpherson's interpretation; and Christopher Thompson, 'Maximilian Petty and the Putney debate on the franchise', *Past and Present*, no. 88 (1980), pp. 63–9, who contends that Petty's position is misinterpreted by Macpherson. See also Brian Manning, *The English People and the English Revolution* (Harmondsworth, 1978), who piles up quotations which emphasize the Levellers' concern for those who sweat, who work with their hands, whose payments of tithes and taxes come out of their bellies, but then suggests that the Leveller leaders were of the 'middle', or even better, sort and their followers more radical, concluding that the Levellers stood for small propertied merchants and farmers.

[2] Richard Overton, *An Arrow Against All Tyrants* (London, 1646; repr. The Rota, Exeter, 1976), p. 3.

[3] Ibid., pp. 19–20.

21 yeares and upwards, be the electors, excepting those that have
or shall deprive themselves of that their freedome, either for some
years or wholly by delinquency'.[4] Unless we suppose that Overton
and Wildman, notwithstanding their being political allies, used the
term 'free born' with two quite different meanings, then the
freeborn who are to be equally respected must be the same free-
born (with the exception of those who are fighting against parliament) who are to be electors.

   The same principle may be discovered in John Lilburne's *Regall
Tyranny Discovered*. His argument against the House of Lords'
tyranny relies upon the equality of men under God and by nature;
thus all are equally under both the negative and the positive
versions of the Golden Rule:

And again seeing nature teacheth me to defend my self and preserve my
life; reason teaches me in the negative, that it is but just that I should not
do that to another, which I would not have another doe to me; but that in
the affirmative I should do as I would be done unto.[5]

From this basic equality, Lilburne infers both that 'it is not lawfull
for any man to subject himself to be a slave' and that among those
'that live in mutual society amongst one another in nature and
reason, there is none above or over another against mutual consent
and agreement'.[6]

   Similar views are put forward in *The True Levellers Standard
Advanced*; although the governing powers have committed themselves to reform and 'to bring in liberty, every man in his place', yet
those who pursue this end are oppressed: 'And all because they
stand to maintain an universal liberty and freedom, which is not
only our birthright which our maker gave us, but which thou has
sworn to restore unto us.'[7] They are also to be found in *Light Shining
in Buckinghamshire*, in which it is argued that man, being created
after God's image, embodies a pure spirit, reason, that implies right
and conscience and so the Golden Rule. From this there follows
men's equality:

---

[4] *The Case of the Armie Truly Stated* (London, 1647), in *Leveller Manifestoes of the
Puritan Revolution*, ed. D. M. Wolfe (London, 1967), p. 212.

[5] John Lilburne, *Regall Tyranny Discovered* (London, 1647), p. 10.

[6] Ibid., p. 11.

[7] *The True Levellers Standard Advanced* (London, 1649), in *Winstanley: The Law of
Freedom and other writings*, ed. Christopher Hill (Harmondsworth, 1973), p. 82.

and the creature Man was priviledged with being Lord over the inferior
creatures, but not over his own kinde; for all men being a like priviledged
by birth, so all men were to enjoy the creatures a like without proprietie
one more than the other, all men by the grant of God are a like free, and
every man individuall, that is to say, no man was to Lord or command
over his own kinde.[8]

Again in *The Law of Freedom in a Platform*, Gerrard Winstanley relies
on a basic principle of equality; common action has recovered land
and liberties from the oppressor, they having been 'recovered by a
joint consent of the commoners, therefore it is all equity, that the
commoners who assisted you should be set free from the con-
queror's power with you'.[9]

Equity, or equality, is according to 'Reason' which is frequently
identified with God; as it applies to human conduct it stipulates
action according to one of the versions of the Golden Rule, that one
should not treat others as one would not be treated or that one
should treat others as one would be treated. In *The Law of Freedom*,
this principle becomes the first root of law: 'The first root you see is
common preservation, when there is a principle in everyone to seek
the good of others as himself, without respecting persons.'[10] All
must have equal privileges, equal rights, equal freedoms. Thus the
Diggers employ the same words as the Levellers. Winstanley, like
Overton, asserts that men by nature possess an equal natural right
which implies equal treatment without respect for persons. Winstanley differed from the Levellers in believing that such a right
immediately implied equality of property. In fact that inference
was so natural that it formed the basis of many arguments used by
'conservatives' in opposing the popular and apparently democratic
rhetoric used by parliamentarians early in the Civil War. Sir
Simonds D'Ewes asserted in 1642 that:

all right and property, all *meum and tuum*, must cease in a civil war, and we
know not what advantage the meaner sort also may take to divide the
spoils of the rich and noble among them, who begin already to allege that
all being of one mould there is no reason that some should have so much
and others so little.[11]

---

[8] *Light Shining in Buckinghamshire* (London, 1648), in *The Works of Gerrard Winstanley*, ed. George H. Sabine (New York, 1965), p. 611.
   [9] *The Law of Freedom* (London, 1652) in Hill, *Winstanley*, pp. 275–6.
   [10] Ibid., p. 315.
   [11] Quoted in Hill, *World Turned Upside Down*, p. 19, from P. Zagorin, *The Court
and the Country* (London, 1969), p. 323.

Similarly the king's *Answer to the Nineteen Propositions* warned that parity and independence would be called liberty, and thereby social distinctions destroyed.[12]

The principle that all must have equal rights had earlier been applied by Overton even to papists and Jews. Lilburne and others used it to denounce the arbitrary actions of the House of Lords (and later the Commons) in imprisoning offenders for no offence against known law and without trial and for demanding that individuals answer questions about their activities on oath. Thus the notion that men are equal is expressed by pointing to the Golden Rule – which is taken to mean that men ought to conform their actions to a rule that holds for themselves as well as others and that there should be no special respect for supposedly superior persons.

The first implication drawn from this principle of equality is that just authority can only be derived from the consent of those who are subject to it. No man is naturally superior to another; equal freedom precludes natural or divinely arranged subordination. This notion lies behind the Levellers' rejection of the authority of the House of Lords and the assertion that only the Commons, as elected representatives of the people, have been entrusted with governing power. It is expressed in the Levellers' dislike of the army officers' proceedings in purging parliament and trying and executing the king before, rather than after, the convening of a truly legitimate assembly, representative of the people. It lies behind their promotion of an 'agreement of the people' as the foundation of government. It rings out in Rainborough's statement at Putney:

For really I think that the poorest he that is in England hath a life to live as the greatest he; and therefore truly, sir, I think it's clear, that every man that is to live under a government ought first by his own consent to put himself under that government; and I do think that the poorest man in England is not at all bound in a strict sense to that government that he hath not had a voice to put himself under.[13]

[12] *His Majesties Answer to the XIX Propositions* (London, 1642); excerpts are included in Andrew Sharp, *Political Ideas of the English Civil Wars 1641–9* (London, 1983), pp. 40–3.

[13] A. S. P. Woodhouse (ed.), *Puritanism and Liberty: being the Army Debates (1647–9) from the Clarke manuscripts with supplementary documents*, 2nd edn (London, 1950), p. 53.

And it is equally sharply put by Winstanley's distinction between kingly government and commonwealth government. The first is tyrannical and oppressive – it makes men slaves. The second makes men free – a freedom that Winstanley, like the Levellers, would implement in annually elected parliaments.[14]

But it was not merely inequality of civil, religious or political rights that was deplored. The Levellers were not merely accused of principles which would produce 'utter confusion' politically; they were accused of principles which would 'deny all property too' and which therefore tended to anarchy.[15] Although these allegations were made against the Levellers generally, and at Putney against such supposed moderate, constitutionalist Levellers as Wildman, they are particularly plausible charges against William Walwyn – who is sometimes therefore hailed as further 'left' than the others.

Undoubtedly Walwyn is the most obvious candidate for this charge. It was put forcefully by John Price:

This Mr. Walwyn, to work upon the indigent and poorer sort of people, and to raise up their spirits in discontents and clamours, &c. did one time professe, he could wish with all his heart that there was neither Pale, Hedge nor Ditch in the whole Nation, and that it was an unconscionable thing that one man should have ten thousand pounds, and another more deserving and usefull to the Common-wealth, should not be worth two pence, or to that purpose.

At another time discoursing of the inequality and disproportion of the estates and conditions of men in the world, had words to this purpose, That it was a sad and miserable thing that it should so continue, and that it would never be well untill all things were common; and it being replyed, will that be ever? Answered, we must endeavour it: It being said, That this would destroy all Government; Answered, That then there would be lesse need of Government, for then there would be no theeves, no covetous persons, no deceiving and abusing of one another, and so no need of Government, &c. but if in such a case they have a form and rule of government to determine cases, as may fall out, yet there will be no need of standing Officers in a Common-wealth, no need of Judges, &c. but if any difference arise, or any criminall fact be committed, take a Cobler from his Seat, or a Butcher from his Shop, or any other Tradesman that is an honest and just man, and let him hear the case, and determine the same, and then betake himself to his work again.[16]

---

[14] *The Law of Freedom*, in Hill, *Winstanley*, p. 338.
[15] These accusations were voiced at Putney by Cromwell and Ireton; see Woodhouse, *Puritanism and Liberty*, pp. 7–8, 57–9.
[16] John Price, *Walwyns Wiles* (London, 1649), in *The Leveller Tracts*, ed. William

Price clearly accuses Walwyn not merely of rabble-rousing among the lowest class, but of being in favour of equality of both political and property rights. Indeed it is difficult to tell if he is more scandalized by Walwyn's advocacy of community of property or by his willingness to allow the vulgar, even those so notoriously crude as butchers, to perform civic duties. On this account, Walwyn was no respecter of persons; he was prepared to take as much notice of a cobbler or a chimney sweep as he did of the well-off.

Significantly, neither Humphrey Brooke, Walwyn's son-in-law, in his defence of Walwyn, nor Walwyn himself in *Walwyn's Just Defence*, denied the charge that Walwyn favoured much greater equality of wealth and even community of property. Brooke excused his father-in-law by passing off the offending words as 'old expressions in the heat of Discourses'.[17] Nor did Walwyn repudiate these positions. In fact he goes further than merely avoiding a categorical denial. Having cited a few well-known passages in Scripture which castigate the rich, he reiterates his egalitarianism and refers his detractors to the Levellers' common programme, the *Agreement of the People*:

And where you charge me, that I find fault that some abound whil'st others want bread; truly I think it a sad thing, in so fruitfull a land, as through God's blessing, this is; and I do think it one main end of Government, to provide, that those who refuse not labour, should eat comfortably; and if you think otherwise, I think it your errour, and your unhappinesse: But for my turning the world upside down, I leave it to you, it's not a work I ever intended, as all my actions, and the Agreement of the People, do sufficiently evince, and doth indeed so fully answer all your remaining rambling scandals, that I shall pray the courteous Reader hereof to reade it, and apply it, and then shall not doubt my full and clear vindication: so far as that is, am I for plucking up of all the pales and hedges in the Nation; so far, for all things common.[18]

Yet the view that extremes of rich and poor were at least objectionable had already been expressed by Walwyn as early as 1643 in *The Power of Love*:

Haller and Godfrey Davies (New York, 1944), pp. 302–3.

[17] Humphrey Brooke, *The Charity of Churchmen* (London, 1649), in Haller and Davies, *Leveller Tracts*, p. 346.

[18] William Walwyn, *Walwyns Just Defence* (London, 1649), in Haller and Davies, *Leveller Tracts*, p. 384.

Consider our Saviour saith, He that hath this worlds goods, and seeth his
brother lack, how dwelleth the love of God in him? Judge then by this rule
who are of Gods family; looke about and you will finde in these woefull
dayes thousands of miserable, distressed, starved, imprisoned Christians:
see how pale and wan they looke: how coldly, raggedly, & unwholsomely
they are cloathed; live one week with them in their poore houses, lodge as
they lodge, eate as they eate, and no oftner, and bee at the same passe to
get that wretched food for a sickly wife, and hunger-starved children; (if
you dare doe this for feare of death or diseases) then walke abroad, and
observe the generall plenty of all necessaries, observe the gallant bravery
of multitudes of men and women abounding in all things that can be
imagined: observe likewise the innumerable numbers of those that have
more than sufficeth. Neither will I limit you to observe the inconsiderate
people of the world, but the whole body of religious people themselves,
and in the very Churches and upon solemne dayes: view them well, and
see whether they have not this worlds goods; their silkes, their beavers,
their rings, and other divises will testifie they have; I, and the wants and
distresses of the poore will testifie that the love of God they have not.
What is aimed at? (sayes another) would you have all things common? for
love seeketh not her owne good, but the good of others. You say very true,
it is the Apostles doctrine: and you may remember the multitude of
beleevers had all things common: that was another of their opinions,
which many good people are afraid of. But (sayes another) what would
you have? would you have no distinction of men, nor no government?
feare it not: nor flye the truth because it suites not with your corrupt
opinions or courses.[19]

Thus Walwyn's religious views and his account of Christian love
lead to his accepting a greater amount of communal sharing than
his opponents wished. It also led to his concern for the poor.
Expressions of concern for the poor – not simply those not well-off,
but those whose children might go hungry, who may not eat very
often, who may be reduced to begging – are not confined to
Walwyn, who is usually regarded as the most 'left' of the Levellers.
Similar concerns may be found in the other, supposedly more
moderate, Levellers. For example, take John Lilburne's views, put
in very similar words:

[19] William Walwyn, *The Power of Love* (London, 1643), sigs. A3–A5 (italics
reversed) in *Tracts on Liberty in the Puritan Revolution, 1638–47*, ed. William Haller (3
vols, New York, 1934), pp. 274–5. Walwyn goes on to urge that men and women
be distinguished only as 'you see the love of God abound in them toward their
brethren' and to argue that government is entrusted to rulers by common
agreement.

Therefore when I seriously consider how many men in the Parliament, and else-where of their associates (that judge themselves the onely Saints and godly men upon earth) that have considerable (and some of them vast) estates of their owne inheritance, and yet take five hundred, one, two, three, four, five, six thousand pounds *per annum* salaries, and other comings in by their places, and that out of the too much exhausted publick Treasury of the Nation, when thousands, not onely of the people' of the world, as they call them, but also of the precious and redeemed Lambs of Christ, are ready to sterve for want of bread, I cannot but wonder with my self, whether they have any conscience within them or no, and what they think of that saying of the Spirit of God: That whoso hath this worlds good, and seeth his brother hath need, and shutteth up his bowels of compassion from him, (which he absolutely doth, that any way takes a little of his little from him) how dwelleth the love of God in him? 1 John 3.17[20]

Richard Overton was another Leveller not unmindful of the condition of the poor; in *The Arraignement of Mr. Persecution*, he contrasts the situation of the Presbyterian ministers, who are making a good thing of their inheritance of the state church, with that of those who have to pay for it: 'poor men, that have not bread to still the cry of their children, must either pay or goe in person to the wars, while those devouring Church-lubbers live at ease, feed on dainties, neither pay nor goe themselves, but preach out our very hearts.'[21]

Nevertheless, these Leveller expressions of solicitude may be no more than a few words in passing and the implication that they are speaking on behalf of those who are pale, wan and hungry and who have no bread for a crying child may be mere rhetorical exaggeration. How far are these concerns part of the Levellers' programme? How far is *The Agreement of the People* for making all things common?

It is usually held that the Levellers were individualists who based freedom on property in one's person and favoured the liberty of small enterprisers to acquire external possessions; they had a notion of community, but it was inconsistent with their conception of individual freedom. They did not reject capitalism; they rejected Winstanley's communism.[22]

[20] John Lilburne, *The Legall Fundamentall Liberties of the People of England* (London, 1649), in Haller and Davies, *Leveller Tracts*, p. 435.
[21] Richard Overton, *The Arraignement of Mr. Persecution* (London, 1645), p. 36, in Haller, *Tracts on Liberty*, III, p. 246.
[22] See Macpherson, *Possessive Individualism*, pp. 154–9; Hill, *World Turned Upside Down*, p. 99. Or at least, for Hill, this is true of the 'constitutional Levellers' if not

Certainly there is evidence which appears to support this view of the Levellers. In the petition of 11 September 1648, a document frequently cited by the Levellers themselves as an authoritative statement of their programme, they list a number of things which they had 'long expected' from the House of Commons. Among these things are that the House 'would have bound your selves and all future Parliaments from abolishing propriety, Levelling mens Estats, or making all things common'.[23] Did not Lilburne repudiate the tenets of the 'poor misguided Diggers'?[24]

Nevertheless, it is worth examining the Levellers' actual words in *A Manifestation*, a collective repudiation by Lilburne, Overton, Walwyn and Prince of the calmunies against them.

First, Then it will be requisite that we express our selves concerning Levelling, for which we suppose is commonly meant an equalling of mens estates, and taking away the proper right and Title that every man has to what is his own. This as we have formerly declared against, particularly in our petition of the 11 of Sept. so do we again professe that to attempt an inducing the same is most injurious, unlesse there did precede an universall assent thereunto from all and every one of the People. Nor doe we, under favour, judge it within the Power of a Representative it selfe, because although their power is supreme, yet it is but deputative and of trust, and consequently must be restrained expresly or tacitely, to some particulars essential as well to the Peoples safety and freedom as to the present Government.[25]

Thus the Levellers' repudiation of levelling is far from absolute. Let the existing House of Commons repudiate it, for no government possesses more than a limited jurisdiction. Nevertheless there is nothing intrinsically sacred about private property; it is not enjoined by God's law. Common property was voluntary among the primitive Christians.[26] It must be equally voluntary for seventeenth-century Englishmen. There would be nothing wrong

for 'unofficial Levellers' or 'True Levellers', although he notes Walwyn's views and Overton's proposal that former common ground, now enclosed, be opened to the poor, pp. 95–6. Overton's proposal is in *An Appeale from the Degenerate Representative Body, the Commons at Westminster* (London, 1647), in Wolfe, *Leveller Manifestoes*, p. 194.
[23] Wolfe, *Leveller Manifestoes*, p. 288.
[24] In *Legall Fundamentall Liberties*, in Haller and Davies, *Leveller Tracts*, p. 449.
[25] *A Manifestation* (April 1649), in Haller and Davies, *Leveller Tracts*, p. 279.
[26] Ibid.

in their abolishing it. But while the Leveller programme did not call for the abolition of private property, it always demanded some sort of effective action so that no one would have to beg.

Levelling and Digging are often contrasted. Yet on this matter, Gerrard Winstanley's views are not far from those of the Levellers: 'I do not say, nor desire, that every one shall be compelled to practise this commonwealth's government; for the spirits of some will be enemies at first, though afterwards will prove the most cordial and true friends thereunto.'[27] Apparently for Winstanley, as for the Levellers, true community could only be established voluntarily.

For the Levellers and for the Diggers a Christian society was not just a society outwardly professing Christianity. It was especially not a society imposing a public form of Christian worship. It was, however, a society expressing its Christianity in its actions. For the conscientious Christian in the sixteenth and seventeenth centuries, some concern about the poor was required. Indeed, many thought true Christianity incompatible with extremes of wealth and poverty. Given the views they published, it was hardly surprising that the Levellers were compared with those they called the 'falsely maligned' Anabaptists of Munster. But even quite conservative divines could denounce the evils of private property and excessive wealth. Robert Crowley felt called upon to denounce 'gredie cormorauntes' who oppressed the poor (as well as rebellious peasants) and preach natural equality:

Which of you can laye for hym selfe any naturall cause whye he shoulde possesse the treasure of this wor[l]de, but *that* the same cause may be founde in hym also whom you make your slave? By nature (therefore) you claime no thynge but that whiche you shall get with the swet of your faces . . . . The whole earth therfor (by byrth right) belongeth to the chyldren of men. They are all inheritours therof indifferently by nature.[28]

Crowley also felt it necessary to deny that he favoured making all things common – although he did think that true Christians ought to sell all and give the proceeds to be common as in the primitive

[27] *The Law of Freedom*, in Hill, *Winstanley*, pp. 289–90.
[28] Robert Crowley, *An Informacion and Petition agaynst the Oppressours of the pore Commons of this Realme*, in *The Select Works of Robert Crowley*, ed. J. M. Cowper, Early English Text Society (London, 1872), pp. 163–4.

church.[29] But Crowley only preached equality to remind well-off
Christians that they had duties toward the less well-off.

For the picture of a commonwealth constructed with Christian
principles in mind, we may turn to another sixteenth-century
thinker, Thomas More. His *Utopia* is not a society in which men
profess Christianity but one in which they act according to its
principles. Utopians do believe in a form of natural religion which
is consistent with Christian doctrine: they believe in a single,
omnipotent god; most believe in rewards and punishments after
death. Their society is constructed to promote virtuous conduct
and the cultivation of the soul. They despise and reject the enjoy-
ments beloved of worldly men: wealth they treat with contempt;
all must work and all who work eat; silver, gold and jewels are the
ornaments of criminal slaves. All necessary wants are catered for
but property is communal. Power is accorded only to the virtuous
by election and brings no overweening position but rather responsibilities to others. Sensual and sexual pleasure are both foreign to
Utopians. Thus it is a Christian-like society which does not know
that it is Christian. Its tastes and institutions accord with Christianity but it lacks revelation.[30]

The society advocated by Gerrard Winstanley in his last major
work, *The Law of Freedom*, is very similar to More's Utopia. Both
propose to exclude private ownership of land, the enclosing and
dividing of the earth's common treasury. Both do without buying
and selling, and in both it is less the profession of Christian doctrine
that is emphasized than the acting of the precept to love one's
neighbour as oneself. (Both muster the whole society's repressive
force to ensure that this shall be the case.) Of course there are
differences: for Winstanley equality means equality of rights as well
as equality of wealth; More's society is an aristocracy, ruled by the
virtuous (those noble by nature). For the Diggers all forms of
inequality are forms of 'kingly power', usurped tyrannical power of
one man over another, power not legitimized by consent. So, it is
not surprising that Winstanley should have seen the execution of
the king and the proclamation of a commonwealth as something to

[29] Ibid., pp. 156–8.
[30] Thomas More, *Utopia*, ed. Edward Surtz, S.J. and J. H. Hexter, in *The
Complete Works of Thomas More*, IV, (New Haven and London, 1965); see 'Introduction, Part I' by J. H. Hexter; see also J. C. Davis, *Utopia and the Ideal Society: a study
of English utopian writing 1516–1700* (Cambridge, 1981), pp. 41–61.

be taken quite literally as the extirpation of all lordly usurped power.[31]

Like the Levellers, Winstanley proposed to bring about the changes he advocated by agreement or consent. The Digger communities were gathered out of those who wished to adhere. Even in *The Law of Freedom*, which sketched a whole commonwealth rather than a gathered community, Winstanley suggested that the landlords would wither away from lack of those to work for hire, not be forcibly expropriated. In all his works he relied on voluntary adherence.

Thus *The Law of Freedom* presents us with a communistic society as disciplined as More's Utopia. It is a society governed by officers elected annually by universal manhood suffrage, excluding from those eligible for election and from the electorate those who have supported the king by arms or money and those who have purchased confiscated lands. The officers are to be forty years old or older; and Winstanley also suggests that 'uncivil livers, as drunkards, quarrellers, fearful ignorant men', pleasure-seekers and windbags are not fit to be chosen.[32] But it is not a secular society: it is a 'platform of commonwealth's government unto you, wherein I have declared a full commonwealth's freedom according to the rule of righteousnesse, which is God's Word'.[33] It cannot be seen as a secular ideal – the point of having a commonwealth is to follow God's rule. For those who believe that God is all in all there can hardly be a distinction between what is religious and what is secular. Winstanley's religious commitment was never repudiated; he announced no conversion to a new belief, but shifted from preaching directed at individuals to proposals aimed at a communal reform. Indeed his first five religious pamphlets were reprinted in 1650.[34] Both Levellers and Diggers adhered to a principle of men's

[31] See G. E. Aylmer, '*England's Spirit Unfould'd, or an Incouragement to take the Engagement*: A newly discovered pamphlet by Gerrard Winstanley', *Past and Present*, no. 40 (1968), esp. pp. 9–10.

[32] *The Law of Freedom*, in Hill, *Winstanley*, pp. 321–4.

[33] Ibid., p. 285.

[34] See *Several Pieces Gathered into one volume* (London, 1650). (I owe this point to Barry Smith.) For a contrary view, arguing that Winstanley developed from a religious to a secular thinker, see George Juretic, 'Digger no millenarian: the revolutionizing of Gerrard Winstanley', *Journal of the History of Ideas*, 36 (1975). The extent of secularization of political ideas during the Interregnum is sometimes overestimated, partly because of the editing of republican views for late seventeenth-and eighteenth-century consumption; see Edmund Ludlow, *A Voyce*

equality which was both natural and in accord with their conception of Christianity; in their writings they supported these views by
citing over and over again the same passages, for example, the
Golden Rule and the requirement of charity from 1 John.

Among the adherents of the principle of equality who expounded
their views using the same rhetoric must be counted the Ranters as
well as the Levellers and the Diggers. Abiezer Coppe, for example,
exhibits the acceptance of the principle of equality in his words and
actions. While proclaiming that God's principle was as far from
'sword levelling, or digging-levelling' as 'the East is from the West,
or the Heavens from the Earth', he prophesied:

Behold, behold, behold, I the eternall God, the Lord of Hosts, who am
that mighty Leveller, am comming (yea even at the doores) to Levell in
good earnest, to Levell to some purpose, to Levell with a witnesse, to
Levell the Hills with the Valleyes, and to lay the Mountaines low.[35]

What is to be flattened is all forms of social hierarchy: 'And as I
live, I will plague your Honour, Pompe, Greatnesse, Superfluity,
and confound it into parity, equality, community; that the neck of
horrid pride, murder, malice and tyranny, &c. may be chopt off at
one blow.'[36]

Disagreeing with the proposals of Levellers and Diggers, Coppe
calls upon all to share what they have, obeying the Biblical
injunctions:

you will find the Dominicall letter to be G. and there are many words that
begin with G. at this time GIVE begins with G. give, give, give, give up,
give up your houses, horses, goods, gold, Lands, give up, account nothing
on your own, have ALL THINGS common, or els the plague of God will rot
and consume all that you have.[37]

He himself does so; resisting the temptation to restrict to two pence
his charity to a 'poor wretch', 'a most strange deformed man, clad
with patcht clouts', he decides to give him six pence. He then
'pulling out a shilling, said to the poor wretch, give me six pence,

---

from the Watch Tower: Part Five, 1660–62, ed. A. B. Worden, Camden Society Fourth
Series, 21 (London, 1978), esp. introduction, pp. 1–13.
   [35] Abiezer Coppe, A Fiery Flying Roll (London, 1649; repr. The Rota, Exeter,
1973), p. 2.
   [36] Ibid., p. 4.
   [37] Ibid., Part II, pp. 3–4.

heer's a shilling for thee'. But the man has no change: 'I have never a penny.' Coppe then expresses a pious wish to have given him something, for which he receives the poor man's blessing. But he cannot ride away; first he turns back to bid him call for some money at a house in the next town, then 'the rust of my silver did so rise up in judgement against me, and burnt my flesh like fire: and the 5. of James thundered such an alarm in mine ears, that I was fain to cast all I had into the hands of him, whose visage was more marr'd than any mans that I ever saw.' Riding away again he feels 'sparkles of a great glory', so he once again accosts the poor wretch, puts off his hat, bows seven times and tells him, 'because I am a King, I have done this, but you need not tell any one.'[38] The story, true in the history, is also true in the mystery; it symbolizes the proper relation between those who have this world's goods and those who do not.

Coppe's conception of true religion is not confined to individual actions. It extends to social relations: 'The true Communion amongst men, is to have all things common, and to call nothing one hath, one's own.' True religion is giving one's bread to those without bread and telling them that it is their bread. Vain religion is exclusive, distinguishing the saints from the worldly.

> But take this hint before I leave thee.
> He that hath this worlds goods, and seeth his brother in want, and shutteth up the bowells of compassion from his, the love of God dwelleth not in him; this mans Religion is in vain.

So Coppe called neither for levelling by the sword nor by the spade, but for *'Bloud-Life-Spirit levelling'*, which is presumably to be accomplished by God's spirit working in men.[39]

Ranters, like the Levellers and the Diggers, advocated levelling. Indeed, Lawrence Clarkson in his spiritual pilgrimage passed from the Levellers to the Ranters. While a Leveller, Clarkson wrote a pamphlet in which he chided the communality for choosing oppressors to represent it: 'for who are the oppressors, but the Nobility and Gentry; and who are the oppressed, if not the Yeoman, the Farmer, the Tradesman, and the Labourer?'[40] He retained his radical social views while a Ranter:

[38] Ibid., pp. 4–6.
[39] Ibid., pp. 21–2.
[40] Lawrence Clarkson, *A Generall Charge or Impeachment of High-Treason* (London, 1647), p. 11.

for I apprehended there was no such thing as theft, cheat or a lie, but as man made it so: for if the creature had brought this world into no propriety, as *Mine* and *Thine*, there had been no such title as theft, cheat, or a lie; for the prevention hereof *Everard* and *Gerrard Winstanley* did dig up the Commons, that so all might have to live of themselves, then there had been no need of defrauding but unity with one another . . . .

But Clarkson perceived in Winstanley 'a self-love and vain-glory nursed in his heart, that if possible, by digging to have gained people to him, by which his name might become great among the poor Commonalty of the Nation'.[41] Still, it is clear that, at that time, his interpretation of the social arrangements implicit in true religion was consistent with that of the Diggers.

Thus for all these radicals, Levellers, Diggers and Ranters, adherence to a fundamental principle of equality implied a rejection of social privilege. This adherence was grounded in a common conception of the meaning of true Christianity. These views were expressed in a rhetoric common to all these radicals, frequently citing the same natural rights and relying on the same Scriptural passages and drawing the same implications from them. That conception implied different social arrangements from those prevalent in seventeenth-century England. Whatever their differences, they also agreed that an egalitarian society would be brought about voluntarily.

[41] Idem, *The Lost Sheep Found* (London, 1660; repr. The Rota, Exeter, 1974), p. 27.

5

The Royalist Party in Arms: the Peerage and Army Command, 1642–1646

P.R. NEWMAN

Edward Somerset, from 1646 second Marquess of Worcester, and to April 1644 the king's lieutenant-general in South Wales, may properly be considered, his catholicism and that of his father notwithstanding, the very type of powerful territorial magnate to whom the king would look for support in his struggle against his parliament. Somerset and his father devoted their enormous fortune to the king's cause, and the son's military rank was due entirely to the wealth of the family and the influence which it wielded in South Wales. Somerset's pre-war military experience was nil, and his military skills negligible. His removal from command to be replaced by Prince Rupert was an inevitable consequence of increasing royalist desperation: that it did not, as similar circumstances did with Lord Chandos, lead to defection from the king's party, indicates how right the king had been to rely upon the power that emanated from Raglan Castle, and Somerset continued to serve his king in other ways. Looking back upon the wartime services of himself and his family, the second Marquess took justifiable pride in having acted, throughout his time as lieutenant-general, in a way entirely compatible with his social standing and its inherent duties and responsibilities. During campaigns around Gloucester, he was later to write, he had been able to make sure that his own troops, at least, paid their way and did not rely upon free quarter. This politically valuable capacity to expend money, however, had brought him into confrontation with the king's Lord-General, Patrick Ruthven, Lord Forth, who claimed that it put the rest of the army in a bad light with the local populace. In the king's presence, Somerset and Lord Forth exchanged words, leading to what amounted to a denunciation by Somerset both of the lord-general and, by implication, of other royalist commanders anywhere in England. He told Ruthven that he:

yielded to his Excellencie to be a better soldier. but still to be a soldier of fortune, here today and God knows where tomorrow, and therefore needed not care for the love of the people, but though I were killed myselfe I should leave my posteritie behind me, towards whom I would not leave a grudge in the people . . .[1]

Somerset's words have a direct bearing upon the debate currently developing around the nature of wartime royalism. Much of the argument contained in Ronald Hutton's 1981 paper 'The structure of the Royalist party 1642–6'[2] turns upon the disappearance from the royalist army of men of the standing of Edward Somerset, and their replacement by men of lower social standing, the whole process being indicative of a change in royalist attitudes, a hardening process which, had the king won the war, might have led to the creation of a different style of monarchy, the appearance of autocratic tendencies similar to those emerging in some European monarchies. In the course of a general discussion of the group characteristics of the royalist officer corps,[3] I have argued in much the same way. In 1984, however, the late James Daly took issue with Hutton's contentions in a paper entitled 'The implications of Royalist politics 1642–6'.[4] The purpose of the present essay is not so much to settle the dispute, which would be premature, but to try to clarify the issues; specifically, to consider the role of the territorial magnates, the peerage, in the royalist army and to look at the men of all conditions exercising the rank of 'general' in that army between 1642 and 1646. The figures to be examined concern all army ranks above that of regimental commander, but excluding the somewhat nebulous rank of 'brigadier'. This excludes holders of the ranks of 'scoutmaster-general' and 'waggonmaster-general', posts

[1] *HMC* 12th Report, Appendix Pt IX, Beaufort MSS, 1891, pp. 56–63, for Somerset's 'memoir'.
[2] *Historical Journal*, 24 (1981).
[3] P. R. Newman, 'The royalist officer corps 1642–60: army command as a reflexion of the social structure', *Historical Journal*, 26 (1983). All individuals mentioned in this paper will be found in the present writer's *Royalist Officers in England and Wales 1642–60: A Biographical Dictionary* (New York, 1981).
[4] *Historical Journal*, 27 (1984).

ordinarily filled by commissioned junior officers, but is inclusive of the rank of 'colonel-general' which might represent some kind of field command within an army, or military authority over a county or over groupings thereof.

The royalist party was rooted essentially in the support for the king of those members of his parliament, peers and commons, that had either always supported him or – a larger group – had grown disenchanted and alarmed by political developments at Westminster in 1641–2. They found themselves keeping company at York in the summer of 1642 with those supporters of the king whom Hutton has termed 'ultra-royalists', a term with which Daly took issue. The 'ultras' appear to be those who fell foul of the parliament as a consequence of personal loyalty to Charles I: whether they were united by anything other than a common experience of parliament's displeasure is hard to say. Such coherent royalist political thought as there was appears to have emanated from 'moderates' like Edward Hyde; it is hard to establish any clear 'ultra' policy. Perhaps we should not expect to find one. What does seem to characterize the 'ultras' was their opportunism and their ambition, which was centred upon the royal court. In such circumstances, even men like George Digby might have all their time cut out surviving and preserving their influence without trying to formulate a positive programme aimed at creating some future royal despotism. Certainly, these 'ultras' did not have the political power and muscle that Charles I needed in 1642, hence his reliance upon 'moderates'. I do not, however, wish to pursue this present study within the context of Hutton's and Daly's terminology, for such classifications serve only to obscure the real issue, which is to establish precisely who controlled and commanded the royal armies which Charles was able to raise as a result of his establishment of a broad basis of support for himself amongst those of his subjects who mattered in terms of their influence, standing or wealth in national or in narrower terms.

Much of the work on royalism seems to have centred upon identifying a few prominent men exercising military command, and making assumptions about the rest. Joyce Malcolm, for example, observed that 'Charles chose as officers men whose extensive lands and noble lineage were believed to entitle them to dictate to their many tenants and sway the lesser gentry of their counties.'[5] This

[5] Joyce Malcolm, *Caesar's Due: Loyalty and King Charles 1642–6* (London, 1983), p. 39.

represented her judgement after citing commissions to the Earl of
Lindsey, the Marquess of Hertford, Lord Strange and Prince
Rupert in 1642. Rupert is rather a special case, fulfilling none of the
qualifications Malcolm properly itemized as requisite in an
'officer'. Hertford had some military experience: he had, like Lord
Strange (whose military experience was nil), some territorial clout.
Lindsey recommended himself to the king by virtue of his extensive
military experience. Malcolm, therefore, cuts the ground from
under her later assertion that 'as the war progressed command
devolved upon the professional soldiers.'[6] Lindsey, the king's first
lord-general, was not a prominent peer, but nor was he a soldier of
fortune, which seems to be what Malcolm means when she writes of
'professional' soldiers. Yet as he was the most militarily experienced peer available, until the Scotsman Patrick Ruthven arrived,
he was appointed to overall command. Charles clearly appreciated
the need to give authority to men who knew about war, but the
function of the peerage was no longer primarily to lead armies.
Anthony Fletcher puts their task clearly. Charles 'intended that
leadership should rest as far as possible with the nobility' so as to
'create royalist factions in the counties'.[7] That is not the same thing
as exercising military command at a high level. It was a function of
the peerage that was recognized by parliament too; hence the
latter's attempts to lure Lord Strange into opposing the king. It
seems that we should distinguish between two distinct functions of
the peerage, both royalist and parliamentarian: that of exercising
military command, and that of exerting political and social influence and money on their respective parties. The two functions
might overlap: Hertford and Strange are cases in point, although
Strange's military position (even after he became Earl of Derby)
was never really clarified, and the king used him as a glorified
recruiting officer in 1643. Lindsey was a peer but, more valuable
still to the king, he was an experienced soldier and, until Ruthven
came along, the best available for high command. Lindsey gave
way to Ruthven, a hard-bitten professional soldier with a recent
Scottish peerage, and was killed shortly afterwards at Edgehill.
Lindsey's son succeeded to the title and to regimental commands,
but lacked the military ability to rise as high as his father had done
in the army.

[6] Ibid., p. 94.
[7] Anthony Fletcher, *The Outbreak of the English Civil War* (London, 1981), p. 323.

Thus from the earliest stages of the war, Charles and his advisers recognized two distinct needs. They had to have soldiers in command of the army, and they also had to have the support of the established nobility. Occasionally, but rarely, a peer could combine political leadership with military competence. When, out of necessity, the king gave high military rank to a peer with important connections or influence, but who lacked military experience, then, from the beginning of the wars, such a man would have 'professional' subordinates to assist his military function. Hertford had Sir Ralph Hopton; the Earl of Newcastle in the north-east had James King (later ennobled), and the Earl of Cumberland (most pacific of all) brought in Sir Thomas Glemham to Yorkshire. So the 'professionals' were always there and, by definition, were always influential. Many factors at the topmost levels of royalist army command – defection, war-weariness, attrition and downright incompetence – gradually opened the way for such 'professionals' to become commanding generals. This was not peculiar to civil war England, nor to the royalist army. The shifts in the high command of British and German armies in the Second World War were quite as frequent and quite as consequent upon similar causes (defection alone excepted).

The question to which Hutton and Daly addressed themselves was whether this perceptible change in the composition of the royalist senior officer corps betokened a new development which had specific implications for England's political future had the king won. Such changes in the personnel of army command are not in themselves sufficient to mean anything other than to signal that a natural wartime process was under way. Hutton's contention that as the war progressed, men of lower social standing pushed their way to the forefront of royalist army command, would have more validity if applied to the corps of regimental commanders. In my discussion of the overall structure of the royalist officer corps inclusive of the generals, I have demonstrated that many socially obscure individuals secured regimental control within the army as the war progressed. Social obscurity is not simply a matter of individuals falling outside the armigerous section of society, or being less than parochial gentlemen. The term applies equally to those who, whatever their precise social origin, failed prior to 1642 to assume positions of importance within their communities. Thus many socially obscure commanders of the royalist army between 1642 and 1646 were younger sons or brothers, whose financial and social predicament, in a society dominated by impartible inheritance, is well known. If Hutton had based his contentions upon regimental command, they would have been well founded. Yet in examining army command, he chose an officer corps that was largely exclusive anyway and that, as has been shown, did not change much in that respect during the course of the war. The peerage was represented in army command throughout the war, since successful generals often found themselves advanced to the peerage as a consequence of their service or as an incentive. Yet the pre-war peerage was not eclipsed politically: as Malcolm said, the king needed their names and their standing to bolster his actions and to enhance the legality of his acts. They would have been needed quite as much during negotiations and after peace. The 'rising men' of the royalist army would, had the king won, undoubtedly have achieved some political influence merely by replacing pro-parliamentarian office-holders in the counties. This is what happened, after all, to parliamentarian officers and others when pro-royalist officials were removed from office.

The Civil War took on a momentum of its own, and for the royalist party, as for their enemies, the objective was victory. There were certainly some around the king who desired a negotiated peace, and such men may have held military command for a time, or even for the duration of the war. The task of the army was to provide the basis for negotiation from strength: essentially the army fought with limited objectives, and the king's politicians waited upon developments in the field to pursue their own war objectives. Hutton's paper does have the merit of showing that politicians could out-manoeuvre war-lords – Rupert's downfall surely epitomizes this.

Hutton made one point about changes in army command that must be considered extremely significant. It has already been observed that the Earl of Lindsey secured the position of lord-general in 1642 primarily because of his military experience. His peerage was additional to that vital qualification. As Hutton said, Lindsey resigned his command to Ruthven, the better soldier. The significance of this change-over, however, lies in the fact that if ever there was a 'professional' soldier elevated to supreme command, it was Ruthven. He was subsequently given a Scottish earldom and then an English peerage. The replacement of Lindsey by Ruthven was far more important, in the context of Hutton's argument, than the case upon which he places more emphasis, that of Lord Capel's

replacement by John Byron in 1643. Byron's ousting of the militarily incompetent Capel is cited as evidence of the widespread ousting
of 'most of the peers and baronets' who had commanded the royal
army since 1642. Yet Byron, unlike Ruthven, was no 'foreign'
professional. He came of perfectly respectable social origins in
Nottinghamshire and his peerage, granted in the year of his preferment to command, was only a little more recent than that of Capel
himself, who was elevated in 1641. Capel was a rich man, of course:
Byron was not, but technically there was little social distinction
between them. It was all a matter of military competence, or the
lack of it. Surprisingly, Hutton so far ignores Ruthven's origins and
background as to imply that when the Scot is himself replaced by
Rupert in 1644, the case is analogous to that of Capel and Byron.
On the contrary, it was merely a question of one 'uninspiring'
professional being replaced by a proven better soldier.

Daly's original criticism of Hutton's paper appears to rest on the
grounds that the latter was mistaken in seeing a general rise of the
socially obscure in royalist army command. This is a question to
which further attention will be paid. The point can be made here,
however, that in considering the royalist generals, it is less a matter
of whence they came than of what they represented. The royalist
army did come under the control of hard, ruthless men as the war
developed. Some of them became peers of the realm or secured
other honours in return for their services. Hutton recognized this,
citing the examples of Grenville, Dyve, Mackworth and others,
None of these were socially obscure (Dyve and Grenville had both
been MPs) but they were men of a different stamp from Edward
Somerset and Arthur Capel.

There are certain incontrovertible facts concerning the royalist
armies which are clear-cut. Command lay from the first with a mix
of professional soldiers, either grandees or gentry, who owed their
ranks to social or familial standing or personal fortunes. During the
course of the war, the half-hearted or the incompetent, as well as
the unlucky (those who were killed or who died) dropped out and
were replaced, naturally enough, by subordinates. This was true of
army and of regimental command. Daly properly stressed the
attrition factor in the turnover of royalist command personnel.
Throughout the war, men rose to high rank who might not have
made a name for themselves in peacetime. The really successful
found themselves drawn by promotion into the hierarchical rank
structure of peacetime society. Ruthven and Byron are cases in

point. So, too, Henry Bard, knighted in 1643, made a baronet in 1644, and given an Irish peerage in 1645. The successful had doors opening for them which the king's defeat slammed shut in their faces.

The crux of Hutton's argument lies in two basic assertions. Firstly, the view that in 1642, the peerage and baronetage exercised control of the royal army; secondly, that by 1644 they had lost that control. Space does not permit an extensive examination of the baronetage as commanders: but this paper is concerned with army command and, as will be seen, the baronetage were barely represented therein. It is possible, however, to define more precisely the military role of the peerage, theoretically the most important social group of all, bearing in mind that this group fulfilled two distinctive functions for the king which might, but need not, overlap.

Rushworth cited 81 peers in his list of those eligible to sit in the Oxford assembly in January 1644 (excluding Rupert).[8] Of these, 43 were present on 27 January, 5 were to arrive later, 22 were on active service of one kind or another, 9 were abroad, and 2 were in enemy hands. Of the peers enumerated by Rushworth, in January 1644 no fewer than 36 exercised military commands: of that number 5 were men who had succeeded to titles since 1642, and 7 were entirely new creations. At first glance these figures compare favourably with the situation in 1642, when although 37 peers held military rank of one kind or another, 3 were Scottish peers and 4 were Irish. Numerically speaking, the peerage had improved upon its representation in army command by January 1644, but the figures conceal the fact that this representation was maintained by new creations as well as by successions to titles. Over the whole period 1642–6 army commanders secured 17 new peerages, whilst a further 5 commanders inherited titles, and of the 17 new titles only 2, John Belasyse and Sir William Widdrington, could claim some kind of connection with the titles they were to receive. Thus military command was certainly a means of achieving social distinction. Nevertheless, had it not been for the new creations, the military involvement of the peerage by 1644 would have been markedly down on 1642. Of those Irish peers of that year who swelled the number of military commanders, 2, Carbery and Cholmondeley, secured English peerages in return for their ser-

---

[8] Rushworth, *Historical Collections*, III, pp. 573–5.

vices, as did a single Scot, Patrick Ruthven, who was created Earl of Brentford.

Our primary concern, however, is with army as opposed to purely regimental command. Some, indeed most, generals actually combined these functions. That is to say, a commanding general might well have his own regiment of foot or of horse of which he was still the colonel, however titular. Between 1642 and 1646 some 59 individual peers exercised some form of military command, and of that figure 29 were at one time or another generals. There were also 2 heirs to peerages who were generals. Of the 37 peers cited in 1642, 16 were acting as generals in various royalist armies. Of the 22 accessions to peerages during the war years, 13 titles came the way of army generals, and of that number 10 titles represented acknowledgement of military service by the creation of new titles. The other 3 succeeded to military rank along with titles to which they were heirs. Thus of the 22 advancements noted, 9 came the way of men exercising ranks of colonel or below, and of that 9, 3 (Arundell, Campden and Peterborough) inherited through the normal course of events. Peterborough, for example, had a father who was of parliamentarian leanings. The son inherited in 1643 but exercised only regimental command. Viscount Campden's father had been more or less inactive prior to his death in 1643, and his son, like Peterborough, exercised only regimental command. Not all of the 22 advancements were English peerages, of course: Lords Bard, Bulkeley and Donamore were Irish peerages, as was that of William Ogle granted in 1645, and there was one Scottish peerage, that of James King, the Earl of Newcastle's 'professional' military adviser. General's rank went with the inheritance of the titles of the Earls of Northampton and Lindsey. Military prowess was recognized in the grant of peerages to James King, and to men like Jacob Astley (1644), John Byron (1643), Charles Gerard (1645), Ralph Hopton (1643), Henry Hastings (1643) and Henry Wilmot (1643), among others. Further movement upwards within the peerage, however, was less common in return for military service. The Earl of Newcastle was created a marquess in 1643 (when James King secured his Scottish title), Patrick Ruthven became Earl of Brentford in 1644, Lord Dunsmore became Earl of Chichester in the same year and, as has been said, Lords Chomondeley and Carbery secured English titles in 1645. By no stretch of the imagination could any of those advanced to peerages in return for military service be considered truly obscure, with the possible exception of

Henry Bard, who was advanced to an Irish peerage in 1645.

However, if we reconsider the peers (37 in all, including a handful of Irish and Scottish peers) exercising military commands in 1642, an interesting fact emerges that may tell us a good deal about the nature of support for Charles I. Of the 37, no fewer than 18 were peerages created by Charles himself, and a further 12 were Stuart creations. Of these, 19 were first-generation holders of the titles; if we extend this survey across the years 1642–6 we find that Charles I was served by no fewer than 36 first-generation peers in military commands. Of the 16 peers who served as generals in 1642, 15 were Stuart creations.

As has been noted, of the 37 peers in military ranks in 1642, 16 were army generals. Of 22 advancements to titles over the war years, 13 were generals and 10 owed their advancement to their military service. The point was made earlier that the Earl of Lindsey owed his lord general's rank to his military experience, which was in turn outweighed by that of Patrick Ruthven, Lord Forth. But how representative was Lindsey of the king's noble supporters exercising army command? Of the 16 in 1642, 8 had pre-war military experience of some kind or another. Lord Caernarfon had served in 1640, the Scottish Earl of Crawford had extensive European experience, as had Lord Forth. Lord Grandison had served in 1640, Lord Hertford had had brief military experience in Europe, Lord Newport had served there also and in the army of 1640, and Lord Wentworth had also served in 1640. Of 13 advanced to titles between 1642 and 1646, a further 8 had pre-war military experience, some extensive, like Jacob Astley.

A study of the royalist armies over the years of the First Civil War reveals, however, a total of at least 94 'generals' of whom only 16 were peers when they were commissioned. We need therefore to look more closely at the whole corps of generals, excluding from consideration for the moment the 16 peers and also excluding Rupert and his brother Maurice, who are in many ways special cases. Who were the remaining 76? Apart from one French nobleman, the rest comprised 4 baronets (these social ranks apply at time of commission), 15 knights, 30 esquires, 9 gentlemen (so styled) and a further 17 about whose status we cannot be sure. The social structure of the military high command underwent change, as various of these generals secured advancement in honours. One baronet became a peer (William Widdrington); 3 knights advanced (2 peers, 1 baronet); 17 esquires advanced (9 peers – 2 by succes-

sion – and 6 knights, 1 baronet and 1 knighthood and baronetcy
conferred at the same time); 4 of the gentlemen were knighted;
whilst 3 of those classified as uncertain received knighthoods and
one, James King, whose origins are obscure and whose background
was European, secured a Scottish peerage. King's case may be an
anomaly: from what evidence there is, it seems that no one, not
even a gifted general, leapt up the social ladder more than one rung
at a time, and so we must suppose that James King would have
qualified as an 'esquire' in his native Scotland. Thus the social
standing of the 92 generals (excluding Rupert and his brother) was
as follows:

Peers	16
Baronets	4
Knights	15
Esquires	30
Gentlemen	9
Uncertain	17
Other	1 [French nobleman]

Perhaps in keeping with the exalted military rank involved, the
royalist generals preponderantly belonged to the upper echelons of
civilian society. In contrast, regimental command had a far higher
number of 'mere' gentlemen represented in its ranks.

Clearly, if social standing and title were important considerations as well as military competence for a general, we might
suppose that much of the bulk of the royalist generals below the
rank of peer would consist of men who had some military experience. It would certainly be the factor that would distinguish them
from their fellows, and cause their promotion to army command.
We have seen that of the 16 peers, 8 had pre-war military experience. Leaving those aside, but including Rupert and Maurice in
our survey, we can look at the military credentials of the remaining
78 generals. Of those, 39 had seen service in Europe, 27 in the
armies of 1639–40, and 12 in Ireland against the Confederacy. Of
the 12 with Irish experience, all had served previously either in
Europe or against the Scots. Only 8 generals of those who had
pre-war experience of one kind or another had seen service only in
1639–40 and 3 of them – Caernarfon, Grandison and Wentworth –
were peers. So, proportionately, the peers were less militarily
experienced than their social inferiors, but on the whole the royalist

armies of 1642–6 were commanded by men who might lay claim to knowing what they were doing. Since the overall number of 94 identified generals includes promotions after 1642 of men some of whom owed their military experience to civil war, it is more than apparent that whatever else Charles I expected from his peerage, he clearly did not look to them to exercise overall military control in his war against Parliament. Whilst the peerage, or that section of it loyal to the king, maintained a presence in the army high command, men were chosen less for their social standing than for their skills. Competent, or at least loyal, service, could lead to social advancement, and the loyal peerage was recruited afresh from military commanders. (Incidentally, three of Charles' generals were former parliamentarian officers: Grenville, Wagstaffe and the Scotsman Urry. They found promotion in the royalist armies where, evidently, their skills – particularly Grenville's savage commitment – were appreciated.) The peerage and baronetage were neither in 1642 nor later in the war entrusted exclusively or in large part with army control. On the contrary, army command was vested in a broad social spectrum of the king's supporters. The peerage maintained a presence throughout the war years partly by recruitment from among their social inferiors. The vast majority of the king's generals between 1642 and 1646 are socially classifiable (at time of commission) and those few that are not (Jerome Brett, Thomas Pert, William Webbe for example) cannot be assumed to have been entirely obscure. It may be that long military service in European armies had created a breed of truly 'professional' soldiers and that subsumed within their ranks were countless younger sons or poverty-stricken gentlemen who sought their fortunes in foreign wars and came home to offer their swords to their king. There is certainly little evidence here of an influx into army command of the socially obscure (nor is there, let it be stressed, any evidence for European mercenaries taking up high commands, or even regimental commands, in England's wars).

Daly's criticism of Hutton's view blinded him to the real significance of what the latter urged. Yet quoting from another of Hutton's works[9] Daly cited the use of the term 'English gentry turned feral' which Hutton employs to describe the new type of commander he sees emerging in the armies under the patronage of men like Rupert and Maurice. Here Hutton's argument pinpoints a

---

[9] Ronald Hutton, *The Royalist War Effort* (London, 1982), p. 104.

stark reality of the Civil War. Men like Edward Somerset, whose criticism of Ruthven will be recalled, did lose ground as the war developed its own momentum: they were not so much ousted, perhaps, as shown to be incompetent. There was a need to have commanders who would pursue the war more ruthlessly than Somerset and men like him who were trying to fulfil several roles at once. The lesser a man's social standing or obligations, the more he might devote himself to military ends. For such men there was more to gain from the war than there was to lose. A commander who had shown himself something more than a mere killer of the king's enemies would recommend himself for eventual promotion. Common sense tells us that this is how things were. John Byron had a good reputation as a soldier before he butchered the defenders of Barthomley church: Byron was by no means socially obscure but he was first and foremost a soldier, and understood the weapon of terror, a weapon that neither Somerset nor Capel (nor the Earl of Newcastle nor the Marquess of Hertford) felt comfortable in employing. War produces such men, and some of them emerge from relative anonymity. Byron, Grenville and others were typical 'English gentry turned feral', products of war and of royalist desperation.

There were many men of humble origin rising in regimental ranks who would feel able to obey the commands of superiors like Byron and Grenville. But royalist army commanders were on the whole a part of the established social order, wherever they stood in its ranks at time of commission. Some improved upon that standing in consequence of their services. They did not 'oust' their social superiors to the degree that Hutton implied, they merely pushed to the forefront of events because there was need of them. It is hardly surprising that Edward Somerset (although he was a trifle unfair to Ruthven personally) disparaged that tendency within his own party. It went against the grain, but he also feared it. Had the Civil War lasted twice as long as it did, what horrors might not Somerset and his kind have had to endure? Society was fortunate in that the war came to an end so quickly and so decisively: there would have been far more 'feral' gentry had it not done so. Perhaps it would have ended in the king's favour if there had been more of Hutton's 'feral' gentry around in 1642–3.

6

Putney Revisited: Political Debate in the New Model Army in 1647

AUSTIN WOOLRYCH

Part of the excellence of Ivan Roots's treatment of the crucial year 1647 in *The Great Rebellion* lies in the generous space that he accords to the political activity of Fairfax's army and to the arguments within it – not only the famous debates at Putney, but also the earlier ones at Saffron Walden and Reading. The Putney Debates deserve their fame, but over-concentration on those three marvellously recorded days, and a corresponding neglect of their larger context, has led elsewhere to some misunderstanding of their significance and of the prevailing trend of army politics. One way towards a reassessment of all the debates among officers and agitators lies through a close study of the institution in which most of them took place, the General Council of the Army.[1]

A swift sketch of the situation in which the New Model Army irrupted into politics can begin with the departure of the Scottish army in February 1647 and the transfer of Charles I to the Long Parliament's custody. This was a triumph for the Presbyterian politicians, led by Denzil Holles and Sir Philip Stapleton, who negotiated it, and it clinched their dominance over the House of Commons. It seemed to open the way for what nearly all the nation wanted: the reinstatement of the king on the terms of an English peace, and an early disbandment of the armed forces, which were maintained by crippling taxes yet were still, all too often, living at

---

[1] I have just completed such a study, which will be published by the Oxford University Press under the title *Soldiers and Statesmen: the General Council of the Army and its debates 1647–8*. Matters which for reasons of space are summarily treated or baldly asserted here will be found fully documented in that book.

free quarter on the civilian population. The New Model numbered about 21,500 officers and men, but the various provincial forces, of which Major-General Poyntz's Northern Association army was the largest, were collectively at least as numerous, and being even less regularly paid they were often mutinous and violent.[2] The Presbyterians' opponents in parliament were the political Independents, and except for a very few radicals led by Henry Marten they wished scarcely less to see Charles back on his throne: but they were unwilling to disarm themselves, and in particular to disband the New Model, until he had been bound to satisfactory terms. Since July 1646 Charles had been treating parliament's formal peace terms, the Propositions of Newcastle, with typical evasiveness. It was an open secret that the Presbyterians would settle for less, but a fatal flaw in their plans was that Charles would never have bound himself even to the laxer terms that they had been covertly suggesting to him. They were committed to a Presbyterian settlement of religion, partly because the Scots, on whose alliance they still depended, had made it the price of their military support in the war, and partly because they depended financially on the City of London, in which the high Presbyterian party was very strong, and bitterly hostile to Fairfax's army.

The New Model, as Mark Kishlansky has demonstrated,[3] had not been in origin or intention a political army, and it scrupulously refrained from any kind of political activity until the spring of 1647. The officers covered a wide religious spectrum, and their politics would prove to be scarcely less varied. But a powerful vein of religious enthusiasm ran through the ranks of the cavalry, especially in the half-dozen regiments drawn from Cromwell's former command in the Eastern Association army, and the impetus that drove colonels and captains and corporals and mere troopers to preach had inescapable political overtones. Thomas Edwards concentrated much of the third part of his *Gangraena* on the army, many months before its revolt, and he had no doubt that religious

[2] *Selections from the Papers of William Clarke*, ed. C. H. Firth, Camden Society Second Series, 49, 54, 61, 62 (4 vols, London, 1891–1901), I, pp. 18–19; J. S. Morrill, 'Mutiny and discontent in English provincial armies, 1645–7', *Past and Present*, no. 56 (1972).
[3] Mark A. Kishlansky, *The Rise of the New Model Army* (Cambridge, 1979); 'The case of the army truly stated: the creation of the New Model Army', *Past and Present*, no. 81 (1978); 'The army and the Levellers: the roads to Putney', *Historical Journal*, (1979); and 'Ideology and politics in the parliamentary armies, 1645–9', in *Reactions to the English Civil War*, ed. J. S. Morrill (London, 1982).

and political radicalism ran together in it. He is a very biased and hostile witness, but his evidence is not to be totally discounted, and it does not stand alone. So in place of Kishlansky's picture of a hitherto apolitical army, suddenly and swiftly politicized in the spring and summer of 1647, it is more plausible to assume that its political awareness developed earlier but remained latent until the parliament rashly provoked it into action. To suppose otherwise makes the fears of the Presbyterians, the City and the Scots, who did not imagine that such officer-MPs as Cromwell, Ireton, Fleetwood, Harrison and Rainborough stood alone in their views, unnecessarily hard to explain.

Of course, the forces in England needed to be reduced, and those holding out in Ireland needed desperately to be reinforced. There could have been no complaint if service in Ireland had been offered to all officers and soldiers who wanted to go on soldiering, and if disbandment had then begun with the provincial forces. But a reduced army would still be needed in England, and it should on grounds of justice and military efficiency alike have been drawn from the regiments of the New Model, since they had the finest fighting record and the best discipline, and numbered more volunteers and veterans in their ranks than the rest. Yet apart from Major-General Massey's disorderly western brigade, which was disbanded in 1646, parliament *began* with the New Model, and offered its members a choice between disbandment or enlistment for Ireland before it even considered the provincial forces. As for a standing army, parliament voted to maintain a mere 6,400 horse and dragoons, with only the foot companies in scattered local garrisons for infantry. The Independents knew that this was not enough, even without our knowledge that the Second Civil War lay only a year ahead, but they were as usual outvoted. Moreover, parliament decided that this small force should include three regiments of Poyntz's northern army, before it even considered the crack New Model horse. Poyntz was a professional soldier, not long home from the German wars, who could be relied upon to obey his paymasters; he would shortly be helping to organize London's attempted counter-revolution. When parliament's plans were fully revealed, six of the New Model's ten cavalry regiments and all its twelve foot regiments faced disbandment, unless they enlisted piecemeal for Ireland.[4]

[4] This paragraph is based mainly on S. R. Gardiner, *History of the Great Civil War, 1642–9* (4 vols, London, 1888–91), and C. H. Firth and G. Davies, *The*

It has been claimed that the Presbyterians had no particular animus against the New Model and that their 'plan for reorganization was the least painful one possible'.[5] This is hard to sustain. Their policy was dictated by their financial dependence on the City and by their own fears lest Fairfax's army should resist their design to strike a dubious bargain with the king and entrench themselves in positions of power. As part of their plan, they restored the powerful militia of London to the City's own control, thereby ensuring that it would have a solid phalanx of Presbyterian officers. The plan might have worked, if they had not tried to disband Fairfax's men with a mere six weeks' pay in cash out of their long arrears. When the soldiers petitioned their general against such treatment, Holles drafted a declaration, which both Houses carried, that all who persisted with the petition would be deemed 'enemies to the state and disturbers of the public peace'.[6] With those ten words Holles wrecked his own design, but they were only one of the gratuitous slights that he and his party put upon the army.

The soldiers' resistance mounted inexorably after that. They, and the agitators whom they chose to represent them, and the many officers who supported them, had three aims from the start: to secure justice for the soldiers over their pay, their indemnity for acts done in war, and other material concernments; to vindicate the army's affronted honour and its members' right to petition; and to frustrate what they saw as a *political* design by the Presbyterians which threatened to give away much that they had fought for. Service in Ireland was not a welcome prospect to most of them, and those who had fought for parliament as volunteers objected to being drafted without their consent, but they would have given it if they had been sent in their old troops and companies under the officers they knew and trusted; 'Fairfax and Cromwell, and we all go!', they shouted to the parliamentary commissioners who came to enlist them.[7] But when they learnt that a reluctant and semi-invalid Skippon was to command them in place of Fairfax, and that instead of Cromwell as lieutenant-general they were to get the ultra-

---

Regimental History of Cromwell's Army (2 vols, Oxford, 1940).

[5] Kishlansky, *Rise of the New Model Army*, p. 158 and passim.

[6] *CJ*, v, pp. 129; Journal of Thomas Juxon, Dr Williams's Library, MS 24.50, f. 106v.

[7] *Clarke Papers*, ed. Firth, I, 7; *Moderate Intelligencer* no. 10, 15–22 April 1647, p. 1022; Rushworth, *Historical Collections*, VI, pp. 457–9.

Presbyterian Massey, who would not be long in turning royalist, they organized a collective refusal. They were quick to perceive the Presbyterians' political purpose. The very first pamphlet put out by the agitators asked: 'Can this Irish Expedition be any thing else but a Designe to ruine and break this Army in pieces? . . . This plot is but a meere cloake for some who have lately tasted of Soveraignty; and being lifted beyond their ordinary Sphere of servants, seek to become Masters, and degenerate into Tyrants.'[8]

Agitators first emerged in eight cavalry regiments late in April, initially at troop level – a troop was a unit of one hundred men – before regimental agitators were elected and an inter-regimental organization developed. Some regiments, perhaps most, kept up an internal system of agitators right through the year; some for longer. The cavalry were the natural seeding-ground, partly because cavalry troopers were more widely literate and politically conscious than foot soldiers, but also because their mounts made them more mobile; they could communicate between regiments and attend common meetings more easily. But the foot regiments followed their example in May, and they sent emissaries to the northern army, where agitators were swiftly organized. Poyntz soon lost all his authority; the northern agitators actually arrested him.[9]

At first only soldiers signed the agitators' pamphlets and petitions, but some officers were closely associated with them from the start, notably Captains John Reynolds and Francis White and Lieutenant Edmund Chillenden. White and one or two others were already in contact with some leading Levellers, and so probably were Edward Sexby and Nicholas Lockyer and perhaps a few others among the original agitators. But the Levellers had very little to do with the initial election of agitators, which was spontaneous, and motivated by the grievances felt by the soldiers as soldiers.[10] The two over-quoted newswriters who reported that the

[8] *The Apologie of the Common Souldiers* (30 April 1647), pp. 3–4.
[9] *Clarke Papers*, ed. Firth, I, 146–7, 163–9; R. Bell (ed.), *Memorials of the Civil War: Correspondence of the Fairfax family* (2 vols, London, 1849), I, pp. 360–4, 370; Bodl. Tanner MS 58, f. 346; H. Cary (ed.), *Memorials of the Great Civil War* (2 vols, London, 1842), I, pp. 298, 300.
[10] My own work confirms the conclusions on this matter of Ian Gentles, 'Arrears of pay and ideology in the army revolt of 1647', in *War and Society: A yearbook of military history*, ed. B. Bond and I. Roy (London, 1976), pp. 44–66, esp. pp. 48–9; J. S. Morrill, 'The army revolt of 1647', in *Britain and the Netherlands*, ed. A. C. Duke and C. A. Tamse (6 vols, 1977), VI; Kishlansky, *Rise of the New Model Army*, pp. 205–6, and 'The army and the Levellers', pp. 796–7.

army was 'one Lilburne throughout', and treated his pamphlets as
statute law, were simply mistaken.[11] One can see why. The soldiers' original petition and the Levellers' so-called 'Large Petition'
were circulating for signatures at much the same time, and people
who were scared of both attributed them to a common source. But
it was only *after* the agitators became an organized force that the
Levellers focused attention on them. How little the Levellers were
influencing them in mid-May can be gauged by the statements of
grievances that the regiments then drew up for the parliamentary
commissioners who had come down to investigate the army's
so-called distempers.[12] The agitators, who were now meeting regularly at Bury St Edmunds, played a large part in preparing these;
indeed they evidently drew up a model return for the regiments to
make use of as they thought fit. Five cavalry regiments adopted it in
whole or in part, and echoes of it can be heard in several other
regiments' returns. Nothing in this model statement or *Ur text* bore
a Leveller stamp; indeed specifically Leveller complaints appear in
only three regimental statements (two of them identical), and in
only one or two articles even in those. Understandably, the main
grievances in these returns were over arrears of pay and uncertain
indemnity, but they express equally vividly the soldiers' resentment
and suspicion towards the army's detractors, inside and outside the
parliament.

The large gathering of officers which met in Saffron Walden
church on 15 and 16 May to report on the army's temper to the
commissioners was almost a rehearsal for the General Council of
the Army. Every regiment was represented, some by agitators as
well as officers. When Colonel Sheffield, a Presbyterian of aristocratic family, objected to admitting mere troopers to speak,
Major-General Skippon, who had risen from the ranks in the Dutch
service, over-ruled him from the chair. 'It is more seasonable for us
to receive all together,' he said.[13] The agitators were overjoyed with
their officers' support; 'stand with your officers,' they wrote to the
regiments, 'and one with another you need not fear.'[14] But
although this solidarity was all very stirring, the agitators faced

[11] Bodl., Clarendon MS 29, f. 195v; HMC, Portland MSS, III, 156.
[12] Returns from twelve regiments and short reports from four other units are in
Worcester College library, Oxford, William Clarke MS 41, ff. 105–26. There is a
useful tabular analysis of them in Morrill, 'Army revolt of 1647', p. 78.
[13] *Clarke Papers*, ed. Firth, I, pp. 40–1.
[14] Ibid., pp. 87–8.

Fairfax with a serious problem. They were acting without his knowledge and beyond his control, and they were inciting soldiers to disobey officers who opposed their line. There were incidents bordering on mutiny when officers who tried to march their men off for Ireland were defied by soldiers who answered the agitators' call to keep the army together until their grievances were redressed. The crucial test came when parliament finally ordered the regiments to various scattered rendezvous, to be paid off and disbanded. The agitators mounted such pressure for a general rendezvous, assembling all the regiments within marching distance, that Fairfax took the advice of his assembled officers and summoned it. He had a choice between defying parliament's commands and losing control of his army. He did order the agitators to meet no more on their own and not to act without their officers' authorization, but he was not obeyed. The agitators first secured the army's train of artillery and then abducted the king from Holmby House, where the parliament held him. Cornet Joyce's party of 500 horse, which executed both these *coups*, was assembled from three or four regiments, and it took its decisions collectively, like a kind of military soviet. Its whole exploit was a remarkable feat of organization.

The Solemn Engagement into which the regiments entered at the general rendezvous on 5 June was a military covenant, explicitly analogous to the Scottish National Covenant of 1638.[15] They pledged themselves not to disband or be divided until their would-be destroyers were removed from power, and until their grievances were remedied to the satisfaction of a council that was to include, besides the general officers, two officers and two soldiers elected by each regiment. This became known by mid-August as the General Council of the Army, though it first sat in mid-July. It gave formal status to the agitators and brought them under a degree of control, but it did not weaken them by including elected officers, for many of the latter were already closely associated with them, and were glad to be called agitators too. The General Council's recorded debates reveal more known radicals among the officer-agitators than among the soldiers.

Not all the New Model's officers shared in this solidarity, for somewhere between a fifth and a quarter of them left the service at

---

[15] Printed with minor omissions in A. S. P. Woodhouse (ed.), *Puritanism and Liberty: being the Army Debates (1647–9) from the Clarke manuscripts with supplementary documents* (2nd edn, London, 1951), pp. 401–3; cf. p. 404 for the Scottish analogy.

about this time,[16] some because they deplored the army's defiance on principle, others because they had lost their men's obedience by trying to engage them for the Irish service against their will. Their departure altered the army's political complexion somewhat, and made it easier for it to agree on the larger objectives which it proclaimed on 14 June, to coincide with its impeachment of Holles, Stapleton and nine other Presbyterian MPs. Proudly declaring that it was 'not a mere mercenary army, . . . but called forth . . . to the defence of our own and the people's just rights and liberties', it called for triennially elected parliaments of limited duration, with their seats reapportioned to make constituencies roughly equal, and affirmed that when the people's liberties had been secured, the king's rights should be settled 'so far as may consist with the right and freedom of the subject'.[17]

The Levellers later made a grievance of the fact that the General Council was rarely summoned before September, and that military decisions continued to be taken by Fairfax and his regular Council of War, a body of about thirty or forty officers, mostly senior. They were to interpret the Solemn Engagement as an original compact which dissolved the army's previous power-structure and vested supreme authority in the General Council, reducing Fairfax, Cromwell and the other high officers to its mere executors. That was never the intention. The original stated function of the General Council was to register the army's satisfaction or otherwise regarding the removal of its political enemies and the redress of its just grievances, and for many weeks too little was done in either matter to necessitate a meeting. But the agitators went on meeting informally, without any sign of resentment. During June and July they sent out a series of letters and emissaries to the various provincial forces and to the seamen of the navy, appealing for their support. They were represented on the committee which framed the army's charges against the eleven impeached Presbyterians. They published an address to Fairfax, asking him to apply pressure from the army to make the City reinstate the Independent officers in its

[16] Kishlansky, *Rise of the New Model Army*, pp. 218–20, reckons that twenty-nine per cent of officers of the rank of captain or above, or 'almost a third of all senior officers', left the army in the early summer. Ian Gentles and I have concluded independently that the proportion was probably more like twenty-two per cent, but the evidence cannot be briefly summarized and must await our respective longer publications.

[17] Woodhouse, *Puritanism and Liberty*, pp. 403–9.

militia. Their letters and addresses were always signed by officers as well as soldiers, their names sometimes interspersed without any distinction of rank.[18]

When the General Council eventually met, at Reading on 16 July, the agitators presented a 'humble petition and representation', calling for an immediate march on London, for the arrest of the eleven Presbyterians, for the release of John Lilburne and other Leveller prisoners, for the City to be forced to pay its arrears of assessment, and for other bellicose actions.[19] It was keenly debated until nearly midnight. Up to a point this session anticipated the more famous debate at Putney, with the junior elements pressing to apply force to the parliament, and Cromwell and Ireton resisting it. But in contrast with Putney, there were no proposals for a radical alternative to a parliamentary settlement, no attacks upon the king, and no challenge to the military authority of the generals.

The chief reason for calling this General Council was revealed next day when Ireton divulged to it the Heads of the Proposals, a set of terms on which it was proposed that the army should treat with the king. As a basis for settlement, they were not only more liberal and reforming than the parliament's impossibly harsh Propositions of Newcastle; they should also have been easier for Charles to accept. They have always been regarded as essentially Ireton's work, but it is becoming clear that Viscount Saye and Sele and Lord Wharton were closely involved with him in their preparation, and that this initiative had the support of the 'royal Independents' in both Houses.[20] But to put the Heads of the Proposals to the General Council before they were presented to the king or communicated to parliament was a remarkable act of confidence. William Allen, agitator of Cromwell's regiment, was impressed. The Proposals were 'things of great weight', he said, and he confessed 'that wee are most of us butt young Statesmen'.[21] He asked for time to deliberate, and after some debate Ireton's

---

[18] The above paragraph is based on contemporary pamphlets and on documents in the Clarke and Tanner MSS, which will be fully cited in *Soldiers and Statesmen*.

[19] *Clarke papers*, ed. Firth, I, pp. 170–5.

[20] This will be demonstrated in a PhD dissertation on 'The peerage in politics, 1645–9', which John Adamson is currently completing at Cambridge. Mr Adamson generously communicated to me a draft of the relevant chapter, which is of the highest interest. For the royal Independents see Valerie Pearl, 'The royal Independents in the English Civil War', *TRHS*, 5th ser., 18 (1968).

[21] *Clarke Papers*, ed. Firth, I, pp. 213.

momentous paper was referred to a committee of twelve officers
and twelve agitators. Further debate in the General Council would
certainly have followed if a major crisis in London had not forced
the army to intervene immediately. Since early June, the Commons
had been subjected to sporadic intimidation by menacing bands of
disbanded soldiers or 'reformadoes'. From 20 July the reformadoes
fused with angry crowds of citizens, protesting at parliament's
recent concessions to the army. At a great meeting on 21 July the
citizens launched their own Solemn Engagement, pledging themselves to reinstate the king on minimal terms. Five days later a
brawling mob of apprentices and others, encouraged by some
Presbyterian aldermen and MPs, invaded both Houses of Parliament and terrorized them into inviting Charles to London forth-
with. The Speakers and many members of both Houses fled to the
army.[22]

All that is a well-known story. What is less well known is that
before the army marched in and London's counter-revolution
collapsed, Cromwell and Ireton tried strenuously to persuade
Charles to agree to the Heads of the Proposals on the spot, and
modified them considerably to meet his objections to them. If he
had pledged himself to accept them and promptly repudiated the
rioting Londoners, Fairfax's army would have escorted him back to
Westminster along with the Speakers and the fugitive members.[23]
Charles and his adviser Sir John Berkeley had a point, of course,
when they asked the assembled senior officers what they would do
if parliament refused to implement the Proposals. They got no clear
answer until Colonel Rainborough burst out: 'If they will not agree,
wee will make them.' Then there was a hum of assent.[24] It was a
realistic offer. A limited purge of diehard Presbyterian MPs would
probably have been necessary before the Proposals could be
ratified, but a substantial body of Independents in both Houses
were ready to welcome them, and the Presbyterians were currently
discrediting themselves. A little more violence to a parliament
already heavily subjected to violence would have been swiftly

---

[22] Valerie Pearl, 'London's counter-revolution', in *The Interregnum: the quest for
Settlement*, ed. G. E. Aylmer (London, 1972).

[23] This claim will be documented in *Soldiers and Statesmen*, but it rests mainly on
the memoirs of Sir John Berkeley, Sir John Ashburnham and Major Robert
Huntington, the dispatches of Bellièvre, and John Wildman's *Putney Projects*.

[24] *Memoirs of Sir John Berkeley*, in *Select Tracts relating to the Civil Wars in England*,
ed. Frances Baron Maseres (2 vols, London, 1815), II, 369.

forgiven if its outcome had been the restoration of the king. But all such speculations rest on imagining Charles to have been other than the man he was. Being what he was, he would not repudiate the citizens' anarchic efforts until they were manifestly beaten, and even then he would make no commitment. Berkeley and the French ambassador thought, surely rightly, that he missed his best chance of regaining his throne on honourable terms.

Throughout August and beyond, the agitators kept pressing for a forcible expulsion of all the members who had sat on at Westminster after the Speakers had fled. That would have meant a massive purge, and it was the main talking-point at the next General Council, at Kingston on 18 August. The pressure for action was evidently difficult to contain, but the meeting was persuaded to approve a carefully worded Remonstrance, which was afterwards read at the head of every regiment. It asked parliament to consider and implement the Heads of the Proposals. It backed its various requests with a strong threat of a purge – nothing less would have satisfied the agitators – but it was a conditional threat, and not aimed indiscriminately at all who had sat in the Speakers' absence. It did not end the agitators' pressure, but it contained it. It also reaffirmed the army's qualified commitment to the king, declaring that 'we shall rejoice as much as any to see the King brought back to his Parliament, and that not so much in place, as in affection and agreement, on such sound terms and grounds as may render both him and the kingdom safe, quiet, and happy.'[25]

Fairfax now moved his headquarters to Putney, where he instituted weekly meetings of the General Council in the parish church, each Thursday from 9 September onward. At the first of them it expelled Major Francis White (as he now was), the senior representative of Fairfax's own regiment, for saying that there was no visible authority in the kingdom but the power of the sword. It then published a declaration that the army intended to maintain the fundamental authority and government of the kingdom.[26] It spent most of its first two Thursday meetings, however, debating amend-

[25] *A Remonstrance from . . . Fairfax and the Armie under his Command* (18 Aug. 1647), repr. in *PH*, XVI, pp. 251–73; quotation from p. 262. I believe Gardiner to have been mistaken in his view (*Great Civil War*, III, pp. 182–4) that Cromwell was now eager for a purge of parliament by the army and that only Fairfax's delaying tactics averted it.

[26] *A Declaration of the Engagements* [etc.] *from Sir Thomas Fairfax and the generall Councel of the Army* (1647), p. 150.

ments to the Heads of the Proposals, and although Charles was now arousing exasperation by his attempts to play off the army and the parliament against each other, and Cromwell was coming under fire for playing the courtier, a consensus was maintained all through September for a settlement broadly on the lines of the Proposals. By then, the General Council had something to show for its continued pressure over arrears, indemnity and other bread-and-butter matters, and not only over those; for the eleven impeached Presbyterians had withdrawn from the Commons, Fairfax had been made commander-in-chief of all the forces in England, and in September parliament approved a standing military establishment of 26,400 horse and foot − 20,000 more men than it had voted in the spring.[27]

Consequently there was a fair degree of harmony between army commanders, agitators and even parliament, and the only people to grumble about it were the Levellers. Lilburne addressed tracts to the soldiery from the Tower, urging them not to keep the same agitators for too long, since standing waters putrify. 'But above all the rest', he wrote, 'be sure not to trust your great officers at the Generalls quarters, no further than you can throw an Oxe', for by their cunning ploys they had 'most unjustly stolne the power both from your honest Generall, and your too flexible Adjutators'.[28] Finding little response, Lilburne and his friends proceeded to engineer the emergence of new agitators who could be better relied on to do the Levellers' business in the army. They appeared only in five cavalry regiments, and they were commonly called 'the agents of the five regiments', or simply 'the London agents'. The first definite news of them is in a letter from Lilburne's crony in the Tower, the royalist Sir Lewis Dyve, to Charles I on 29 September. 'Mr. Lilborne set this busines first on foot and hath a great influence upon their counsells,' wrote Dyve.[29] But as a prisoner Lilburne was handicapped, and the chief organizers were probably the civilian John Wildman and the agitator Edward Sexby. The new agents were indoctrinated and briefed in daily meetings with their Leveller mentors in London.[30] Together they formed a little caucus quite separate from the General Council, on which the new

[27] Firth and Davies, *Regimental History of Cromwell's Army*, I, p. xx.
[28] J. Lilburne, *The Juglers Discovered* (1647), pp. 10, 12 (misprinted as 11).
[29] *The Tower of London Letter-Book of Sir Lewis Dyve, 1646–7*, ed. H. G. Tibbutt, Bedfordshire Historical Record Society (1958), pp. 90–1.
[30] Ibid., pp. 91–2.

agents never displaced their regiments' old agitators. It is indeed very doubtful whether their regiments ever elected them; Fairfax and his Council of War publicly denied it.[31] There is some evidence, however, that they sought a mandate of a kind several weeks after they had begun meeting, and indeed after they had published a manifesto called *The Case of the Armie truly stated*.[32]

This pamphlet, which was mainly Wildman's work, attacked the army commanders harshly for reneging on the pledges that they had given in June. It called for an immediate and drastic purge of parliament, and thereafter for biennial parliaments elected by 'all the freeborn' aged twenty-one or more except those who forfeited their freedom through delinquency. It was presented to Fairfax, who simply referred it to the next General Council, on 21 October. There its sweeping charges of backsliding and bad faith were ill received, and Cromwell and Ireton in particular attacked it roundly. The authentic agitators of the five regiments whose self-styled agents had signed it were present, and they disowned it. So the General Council appointed a committee, which naturally included agitators, to inquire into its accusations and its authors, and to prepare a vindication of the army from its aspersions.[33] At this stage the generals were plainly hoping to flush a subversive movement (as they saw it) into the open and to scotch it.

The committee, however, communicated with the new agents through three agitators, Sexby, Allen and Nicholas Lockyer, who were more sympathetic towards them than most of the General Council had been. Thanks largely to these three, the authors of *The Case of the Armie* were invited to come and present their own case to the General Council. That is how the famous debates that William Clarke recorded came about: as a confrontation between the Leveller caucus and the General Council of the Army. The latter met on 28 October to receive its committee's report and to give a hearing to delegates from the rival meeting. Sexby as go-between intro-

[31] *A Remonstrance from . . . Fairfax and his Council of War* (14 November 1647), printed in *LJ*, IX, p. 529.
[32] *Select Tracts*, ed. Maseres, I, pp. xv–lxvii. *The Case of the Armie* is printed in *Leveller Manifestoes of the Puritan Revolution*, ed. D. M. Wolfe (New York and London, 1944), pp. 198–222.
[33] *Papers from the Armie concerning His Excellency and the Generall Councell* (22 October 1647), pp. 2–4; *Perfect Diurnall* no. 221, 18–25 Oct. 1647, pp. 1775, 1778; *A Cal to all the Souldiers of the Armie* (1647), p. 5; Rushworth, *Historical Collections*, VII, pp. 849–50; *Clarke Papers*, ed. Firth, I, p. 234.

duced them: two as yet unnamed new agents (one was Robert Everard) and two civilians, Wildman and Maximilian Petty. They came, however, not just to defend *The Case of the Armie* but to promote a new document that their meeting had approved and submitted only the day before. They called it An Agreement of the People, and it proposed that the nation's future government should be settled not by parliamentary enactment and royal assent but by the sovereign people's individual assents to the Agreement itself. Even while the Putney debates were in progress, the Agreement was circulating among the soldiers for their signatures. So were pamphlets which blatantly incited them to mutiny. *A Cal to all the Souldiers of the Armie*, for instance, reviled Cromwell and Ireton for presuming to treat with the king in the army's name. 'Hold not parley with them,' it urged; 'ye have men amongst you as fit to govern as others to be removed. *And with a word ye can create new officers* . . . Establish a free parliament by expulsion of the usurpers.'[34]

There were three reasons, besides their objections to the Agreement in principle, why the generals felt compelled to take a stand against the army Levellers. One was that the Leveller agents were stirring up serious disorder in the ranks; Colonel Robert Lilburne's regiment was already in full mutiny, and others were being subverted.[35] Secondly, the Agreement contained much that was incompatible with the pledges and engagements that the army had published to the world since June. Thirdly, it could only have been implemented by direct military action, including a violent dissolution of parliament, since only a tiny band of members, such as Henry Marten and Colonel Rainborough, were favourably inclined towards it. Such a dissolution was just what most Levellers wanted, but at that time, before serious negotiation with the king had begun and before the Independents' alternative to the Propositions of Newcastle had even been debated, it would have utterly alienated the political nation, and would probably have driven Charles into the arms of the Scots with considerably more hope of success than he and they were to enjoy in 1648. To Cromwell and Ireton it naturally seemed premature to abandon the formula for settlement that they and Lord Saye and his circle had been working on since

[34] Extract in Woodhouse, *Puritanism and Liberty*, pp. 439–43; italics in original.
[35] *Letter-Book of Sir Lewis Dyve*, p. 94; *Perfectly Weekly Account* no. 43, 26 October–2 November 1647; *The Justice of the Army against Evill-Doers Vindicated* (1649); *Clarke Papers*, ed. Firth, I, p. 367.

July, a formula that still sought a balance between king, Lords and Commons. So when Sexby led off the debate with a full-throated attack on both king and parliament they naturally kept urging that the first question must be to establish how much of the Agreement the army was free to consider, in view of its previous promises and engagements. This was not just an exercise in the lower tactics of debate, as Woodhouse called it, and it was more than a procedural device to secure consensus.[36] If Ireton and Cromwell could demonstrate that the army's public declarations debarred it, in honour, from espousing the more extreme courses proposed by the Agreement, they could hope to hold the General Council on course towards a settlement by constitutional means and to head off the Leveller attempt to deflect it towards a revolutionary solution requiring the use of force. They did not do badly that first day, the Thursday. They put off a discussion of the content of the Agreement, and they got a committee appointed to compare its proposals with the army's previous engagements. The next meeting of the General Council was scheduled for the Monday, after the committee had done its business.

Friday morning was set aside for seeking the Lord in prayer, not in Putney church but in the Quartermaster-General's lodgings. The officers were still at their religious exercises there when Wildman, Petty, Everard and other agents arrived in the early afternoon, presumably to meet the committee appointed the day before. Finding a larger company, they and Rainborough, who had probably come down from London with them, pressed for an immediate debate on the Agreement, clause by clause. Cromwell was understandably against it, for this was not a scheduled session of the General Council and the committee had not yet met, but he was overborne.

What followed must be the best-known debate in British history. Ireton pounced on the Agreement's first clause, which declared 'That the People of England being at this day very unequally distributed . . . for the election of their Deputies in Parliament, ought to be more indifferently proportioned, according to the number of the Inhabitants.'[37] Did that mean, he asked, that every male inhabitant should have the vote? It did, of course, but it was

[36] Woodhouse, *Puritanism and Liberty*, p. 28; Mark A. Kishlansky, 'Consensus politics and the structure of debate at Putney', *Journal of British Studies*, 20 (1981).
[37] Wolfe, *Leveller Manifestoes*, p. 226.

not explicit, and Ireton committed a tactical blunder by focusing
on it. One cannot regret it, in view of the marvellous debate that
ensured; but the notion that every free man had a right to a voice in
electing the people's representatives, at least unless he somehow
forfeited it, had a predictably wide appeal, and in opposing it
Ireton and Cromwell almost isolated themselves. They would have
been wiser to direct discussion towards those matters in the Agreement on which consensus was possible, such as liberty of conscience, an early dissolution followed by biennial parliaments, reappor-
tionment of constituencies, and reform of the law. By so doing they
could have appealed to the General Council's genuine desire for
unity and deflated the pressure for a physical challenge to the
parliament, which was the main danger and the Levellers' avowed
objective. Manhood suffrage was not such a danger, nor so revolutionary a proposal as Ireton supposed, in view of what we now
know about the great enlargement of the electorate in the previous
half-century and the strong consensus in the Long Parliament in
favour of admitting 'the commonalty' to vote in borough elections
unless there was a statute to the contrary.[38]

   If Ireton and Cromwell might have foreseen their rough passage
over the franchise, they could hardly have anticipated Rainborough's passionate championship of the Leveller cause. Rainborough had been little seen lately in the General Council, though he
had quarrelled with Cromwell at its meeting on 16 September.
Soon afterwards he was appointed vice-admiral, a post that he had
eagerly sought, and he was furious with Cromwell for having
opposed his appointment. When he got it, Fairfax gave his regiment to Richard Deane. Rainborough resented that too; he had
evidently hoped to draw his pay for both commands, and that is
what brought him to Putney on 28 October. By his own account
Everard, the new agents' chief spokesman, was a stranger to him,
and he had first seen the Agreement the day before, by chance.[39] In
the famous debate on the franchise he sometimes sounds like a
starry-eyed fellow-traveller whose enthusiasm was a shade embar-

[38] Derek Hirst, *The Representative of the People?* (Cambridge, 1975), chs. 3–5.
Although the commonalty was often equated with the freemen, some very
prominent MPs favoured extending the franchise to all inhabitants (ibid., pp. 83,
92–3). Hirst is illuminating about the ignorance on both sides at Putney concerning contemporary electoral practices (pp. 21–3).
[39] D. E. Kennedy, 'The English naval revolt of 1648', *English Historical Review*,
77, (1962), 247–56; *Letter-Book of Sir Lewis Dyve*, p. 89; *Clarke papers*, ed. Firth, I,
pp. 244–5, 273.

rassing to the seasoned party operators, who did not want to be too literal about 'the poorest he that is in England'; Petty was ready that very afternoon to talk about disfranchising servants and alms-takers. Rainborough's attachment to the Levellers would cease within two months, when the Commons suspended his vice-admiralship because of it; he then made a full submission to the General Council and got it to intercede for him. But on that Friday he offered the dangerous motion 'That the Army might bee called to a Rendezvous, and thinges setled'.[40] He evidently hoped for a re-run of the June rendezvous, and for the Agreement to be carried by acclamation as the Solemn Engagement had been. Nobody seconded him, and it may be that Cromwell told him, off the record, that this unconstituted meeting could not possibly take such a decision.

In a pamphlet which the new agents addressed to their regiments on 11 November, they claimed that in one of these debates they carried a vote against only three dissentient voices 'That all soldiers and others, if they be not servants or beggars, ought to have voices in electing those which shall represent them in Parliament'.[41] Their statements are not always trustworthy and their chronology in this tract is self-contradictory, but if such a vote *was* passed (and it is not implausible) it was almost certainly on either 29 October or 2 November, and more probably on the 29th, after Clarke gave up his shorthand record, which is manifestly incomplete.[42] What certainly happened before that meeting broke up was the briefing of a fresh committee to find what common ground it could between the Agreement and the army's previous engagements, 'and prepare somewhat to be insisted upon and adhered unto for settling the kingdom'.[43] The committee met next day, with Cromwell, Ireton and Rainborough among its twelve officers and Sexby and Allen among its six agitators, and it made much more headway than might have been expected.

When the General Council met again in formal session on Monday 1 November, a succession of officer-agitators and Level-

[40] Ibid., p. 346.

[41] *A Letter sent from several Agitators to their Respective Regiments*, substantially repr. in Woodhouse, *Puritanism and Liberty*, pp. 452–4.

[42] The evidence is complex and must await the publication of *Soldiers and Statesmen*. Most historians have dated the vote 4 November, but the General Council almost certainly did not meet that day.

[43] *Clarke Papers*, ed. Firth, I, p. 363.

lers spoke out against any further negotiation with Charles and even against kingship itself. Wildman and Sexby were specially severe, but Rainborough and Allen dissociated themselves from such anti-monarchical views, which were still untypical. Rainborough had visited Lilburne in the Tower the day before, and remonstrated with him about the evil intentions towards the king that the Levellers had been expressing at Putney, intentions 'which he said he well knew the greatest part of the army abhord to thinke of'. Lilburne himself shared no such intentions, for he had been trying through Dyve to put Charles in touch with several leading army radicals, incuding Reynolds, White and Sexby, assuring him that if he would send for them and win them over he could have the whole army at his devotion within six weeks.[44] Sometimes one is left wondering whether John Lilburne or Charles Stuart had the weaker grasp of political realities.

Clarke's precious record gives out tantalizingly after 1 November, though the General Council sat again on the 2nd, 5th, 6th and 8th. Very possibly it confirmed on the 2nd the straw vote of the previous Friday to give the vote to all but servants or beggars, for two newspapers have in their curt reports of its conclusions the words 'Elections free to freemen'.[45] The session on the 5th went more seriously wrong for the generals. Fairfax was in the chair; Cromwell was probably in the Commons for a crucial debate on parliament's revised propositions to the king. The General Council was again debating its committee's draft statement of the army's desires regarding the kingdom's settlement, which still envisaged a strictly limited monarchy. Rainborough, though a member of the committee, now urged that the army should oppose any further addresses to the king whatsoever. Certainly the General Council sent a letter to the Speaker that day, saying that if the Commons were sending propositions to the king because they had been told that the army desired it they were misinformed. Ireton correctly interpreted this as a censure upon himself and Cromwell, and opposed it strenuously. When the letter was nevertheless approved he stormed out of the meeting, and refused to return until it was recalled.[46]

[44] *Letter-Book of Sir Lewis Dyve*, pp. 92, 95–6.

[45] *Perfect Diurnall* no. 223, 1–8 November, pp. 1, 792–3; *Perfect Occurrences* no. 44, 29 October–5 November, p. 312. They may have a common source in John Rushworth.

[46] *Clarke Papers*, ed. Firth, I, pp. 440–1; Rushworth, *Historical Collections*, VII, p. 864; *Clarendon State Papers* II, App. p. xli.

The new agents claimed that their friends secured a decision at this meeting to call a general rendezvous of the whole army.[47] This is inherently implausible, and Fairfax would undoubtedly have informed parliament if such a decision had been taken. He may, however, have responded sympathetically to proposals for a rendezvous, without committing himself to assembling all the regiments in the same place on the same day, as the Levellers desired.

Next day, a Saturday, the General Council continued to debate its committee's draft proposals, which were an interesting attempt to blend and reconcile the principles of the Heads of the Proposals with those of the Agreement of the People. The Leveller faction, however, pressed for a free debate on whether it was safe to leave any power at all in the crown, and by their account Cromwell promised that they should have one on the Monday. Perhaps, as so often, they exaggerated, but there is no doubt that over the weekend Fairfax and Cromwell changed their tactics. They gave up the long struggle to secure an agreed statement of the army's political objectives. Three considerations may have weighed with them. They may have judged the prospects of achieving a consensus to be worsening, and reckoned that by prolonging the debate they were only giving a platform to ideologues who were tearing the army apart. Secondly, the Leveller agents were stepping up their efforts to subvert the soldiery, and it was becoming daily more urgent to restore order and discipline. Thirdly, intelligence may have reached headquarters of the king's intention to flee from the army's custody, for he had been incurring suspicion for over a week, and he finally made up his mind to bolt at some point between 3 and 7 November.

Consequently, the General Council on Monday 8 November did not go as the Levellers had expected. It approved a second letter to the Speaker, explaining that the one that had so angered Ireton did not mean that the army opposed the sending of propositions to the king, but simply that it wanted to uphold parliament's freedom of decision. Then Cromwell moved that in view of Fairfax's intention to call the army to a rendezvous shortly, and because of public concern over the distempers in several regiments, the elected officers and agitators should return to their regiments until Fairfax reconvened them. This was apparently carried without opposition;

[47] *A Letter sent from several Agitators*; extract in Woodhouse, *Puritanism and Liberty*, p. 452.

indeed Fairfax reported to parliament that the officers and agitators unanimously *offered* to return to their units and assist in
'recovering the ancient discipline of the army'.[48] There were indeed
some other signs of a revulsion against the protracted, divisive
debates, and Henry Denne, a repentant ex-Leveller, recalled in
1649 that most of the regiments petitioned Fairfax to dismiss the
agitators shortly before this meeting.[49]

How does one explain the change in temper, to put it no higher,
between the warm response to the Levellers' franchise proposals on
29 October and the ready acquiescence in the indefinite (and as it
proved permanent) dismissal of the agitators ten days later? In the
first place, those who thought it right for all free men to have the
vote were not necessarily Leveller converts; they did not necessarily
underwrite the whole Leveller package, which involved imposing a
chimerical sketch of a constitution by direct action instead of
continuing to seek a settlement through parliamentary channels.
The words of the Agreement had a bright ring, but few found them
worth breaking the unity of the army for, especially when the army
might soon have to fight the common enemy again. Within three
days of the agitators' departure Charles escaped from Hampton
Court, and thereby demonstrated how urgent it was for the army to
close its ranks. He claimed to be in fear of assassination, and there
was indeed some shadowy conspiracy among certain agents and
other extremists, though perhaps to abduct him rather than to kill
him. But Charles's chief motive for his flight was what it had been
for weeks: to negotiate with the commissioners recently arrived
from Scotland without having the army officers breathing down his
neck. The lure was a Scottish army. Carisbrooke Castle on the Isle
of Wight proved an ill-chosen venue, but that is another story.

Fairfax had already ordered all the regiments to one of three
rendezvous, on 15, 17 and 18 November. There was nothing
machiavellian about holding three rendezvous instead of one. The
twenty-two regiments were quite widely dispersed, and seven or
eight were as many as Fairfax could personally address in a short
winter's day. The first rendezvous, at Corkbush Field near Ware, is
famous because two regiments arrived there against orders, with
copies of the Agreement stuck in the soldiers' hats. But the little
mutiny swiftly collapsed in face of the firm determination of

[48] *Clarke Papers*, ed. Firth, I, pp. 411–13; Rushworth, *Historical Collections*, VII,
pp. 866–7.
[49] Henry Denne, *The Levellers Designe Discovered* (1649), pp. 4–5.

Cromwell and Fairfax and the vociferous loyalty of the other seven regiments on the field.[50] It was not only their general whom they cheered; several shouted repeatedly 'For the king and Sir Thomas!'[51] This and the other two rendezvous succeeded spectacularly in restoring the unity and discipline of the army, not by an act of repression but by a new mutual covenant between commanders, regimental officers and soldiers, comparable to the Solemn Engagement of June. This Remonstrance, as it was called, was read to each regiment, commended in a short speech by Fairfax, and subscribed by officers and men on the spot. It castigated the subversive activities of the Leveller agents, and affirmed that the army commanders and the General Council had done all they could to fulfil the army's undertakings 'without present destruction to the Parliament, which in their opinions would inevitably put the Kingdome into blood and confusion'. There followed a mutual pledge that all officers and soldiers would obey their superiors, and that Fairfax and his fellow-generals would 'live and die' with the army to secure not only the soldiers' pay and other material interests but also the earliest safe dissolution of the present parliament, a guaranteed and regular succession of parliaments thereafter, 'and for the freedom and equality of elections thereto, to render the House of Commons (as near as may be) an equal representative of the people that are to elect'.[52]

The almost eager closing of the ranks showed how shallow the Levellers' penetration of the army had been so far. The Levellers had set their hopes on a re-enactment of the heady days of June, with the Agreement acclaimed by the soldiery as the Solemn Engagement had been. But the situation was very different. In June, most of the army had faced disbandment; in November it had an approved establishment of 26,400 men. It was the Levellers who wanted it disbanded, once the soldiers' grievances had been met. In June the Presbyterians had been contemplating a sell-out peace with the king; that had been averted, if only temporarily. In June the soldiers had had no remotely adequate security for their arrears of pay; in November they were still too irregularly paid, but their

[50] I am unable to understand Mark Kishlansky's statement in 'What happened at Ware?', *Historical Journal*, (1982), 827–39, that 'there was no mutiny at Ware' (p. 839), and I shall offer evidence in *Soldiers and Statesmen* that Cromwell's personal role in cowing the mutineers was no mere legend.

[51] 'John Lawmind' [Wildman], *Putney Projects* (1647), p. 27.

[52] *LJ*, IX, p. 529.

arrears were being looked after, and their wiser heads appreciated the unwisdom of killing the only goose that could lay even under-sized golden eggs. But the crucial difference was that in June the great majority of officers, from Fairfax and Cromwell downward, had stood foursquare with their soldiers and championed their protest. In November, by contrast, the great majority of officers, though divided on such questions as who should vote in elections and how much rope should be given to the king and to the present parliament, held firm against the military *coup* that the Levellers demanded as the first step into an unknown future.

The Levellers were splitting the army at a very dangerous time. It is possible to feel the warmest sympathy with the democratic principles that they advanced at Putney, and yet to recognize that their prescriptions for action in the last three months of 1647 would, if followed, have been disastrous. On 26 December the king did what he had been looking forward to for over two months: he signed the Engagement with the Scottish commissioners which led, directly and deliberately, to the Second Civil War. Thanks to the actions that Fairfax and Cromwell had taken in November, the army was ready for it. If (to imagine the very improbable) the Leveller mutinies had succeeded, the likely consequences would have been a massive exodus of seasoned officers, from the generals downward, a premature purge or dissolution of parliament, and a royal restoration – virtually unconditional – by Scottish arms.

7

The Problem of Indemnity, 1647–1648

ROBERT ASHTON

The Indemnity Ordinances of 1647 establishing a mechanism for suspending normal legal process in certain cases are frequently cited as a prime example of revolutionary illegality.[1] As far as the government was concerned, there were, as G. E. Aylmer has observed, distinct advantages in granting soldiers immunity in suits for debts incurred in the public service rather than having to satisfy their enormous arrears of pay, whose accumulation had given rise to the institutionalization of the hated practice of free quarter.[2] The connection between indemnity and arrears of pay is crucial, but this is not the only, nor even the main, reason why the former loomed as large as the latter among the soldiers' demands in the spring and summer of 1647.[3] As well as these and other matters, the *Vindication of the Officers of the Army*, presented to the House of Commons on 27 April, stressed the need for 'indemnity for such actions as, being not warrantable by Law in tyme of Peace, we were inforced unto . . . by the necessity and exigence of the war'. The matter was particularly urgent, stressed the officers, because soldiers were already being indicted, and indeed convicted, for such actions. If such things could go on with parliament still in session, 'what cruel and violent proceedings are we like to find after you are pleased to dissolve?'[4] Nor were soldiers the only vulnerable per-

---

[1] See e.g. J. S. Morrill, *The Revolt of the Provinces* (London, 1976), p. 76.
[2] G. E. Aylmer, *The State's Servants. The Civil Service of the English Republic 1649–60* (London, 1973), p. 13.
[3] *The Petition of Colonels, Lieutenant Colonells* [sic], *Majors and other officers* (March 1647), BL E382(4), p. 5; *Letters from Saffron-Walden . . .* (3 April 1647), BL 383(24), p. 10; *PH*, XV, pp. 339, 343.
[4] *The Vindication of the Officers of the Army* (1647), BL E385(19), pp. 3–4; *PH*, XV,

sons. As the cases which were to come before the Indemnity Committee clearly demonstrate, civilians in the service of the government stood equally in need of protection.

A further cause for alarm was the soldiers' apprehension that those presiding at the trials of their fellows might be, at worst, former Cavaliers or, at best, conservative gentlemen noted for their dislike to the army; that as some frantically worried soldiers put it on 3 May, 'our very enemies are made our Judges.'[5] For there can be no doubt that, for example, the reconstituted Commissioners of the Peace in some counties after the end of the First Civil War did contain former Cavaliers[6] nor that the subsequent parliamentary ordinances of 9 September and 4 October 1647 against the appointment of such persons to places of trust and authority were widely disregarded,[7] though the position was certainly worse before the ordinances were passed. A Hertfordshire petition of 18 June told of a warrant obtained by a certain Cordwell, 'a Man of most notorious lewd life and Conversation, and withal a most desperate Malignant', for apprehending three soldiers and bringing them before a magistrate in St Albans. The magistrate, while acknowledging the soldiers' plea that they had done the things of which they were accused as soldiers acting under orders, would nevertheless have committed them had it not been for their captain's and colonel's willingness to become bound for their appearance at the next Sessions. Cordwell then proceeded to prepare his indictment and a true bill would almost certainly have been found, 'had it not been for Two or Three honest Men . . . on the Grand Jury'. Beyond all doubt the soldiers' lives had been in real danger, 'there being but little Favour or Mercy to be had for Parliament Soldiers by the Justices of our County'.[8]

----

pp. 353–6. For similar views expressed by the common soldiers, see *The Apologie of the Common Souldiers*, 3 May 1647, BL E385(18), pp. 3, 6–8.

[5] *The Apologie*, BL E385(18), p. 6. See also *Divers Papers from the Army*, 15 May 1647, BL E388(18), p. 8.

[6] See the army's charges against Recorder Glyn in R. Bell (ed.), *Memorials of the Civil War* (1849), II, 380. See also *LJ*, IX, p. 278; *PH*, XV, p. 486: *Vox Militaris*, 11 August 1647, BL E401(24), p. 10.

[7] *A & O*, I, pp. 1009, 1023–5. The proceedings of the Indemnity Committee, which was given an oversight of such matters, provide ample evidence of evasion. See below, pp. 137–8.

[8] *LJ*, IX, p. 278; *PH*, XV, pp. 486–7.

II

Following weeks of intensive agitation and lobbying,[9] the first Indemnity Ordinance passed through parliament on 21 May 1647. It ordained that proof that the acts for which suits had been brought had been committed by the authority or for the service of parliament could be admitted in a court of law, not simply in extenuation of the offences of which defendants were accused, but as sufficient to justify their acquittal. Even more radical were the provisions of the ordinance which were to be the occasion of most of the complaints that it involved an interference with the due process of law. Recognizing that many such defendants 'may be poor and not able to defend a Suit at common Law', provision was made for the creation of a parliamentary Committee of Indemnity with power to order the termination of suits when it was convinced that the plaintiff had acted in the service of parliament, as well as to award damages of up to treble the costs incurred by defendants and to commit recalcitrant plaintiffs to custody if they refused to desist from their actions or pay the damages awarded. The committee contained twenty-nine peers and forty-nine commoners and had a quorum of as little as five. Its composition and effective membership will be examined later.[10]

Far too radical for the taste of professional lawyers, revenge-seeking Cavaliers and parliamentary conservatives, the ordinance seems also to have disappointed those whom it was designed to help.[11] According to one of the soldiers with Cornet Joyce at Holdenby in June, soldiers continued to be prosecuted notwithstanding the ordinance.[12] An additional ordinance of 7 June seems to have done little to allay the soldiers' misgivings,[13] and a pamphlet published early in August denounced the indemnity arrangements as 'a meer baffle, a pure nullitie, and not so much as the least securitie; so that this was our case as souldiers . . . we must disband, starve and be hanged.'[14] The general objections of the

---

[9] For agitation in the week before the passing of the ordinance, see *Divers Papers from the Army*, pp. 5, 7–8, 12; *The Declaration of the Armie Under . . . Sir Thomas Fairfax*, 16 May 1647, BL E390(26), pp. 2, 7, 13.

[10] *A & O*, I, pp. 936–8. See below, p. 124.

[11] *A Motion from the Armie* (1647), BL E391(5), no pagination.

[12] *A true and Impartiall Narration* (1647), BL E393(1), p. 2.

[13] *A & O*, I, pp. 953–4.

[14] *Vox Militaris* (1647), p. 12.

soldiers are nowhere more clearly stated than in *The Humble Representation of the Dissatisfaction of the Army* of 4 June. They feared with reason that when indemnity was pleaded in the courts, it would be both difficult and costly to prove a clear parliamentary authority for the acts of which they were accused. Moreover, while the alternative procedure of appeal from the courts to the new Indemnity Committee might offer a more practical and radical solution, how could poor and humble men be expected to sustain the expense of journeys to London, often for a number of sittings weeks or even months apart since it was only very exceptionally that the Committee made its decisions after a single hearing? Better, argued the soldiers, a blanket ordinance of oblivion covering 'all things done by soldiers in the war', which would have the additional advantage of saving the kingdom from yet another arbitrary and tyrannical committee.[15] Essentially the same point was to be made by the army's remonstrance later in the month, which demanded 'That in no case malignants or others may be admitted to prosecute those who have acted for the Parliament . . . in any court whatsoever.'[16]

The important snag presented by the expenses of travel was made much of by the Levellers,[17] but was also not lost on the lord-general and the Council of the Army. In their sweeping proposals of 5 December 1647 for dealing with the manifold discontents of their soldiers they made some very practical suggestions on the matter of indemnity procedures. In the absence of any Ordinance of Oblivion freeing parliamentary soldiers from all legal responsibility for acts done in the war, judges who continued to hear cases where the service or authority of parliament was pleaded on behalf of the defendant should themselves be subject to swingeing legal penalties, a proposal which, needless to say, was never adopted. Their other major recommendation was for a decentralization of indemnity procedures by setting up indemnity commissions in every county, thus radically reducing the cost of attendance.[18]

[15] Morrill, *Revolt of the Provinces*, p. 175.

[16] *A Remonstrance of the Representatives of the Army* (21 June 1647), BL E393(17), no pagination.

[17] D. M. Wolfe (ed.), *Leveller Manifestoes of the Puritan Revolution* (London, 1967), p. 217.

[18] *A Humble Representation from . . . Sir Thomas Fairfax And The Councel of the Armie* (1647), BL E419(16), pp. 23–4.

The following April, parliament took a solitary step in the recommended direction when it set up a commission in Kent to deal with local cases.[19] But if in Kent, why not also in Cornwall and Northumberland, for the inhabitants of which the expenses of journeying to London in search of indemnity were enormously greater? The terms of the new ordinance remind us that provision for indemnity was not confined to soldiers, and it may be that the excesses of the Kent county committee had rendered its members particularly vulnerable.[20]

It must be obvious from the foregoing account that even an altered and improved indemnity along the lines suggested by the army and its parliamentary allies was very much a *pis aller* compared with an Ordinance – or better still an Act – of Oblivion exempting men from acts done in the service of the parliament during the war. Moreover, a further matter for concern was that, in the words of a long pamphlet of October 1647, the Indemnity Ordinances did not extend to acts done since the war, more especially in connection with the petitioning activity in the army in March 1647 and the agitation of the subsequent weeks.[21] The soldiers' fears that they would be victimized for such matters find notable expression in the army's Solemn Engagement on Newmarket Heath on 5 June and in the Council of the Army's representations of the soldiers' desires on 21 September.[22] But where was this claim for an extension of the scope of the indemnity provision to end? As a royalist newsletter pointed out in November, the soldiers at Bristol who, unwilling to wait any longer for their pay, 'secured an Alderman, which is as good security as heart can wish; and so agreed to put the Lobster in pickle' till their needs were met: these being not only a month's pay, but also indemnity for their outrageous behaviour.[23]

From both the parliamentary Presbyterian and the radical Leveller viewpoints the idea of an Act of Oblivion was especially dangerous since – necessarily if it was to be an act as distinct from an ordinance – it raised the question of whether the army might itself come to a private arrangement with the king. 'How', per-

---

[19] *A & O*, I, pp. 1119–20.
[20] See its petition of 23 October 1647, *CJ*, V, p. 341.
[21] *A Full Vindication of the Armie* (1647), BL E410(18), pp. 24–5, 51.
[22] Wolfe, *Leveller Manifestoes*, p. 150; *A Representation from his Excellency Sir Thomas Fairfax And the generall Councell of the Army*, BL E408(11), pp. 5–6.
[23] *Mercurius Pragmaticus*, no. 11, BL E417(20), no pagination.

tinently argued a royalist pamphlet of early July 1647, 'can you expect an Act of Indemnity? so long as the King remaines in Captivity; the Parliament cannot grant it unto you, for they cannot give it to themselves.'[24] The soldiers were at least as concerned about the need to safeguard themselves against a restored monarch's desire for vengeance – from which an ordinance would afford no protection – as against the hostility of conservative parliamentarians. Accordingly among the army's articles presented to Charles at Newmarket in June was a demand for 'an Act of Oblivion wherin they may bee secured as well as his owne party'.[25] Given the king's decided preference for the terms of the Heads of the Proposals over those of the Newcastle or Hampton Court propositions, this possibility presented a real threat to conservative Presbyterian politicians. But it was no less unwelcome to the Levellers, though for different reasons. A Leveller pamphlet of December 1647 reiterates all the deep radical suspicions which had been expressed a few weeks earlier at Putney about the courting of the king by the army grandees. In particular, it scorns their search for royal consent to an Act of Indemnity or Oblivion, 'which is as much as to cry PECCAVI and to come on your knees . . . and aske . . . that he may grant . . . you a pardon for what you have done as though ye could not indempnifie your selves'.[26]

The Second Civil War, of course, changed everything. Although a declaration by the Prince of Wales with the revolted fleet on 27 July 1648 mentions an Act of Indemnity and Oblivion as one of the insurgents' war aims,[27] after the renewed bloodshed of that year, the views of the army grandees came – in this at least – to approximate to those of the Levellers which they had so roundly condemned the previous autumn. Denouncing the impending treaty in the Isle of Wight, an army declaration of 26 September also spurned 'acceptation of an odious act of Oblivion or Indemnity, as if wee were Traytors or Thieves',[28] reflecting a new intransigence which was to find its most celebrated expression in the army's Remonstrance of November.

---

[24] *Lex Talionis, or a Declamation Against Mr Challener* (1647), BL E396(20), p. 10.

[25] 'Certain Independent Articles presented by the Army to his Majestie att Newmarkett, June 19th 1647', BL E393(11), no foliation.

[26] *The Coppy of a dangerous Paper published, called an Alarum to the Headquarters* (1647), BL E420(5), pp. 12–13, 16–17.

[27] *The Declaration of His Highnesse the Prince of Wales*, BL E456(11), p. 5.

[28] *The Demands, Resolutions and Intentions of the Army*, BL E464(41), p. 8.

III

In the meantime the parliamentary Indemnity Committee set up in May 1647 had, following slow and rather tentative beginnings between June and October, dealt with an enormous number of cases. Business accelerated very markedly in November when more cases were heard than in all the previous months together, and reached its peak in February 1648. Between June 1647 and 19 December 1648 the committee met on 229 occasions[29] and heard 876 cases, comprising 2,069 items of business. In the five months before November 1647 it met forty times but heard only fifty-eight new cases. The volume of business month by month thereafter is illustrated by table 7.1.[30]

Table 7.1   Volume of Indemnity Committee Business,
November 1647–19 December 1648

Month	Number of meetings	Number of items of business	Number of new cases
November 1647	12	101	60
December 1647	13	116	53
January 1647–8	15	121	52
February 1647–8	18	278	151
March 1647–8	16	138	42
April 1648	13	155	53
May 1648	15	250	96
June 1648	20	260	97
July 1648	10	120	35
August 1648	10	72	25
September 1648	10	76	23
October 1648	13	69	35
November 1648	20	194	76
To 19 December 1648	4	48	20

[29] No distinction is here made between morning and afternoon sessions.

[30] Figures are compiled from the Order Books of the Indemnity Committee, PRO SP 24 (1–3), which probably understate the totals for December 1648.

It will be recalled that the original committee contained 26 peers and 60 commoners; the latter including the Irish peer Lord Mounson who attended very frequently (55 appearances) and took the chair on 29 occasions down to 19 April 1648, more often than any other member.[31] The attendance of the English peers was negligible. Of the commoners, radical Independents, as well as being in a substantial majority, attended more frequently than conservative Presbyterians, and the fact that Oliver Cromwell attended only twice and Philip Skippon only 8 times can confidently be ascribed to their preoccupation with other business. Quite different and obvious causes explain the failure of 7 Presbyterian MPs, including 5 of the 11 MPs whom the army tried to impeach in the summer of 1647, to attend at all, and of 4 more, including another of the '11', Sir Philip Stapleton, to put in only one appearance, though the two ex-middle-groupers Oliver St John and William Pierrepoint never attended either. Of those members of the committee whose political affiliations are known, 35 were undoubtedly Independents as against 18 whose political affiliations were of a more conservative pro-Presbyterian sort. Moreover, in the matter of attendance at meetings, at which the quorum was very low, the more radical 'Independent' members dominated even more impressively, 35 commoner Independent members recording 640 attendances as against the 111 attendances recorded by the 18 'Presbyterians' down to 19 April 1648. The most assiduous attender of all was the radical Independent MP, Colonel William Purefoy, who put in 71 appearances, 15 of them in the chair.[32] Five other members attended more than 20 times.

IV

Most cases came before the Indemnity Committee in response to petitions from persons who were usually defendants in suits brought against them in courts ranging from Quarter Sessions to King's Bench, Common Pleas and Exchequer. Most petitioners pleaded indemnity from such proceedings on the grounds of having

---

[31] Details of attendance cease to be recorded in the Order Books from 19 April 1648.

[32] The figures are derived from PRO SP 24/1–2, passim, and relate only to the period down to 19 April 1648, after which attendance ceases to be recorded.

been engaged in the service of the government. At this point it was not usual for the committee to reach a decision though there are a few exceptions to this rule. Normally, it would call the plaintiffs in the suit before it to answer the petitioners' complaints. If, as was very often the case, a plaintiff did not observe the formal summons to attend, the committee usually commanded him to stay proceedings at law, and, if he refused to comply, called him before it under escort to answer his contempt. If he again failed to attend, the complaint against him was usually sustained and the suit ordered to be discharged and damages paid to the petitioner, which, of course, also happened if he obeyed the summons and failed to show that the petition was not justified. Often, however, extra time was needed for further evidence to be gathered, sometimes by reference to local authorities such as county committees or JPs, in which circumstances the suit at law would be stayed rather than discharged outright. But even at this point many plaintiffs clearly did not think it worthwhile to attend, doubtless regarding the committee as being hopelessly biased in favour of the petitioners.

The actual success rate of petitions does not, however, altogether bear out this connection. While it is certainly true that the Indemnity Committee decided in favour of the petitioners in the great majority of cases coming before it, 54 net failures[33] out of a total of 876 cases is by no means an insignificant proportion, even if not a spectacular one. Moreover, in 8 cases where the decision did go in favour of the petitioners, the Committee made arrangements for some compensation to be paid to the plaintiffs against whose suits they complained.[34] On one occasion the Committee refused to order the discharge of a suit on receiving the plaintiff's assurance that he would forbear it.[35]

Common reasons for the Committee's refusal to grant indemnity to petitioners were their absence from the meeting fixed to hear their petitions (20 cases), though on one occasion they pleaded that they had been tricked into neglecting to attend;[36] rulings that the

---

[33] By 'net failures' is meant the total number of failures minus the cases where petitions which had failed were successfully re-presented at a later date.

[34] For two examples see, PRO SP 24/1, ff. 71, 133. There are also 3 cases of petitioners who had failed to make their cases good receiving compensation.

[35] PRO SP 24/3, f. 109(b).

[36] The case of Sheppard *versus* Anderson. See PRO SP 24/1, f. 158; SP 24/2, ff. 18(b), 57(b), 102(b), 168(b)–9.

cases did not fall within the Committee's terms of reference (15 cases); and, of course, the simple failure of the petitioners to make out a convincing case (20 cases). In one case the reasons for the Committee's negative decision is unclear, while on another it simply decided not to proceed on the grounds that the judge in this case could be relied on to ensure a just trial for the petitioner.[37] The fact that this case is unique is an interesting oblique comment on the biased nature of most proceedings. While it may be true that the dice were on the whole loaded in favour of petitioners before the Indemnity Committee, that body owed its very existence to the assumption that they were even more heavily loaded the other way in the courts of law.

V

There now follows an attempt briefly to describe the main categories of cases which came before the Indemnity Committee. It has already been remarked that it was the government's failure to satisfy the soldiers' demands for full payment of the arrears due to them which made the adoption of the cheaper solution of protecting them against suits by granting them indemnity inevitable. Certainly the main and most contentious aspect of such cases was the debts for free quarter which failure to satisfy the soldiers' arrears of pay had precipitated. Many unfortunate householders who had had soldiers billeted on them took to the law as a means of obtaining what was due to them and many of the defendants in such cases sought protection from the Indemnity Committee. Among the cases which it considered were suits against those responsible for assigning soldiers to billets, ranging from an army quartermaster to village constables.[38] Most cases, however, related simply to pleas for indemnity from suits for quartering charges. In 10 out of 16 such cases indemnity was granted to the petitioners within the period covered by this essay, a frequent solution being to assign to the plaintiff a claim on the petitioner's arrears of pay with the same dim prospect as he of receiving satisfaction at the Greek Kalends.[39]

---

[37] PRO SP 24/1, f. 183(b).

[38] PRO SP 24/2, ff. 163, 172–2(b); SP 24/3, ff. 6, 22(b), 58–58(b), 63, 143, 154.

[39] For examples, see PRO SP 24/1, ff. 13, 28(b); SP 24/2, ff. 107, 172(b). Nine debts for other than quartering charges were similarly treated. On this, see the order of the House of Commons of 15 June 1647 (*CJ*, V, p. 212).

Three of the 7 petitions for indemnity from suits relating to soldiers' pay were made by army paymasters, one of whom, Malachi Dudeney, who had been paymaster in Sir Wiliam Waller's army, was indemnified on two separate suits.[40] Less fortunate was Thomas Egerton, former provost-marshal in Essex's army, who failed to obtain indemnity from a suit against him by his successor about funds allegedly due to the latter, the committee regarding this as a purely private matter 'betweene partye and partye'.[41]

There are many examples of petitions for indemnity against suits for acts done by soldiers and others in the line of duty and under orders, among them 3 cases relating to the confiscation of the arms of suspected delinquents.[42] Of the 53 petitions relating to suits for wrongful arrest or imprisonment, 26 were brought by soldiers and ex-soldiers (incuding officers), 12 by petty local officers such as constables and headboroughs, 4 by local magistrates and 1 by an excise officer. Most striking of all were the 12 petitions for indemnity from suits concerning the acts of physical violence in the course of conflict, and there is one case involving homicide in a duel.[43] The petitioner here had previously been acquitted by a Council of War and was granted indemnity from further prosecution as were the petitioners in 5 cases involving the death or wounding of enemies of parliament in what seem to have been casual affrays rather than pitched battles.[44] Property was another casualty of war, and among those seeking indemnity from suits relating to the demolition of buildings to construct fortifications or improve fields of fire were the former military governor of Crowland in Lincolnshire[45] and – very unfairly – the unfortunate tenants of demolished houses in Southwark and Taunton, who were sued by their landlords and indemnified by the Committee.[46]

No doubt many suits were occasions for disgruntled Cavaliers to

[40] For Dudeney, see PRO SP 24/1, ff. 100, 105(b), 108, 111(b), 122, 127(b), 129; SP 24/3, ff. 113–3(b), 121(b), 139. For the other case involving a paymaster, see SP 24/3, f. 59(b).

[41] PRO SP 24/3, ff. 20(b)–21, 30–30(b), 66.

[42] PRO SP 24/1, ff. 37(b)–38, 39, 40, 41; SP 24/3, ff. 65(b), 118.

[43] For this case see, PRO SP 24/1, ff. 182, 193(b); SP 24/2, f. 9(b).

[44] PRO SP 24/1, ff. 29, 76(b), 106, 121(b)–2; SP 24/2, ff. 105(b), 175(b)–6; SP 24/3, ff. 35–35(b), 59(b), 82.

[45] PRO SP 24/2, ff. 36, 110, 138–8(b); SP 24/3, ff. 87(b)–88.

[46] PRO SP 24/1, ff. 112, 116, 122; SP 24/2 f. 3. A similar case was the petition of the Staffordshire borrower who had mortgaged houses which were subsequently demolished: (SP 24/3, ff. 7(b), 51(b)).

pay off old scores. However, former Roundhead soldiers were not immune from the infection. There were two successful petitions by officers for indemnity from suits brought against them by ex-soldiers whom they had struck for disobedience, and another against a suit for false imprisonment brought by a former corporal against his officer.[47]

There were a number of pleas for indemnity from suits brought by ex-Cavaliers on bonds or other obligations which had been extorted from people at their mercy during the war: in 2 cases under threat of plunder for non-compliance,[48] and in a further 6 as a condition of obtaining release from captivity.[49] Soldiers on both sides in the war probably engaged in this sort of extortion, although it is in the nature of things that complaints coming before the Indemnity Committee were all against suits brought by former Cavaliers. Far more frequent were suits against soldiers for prize goods or booty obtained during the war, and on occasions not against them but those who subsequently purchased such goods from them. There were 58 petitions for indemnity from such suits, 35 of which were stayed (27 of them finally discharged). Only 2 petitions were disallowed, the remaining cases not being decided by the end of 1648.

It is not always easy to distinguish cases of prize and booty from the even more numerous cases of petitions against suits arising out of the requisitioning of animals and goods for parliament's service in wartime. This was unquestionably one of the most potent causes of the soldiers' discontent, and one which, according to Major-General Poynz in June 1647, was unscrupulously exploited by the Leveller agitators who were trying to corrupt his troops, telling of fourteen soldiers who had already been hanged 'which took horses by order of their officers'.[50]

It will be convenient to represent these cases in tabular form. By far the largest number of them relate to the requisitioning of horses, sometimes with horse furniture and sometimes with carts; often but not always from royalists or suspected royalists. The second and smaller group is made up of cases of requisitioning sheep and

---

[47] PRO SP 24/1, ff. 78, 89(b); SP 24/2, ff. 7, 19–19(b), 29, 36–36(b), 42(b), 49, 54, 54(b), 55; SP 24/3, ff. 154(b), 163(b).

[48] PRO SP 24/2, f. 142(b); SP 24/3 ff. 34–34(b), 104(b)–5, 147.

[49] For an example, see PRO SP 24/1 f. 191(b); SP 24/2, ff. 13, 24, 175.

[50] H. Cary (ed.), *Memorials of the Great Civil War in England, 1642–52* (2 vols, 1842), I, pp. 233–4.

Table 7.2 Petitions against suits relating to requisitioning

Item requisitioned	By military personnel	By civilians		
		By constables	By other civilians	Unspecified
Horses and mares	56	15	7	8
Cattle and sheep	7	NIL	2	NIL
Transport facilities	1	2	NIL	NIL
Miscellaneous foodstuffs	15	1	4	7
Miscellaneous other goods	12	NIL	4	6
Total	91	18	17	21

cattle; the third requisitioning transport (sometimes along with horses); the fourth, foodstuffs other than cattle or sheep, including cheese, meat, wine (*en route* for the enemy on two occasions), malt, hops, hay and oats; and the fifth, a great miscellany of objects including arms and ammunition, gunpowder, lead to make bullets, seed, jewels, money and plate, canvas, wool and cloth for uniforms. In table 7.2 an attempt has been made to distinguish requisitions made by military personnel (officers and men) from those made by civilians, who are in turn sub-divided into constables (including headboroughs and tithing men as well as one high constable)[51] and others. In these matters, of course, soldiers and civilians had often acted in concert.

In addition there are 10 cases recorded of petitions by sea captains and others against suits relating to the seizure of goods – and sometimes of ships – at sea when bound for or sailing from ports in royalist hands. One petitioner, a certain Captain Plunkett, was involved in 3 such cases, in one of which (against which he was indemnified) the plaintiff, a Scottish merchant, received compensation by order of parliament for the wines which Plunkett had seized at sea and which had been ultimately consumed, 'in case of great extremetie', by Lord Inchiquin's troops in Munster.[52]

Needless to say, royalist officers had also done their share of requisitioning in their day, but, unlike their Roundhead equiva-

[51] PRO SP 24/2, ff. 42, 76.
[52] PRO SP 24/1, ff. 15(b)–16, 108(b)–9; *LJ*, IX, pp. 453–4; *CJ*, V, p. 355.

lents, were completely vulnerable to attacks in the courts. Indemnity was emphatically for the victors not for the vanquished and even when specifically granted in articles of surrender seems to have been more honoured in the breach than the observance. Accordingly, the only cases to which royalist requisitioning gave rise were petitions for indemnity from suits against persons who had endeavoured to recover their property which had been seized by the royalists. The fact that one such petition was disallowed is almost certainly accounted for by the fact that, in contrast to the two successful cases, the petitioner had acted without first obtaining permission from the appropriate civil authority.[53]

The civilian officers most in need of indemnity were constables. Something has already been said about constables' applications for indemnity from suits for wrongful arrest or requisitioning. Of the other 12 cases affecting constables, one relates to a variety of matters and 11 to distraints made for arrears of tithes and taxes such as the Excise, the weekly assessment and the fifth and twentieth part. Other indemnity suits concerning taxation include 20 cases relating to the hated Excise and 12 to the weekly assessment, many of them relating to distraints for non-payment. Thirteen of the Excise suits were against officers in the Excise service, and the evidence for 1647–8 neither supports nor confutes G. E. Aylmer's contention that the Indemnity Committee did not look on such petitioners with great favour.[54] It is true that only 4 of these 13 suits were formally discharged by the end of 1648, which may not argue for great urgency on the Committee's part. On the other hand, however, there is no evidence of any petition from an Excise officer being rejected. As to the weekly assessments, cases arising out of distraint for non-payment or over-assessment (12 cases) were less numerous than disputes in which landlords were suing tenants who had deducted the tax they had paid from their rent (30 cases) as permitted in an ordinance of 24 February 1643.[55] This right, which turned on the ordinance's careful distinction between economic and beneficial rents, obviously afforded great scope for litigation, and it is not surprising that only 9 of the cases coming before the Committee in 1647–8 finally were decided by the end of the latter year. Of these 9, 5 petitioners were indemnified, 2

---

[53] PRO SP 24/1, ff. 115, 144(b)–5; SP 24/2, ff. 21(b), 28(b), 104(b), 119(b), 125(b), 143(b); SP 24/3, ff. 14, 128(b), 145, 148(b)–9, 160(b).
[54] Aylmer, *The State's Servants*, p. 299.
[55] *A & O*, I, pp. 96–7.

were unsuccessful and 2 more were referred to other, and presumably better informed, bodies, in one case to the Kent county committee.[56]

Not all of the revenue collectors who petitioned the Indemnity Committee were pleading for protection against recalcitrant and litigious taxpayers. There are 13 Exchequer suits involving collectors where the plaintiffs were Exchequer officials and all but one of the petitioners collectors of parliamentary subsidies. Six of them were sued for parts of these collections which had been appropriated by the enemy in war-torn counties such as Somerset, Wiltshire and Oxfordshire,[57] while a further 5 were sued in the Exchequer for sums which they had paid out locally,[58] as was the Warwickshire Treasurer of Sequestrations for paying out money on the order of the Coventry committee.[59] The Indemnity Committee was usually sympathetic to such petitions.

Among the most numerous indemnity cases were those concerning sequestration. Of the petitions for indemnity against suits brought by sequestered persons, 45 were against sequestrators and their associated officers and helpers, including constables;[60] 9 against purchasers of sequestered goods and animals, and one case of simple harassment without any lawsuit, of an unfortunate purchaser of sequestrated timber;[61] 13 against purchasers or tenants of sequestered lands on charges such as trespass,[62] including one case of violent molestation of the purchasers of woodland formerly belonging to the Earl of Worcester, in which the enormous damages of £777 18s. were awarded;[63] 63 cases against those who paid

---

[56] PRO SP 24/1, ff. 99(b), 150(b); SP 24/3, ff. 55(b)–56; SP 24/3, ff. 52, 60. Among the undecided cases (in 5 of which the suits against petitioners were stayed) was a petition from Lord Mounson, himself one of the most prominent members of the committee (SP 24/3, f. 70(b)). In 2 cases the petitioners had deducted expenses for free quarter as well as assessments from their rent: SP 24/2, f. 66(b); SP 24/3, f. 106(b).

[57] PRO SP 24/2, ff. 78(b), 83–83(b), 89, 96, 107(b)–8(b); SP 24/3, f. 136(b).

[58] PRO SP 24/1, ff. 75, 90, 145, 151; SP 24/3, ff. 130(b), 140(b)–1, 159(b).

[59] PRO SP 24/3, ff. 157(b)–8.

[60] Three petitions had been disallowed, and 27 suits were stayed (19 of which were formally discharged) by the end of 1648.

[61] PRO SP 24/1, f. 177; SP 24/2, ff. 63–63(b), 68(b)–69, 82(b)–83, 128(b)–9. Five suits were stayed (4 of them permanently discharged) before the end of 1648.

[62] In one of these cases the tenant was also being sued for arrears of the recusancy fines due from the sequestrated owner. (PRO SP 24/3, f. 139(b)). Three of these petitioners were indemnified.

[63] PRO SP 24/3, ff. 82(b)–3, 158(b), 164(b)–5.

sequestered rents, and 86 against those who paid sequestered debts, to sequestration authorities. Twenty-three of the rent suits were stayed by the Committee (16 of them permanently discharged), 5 petitions were dismissed, while 59 of the debt suits were stayed (41 of them permanently discharged) and only 6 petitions dismissed. In the other cases no decision had been reached by the end of 1648. One of the reasons for the greater delay in reaching decisions about petitions in cases of sequestered rents may well have been the Committee's insistence on proof of the fact of sequestration which sometimes involved reference to local committees which were not always prompt in their replies.

One interesting category of indemnity cases relates to suits for opprobrious words usually uttered to Cavalier sympathizers. Excluding 3 cases already included under other headings (confiscation of arms, distraint of animals and sequestration proceedings), most cases fall into two categories: abuse of private persons, such as that uttered by a much-enduring soldier when being plundered by a Cavalier, and for which he would have had to answer in the courts if the Committee had not indemnified him (2 cases); and treasonous words against the king, queen and Prince of Wales (3 cases). The words against the Prince of Wales were a product of the Second Civil War when he had taken command of the insurgent ships of the fleet against parliament. In July 1648 a certain Peter Way was arrested for words allegedly spoken against the prince while 'endeavouringe to secure one John Maunsell for his abusive language and disaffection . . . against the proceedings of Parliament'.[65] The question of abuse of the royal family presented real problems especially when provoked by Cavalier insolence. Fairfax himself showed that he was acutely aware of the difficulties when, without in any sense justifying potentially treasonous words, he informed the Speaker in September 1647 of extenuating factors in the cases of four persons who, under extreme provocation from delinquents, had given vent to ill-advised but understandable sentiments out of excessive zeal for the parliamentary cause. Of these, only the case of one James Symball came before the Indemnity Committee. Symball, a former Deputy Keeper of Peterhouse prison

[64] PRO SP 24/1, ff. 61(b)–2, 93(b)–4, 98(b), 104(b). For the other case, SP 24/2, f. 158(b).
[65] PRO SP 24/3, f. 45(b). For cases of words against the king and queen, see SP 24/3, ff. 1(b), 8(b), 84. For a parson charged with attacking the king in a sermon, see SP 24/1, ff. 84(b), 113, 116(b).

but now himself lying in irons in the White Lion prison in Southwark, had allegedly been provoked by a disputatious Cavalier formerly his prisoner into the rash remark that 'he hoped to see the King's head upon the Tower block.' He was to remain in gaol for a further four months before the Committee finally indemnified him in January 1648.[66]

An early parliamentary measure which had aroused deep conservative misgivings was the ordinance of 1 November 1642 stipulating that enlisted apprentices might reckon their time in the army towards their period of apprenticeship, 'as if', as Clarendon scornfully puts it, 'they had been still in their shops'. To many conservative people, and not all of them royalists, the ordinance was pernicious for setting sons against fathers and apprentices against masters. To its devisers, on the other hand, it was a necessary recognition of the principle that 'in Times of common Danger and Necessity the Interest of private Persons ought to give Way to the Public.'[67] What was too easily and conveniently forgotten was that the same ordinance also stipulated that there would be public provision for recompensing those masters 'who have received any considerable Loss by the Absence of their Apprentices'. Indeed the neglect of the provision may have been at least partially responsible for the refusal of many masters to recognize military service as counting towards apprenticeship. Complaints about their neglect to do so multiplied, and there was a formal recommendation from the Army Council to parliament in December 1647 that stiff legal penalties should be imposed on such recalcitrant masters.[68]

This was the background against which the Indemnity Committee entertained complaints from petitioners on this matter. There were 14 such petitions in 1647–8,[69] 7 and perhaps more of which related to London crafts. The other petitioners include a mariner from Wapping, a Barnstaple cordwainer, a Yorkshire saddler and a

---

[66] PRO SP 24/1, ff. 34, 134(b); SP 24/2, f. 42(b); *An Humble Remonstrance from his Excellency Sir Thomas Fairfax*, BL E407(15).

[67] Edward, Earl of Clarendon, *The History of the Great Rebellion and Civil War in England*, ed. W. D. Macray (6 vols, Oxford, 1888), II, p. 380. For the ordinance and its confirming ordinance of 24 December 1647, *A & O*, I, pp. 37, 1054–5.

[68] *LJ*, IX, pp. 563; *Divers papers from the Army* (1647), BL E388(18), pp. 9–10; *A Motion from the Armie* (1647), BL E391(5), no pagination; *An Answer from Parliament to a Declaration*, BL E392(18), no pagination; *An Humble Representation from Sir Thomas Fairfax and the Councel of the Armie* (1647), BL E419(16), p. 24; *The Moderate Intelligencer*, no. 144, (16–23 December 1647), BL E421(7), p. 1065.

[69] There were at least another three in January 1649.

Kentish blacksmith.[70] Strictly speaking only three of the petitions
were indemnity cases. These were petitions against suits brought
by masters for breach of contract by their apprentices in joining the
army and for practising trades after demobilization without serving
a full apprenticeship.[71] When military service was added to
apprenticeship previously served, the total usually exceeded the
customary term of apprenticeship, though this does not mean that
masters were predisposed to accept the ordinance when it did not,
as is shown by a petition from a Kentish blacksmith who, even after
service in the army, still had half a year's apprenticeship to serve.[72]
On the face of it, the objections of the London master-baker when
an ex-soldier had served him for eight of his customary nine years
apprenticeship seems unreasonable; more so than the Watermen's
objection to a case when the apprenticeship requirements were
decreed to be fulfilled by eighteen months' apprenticeship and five
and a half years' military service.[73] The Watermen, who were
rebuked for making difficulties about the Indemnity Committee's
order to this effect, were reputedly a strongly pro-royalist body, and
on another occasion removed from their hall-book the name of one
who had left his master's service to serve with Fairfax at the siege of
Colchester in 1648. The Committee ordered that he should be
reinstated and paid £4 damages.[74]

Too much importance ought not to be attached to the fact that
no decisions are recorded in 1647–8 in 9 out of the 14 apprenticeship cases. It is not unlikely that in some cases the Committee's
summons to a recalcitrant master would produce compliance without further ado. This is suggested by the fact that the other 5 cases
were decided in favour of petitioners with unusual promptitude: a
matter of days after the petitions had been presented, rather than
months as was so often the case with petitions on other matters.

On 20 August 1647 the House of Lords heard the petitions of
four intruded parsons, one of which was later to come before the
Indemnity Committee. The indignant petitioners complain,
amongst other things, of 'a sudden Surprizal, not only of our
Tithes . . . but of our proper Goods and Corn growing upon the

[70] In one petition both trade and location are unspecified; in two others, from a
barber-surgeon and a grocer, the location is not given.
[71] PRO SP 24/1, ff. 100(b), 137, 152(b), 171(b); SP 24/3, f. 134.
[72] PRO SP 24/2, f. 64.
[73] PRO SP 24/1, ff. 127(b), 137(b), 139(b)–40; SP 24/2, ff. 28, 40(b).
[74] PRO SP 24/3, ff. 81–81(b), 86, 91–91(b), 132(b).

Glebe . . . having our Houses . . . seized . . . with Threats to plunder us of our Estates, as some have already attempted.'[75]

Historians of the radical religious changes of the time have paid insufficient attention to the light thrown by the Indemnity Committee records on the resistance to the intrusion of new incumbents and new forms of worship, which has recently been emphasized in the work of J. S. Morrill.[76] The 55 cases concerning tithes coming before the committee are petitions against a wide variety of prosecutions and not just those brought against intruded parsons (13 cases only). They include suits by impropriators; suits against payers and collectors of tithes to and on behalf of intruded parsons; and suits against one set of tithe-farmers by another. Most of these cases provide abundant evidence of lively opposition to the intruded parsons, who were, however, normally supported by the Indemnity Committee. Of the 54 petitions, of which admittedly only 16 were finally decided in 1647–8, only 3 were rejected.

At least 16 of the other suits complained against were on actions of trespass or similar charges, while 4 related to suits by extruded parsons against those responsible in one way or another for their exclusion. In one of these cases those sued were alleged bearers of false witness against the plaintiff at the Committee for Plundered Ministers. This was discharged by the Indemnity Committee only fifteen days after its first hearing on 4 May 1648.[77] There were 5 petitions for indemnity from suits brought against parishioners and other persons for acts of violence in support of intruded parsons, 2 of them involving homicide.[78] But violence was by no means a one-sided matter. Dr Thomas Browne, for example, the intruded parson of Weston [Longueville] in Norfolk who pleaded indemnity in September 1648 from the extruded parson's suit against him, had been driven from his parish by force.[79]

Other pleas for indemnity came from a Ripon alderman who was being sued for battery in King's Bench as a result of his forcible interruption of the burial service of a child conducted according to

<hr/>

[75] *LJ*, IX, pp. 389, 390–1.
[76] J. S. Morrill, 'The church in England, 1642–9', in *Reactions to the English Civil War*, ed. Morrill (London, 1982).
[77] PRO SP 24/2, ff. 76, 121(b).
[78] PRO SP 24/1, ff. 24, 42(b), 62(b)–3, 69(b)–70, 85(b)–6, 148; SP 24/3, ff. 19, 28(b)–9.
[79] PRO SP 24/3, f. 79(b).

the Book of Common Prayer,[80] from five Cambridgeshire parsons who were sued for administering sacraments according to the Directory of Worship rather than the Book of Common Prayer, and whose case was referred to the Cambridgeshire county committee for further evidence;[81] and from three Norfolk parsons who were sued for putting into effect the controversial ordinance for the suspension of scandalous sinners from the Communion.[82]

A no less contentious issue was the enforcement of the Sabbath and of officially ordained fast days, on which subject the Indemnity Committee heard 5 petitions from godly magistrates, constables and headboroughs. By the end of 1648 two of these suits had certainly been stayed in answer to such pleas (one of them finally discharged), but a decision had not been reached on the other three.[83]

It is perhaps surprising, in view of the variety of persons who clearly stood to benefit from the Indemnity Committee's operations, that, with one exception, there are no petitions for indemnity from members of parliamentary committees, and especially of the hated county committees. The exception is provincial sub-committees of the Committee for Taking the Accounts of the Kingdom, which, as the work of D. H. Pennington has shown, had power to investigate anyone who had been entrusted with public funds on any account.[84] Even here, however, there were only three pleas for indemnity in 1647–8, two from members of the Leicester-shire and one from a member of the Worcestershire Accounts Committee. Indeed such persons were not formally brought within the ambit of the Indemnity Ordinance until the House of Commons made an order to that effect on 11 March 1648.[85] One petition which had previously been dismissed was re-opened on account of the new ruling, and the suits against petitions in the 2

---

[80] PRO SP 24/2, ff. 99(b), 171(b); SP 24/3, f. 42–42(b). The alderman was granted indemnity.

[81] PRO SP 24/3, ff. 118(b)–9, 152(b), 163. On 12 January 1649 a further hearing was arranged for 30 January, which was to be the date of the king's execution.

[82] PRO SP 24/1, ff. 120(b), 198; SP 24/2, ff. 66(b)–7. There is record of a decision being reached (in favour of the petitioner) in only one of these cases before the end of 1648.

[83] PRO SP 24/1, ff. 17–17(b), 68(b), 77, 92(b); SP 24/3, ff. 72, 133(b).

[84] D. H. Pennington, 'The accounts of the Kingdom 1642–9', in *Essays in the Economic and Social History of Tudor and Stuart England*, ed. F. J. Fisher (Cambridge, 1961).

[85] *CJ*, V, p. 492.

other cases were stayed, one of them being permanently discharged.[86]

Most, though not all, of the categories into which the business of the Indemnity Committee falls have now received mention. An important exception has deliberately been left to the last because there was no logical reason why it should fall within the Committee's terms of reference since the question of indemnity was in no way involved. It must simply have been a matter of administrative convenience that it was given the task of investigating complaints about the violation of the ordinances of 9 September and 4 October 1647 against ex-Cavaliers who held public office or exercised public functions such as voting in elections.[87] Over 1647–8 the Committee took cognizance of 32 such complaints, coming to recorded decisions in 13 of them, though some of the persons complained against may have withdrawn voluntarily, thus removing the need for action by the committee. Steps were taken for the removal of two of the municipal governors of Stamford, two others voluntarily withdrawing;[88] the mayors and several aldermen of Wigan and Carlisle and several common councilmen of the latter town;[89] three municipal burgesses of Abingdon;[90] an undersheriff of Herefordshire and a Croydon constable; while a Somerset attorney was disabled from practising in the courts.[91] Ex-Cavaliers who had voted in the election of the mayor of Maidstone in 1647 and a ward election in the City of London were punished and disabled from voting in the future.[92]

Three of the Committee's decisions definitely went against the complainants. Insufficient proof was available to warrant the dismissal of the town clerk of Southampton.[93] The loyally parliamentarian city fathers of Norwich appeared to have had a good case against Francis Cory whom they had dismissed from the office of

[86] PRO SP 24/1, ff. 18, 107, 176; SP 24/2, ff. 17, 167; SP 24/3, ff. 22(b), 120(b)–1, 137–7(b).
[87] A & O, I, pp. 1009, 1023–5.
[88] PRO SP 24/1, ff. 147(b)–8. There is no record of a decision in the cases of two others.
[89] PRO SP 24/1, ff. 103(b), 119–9(b), 162–2(b); SP 24/2, ff. 115, 161–2, 176–6(b).
[90] PRO SP 24/3, ff. 57, 84(b).
[91] PRO SP 24/1, ff. 145; SP 24/2, ff. 65, 70, 89, 125, 167(b), 179(b); SP 24/3, ff. 32(b), 42(b).
[92] PRO SP 24/1, ff. 66(b)–7, 73–73(b); SP 24/3, ff. 126(b), 150; CJ, V, p. 349.
[93] PRO SP 24/3, ff. 54, 104(b).

Recorder in 1644 for obstructing the implementation of parliamentary ordinances in Norwich but who had since obtained a judgement in King's Bench against his dismissal. But their failure to
appear to make good their petition on 24 April 1648 resulted in its
being disallowed.[94] A similar fate befell the self-styled well-affected
Fellows of Gonville and Caius College, Cambridge, against the
allegedly delinquent Master and three other Fellows.[95]

Of the 18 cases such as that against ten of the Worcester city
fathers,[96] where no final decision about the complaints coming
before the Committee is recorded, there is a strong likelihood that
the alleged delinquents in question had yielded to pressure and
resigned, though one should not completely discount the possibility
that some complaints were malicious settling of private grudges
rather than founded on incontrovertible fact.

VI

If the essence of tragedy does indeed consist in conflict between
right and right, then the indemnity problem has a genuinely tragic
dimension to it. It was obviously right to afford protection to
soldiers and others from prosecution for acts done in the heat of
battle or under orders and for debts which they could hardly be
expected to pay when their own pay was months in arrears. But it
was no less right that the free access of Englishmen to legal redress
for wrongs done to them should not be curtailed. One index of the
hostility aroused by the indemnity arrangements is the fact that in
as many as 85 out of the 876 cases heard by the Indemnity
Committee before 19 December 1648, persons had to be called
before the Committee again to answer their contempt for refusing
to discharge suits, pay damages or give up official positions, when
ordered to do so.

To the rapidly swelling conservative opposition to the indemnity
arrangements in 1647 there is one notable exception: an ordinance
of 19 June offering indemnity to a distinct group, that is, 'those
Officers and Souldiers that are come off from the Army, that they

[94] PRO SP 24/1, ff. 181(b); SP 24/2, f. 54(b); Norfolk and Norwich RO, *Norwich Assembly Book 1642–68*, f. 20; J. T. Evans, *Seventeenth-Century Norwich* (Oxford, 1979), pp. 125, 131, 185.
[95] PRO SP 24/3, ff. 151(b)–2, 163(b).
[96] PRO SP 24/3, f. 11.

may not be tried by a Council of War.'[97] It was for a time an object both of the parliamentary Committee of Safety and the City Militia Committee to recruit not only reformadoes, but also deserters from the New Model, so that the ordinance of 19 June fitted well with the objective of creating a counter-revolutionary anti-army force.

Already by the beginning of August, in a vain attempt to stave off the army's occupation of the city following the counter-revolutionary coup of 26 July, the formerly irate citizens and some of their conservative parliamentary allies were eating humble pie and declaring their readiness to abandon this plan and accede to many of the soldiers' demands, including improved conditions for indemnity.[98] Nevertheless, despite their climbdown, it was to remain an article of counter-revolutionary faith that the soldiers' stress on grievances such as arrears of pay and inadequate indemnity were first and foremost a device to keep the army in being. Indemnity ordinances had been passed, complained one such pamphleteer in December 1647, but nothing significant had been done about disbandment.[99]

The indemnity ordinances, argued one conservative Presbyterian pamphleteer early in January 1648, 'were only made to free those who acted for the Parliament from unjust suits and vexations, for acting according to their duties, and not [to exempt] any from legal prosecutions for . . . unjust, malicious and oppressive actions and abuses of their trust and power'.[100] But this is exactly what they had become, violating Magna Carta at every turn, and debarring men from their legal rights of sueing those who had wronged them. Thus if the issue of indemnity had been a major factor in the army's dissatisfaction with parliament in 1647, it also contributed to the frustration and sense of injustice which made moderate and conservative people, as well as ex-Cavaliers, swell the ranks of the insurgents in the Second Civil War. Prince Charles might stress full indemnity as a royalist war aim, but his allies in beleaguered Colchester were probably more typical of insurgent

[97] *A & O*, I, 957–8; BL 669, f. 11 (27).
[98] BL 669, f. 11(54); *A Declaration of the . . . Committee for the Safety and the Militia of London*, BL E401(6), pp. 5–6: *A Declaration from the Lord Mayor, Aldermen and Commons of the City of London Presented to . . . Sir Thomas Fairfax*, BL E401(11).
[99] *A Word to Lieut. General Cromwel and his Privy Council* (1647), BL E421(20), pp. 10–11.
[100] *The Petition of Right of the Freeholders and Free-men of the Kingdom of England* (1647), BL E422(9), pp. 7–10, 18.

opinion in their round condemnation of 'the obstructing [of] justice in our Courts of Judicature . . . by the . . . Committee of Indemnity, perverting judgement and exercising arbytrary power'.[101] On the other hand, for those numerous people for whom the Second Civil War was the final and unequivocal demonstration of the untrustworthiness of Charles I, this also underlined the unreliability of royal promises of indemnity. Might not the safer course be an end to monarchy and the establishment of a regicidal regime which would have at least as much to fear from a royal restoration as humbler men whose experience of the sharp pains of Cavalier retribution had occasioned the need for indemnity in the first place?

[101] *The Remonstrance and Declaration of the Knights, Esquires, Gentlemen and Freeholders in Colchester* (1648), BL E451(11), p. 4.

8

'A World Elsewhere': Aspects of the Overseas Expansionist Mood of the 1650s

DEREK MASSARELLA

The historiography of the English Revolution has tended to become introspective. We now have many fine studies of individual trees but are in danger of losing our appreciation of the wood in which they are situated. Introspection, encouraged by such factors as scepticism about the contemporary relevance of seventeenth-century Utopian philosophy in the light of twentieth-century experience, a further faltering of the spirit of optimism, the retreat from empire and the gradual realization of Britain's diminished political and economic status in the world, has made historians increasingly reluctant to attempt any grand interpretation of events from 1640 to 1660. This attitude is best summed up in the words of J. S. Morrill: 'In scholarship as in everything else, if we look after the pennies, the pounds will look after themselves.'[1] In some respects the tendency can be seen as positive when the inadequacies of the comfortable assertions and generalizations of past historians are highlighted, especially after subjection to rigorous examination in numerous empirical studies. But this has also made it enormously difficult to see the events of those two decades in a wider context, to see their place in the broader sweeps of European, even world, history, or their significance within contemporary developments outside the British Isles. There is not even any consensus as to what they should be styled: 'Puritan Revolution', 'Great Rebellion', 'English Revolution', more neutrally 'Civil War

---

[1] 'Proceeding moderately', *Times Literary Supplement*, 24 October 1980. See also G. R. Elton's inaugural lecture, *The History of England* (Cambridge, 1984), passim.

and Interregnum', or merely 'the 1640s and 1650s'. Indeed, it is regrettable that there are still no adequate, comprehensive modern studies of the foreign relations, diplomatic and commercial, of successive governments during the period. Nevertheless, in the words of Shakespeare's Coriolanus, 'there is a world elsewhere', and by the outbreak of civil war in 1642 a growing number of Englishmen, and other Britons too, already had direct experience of new worlds and old civilizations with different cultures and traditions, offering new commodities and economic opportunities, even a new life, beyond the frontiers of the country's seaboards.

It is only recently that major reassessments of England's early overseas expansion have been attempted, reassessments made easier by the discarding of the Whiggish view of overseas history which detected an organic development from the Elizabethan seadogs to the late nineteenth- and early twentieth-century empire at its height. Unfortunately, two recent substantial revaluations, by D. B. Quinn and A. N. Ryan and by K. R. Andrews,[2] stop in 1642 and 1630 respectively, before reaching the 1650s and policies and developments which emerged under the republic. Nevertheless, interesting claims have been made for these policies, especially by those who would like to interpret the English Revolution as having contributed something enduring to English history, not merely as a series of events to be written off as a revolution that failed. It has been asserted that one of the consequences of the revolutionary upheavals of the 1640s and early 1650s was that English governments, prompted by a new breed of go-getting merchant, became very interested in those worlds elsewhere, and in pursuing a more active commercial policy; it is said that this represented a new development in English overseas enterprise, that it played some part in establishing the foundations for later imperial success, and that some of the proposals advanced anticipated later developments. The aim of this chapter is to look at one of the 'worlds' for which such claims have been made, the East Indies – and in particular Japan which, for much of the seventeenth century, including the 1650s, was considered a market of great potential for English trade – in order to test some of these assertions and try to see the expansionist mood of the 1650s in a somewhat wider perspective.

[2] D. B. Quinn and A. B. Ryan, *England's Sea Empire 1550–1642* (London, 1983), and K. R. Andrews, *Trade, Plunder and Settlement* (Cambridge, 1984).

In Christopher Hill's view, the governments of the 1650s were the first in English history to have a world strategy. He sees the vigorous foreign policy of that decade as the rich harvest of seeds that were sown in the Elizabethan period by Sir Walter Ralegh and Richard Hakluyt, who 'put forward a national policy which offered something to all sections of the community' and which, Hill suggests, reached fruition under the Lord Protector.[3]

Sharing this interpretation, and the view that the 1650s represent a bold new phase in commercial attitudes and policies, J. C. Farnell argues that the sponsors of the Navigation Act of 1651, often credited as a landmark in the evolution of the British empire, were 'Maurice Thompson and a group of his friends and relatives engaged in the colonial trade – an area dear to the Independents . . . – and also interested in a programme of expansion in the Far Eastern trade of England.' Farnell identified Thompson, whose earlier mercantile career was associated with business enterprise in Africa, North America and the Caribbean, very much with what he styles 'the non-Company, interloping free merchant.'[4] This type was not entirely new, of course. Condemnation of monopolies by advocates of free trade had existed from the earliest days of chartered companies, and opposition to them had ebbed and flowed since the early seventeenth century. However, in Farnell's view what made Thompson different was his vision. This emerges as a kind of commercial counterpoint to the foreign policy vision which Christopher Hill finds in Oliver Cromwell, although there were important differences of emphasis and interest, even if Thompson chose to ally himself with the anti-Spanish direction of Cromwell's foreign policy.[5] Thompson wanted to overturn the existing multiplicity of trading companies, using their monopolies mainly to export cloth from England in exchange for the local commodities of the regions in which they traded. According to Farnell, Thompson could see that the intrusion of the colonial and East India trades, with their diversified commodities, was altering this comfortable two-way relationship and required a new framework, 'a reorganization of English trade policy from one

[3] Christopher Hill, *God's Englishman* (London, 1970), p. 166; idem, *The Intellectual Origins of the English Revolution* (Oxford, 1982 edn), pp. 157, 159, 164–5.
[4] J. C. Farnell, 'The Navigation Act of 1651, the First Dutch War, and the London merchant community', *Economic History Review*, 2nd ser., 16 (1963–4), pp. 439–54, esp. pp. 443, 446, 454.
[5] Ibid., pp. 452–4.

based on monopoly companies to one based on national monopoly'. It is this insight which Farnell sees as original in the conception of the Navigation Act.[6]

Developing Farnell's analysis, Robert Brenner produced a detailed interpretation of 'The Civil War politics of London's merchant community',[7] which relates the Civil War politics of the London merchants to changes in the nature of England's overseas trade before the war, and especially to the rise of a new breed of merchants who had cut their commercial teeth and acquired financial power from activity, mainly in the New World, quite different in character and style from the established merchants of the monopoly companies. Brenner labels the latter the 'Levant-East India Complex' and sees its members as largely conservative socially and politically, having everything to gain from the maintenance of order during the crisis years 1640–2, and therefore associating themselves with the royalist cause. He also claims that a small but significant number of them had been allied to the court during the 1630s. The 'Colonial-Interloping Complex', on the other hand, the thrusting men who were determined to overturn the existing cosy relationship between the merchant elite and the crown in order to redefine commercial assumptions and practice in accordance with their experience in the New World, supported parliament. According to Brenner, the colonial-interloping group reached its zenith under the Commonwealth when its influence, derived from the holding of key administrative offices, representation in the Rump and personal connection, was felt not just in London politics but at the national level as well. Brenner credits the merchants of the group with 'powerful influence' in shaping what he sees as the 'expansionist commercial policy of the commonwealth . . . especially in those areas of interest to them, the Americas and the East Indies'.[8]

Naturally these views have not gone unchallenged. Robert Ashton has questioned the determinism of the proposition that East India-Levant merchant equals royalist and colonial-interloper equals parliamentarian. He convincingly shows that there is no simple correlation between a merchant's position as a member of the established London mercantile elite and support for the crown,

[6] Ibid., p. 445.
[7] R. Brenner, 'The Civil War politics of London's merchant community', *Past and Present*, no. 58 (1973).
[8] Ibid., p. 103.

and that Brenner's conservative merchants, especially those in the East India Company, had good reason to resent royal policies in the 1630s. After all, Charles I had supported the rival East Indies trading company, the Courteen Association, under the leadership of Sir William Courteen and the king's favourite, Endymion Porter. In Ashton's view, it was fear of a breakdown in social order that brought many of the established merchants back to the crown in 1642.[9]

Elsewhere, Blair Worden has shown that Henry Marten and Thomas Chaloner, both members of the Rump, were sympathetic to economic reform that would promote trade, even possibly to the idea of abolishing monopoly companies (one of Maurice Thompson's strategic objectives), and that a number of merchants, including Thompson's brother George, were MPs who formed a cohesive group and sat together on many committees. However, he cautions against reading too much into this because the evidence suggests that the Rump's aversion to anything that smacked of social change (and throwing open foreign trade to all merchants would have involved just that), and its conservative instincts, ensured that in the interests of social and economic stability it preferred to cooperate with monopoly companies rather than abolish them.[10]

A similar note of caution is sounded by J. P. Cooper, who warns against seeing too much consistency in the Rump's economic policies, especially in relation to loosening controls over trade. He questions Farnell's contention that the Navigation Act was inspired by an aggressive interloping group led by Maurice Thompson, pointing out that George Thompson had supported an act in 1650 less restrictive to foreign vessels than the one passed in the following year, and that the 1651 act did not go against the interests of the established monopoly companies. Cooper concedes that there is some contemporary evidence to support the view that generally speaking the Rump appeared more favourable to trading interests when compared with the Protectorate.[11]

---

[9] R. Ashton, *The City and the Court 1603–43* (Cambridge, 1979), passim but esp. pp. 127–9, 139–41. See also K. N. Chaudhuri, *The English East India Company* (London, 1965), p. 73.

[10] A. B. Worden, *The Rump Parliament* (Cambridge, 1974), pp. 254–9, 301n. The preference for regulation in the interests of social stability echoes early seventeenth-century government views.

[11] J. P. Cooper, 'Social and economic policies under the Commonwealth', in *The Interregnum: the quest for Settlement, 1646–60*, ed. G. E. Aylmer (London, 1974),

Unfortunately, both Farnell's and Brenner's analyses end with the dissolution of the Rump, although both have some things to say about commercial policy under the Protectorate. They agree with Menna Prestwich that during the Protectorate commercial considerations were subordinated to the greater goals of Cromwell's vision of England as the leading protestant power. This vision dragged the country into war with Spain, a war which Farnell says Maurice Thompson supported although it benefited the Dutch, England's commercial rival, who reaped the harvest of the Spanish trade (wool, fish, wine) and even made inroads into the English carrying trade at the expense of English merchants and shippers.[12] Thus they would agree with the view that there is no consistency in foreign and commercial policy in the 1650s. The policies pursued under the Commonwealth were not as radical as the colonial-interlopers might have wished and, under the Protectorate, not always in accord with their alleged hopes and ambitions.

With regard to the East Indies this is clearly illustrated by Cromwell's ambivalent attitude towards English policy there. The amazing proposals for a kind of protestant version of the Treaty of Tordesillas between England and the Dutch, submitted to the Dutch commissioners by Sir Cornelius Vermuyden in June 1653, according to which England would have ceded her interests in the East Indies to the Dutch, seem unlikely to have been made without Cromwell's knowledge, if not his connivance. If pursued, these proposals would have been a disaster in the long run for British overseas expansion: the British were to benefit from their first empire in North America, but it was to be their dominant position in Asia, especially in India, that eventually turned them into a world power.[13] Yet in 1654 Cromwell, as Lord Protector, was reported to favour establishing 'a national interest in India'.[14] The

---

pp. 121–2. It is not entirely clear, however, how this evidence supports Farnell's contention about the emergence of a colonial-interloping group.

[12] Farnell, 'Navigation Act', pp. 452–4; Brenner, 'Civil War politics', pp. 106–7; Menna Prestwich, 'Diplomacy and trade in the Protectorate', *Journal of Modern History*, 22 (1950). See also Maurice Ashley, *Financial and Commercial Policy under the Cromwellian Protectorate* (Oxford, 1934); Austin Woolrych, *Commonwealth to Protectorate* (Oxford, 1982), pp. 280, 282.

[13] For the proposals, see *Thurloe State Papers*; II, pp. 125–6; S. R. Gardiner, *History of the Commonwealth and Protectorate, 1649–56*, (4 vols, London, 1903), III, pp. 49–50. See also Prestwich, 'Diplomacy and trade', p. 105, and Woolrych, *Commonwealth to Protectorate*, pp. 283–4.

[14] E. B. Sainsbury (ed.), *A Calendar of the Court Minutes of the East India Company 1635–79* (11 vols, Oxford, 1907–38), *1650–4*, p. 374.

discrepancies are understandable. Cromwell's awareness of the East Indies and his curiosity about them were minimal and his views and attitudes concerning them were not shaped by any perception of strategic concern for England. Cromwell was an Atlanticist; a man who had associations with the Providence Island Company and who is alleged to have contemplated emigrating to North America.[15]

Regardless of whether or not the colonial-interlopers should be considered as a set-off to the established East India-Levant merchants, or of whether the Navigation Act was the work of Maurice Thompson and his associates, or of how far the Rump was favourable to trading interests and preoccupations, or of the policy differences between the Commonwealth and Protectorate, it is certain that the English Revolution provided opportunities for new men seeking to challenge established ideas and practices in commercial matters as in other areas. The existence of such men is not open to doubt, whether one agrees or disagrees with the argument that they formed a colonial-interloping 'complex'; fuller study of the composition, cohesiveness, aims, conduct, connections and influence of its members is needed to determine this. Thompson, who despite his antipathy to monopoly companies rose to become governor of the East India Company, certainly tried to grasp such opportunities. He has been credited with having a 'comprehensive' and 'not unrealistic' programme for expansion in Asia which not only anticipated eighteenth-century developments but was actually revived by Alexander Dalrymple; and with being the link between an expansionist East India Company and the ambitions of the Western Design.

Thompson was certainly a man of vision and his proposals shook up the East India Company establishment, even if his desire to see the Company's monopoly broken was not fulfilled. In this respect he is symbolic of three characteristics of the English Revolution: an intellectual and moral conviction of the righteousness of overturning established institutions if circumstances required it; a questioning of accepted values; and a belief in the merits of pursuing bold

[15] Cf. Hill, *God's Englishman*, pp. 166–8. The discussion of foreign policy under the Protectorate in Charles P. Korr, *Cromwell and the New Model Foreign Policy* (Los Angeles and London, 1975), confines itself largely to relations with France. The Baltic gets scant attention, the East Indies none. Moreover, Cromwell's relations with the Rump are poorly understood and his power and influence before the establishment of the Protectorate over-rated.

aggressive policies. But on what kind of information were his plans and proposals based, and what does this tell us about the expansionist mood of the 1650s? Fortunately, it is possible to attempt an answer to these questions by taking as an example the East India Company's attempts to conduct direct trade with Japan, one of the places on which Thompson had set his sights.[16]

The East India Company had already traded directly with Japan, where it had had a factory from 1613 to 1623, one of a number in the Far East. The Company's trade in this region was not very successful, mainly because of competition from the Dutch, especially in the Spice Islands, where the English made considerable, and ultimately unsuccessful, efforts to establish a foothold. There was also competition in the Japan trade from the Portuguese who made good profits on their Macao-Nagasaki voyages. Furthermore, the Dutch East India Company was better organized than the English, having servants of high ability, and a clear idea about what it wanted: uncontested control of the Spice Islands. It was also better capitalized, better supplied from Europe, and enjoyed naval superiority vis-à-vis the English, even if it used up much of its precious resources in attacking the Spanish and Portuguese in a manner which shows that commercial rivalry could be used to pursue war aims under a different guise. By 1623, but before the infamous 'massacre of Amboyna', which remained a thorny issue in Anglo–Dutch relations into the 1650s, the Company had decided to cut its losses in the Far East and close a number of unprofitable factories, including the one in Japan. The factory, situated at Hirado in the south-west of the Japanese archipelago, was closed at the end of 1623 and the merchants, some of whom had been in Japan throughout the factory's existence, left the country after placing the Company's property in trust with the local lord and authorizing the Dutch to collect outstanding debts.[17]

The experience of these early Britons in Japan is especially memorable because the records of the factory are a rich storehouse

[16] Sainsbury, *Calendar of the Court Minutes 1650–4*, p. 354.

[17] Ludwig Riess, 'History of the English factory at Hirado', *Transactions of the Asiatic Society of Japan*, 1st ser., 26 (1898), provides a narrative. For a general discussion of Anglo-Dutch rivalry in the Far East, see Andrews, *Trade, Plunder and Settlement*, ch. 12, and for a more detailed discussion of the Company's policy on trade in the region, see the important articles by D. K. Bassett, 'Trade of the English East India Company in the Far East, 1623–85, *Journal of the Royal Asiatic Society* (April, October 1960).

of source material. They constitute the fullest archive of any of the Company's factories in the Far East in the seventeenth century (the only comparable one is for Tonkin, in present-day Vietnam, later in the century) and include numerous letters, both business and private, the two-volume diary of the chief factor, Richard Cocks, and a valuable set of accounts. The records provide information about the factory's business operations, the social life of its members, their relationships with each other, with the officers, crews and merchants of Japan-bound Company vessels, with other Europeans (especially Dutch and Iberian), and with the Japanese. They also provide important information about Japan at a time when the Tokugawa regime was still trying to consolidate its power both within Japan and in relation to foreign powers, a process not without its parallels to the quest for legitimacy of successive regimes in England after 1649.[18]

If the records of the Hirado factory are so rich, what use, if any, was made of them to help the Company chart its strategy when it contemplated reopening direct trade with Japan at various times after 1623, including the period of Thompson's governorship? To answer this question it is necessary to be clear about how the Company organized its business in order to formulate the policies it intended its servants overseas to carry out, how it conveyed its orders to them, and how it was informed of the results and provided with any other relevant information.

The policy formulating body was the Court of Committees, comprising the governor, deputy governor and the ordinary members (final authority rested with the General Court, made up of all the shareholders).[19] Letters, instructions and commissions to voyage commanders were the principal methods of conveying decisions and orders. The Company's servants overseas were expected to send back information in letters and were supposed to keep diaries and accounts, although the Company was to complain frequently about the sloppy book-keeping of its servants. There was also correspondence between the various factories and the presidencies, at Bantam in Java for the southern region and Surat for the northern one, and between individual factories. Valuable as much of this correspondence was, dealing with a whole range of

[18] See Ronald P. Toby, *State and Diplomacy in Early Modern Japan* (Princeton, 1984).
[19] Chaudhuri, *English East India Company*, pp. 31–2.

matters from commodity prices, policy recommendations and relations with local rulers and officials, to petty complaints and tale-telling about others, the Company did not treat its records with care or respect, even after 1613 and the establishment of joint stock voyages in which capital was tied up for several years. This was true from the Company's earliest years. In 1604, for example, when certain documents were sought for consultation they could not be found. The Court ordered that in future records should be better preserved, but the order met with little success.[20] There were occasional bursts of enthusiasm for putting into order the vast amount of documentation that accumulated in London. In March 1669 the secretary was instructed to supervise the indexing of the Court Books (the minutes of the Court of Committees) from the Company's foundation. However, in April 1682 it was reported that there were many 'old books and papers which are in a confused manner layd in the upper garret of the [East India] House'.[21]

Confusion and neglect of documents no longer considered to be of any worth persisted until the end of the Company's history. Between 1858 and 1860 literally tons of documents were sold as waste paper, ironically coinciding with a recognition in other quarters of their value as historical material and the first efforts to calendar them as state papers.[22] This does not, however, mean that the Company did not use the material it received. In the 'Factory Records Miscellaneous' among the India Office Records, where most of the Company's archive is now located, there is a volume dating from 1619 which briefly abstracts letters received from the Indies (it also includes a few from before 1619). The letters are abstracted in the order in which they were received, point by point in some detail for quick reference, presumably by the Court.[23] Some of the letters so abstracted are no longer extant in their original form in the 'Original Correspondence' series. The

[20] F. C. Danvers and William Foster (eds), *Letters Received by the East India Company* (6 vols, London, 1896–1902), I, pp. xv–xvi.

[21] Sainsbury, *Calendar of the Court Minutes 1668–70*, pp. 72, 180; William Foster, *A Guide to the India Office Records, 1600–1858* (London, 1919), p. 1ff.; idem, *The East India House* (London, 1924), p. 51 and n.

[22] The details of the weeding out, or more properly disafforestation, can be followed through in India Office Records, Home Miscellaneous Series, 722, which makes it clear that the process had been under way since the early eighteenth century.

[23] India Office Records, G/40/1.

seemingly casual attitude to its papers, however, did not prevent
the Company from jealously guarding access to them. When
Samuel Purchas applied for permission to consult documents in the
Company's possession in February 1622, he was permitted to do so
on condition that he made notes only about 'that which is proper to
a history and not prejudiciall to the Companie'. He also had to
submit his notes for examination by the deputy governor before he
could take them home. Some of the materials relating to Japan
which he used in *Purchas his Pilgrimes* must have been copied from
the Company originals, but now survive only in that work. It is
against this background, an archivist's nightmare, that the subsequent discussions and attempts to re-establish direct trade with
Japan and the schemes of Maurice Thompson must be viewed.

In February 1626, the Batavia presidency (in present-day Jakar-
ta, its location from 1620–8 when it was moved during a Dutch
blockade of Bantam, its original site) wrote enthusiastically about
the prospects for profitable trade in the Far East, including Japan.
The following year in a detailed report the president, Henry
Hawley, and his colleagues declared that 'this trade of Japan is the
summum bonum of East India' and urged the Company to obtain
letters patent from the king addressed to the Japanese emperor (in
fact the shogun, whom Europeans confused with the real emperor
in Kyoto until the nineteenth century, assuming the latter to be a
religious figure like the pope) 'to countenance your first expedition'
thither. Hawley claimed that English cloth would sell well (he was
confident of a turn-over of 100,000 cloths per annum) and could be
traded for silver and copper, then major Japanese exports. The
assessment was based on information obtained locally from
Japanese who would either have been residents of Batavia or crews
trading from Japan.[25]

This was barely three years after the closure of the Hirado
factory, whose existence had shown that English cloth would not
sell in any significant quantity. The assertion that the Company
should send its first expedition to Japan seems puzzling, especially

[24] William Foster, 'Samuel Purchas', in *Richard Hakluyt and his Successors*, ed.
E. Lynam (London, 1946) p. 56. The Company's jealousy was probably occasioned rather by fears of information falling into the wrong hands, competitors and
critics, than by an interest in 'preserving their journals' as Foster oddly implies
(ibid., p. 53.)
[25] India Office Records, E/3/11, ff. 207–210v, esp. ff. 207v, 208v; Peter Pratt,
History of Japan Compiled from the Records of the English East India Company, ed.
M. Maske-Smith (2 vols, repr. London and New York, 1972), pp. 119–26.

as Hawley had signed the presidency's report on the closure of the factory in 1624.[26] Amnesia is an unlikely explanation. Perhaps what Hawley meant was 'your first ['renewed' understood] expedition with a chance of success'. Whatever the reason, there is no hint that a search of the presidency's records was made. In theory, copies of all 'out' correspondence and the originals of all 'in' letters to the presidency should have been available. Some of these may have been lost in the disastrous attempt to relocate the presidency in 1624. A more likely explanation is that, as with the Company in London, papers were not kept systematically, but were used for immediate purposes and, if not considered important, then stored away, running the risk of deterioration in the tropical humidity. Under these circumstances what survived, such as the journal of the master of the *Hoseander* (which had gone to Japan in August 1615) which turned up among the presidency's papers in 1664, was very much a matter of chance.[27]

The Company in London, where memories were a bit longer – helped no doubt by the fact that the Hirado factory's deputy during its last years, William Eaton, had arrived back in England after service in India and was questioned about the factory's affairs, and by the continuing dispute with Cocks's executors over his will[28] – did not take Hawley seriously. This did not stop Thomas Smethwick, a freeman of the Company and an adventurer in the third joint stock, from suggesting to the Court in March 1633 that trade with Japan should be re-established because the market there for English cloth was vast and lucrative. He envisaged profits of 400 per cent and claimed that his information was based on a study of Company records which he submitted to the Court – what these were is unknown – and on the Hawley paper. Smethwick was a frequent critic of the Company, but far from being simply 'a troublesome eccentric' he enjoyed the backing of the crown and, with almost gangster-like audacity, was attempting to extort money from the Company in return for royal protection. The Court gave Smethwick's proposals very short shrift, concluding that they were derived from the Hawley paper, which it dismissed as 'ridiculous and the thing impossible'. In its comments the Court also drew

[26] Ibid., I, pp. 482–5.
[27] Ibid., II, p. 137. The journal is now located in the India Office Records (L/MAR/A/XXIII).
[28] *Calendar of State Papers, Colonial Series, East Indies, China and Persia, 1625–9*, pp. 261, 266, 267, 276, 359, 571, 599, 620, 656, 666; ibid., *1630–4*, p. 32.

upon its own collective memory, and most likely on papers from its own records, stating that it 'well-remembered the ill success [it] had upon [its] attempt at Japan, having not vented in 22 months above 32 cloathes, and in 5 yeares not above 165, and many of them by retayle'. Interestingly, a subsidiary reason for rejecting Smethwick's proposals was that the Court felt that a profitable trade with Japan could be pursued only if it was part of a triangular relationship with China (to obtain silk, much in demand in Japan) and south-east Asia (to send Japanese silver), which shows that the Company was at last beginning to appreciate the trade flows in the region. Smethwick was not unduly put out by the rejection and advanced similar, if not identical, proposals in November 1635, in which the ghost of Hawley is again evident. Once again the Court threw them out.[29]

Meanwhile the southern presidency made some suggestions for possible trade with China and Japan in a wide-ranging report at the beginning of 1635. There was a realization of the need to see the Japan trade within its regional context, but there still remained a firm belief that English cloth could become the principal trading commodity. The report appears to indicate an awareness of the Hirado factory, although this is somewhat ambiguous. The following year in its reply the Court was not as scathing as it had been to Smethwick, and while it recalled its unsuccessful experience in Hirado it showed that its detailed knowledge of those years was fading, for it stated that the factory had lasted 'not lesse than 15 or 16 yeares'; it had in fact lasted just over ten. The Court generously acknowledged that Coulson, the president, was not simply relying on local hearsay and harbour gossip, in contrast to Hawley (although many of the suggestions look like a rehash of Hawley's), and urged him to make further detailed enquiries and do some research to find out what European commodities could be sold in Japan and what could be exported from there.[30]

In December 1636 Coulson replied, saying that there was not much information to go on concerning the Japan trade because nobody resident at Bantam had been there or was acquainted with

[29] Pratt, *History of Japan*, II, pp. 127–9; Sainsbury, *Calendar of the Court Minutes 1635–9*, p. 119; Bassett, 'Trade . . . in the Far East', p. 40; Chaudhuri, *English East India Company*, pp. 58–9; Ashton, *The City and the Court*, pp. 127–9.
[30] Pratt, *History of Japan*, II, pp. 129–31. Cf. Bassett, 'Trade . . . in the Far East', p. 40.

it.[31] In reality he does not seem to have bothered himself very much to find out additional information; the shipmaster's journal which turned up in 1664 must have existed in 1636, which adds strength to the argument that by this time whatever papers about Japan had survived at the presidency had been stored away and forgotten. There is no intimation that any effort had been made to appraise developments within Japan by consulting the Dutch or overseas Japanese and Chinese, for there is no mention of the shogunal decrees restricting direct foreign trade by Japanese vessels.

By the end of the 1640s the challenge to the Company's monopoly had grown in strength and confidence, especially after the establishment of the Commonwealth in 1649. It was at this time that Maurice Thompson emerged onto the national scene. In 1649 the Assada merchants, among whom Thompson was the leading figure, made a bid to break the East Indies monopoly by attempting to establish a colony on the island of Assada (Nosy Bé, off the north-west coast of Madagascar), which it was believed had friendly natives, fertile ground and a climate ideally suited to colonization. The Assada merchants intended to use the island as a base for trade with the Indies. The East India Company tried to have the scheme suppressed and the matter was taken before the Council of State where it developed into a more general consideration of how the Company ran its affairs. Among other things, the Assada merchants were convinced that the Company was not exploiting the potential of the East Indies trade to the maximum, and in the compromise that was thrashed out in December 1649, and approved by the Rump on 31 January 1650, provision was made to allow any member to explore the possibilities of trade in the Far East, including Japan, even if the Company itself decided against it. The compromise also created a united joint stock which allowed the Assada merchants to trade in the Indies as part of the Company, pending a permanent solution of the dispute by parliament.[32]

Taking full advantage of the confusion that clouded the Com-

[31] Pratt, History of Japan, II, p. 131.
[32] Sainsbury, Calendar of the Court Minutes 1644-9, pp. xxi–xxv, 358–9, 360, 261, 364, 365–7, 369–72, 374–8, 382–4; Brenner, 'Civil War politics', p. 104. The history of the ill-fated first attempt to settle Assada, originally one of the Courteen Association's pet projects, is discussed in William Foster, 'An English settlement in Madagascar in 1645–6', English Historical Review (1912), pp. 239–50. The second effort fared no better and was soon abandoned: Sainsbury, Calendar of the Court Minutes 1650-4, pp. ix–xi.

pany's future – confusion which became even murkier under the Protectorate because of uncertainty as to whether or not the Protector would grant a new charter, competition from private merchants despatching vessels to India, and the formation of a syndicate which included Company members to trade in the Indies[33] – Thompson's attacks on the Company's nominal monopoly increased. He put forward his own proposals advocating a more aggressive East Indies trade. Unlike critics of the Company earlier in the century who objected to the East Indies trade because it allegedly drained bullion out of the country, Thompson wasted no words in extolling the advantages of the trade. In a paper of August 1654 he argued that the Indies trade benefited the nation by stimulating economic activity and creating investment opportunities, increasing its naval power, adding to its talent pool by enriching the skills of its seafarers, and enhancing its 'reputation' as a major power. The nation could ill afford not to participate to its utmost in this fast growing trade, otherwise it ran the risk of being pushed out of it altogether by the Dutch and Portuguese. This (in language reminiscent of army rhetoric in the late 1640s) he felt would 'mean an irreparable loss of what has been obtained with much difficulty, hazard, and expense of blood of the nation'. He also asserted, and this is where Thompson's views differ radically in emphasis and implication from those of the established Company merchants, that Dutch and Portuguese strength was derived from military prowess and a programme of colonization:

The extraordinary wealth, potency and strength of the Portuguese and Dutch East India Company, who, having made it their concern to follow and improve the said trade, have, in spite of most powerful potentates in those parts, been able to build forts, plant garrisons, and settle factories, colonies and jurisdictions of their own independently of the said princes and in the midst of their domains.[34]

Thompson became governor of the Company in December 1657. By that time it had received a new charter from the Protector in October, easing the way for a fresh subscription and infusion of new capital, and during the period of his tenure, until July 1659, years of renewed political instability in England, only modest efforts were made to implement any of this. Plans for a settlement

---

[33] Ibid., 1655–9, p. ix; Ashley, *Financial and Commercial Policy*, p. 114.
[34] Sainsbury, *Calendar of the Court Minutes 1650–4*, pp. 333–4, esp. p. 334.

on Pulo Run (Run, one of the Banda Islands, in present-day Indonesia) recognized as English by the Dutch in 1623, ran into the sand in the face of Dutch resistance to handing it back (it was eventually ceded to the Dutch in 1667), but as a spin-off from these efforts a settlement was set up on St Helena.[35] However, some nine months after Thompson became governor, a new attempt at the Japan trade was made. A decision to send a ship for Japan, and one for China, was taken in September 1658 and preparations, including the securing of a letter from the new Protector to the Japanese and Chinese 'emperors', went ahead at full speed until they were abruptly cancelled on 3 December because of the threat of renewed warfare with the Dutch.[36]

There is little indication about the information on which the Company based its decision. However, one thing is clear: there is no mention in the minutes that the Court looked into the Company's records. Quarles Browne, who was appointed head of the proposed Japan factory, and who had gained valuable experience in the East Indies as chief factor at Cambodia from 1651 to 1656 in addition to his service at Bantam, undoubtedly provided some information, as well as enthusiasm. He was an able, perceptive man who would have made a worthy successor to Richard Cocks as an informant about Japan. In 1661 in a paper presented to the deputy governor, Sir Thomas Chamberlain, outlining prospects for trade in the Far East, he noted that in Cambodia the Japanese merchants were 'the noblest Merchants in those parts, free from baffleinge, constant in his [sic] bargaines and punctuall in his tymes for payments, a ffirme ffriend'. More significantly, in September 1658 when the project was getting under way, the Court of Committees ordered that the Company's agent at Amsterdam was to be instructed to find out what he could about the 'traffique and custom of Japon' and to obtain any other relevant information. There is also evidence to suggest that Thompson himself did some homework. In 1668 when the Company was again seriously considering reopening direct trade with Japan, a special committee set up to investigate the matter heard from Captain Robert Bowen, who had been in Japan in 1622, that he had given the journal of his voyage thither (which should have been handed over to the Company on his return from the voyage) to Thompson 'about eight

---

[35] Ibid., *1655–9*, pp. xxvii–xxxi.
[36] Ibid., pp. 281–3, 286, 290, 295–6, 297, 300 and n.

years ago'. Since Bowen would have been fairly old at that time it would be unreasonable to pin him down to 1660.[37]

Somewhat more systematic efforts were made after the Restoration, by which time Thompson and the colonial-interlopers had lost influence and the Company's monopoly was assured once more by a charter from Charles II. The special committee set up in 1668 not only called upon some veteran servants who had been in Japan during the early 1620s to appear before it, but it also consulted some of its records to establish that, contrary to rumour put about by the Dutch, the Company had not left Japan indebted but with debts outstanding to the tune of £2,400. A document purporting to be a copy of the original trading privileges granted to the Company was also found. In reality this was a copy of the Japanese version of the petition to the Japanese government for privileges; the mistake was not discovered until the nineteenth century. The document had been published by Purchas and it is not at all clear whether that carried aboard the Company's ship *Return*, which made an unsuccessful call at Nagasaki to request the resumption of trade in 1673, was not in fact a copy made from Purchas.[38]

The post-Restoration agency at Bantam (for some years after 1652 the factory was downgraded in status) was staggeringly ignorant of the original factory and about recent developments in Japan, imagining that the Japanese were just waiting for the English to come back and reopen their old factory. It believed that the Japanese had rejected numerous Dutch overtures to purchase the factory and the island on which it was situated. The reason for this optimism is unknown, as is the presidency's impression that the Hirado factory had itself been on an island. This would seem to be a much garbled understanding of the reality of Deshima, the man-made island in Nagasaki harbour to which the Dutch had been confined since 1641. Odder still were the instructions issued at Bantam for an aborted mission to Japan in 1671 which urged the supercargoes to make discreet inquiries about the Hirado factory in order to find out where it was located (presumably the site) and

---

[37] India Office Records, G/21/4, p. 5, printed in D. K. Bassett, 'The trade of the English East India Company in Cambodia', *Journal of the Royal Asiatic Society* (1962), pp. 55–61, esp. p. 57; Sainsbury, *Calendar of the Court Minutes 1655–9*, pp. 282–3; ibid., *1668–70*, p. 105.

[38] Ibid., pp. 104–5, 111; Pratt, *History of Japan*, I, pp. 479, 482–4; II, pp. 143n., 164; Samuel Purchas, *Purchas his Pilgrimes in Japan* ed. Cyril Wild (Kobe, 1939), pp. 156–7, 219–20.

why it had been removed (whether in the sense of 'physically' or 'closed down' is unclear). There was also the bizarre expectation of finding some Scots and Irish to whom English cloth was to be given in the hope of stimulating demand for bulk purchases, another reminder, albeit unusual, of how important the export of English cloth remained.[39] The Company persisted for some time after the rejection at Nagasaki in 1673 (the Dutch, knowing that catholicism was by then anathema to the Japanese, had tipped off the Japanese authorities that Charles II was married to a Portuguese catholic) in its efforts to obtain a foothold in Japan before finally shifting its attention to China, a market which appeared to hold more promise.

To sum up, the Company's efforts to re-establish direct trade with Japan in the years after 1623 have three aspects. Firstly, in the Indies, the southern presidency quickly forgot about the Hirado factory. It, and presumably the other factories closed down at around the same time, was soon forgotten, probably on the assumption that failure could teach no lessons. When the presidency came up with fresh initiatives for expanding trade in the region, information about past efforts was not available. Material which had not been sent back to London had either been lost or stored away, out of mind. Even the proposals of Quarles Browne, a man of obvious ability, were based on his experience in Cambodia and his own shrewd assessment of existing trade patterns. Secondly, while the Company in London initially retained very vivid memories of the losses incurred at Hirado and had some records available to consult, by 1636 facts could no longer be taken for granted. Moreover, while these memories lingered – and by the 1650s they had largely been erased – the Company's assessment of the factory was very much conditioned by its conviction that its servants, especially Cocks, had let it down. The Court of Committees never admitted the possibility that imperfections in the Company's strategy might have been a major reason for failure. This attitude ruled out any possibility of studying the records objectively to find out what had gone wrong. Thirdly, when more serious efforts to reopen the trade were made from the 1650s, the Company's information about Japan was based, for the most part, on recently

[39] Pratt, *History of Japan*, II, pp. 141, 153–7. A series of edicts expelling the Japanese wives and children of Europeans, including those of the English, was passed from 1636. Even if these were not completely enforced, it is inconceivable that any children who remained in Japan were conscious of their Scottish or Irish identity.

acquired information, especially what could be discovered about the Dutch trade there. There was no methodical search of the Company's records, which were in any case not in a state to permit this, and no recognition in the Court of the value of such an exercise. When records were consulted it was for a specific purpose, not as a necessary precondition for planning to help avoid previous mistakes or to form a clearer picture of the polity and society the Company's servants would encounter in Japan. The merchants who managed the Company's affairs were not avatars of the civil lawyers, placing a high value on the examination of records to find precedents to guide them forward. They were interested in short- to medium-term considerations. The view that by the 1660s the Company was a rational business organization with a well-developed sense of corporate history is very questionable.[40]

In this respect, whatever the novelty and originality of his vision, Maurice Thompson's disregard of what could have been learned from the past is no different from the attitude of the established merchants. Certainly political circumstances greatly reduced the chances of translating his vision into action, especially under the Protectorate. In the Elizabethan period of English overseas expansion, privateering voyages into the Atlantic and down the west coast of Africa had linked together merchants from London, the outports, members of the aristocracy and gentry, and, because of limited government resources for building up a navy, the court.[41] During the Protectorate there was no such fusion of key elements of the political nation behind the government's foreign policy. This policy was flawed anyway by a failure to square up to the challenge posed by the Dutch which alienated sections of the merchant class.[42] There is also no way of knowing what difference, beneficial or otherwise, Thompson's advocacy of free trade would have made to English trade with the Indies had it been implemented. As K. N. Chaudhuri has observed, the decision to entrust the trade to monopoly bodies 'was derived on the basis of conditions in Europe

[40] The view is central to the argument of K. N. Chaudhuri's monumental work *The Trading World of Asia and the English East India Company 1660–1760* (Cambridge, 1978), esp. p. 79, and is restated in his *Trade and Civilization in the Indian Ocean* (Cambridge, 1985), esp. pp. 82–3. See also D. K. Bassett's review of *Trading World* in the *Bulletin of the School of Oriental and African Studies*, 44 (1981), p. 191.
[41] Quinn and Ryan, *England's Sea Empire*, pp. 88, 126.
[42] Prestwich, 'Diplomacy and trade', p. 120.

rather than those in Asia', in this instance the Protector's decision to endorse the East India Company's monopoly.[43]

Much of Thompson's programme was based on what was mistakenly believed to have been successful Dutch and Portuguese plans in the East Indies. This reflected a similar outlook to that of the established Company merchants who, for most of the seventeenth century, were trying to imitate what they felt to be Dutch success, whether it was in the efforts to break into the Spice Islands, or to re-establish trade with Japan in the hope of getting access to Japanese silver and copper. Thomson's belief that the Dutch and Portuguese owed their strength to a programme of settlement was wrong. Enclaves existed, but mostly they had been granted by local potentates, not seized (the major exception was the Spice Islands where the Dutch were ruthless in attempting to gain a monopoly, especially under the leadership of Jan Petrz. Coen). The Europeans in Asia owed their strength to the fact that they were strong naval powers in Asian waters. However, they came largely as merchants intent on seeking profitable trade not conquest or the enhancement of national 'reputation'. The directorate of the Dutch Company were quite explicit about this, writing in 1622: 'No great attention should be paid to the question of reputation or honour . . . in our opinion (for we are merchants) he has the honour who without doing unright or violence has the profit.'[44] In the case of the English in the seventeenth century, the Company preferred diplomacy to force in obtaining its objectives, even if the 'idea' of force to protect English interests, whether motivated by defensive concerns (the need to protect legitimate English settlements) or offensive ones (to win more concessions by instilling fear into the local population), gradually became more acceptable, particularly in India.[45] Thompson's proposals very much echo Coen's schemes

[43] Chaudhuri, *Trading World*, p. 45, Ashley, *Financial and Commercial Policy*, pp. 111–31.

[44] Quoted in Niels Steensgaard, 'The Dutch East India Company as an institutional innovation', in *Dutch Capitalism and World Capitalism*, ed. Maurice Aymard (Cambridge, 1982), p. 255. On the importance of *reputación* in formulating Spanish strategy during the struggle with the Dutch, see Jonathan I. Israel, *The Dutch Republic and the Spanish World 1606–61* (Oxford, 1982), esp. pp. 32, 71.

[45] However, the Indian experience should not be considered typical of the Company's relations with polities elsewhere in Asia, a reservation which has to be made about the argument in I. Bruce Watson, 'Fortifications and the "idea" of force in early English East India Company relations with India', *Past and Present*, no. 88 (1980), pp. 70–87.

in tone; it is not improbable that he had some familiarity with them. They also appear to have been based on personal experience, on the conviction that what had worked well in the New World could be applied in Asia. This was a mistaken assessment of the situation at this time: North America, peopled by Indian tribes which seemed primitive both culturally and economically by contemporaries, lent itself to conquest and settlement; Asia, with old-established civilizations, some of them at least equal to that of Europe, with a long commercial history, and such major powers as Mughal India, China and Japan, did not.[46]

As far as English trading activity in the Indies was concerned, the 'age of reconnaissance', that is the acquisition of knowledge through an unsystematic, haphazard process of discovery, was to continue for much longer before it was finally succeeded by the age of conquest, and the pursuit of power and 'reputation'. It is from this perspective that the confident expansionist mood of the 1650s must be considered.

---

[46] On this point see also Quinn and Ryan, *England's Sea Empire*, pp. 168–9, and Andrews, *Trade, Plunder and Settlement*, pp. 9–10.

9

Law-Making in the
First Protectorate Parliament

PETER GAUNT

Their History shall remain blank, to the end of the world. I have read their Debates, and counsel no other man to do it. Wholly upon the 'Institution of Government', modelling, new-modelling of that: endless anxious spider-webs of constitutional logic; vigilant checks, constitutional jealousies, &c. &c. To be forgotten by all creatures.

Carlyle's assessment of the First Protectorate Parliament was emphatic, magisterial and unremittingly condemnatory. It was, he tells us, 'a refractory Parliament', 'a most poor hidebound Pedant Parliament', which ignored the pressing needs of the government and people and spent its time instead revising the written constitution. The whole session was devoted to 'constitutional air-fabrics', to 'painful new-modelling and rebuilding of the Instrument of Government', relieved only by occasional displays of religious intolerance and persecution. The process of rewriting the constitution was unnecessary, dangerous and divisive and the finished product unrealistic and unworkable. The five-month session was squandered in fruitless constitutionalizing, in 'Sheepskin Formulas' irrelevant to 'the facts and clamorous necessities of the Present', and nothing constructive was achieved. An abrupt dissolution at the earliest opportunity ended a parliament which had proved very unsuccessful – a judgement repeated four times within a hundred pages – and MPs and their draft constitution together 'disappear[ed], regretted or remembered by no person, – not by this

An earlier version of this paper was presented to a conference of the New Zealand Early Modern Studies Association held in Wellington in April 1985; I am grateful to all who attended for their comments and criticisms on that occasion.

Editor for one'. In short, Carlyle condemned the parliament for
concerning itself with unproductive and irrelevant constitutional
reform to the virtual exclusion of everything else, including many
more pressing and important matters. It was, he concluded with
supreme contempt, a parliament 'hardly worth naming!'[1]

Shorn of their colourful excesses, these views have proved remarkably durable. If not 'forgotten by all creatures', the First
Protectorate Parliament has certainly languished in relative neglect, bereft of the detailed attention afforded the Long Parliament,
Rump and Nominated Assembly. Wider narratives of the period
have generally followed the Carlyle line, dismissing the parliament
with a few brief and bleak references to the destructive and futile
nature of its work. The customary picture remains that of a session
passed in major political conflict, wholly absorbed by an antagonistic constitutionalizing which provoked continual division, both
within the House and between Protector and parliament. Even the
most detailed and judicious account of the session, that of
S. R. Gardiner, rarely progresses far beyond the sorry tale of confrontation and recrimination, empty constitutional struggle and
wasted opportunity.[2] Trevor-Roper's account of executive trickery,
purges and mismanagement, of opposition leaders scrambling for
the front bench and of party conflict and utter failure, does nothing
to alter the image.[3] The most recent narratives of the Interregnum
follow essentially the same line, with 'most' or 'all' of the session
spent in destructive constitutional reform, producing not healing
and settling, but distemper and relapse.[4] Yet even a cursory glance
at the official and unofficial records of the session reveal that there
was much more to the parliament than this tale of unrelieved and
unmanaged chaos allows. Contemporary sources demonstrate that
amid the supposed cauldron of major political strife, MPs found
time to engage in less frenetic parliamentary business, to work in
relative harmony on a wide range of projects, to promote public

[1] Thomas Carlyle, *Oliver Cromwell's Letters and Speeches: With Elucidations*, (5 vols, London, 1871-3), IV, pp. 17-19, 42-5, 70-6, 79-81, 108-9.

[2] S. R. Gardiner, *History of the Commonwealth and Protectorate 1649-56* (4 vols, London, 1903), III, pp. 167-255.

[3] H. R. Trevor-Roper, 'Oliver Cromwell and his parliaments', in *Essays presented to Sir Lewis Namier*, ed. Richard Pares and A. J. P. Taylor (London, 1956), pp. 31-5.

[4] T. C. Barnard, *The English Republic 1649-60* (London, 1982), pp. 43-7; A. H. Woolrych, *England Without A King 1649-60* (London, 1983), pp. 36-7.

and private legislation and to meet many of the requirements for which they had been summoned. This chapter attempts to explore the positive and constructive aspects of the session, as well as briefly to re-examine the more familiar images of conflict and mismanagement.

The parliament which assembled on 3 September 1654 was like no other before it, for it was the first to meet under the terms of a written constitution. The Instrument of Government not only set out the general positions of executive and legislature but also quite closely defined the composition, operation and powers of parliament. The constitution restored a powerful and largely independent executive in the form of a Lord Protector and a permanent Council, while guaranteeing the legislature a significant and continuing role in central government. Single-chamber assemblies comprising 460 elected members representing Scotland and Ireland as well as England and Wales were to meet triennially and to sit for at least a set minimum period; additional assemblies could be summoned as required. Parliament was given apparently extensive and supreme legislative rights and was empowered to examine and oversee the actions of the executive in all important matters of government and administration. However, the impression of parliamentary omnipotence was illusory, for the legislature was surrounded by potentially severe restrictions, including the prerogative of the Protector to veto any legislation which in his sole and unquestionable opinion ran counter to the constitution. Several important provisions of the Instrument were specifically deemed inviolable and beyond alteration or revision by future legislation. Indeed, there was no provision for any form of constitutional amendment and Cromwell may initially have considered that the whole document was sacrosanct. In such manner was the ground prepared for co-operation and conflict.[5]

How, then, did these arrangements work in practice during the 1654–5 session? It must be admitted at the outset that our knowledge of proceedings is incomplete and based upon a range of limited and often flawed sources. The official record of the session, the parliamentary roll, has disappeared, almost certainly destroyed at the Restoration. No legislation had been completed and had

[5] The Instrument is printed in S. R. Gardiner, *The Constitutional Documents of the Puritan Revolution 1625–60*, 3rd edn (Oxford, 1906), pp. 405–17.

reached the Statute Book or the government presses by the time of the dissolution. With the exception of the Government Bill, two copies of which are extant,[6] none of the Bills considered during the session survives in manuscript or print. In consequence, the *Commons Journal* becomes our principal source for the legislative achievements of the session as well as for general proceedings within the House. It is, however, a decidedly limited source. It comprises a sparse record of decisions and divisions, and carries no details of speeches or debates. Even formal divisions and resolutions were omitted when parliament was functioning as a Committee of the Whole House, and this is particularly unfortunate as the House moved into Grand Committee almost fifty times in 1654–5 and settled many important aspects of the Government Bill and other legislation there. Worse still, it seems that the *Journal's* account of proceedings is often at fault: from time to time names appear on committee lists which belong to no known MPs; unofficial sources report the existence and operation of several parliamentary committees whose initial appointment passed unnoticed in the *Journal*; at several points the manuscript copies of the Government Bill differ in wording, phraseology or content from all original and amended versions of those clauses found within the *Journal*; and, as we shall see, the clerk may also have failed to record the receipt of, and response to, several bills which apparently came before the House some time during the session.

Unofficial reports and commentaries fill some of the gaps. Despite a parliamentary order of late September permitting publication of proceedings only by direction of the clerk,[7] accounts of parliament's business continued to appear in the weekly newspapers. The reports should be treated with caution – one newspaper obviously went to press before receiving word of the dissolution and instead carried a long and completely fanciful account of proceedings in the House on 22 January.[8] On the whole, however, their reports of debates and decisions, of committee meetings and progress on the Government Bill and other legislation appear quite accurate and are frequently corroborated by other sources. Several

---

[6] Gardiner, *Constitutional Documents*, pp. 427–47, prints a manuscript then 'in the possession of Lord Braye'; a slightly different version, correcting several copy errors in the Braye draft, is now amongst the Clarke manuscripts at Worcester College, Oxford, clxxxi, box 2 (unbound and unfoliated papers).

[7] *The Weekly Intelligencer*, 26 September–2 October 1654.

[8] Ibid., 16–23 January 1655.

broadsheets and pamphlets which appeared during or after the session described events in the House in order to defend Protector or parliament, but their generally sketchy accounts of parliamentary proceedings and their unmistakably propogandist intent make them very dubious sources.[9] A partial exception is *A Representation Concerning the Late Parliament*, a detailed and well-informed account, probably written by a member whose defence of parliament's action, though clearly politically motivated, is lucid, informative and, where it can be checked, factually accurate.[10] A number of contemporary commentators, including Ludlow, Whitelock and the Venetian and French ambassadors recount major events in parliament and occasionally add useful information as well as generally venomous interpretation.[11] Unfortunately, for much of 1654 the newsletters sent from London to William Clarke in Scotland were written or transcribed in cypher and only for the closing weeks of the session do Mabbott's and Downing's accounts of parliamentary, political and military events in the capital survive in long-hand.[12]

What of descriptions of the session written by Protectoral politicians themselves? Sadly, the two leading figures, Cromwell and his Secretary of State, wrote very little at this time. Both were injured in a coach accident in late September and Thurloe in particular spent much of the autumn convalescing, despatching few letters and recounting generally second-hand news.[13] Perhaps for this reason, his collection of state papers becomes noticeably shallow

[9] See, for example, *A Declaration of the Members of Parliament Lately Dissolved by Oliver Cromwell, Esquire* ([27 January] 1655).

[10] *A Representation Concerning the late Parliament in the Year 1654, To Prevent Mistakes* ([9 April] 1655). The author claims to have known most of the members; he also asks the reader not to consider the pamphlet 'the sense of the Parliament, which no single Member may undertake, much less the meanest of them all.'

[11] C. H. Firth, *Memoirs of Edmund Ludlow* (2 vols, Oxford, 1894); Bulstrode Whitelock, *Memorials of the English Affairs* (4 vols, Oxford, 1853); A. B. Hinds, *Calendar of State Papers and Manuscripts Relating to English Affairs Existing in the Archives and Collections of Venice and other Libraries of North Italy*, xxix–xxx (London, 1929–31); for transcripts of the French ambassador's despatches, see PRO 31/3/90–102.

[12] Worcester College, Oxford, Clarke MSS xxvi–xxvii.

[13] Although Thurloe's letters are now widely scattered, the best series from this period is to be found in Robert Vaughan, *The Protectorate of Oliver Cromwell and the State of Europe during the early part of the Reign of Louis XIV* (2 vols, London, 1838). The letters indicate that Thurloe did not resume work until late October, and parliamentary committee lists suggest that he did not retake his seat in the House until December.

during the closing months of 1654 and contains little of real
importance on political and parliamentary events beyond a dozen
or so intercepted letters from the Dutch and French representatives
in London.[14] Councillors and other prominent members seem to
have been remarkably coy about committing to paper simple
accounts of parliamentary proceedings, let alone details of the
mood, intentions, divisions or leadership of the House. Careful
research in local and private archives may turn up caches of letters
or diaries, but at present we know of only one substantial account
of the 1654–5 parliament written by an MP, that of Guibbon
Goddard, member for King's Lynn.

Goddard's diary is incomplete, closing in mid-sentence on 18
December and omitting much that occurred in the preceding three
and a half months. The author fails to record many debates and
decisions, presumably through lack of interest or absence from the
House. He left London for five days in mid-September and missed
at least one further sitting day when he 'took physic'. Many other
entries are very brief and apparently copied from the *Journal*,
suggesting that Goddard was absent from parliament quite frequently during the autumn. Even when describing proceedings in
greater detail, the diary usually recounts a debate in a single
compact paragraph, identifying neither individual speeches nor the
MPs who made them; less than a dozen members are named in the
entire diary. The account of a day's business could run to over
1,000 words, but most sittings were described in 200 or less.
Inevitably, therefore, a great deal was completely omitted and the
remainder was recounted in a very sketchy and compressed manner. Goddard's cramped style can obscure meaning and produce
uncertainty and confusion. The author himself was sometimes
confused, misdating certain debates or decisions. But confused,
cramped and incomplete though it is, Goddard's diary is of vital
importance to our understanding of the session, for it is the only
surviving source to describe in any detail the course and contents of
debates within the Chamber.[15]

The diary opens with Goddard travelling from East Anglia to
London to attend the House. The journey was quite short, prob-

---

[14] *Thurloe State Papers*, II, III, passim.

[15] Goddard's diary is printed as an introduction to vol I of the *Diary of Thomas
Burton, Esquire*, ed. J. T. Rutt (4 vols, London, 1828). The original manuscript is
now deposited at the Wiltshire RO, Trowbridge, Marquis of Aylesbury (Saver-
nake) Papers, box 9.

ably taking no more than two days, and Goddard arrived in the capital on 2 September, in good time for the formal opening.[16] Other members had had much longer and more difficult journeys. The Scottish representatives had left Edinburgh on 23 August, the Irish Dublin on the 24th, but still many did not reach London until several days after the session had begun.[17] The Yorkshire members had set off from York during the last week of August and had travelled south bearing not only the good wishes of their constituents but also their expressions of hopes and aspirations for the coming session: 'The People have great expectations of this Parliament in hearing grievances; that they will not make Acts with unreasonable penalties; that they will ease the heavy burthens and let the oppressed go free.'[18] Expectations were indeed high as over 300 MPs, Goddard amongst them, packed Westminster Abbey and St Margaret's for special services on 3 and 4 September and crowded into the Painted Chamber – standing room only – to hear Cromwell's opening speech, at which 'all seemed abundantly to rejoyce by extraordinary expressions and hums.'[19] It was, thought Cromwell, 'the hopefullest day that ever mine eyes saw, as to considerations of this world'.[20]

If many of these hopes and aspirations remained unfulfilled at the dissolution, it was through no lack of effort or progress during the intervening twenty weeks. Very occasional long weekends and days of fasting, prayer and humiliation aside, MPs met daily, Monday to Saturday, throughout the session. During the opening weeks the House usually adjourned around midday, but in November it began to meet both morning and afternoon and on the 30th members resolved to sit all day every day (Sunday excepted) until further notice, a resolution observed until the dissolution.[21] From time to time during the autumn the House reportedly sat until 'late at night' and in January 1655 there were several very late or

---

[16] *Burton's Diary*, ed. Rutt, I, xvii.

[17] *Mercurius Politicus*, 24–31 August, 31 August–7 September 1654; *Certain Passages of Every Dayes Intelligence*, 1–8 September 1654.

[18] *A Perfect Diurnall; or, Occurrences of Certain Military Affairs*, 21–8 August 1654.

[19] Detailed accounts of the events of 3 and 4 September are to be found in most newspapers, particularly *Severall Proceedings of State Affairs*, 31 August–7 September 1654; *Burton's Diary*, ed. Rutt, I, xvii–xx.

[20] W. C. Abbott, *The Writings and Speeches of Oliver Cromwell* (4 vols, Cambridge, Mass., 1937–47), III, p. 579.

[21] *CJ*, VII, pp. 365–421.

all-night sittings, until 4 a.m. on one occasion.[22] Attendances
inevitably fell when Cromwell imposed a written test on members
on 12 September and they sagged again during December, but the
House was never found to be inquorate, the total vote recorded in
division only twice fell below one hundred, and there were usually
between 150 and 200 members present when the House divided.

Nor was this energy expended solely on the supposedly irrelevant
and ultimately abortive Government Bill. The range of issues
handled by the House can be introduced most easily by following
proceedings over a fairly brief and manageable period. The fifteen
sitting days from 30 October to 15 November were apparently
typical of the session as a whole. Throughout these two and a half
weeks the House assembled daily, usually in the morning alone,
but with occasional afternoon sittings as well; MPs also gathered
on Sunday 5 November for a thanksgiving service. The Government Bill was considered during all but one of the sittings, debated
either in Grand Committee, where the clauses were first drafted, or
in the House itself, where they were considered for a second time.
Debates could be long and acrimonious, and the relevant clauses
either shelved for reconsideration or eventually settled amid 'great
confusion and discontent'. Thus the provision granting the Protector a limited veto over parliamentary legislation led to a fundamental questioning of the role and powers of the 'Single Person',
provoked some of the longest and angriest exchanges of the session
and gave rise to 'fears and imminent dangers' and rumours of 'an
ominous and sudden dissolution'. Yet even in the midst of this
apparently bitter constitutional battle the mood could suddenly
change, and anger collapsed into humour as a witty defence of an
inflammatory speech led other members to make 'a little merry
with . . . puns'.[23] Moreover, official and unofficial sources indicate
that during this period, as during the session as a whole, most of the
new constitution was drafted and agreed not amid serious conflict,
division and hostility but in a constructive spirit of consensus and
co-operation. Veto powers aside, the Government Bill made fairly
smooth and peaceful progress during the first half of November,
both in the House and in Grand Committee.

Despite the long hours spent on the Government Bill, a mass of
other business was raised and despatched over these fifteen days.

---

[22] *Severall Proceedings of Parliament*, 2–9 November 1654, 11–18 January 1655.
[23] *Burton's Diary*, ed. Rutt, I, lxiii–lxxi.

Constitutional revision itself led the House, into several wider fields, including a thorough review of the state's finances, a long and rambling debate on the legality of sheriffs serving as MPs, consideration of a set of Articles of Faith, the appointment of a sub-committee to confer with Cromwell on religious toleration and the receipt of several petitions relating to property disputes raised under article forty of the Instrument. After initial discussion in the House, these and other petitions were referred to committees for detailed examination. Trade and religion were considered by Committees of the Whole House which met semi-regularly throughout the session, but most other matters were handled by select committees. Five of the forty or so committees of the First Protectorate Parliament were appointed during the first half of November and several others were granted additional powers or personnel. Committees comprised anything from six to over a hundred members – between thirty and sixty was the norm – and usually met after the House had risen for the day. Their meetings are not recorded in the *Journal* but unofficial sources indicate that on most afternoons or evenings up to six different committees would be at work at Westminster. Thus the committees for privileges, Ireland, petitions, creditors and poor prisoners, cloth and state finance all met on the afternoon of 6 November and a week later those for Scotland, Ireland, the Chancery, petitions, privileges and cloth gathered to continue their work.

There was a constant interchange between the House and its committees as business was referred or reported back. On 31 October, MPs passed a long series of regulations for the export of agricultural produce but left the question of beer exports unresolved, to be examined by a committee. The House formally divided over the proposal to export butter, the first of seven divisions during this period. A week later MPs narrowly voted against suspending a conciliar ordinance.[24] On 4 November members debated the misuse of *certioraris* and *habeas corpus* and appointed a committee with the wide-ranging brief of examining these and all other abuses in the law courts. The finance committee had all but completed its investigations by mid-November and its report to the House on the 15th gave rise to the first of many debates on national finance, assessments and the armed forces. The House could be diverted by quite minor or passing incidents. On 7 November, for

[24] The remaining five divisions concerned aspects of the Government Bill.

instance, debate on the Government Bill was interrupted when Colonel Shapcott, MP, rose to complain about a libellous and inflammatory pamphlet circulating in his name;[25] the offending publication was read and condemned and orders passed for its suppression and the apprehension of the authors, printers and publishers. Individual members were granted leave of absence from the House, money was voted to pay a long-standing military debt owed to Colonel John Birch, MP, and Speaker Lenthall announced his decision to sit for Oxfordshire, waiving his election for Gloucester and ordering a bye-election for the vacated seat. All this and a lot more besides was handled in just fifteen days.

Only two bills came before the House during this period, the Government Bill and the bill for ejecting scandalous, ignorant and insufficient ministers and schoolmasters, given its first reading on 6 November when a date was set for the second. Other legislation, however, was in progress at this time. A drafting committee failed to have the bill for the relief of creditors and poor prisoners ready for its planned introduction on 2 November and was instructed to sit daily until the draft was complete. Committees were appointed to convert into legislative form resolutions of the House regulating the export of produce, confirming the abolition of the English Court of Wards and removing the Court of Wards and tenure *in capite* in Ireland. Another committee was instructed to prepare legislation 'for the better regulation of weights and measures through the whole Nation' and a Councillor MP was given leave to introduce a naturalization bill. Legislation was to be drafted to compel the sheriff of Surrey to use money, collected under an earlier act, to pay for a common gaol and house of correction for the county. Although some of these bills disappeared without trace, others were in due course introduced and began their passage through the House. None completed the journey.[26]

Parliament's failure to place any acts on the Statute Book has resulted in the session being portrayed as a legislative wilderness in which nothing but the Government Bill flourished. The reality is quite different. The *Commons Journal* shows that thirteen bills had

[25] *The Speech of Colonell Shapcott, Knight for Devonshire, in behalf of K Charles the Second* ([30 October] 1654); *CJ*, VII, p. 383.
[26] This and the preceding three paragraphs are based upon *CJ*, VII, pp. 379–85; *Burton's Diary*, ed. Rutt, I, lx–lxxviii; and the newspapers of the period, particularly *Severall Proceedings of Parliament*, 26 October–2 November, 2–9 November, 9–16 November 1654.

been given one or more readings by 22 January and that at least fifteen more were considered at some point during the session. Some of these probably never progressed very far: the case of the sheriff of Surrey, for instance, was referred to a drafting committee after a brief examination of the complainants' petition in the House and neither Bill nor committee was ever heard of again. Other legislation which failed to receive a first reading had nonetheless been considered in detail in the House and committee. The bill for the relief of creditors and poor prisoners was in preparation from mid-September; in October the drafting committee examined and reported defects in the conciliar ordinance of the same name; the matter was debated in the House on several occasions during the autumn; and in November and December members repeatedly set a date for the first reading, only to postpone it because the draft was incomplete or as other business intervened.[27]

Further information can be gleaned from an apparently contemporary list of legislation, now amongst the Stowe manuscripts in the British Library.[28] The first folio is missing and with it not only the titles of eight bills but also any heading, date or explanatory note which the document may once have carried. The surviving pages list the titles of thirty 'Acts', numbered '9' to '38' in the left-hand margin. Many of these, including the thirty-eighth and last, 'An Act for settling the Government, which containes 60 Articles', can be identified from the *Journal* as bills considered during the 1654–5 session, and the document is clearly a list of legislation proposed or prepared by the First Protectorate Parliament.[29] Several items of public legislation recorded in the *Journal* are not listed in the manuscript and in this way the eight missing bills can easily be identified and added. The Stowe manuscript also omits all private legislation, including the two bills known to have been read in the House during January 1655. Greater difficulties are caused by the appearance on the Stowe list of around ten bills which are mentioned nowhere in the *Journal*. This seems to suggest that the *Journal* carries an incomplete record of legislative proceedings, omitting decisions to initiate legislation, referrals to and reports from drafting committees, perhaps even formal readings themselves. In some cases the origins of these

[27] *Burton's Diary*, ed. Rutt, I, xxxix, lviii–lix; *CJ*, VII, pp. 368, 377, 378–80, 392, 394.
[28] *BL*, Stowe MSS 322, 74ff.
[29] *CJ*, VII, pp. 365–421.

otherwise unrecorded bills can be tentatively identified; 'An Act for
repealing the Act for digging Salt Petre' and 'for transportation [i.e.
export] of geldings' may have been initiated in committee, possibly
the Grand Committee on Trade or the select committee on exports,
without any reference or order from the House. Others seem a
complete mystery, including the very curious 'Act for Restoring
Cathedralls upon the several citties and counties where they stand'.

The Stowe manuscript and printed *Journal* together reveal that at
least eleven public and two private bills were read once or more
during the session and that a minimum of twenty-seven other
public bills and an unknown number of private were in preparation
or in progress. Thus something over forty bills had been seriously
considered in the course of twenty weeks, not perhaps the most
industrious session of the period – during the forty-two weeks of the
1656–7 session, the Second Protectorate Parliament drafted or
passed around 180 bills[30] – but certainly not the legislative desert of
tradition either. Despite the time and effort devoted to the Government Bill, MPs had promoted and maintained a fairly broad and
extensive legislative programme, and one by no means untypical of
an early modern parliament.

Bills could spring from petitions presented to the House, debates
in the chamber, the initiative of individual members or grand and
select committees, and from entirely unplanned and unexpected
incidents; the arrest of a swashbuckling Quaker at the door of the
Chamber led the House to initiate a bill 'touching Quakers'. Most
legislation was drafted in committee, a process which could take
weeks or even months. In some cases the first record of a bill is its
introduction and first reading in the House and the processes by
which it was prepared and brought to parliament are completely
unknown. As we have seen, the *Journal* omits all record of several
other bills apparently considered during the session. The text of
only one bill has survived and of the rest, little is now known except
their titles. Bills for the relief of creditors and poor prisoners, the
ejection of ignorant ministers and schoolmasters and the reorganization of chancery were designed to replace conciliar ordi-

[30] I. A. Roots, 'Law-making in the second Protectorate parliament', in *British
Government and Administration*, ed. H. Hearder and H. R. Loyn (Cardiff, 1974),
pp. 134–6. As the title and contents indicate, the present article attempts to follow
for the first Protectorate parliament the course chartered by Professor Roots
through the second; I gladly acknowledge my debt – one of many – to Professor
Roots.

nances on the same subjects, deemed unworkable or unjust in some way.[31] The Marriage Bill was aimed at correcting 'many inconveniences' in the existing Marriage Act, particularly its vague definition of a lawful marriage and the resulting uncertainty over bastardy.[32] Legislation ranged from the highest matters of state – the constitution, treason, printing and censorship and the uniting of Ireland with England – to purely regional or local issues, such as the establishment of courts at York and the financing of the Surrey gaol. Scotland and Ireland were well served, with separate bills for assessments, printing and the abolition of Courts of Wards in each country. Several aspects of the legal system were to be reformed and other legislation touched upon trade and finance, religion (including restraints on Quakers, the ejection of inadequate ministers and the better maintenance of the rest) and society (bills on drunks, idiots and lunatics, marriage, naturalization and the relief of maimed soldiers, widows and orphans). Private bills were introduced to settle the estates of the late Samuel Dingley and William Massham.

Most legislation made rather slow progress through the House and long periods often elapsed between the drafting of a bill and its introduction and between readings and committee stages. Legislation due to be debated on particular days was constantly being jostled out by other business. For example, on no less than five occasions between 11 and 21 November members agreed a date for the second reading of the Ejection Bill and five times it had to be postponed as other business intervened.[33] However, the legislative programme never came to a complete halt and even during the closing days of the session, when MPs were working day – and often night as well – on the Government Bill, time was found to introduce and read other legislation.

By the end of the session several bills had almost completed their passage through the House and many others were in progress. The Government Bill had been fully drafted, read and agreed and was all but ready for presentation to the Protector; one report suggests that the bill was actually 'in the birth' and within an hour of completion when Members were summoned to the Painted Chamber to be dissolved, though others claim that 'near 80 provisoes'

---

[31] *Burton's Diary*, ed.Rutt, I, xli, xlviii–xlix, lviii–lix, lxii, xcvi.
[32] Ibid., xxxix.
[33] *CJ*, VII, pp. 384–7.

were still to be considered.[34] The bills for ejection of ministers and abolition of purveyance and Courts of Wards had each received their second reading during November and December and by the end of the year the Assessment Bill had been read twice, committed, read a third time and engrossed.[35] However, in late December MPs decided that no legislation should be presented or passed until the new constitution was in place. The completed Assessment Bill was held up while the House worked on the constitutional legislation; the bill was to be presented to Cromwell with, or immediately after, the Government Bill.[36] In early January, several newspapers reported parliament's unwillingness to present any legislation until the Government Bill was complete, adding that, if Cromwell approved the constitution, MPs 'will desire that some longer time may be given for the finishing of the several Bills, as for the Regulation of the Chancery, the Relief of Creditors and Poor Prisoners, and many others for the honour and advantage of the Commonwealth'.[37] In the event, dissolution killed both the Government Bill and all the other honourable legislation then in progress.

If this is all a long way from the usual picture of a session devoid of legislation, so parliament's work outside the legislative field reveals a side far removed from the familiar image of intense and incessant constitutional warfare. Despite occasional attempts to limit or halt temporarily the receipt of petitions, an array of local and private grievances was constantly coming before the House. Petitions were received on a range of subjects, from fen-draining and legal mismanagement to property disputes and personal appeals for liberty or payment, reward or redress. The Earl of Clanrichard was given leave to remain in England for six months and the Earl of Worcester released from the Tower on bail because 'he was an old man, had lain long in prison, and the small-pox was now in the same roof where he lay'.[38] Members referred petitions from Lord Craven, Sir John Stowell and others concerning long-standing property disputes to a committee for further examination, unwittingly stirring up a hornets' nest involving a swarm of titled

---

[34] A Representation, pp. 26–7; Severall Proceedings of Parliament, 18–25 January 1655.
[35] CJ, VII, pp. 387, 392–5, 405–7.
[36] A Representation, pp. 27–8; Worcester College, Oxford, Clarke MSS xxvi, f. 137v.
[37] The Weekly Post, 1–8 January 1655; The Weekly Intelligencer, 2–9 January 1655.
[38] Burton's Diary, ed. Rutt, I, xlviii; CJ, VII, pp. 371, 373.

witnesses, testimony from the Protectoral Councillors and a number of printed expositions of the case.[39] On 12 October the House considered a petition concerning the 'late disappointment' of the Greenland fleet and the consequent shortage of whale oil. A broader discussion of the activities of the whaling fleets and the supply of oil and other products led in turn to a review of the import and export of corn and other agricultural produce and a wide-ranging examination of existing trade legislation. The debate lasted all morning and ended with a resolution that the House sit as a Grand Committee on Trade once a week. Thus the main business of the day, consideration of the Government Bill and in particular a crucial debate on the elective or hereditary nature of the Chief Magistracy, was cut short or jostled out by whale oil and corn carriers.[40]

Far from ignoring 'the facts and clamorous necessities of the Present', as Carlyle alleged,[41] Protectoral MPs in fact spent much of their time trying to meet the needs of the nation and its people. Affairs of state were examined, regulated and advanced, a broad programme of public and private legislation was promoted and petitions and disputes were heard and resolved. All facets of government, including the constitution, law, religion, trade, finance, society, morality, Scotland, Ireland and the localities, were debated and developed during the session. The House was also careful of its own rights, reacting swiftly to any infringements of the privileges of parliament, its members or their servants.[42] This was not a parliament constantly locked in major political conflict or the pursuit of a single, constitutional goal, and members were called upon to handle a mass of issues, important or trivial, predictable or unexpected, long-standing or fleeting, holding the House for an instant and then disappearing for ever. There were flashes of anger and moments of humour, but for the most part debate was steady and serious. Parliament generally worked in something

[39] *Burton's Diary*, ed. Rutt, I, lxi; *CJ*, VII, pp. 380–2, 384–5; *The Lord Craven's Case briefly Stated* ([2 November] 1654); *To Parliament. The Petition of John Stawell ([December] 1654); Severall Proceedings of Parliament*, 2–9 November, 9–16 November, 16–25 November 1654.

[40] *Burton's Diary*, ed. Rutt, I, xlix–l; *CJ*, VII, p. 375; Bordeaux's account of the succession debate records that the subject was dropped when the House moved on to consider whale oil, thus fixing the date as 12 October, PRO 31/3/96 f.77v.

[41] Carlyle, *Cromwell's Letters and Speeches*, IV, p. 108.

[42] *Burton's Diary*, ed. Rutt, I, xx, xlvi–xlviii, lxxi–lxxiii; *CJ*, pp. 365, 371, 373, 376, 382–3, 398–9, 404, 410; Bodl., Tanner MSS 52 f. 132.

approaching harmony as it fulfilled what might be called its traditional role, that of the grand court of the nation, a forum for discussing and advising on questions of the moment, for hearing appeals, receiving petitions and redressing a wide range of grievances. On the way MPs doubtless sought to aid their friends, family and constituents and to promote the interests of their localities, but the debates and resulting legislation also reveal a genuine interest in the well-being of the nation as a whole. This picture of the First Protectorate Parliament peacefully conducting the customary business of an early modern parliament in the customary ways contrasts not only with the image of a rootless and unmanageable assembly wildly adrift in a sea of constitutional turmoil but also with the portrayal of Protector and parliament as incessant and implacable adversaries.

In September 1654 Cromwell had high hopes of the coming session, though he apparently had few concrete demands or requests to put to members as they assembled in the Painted Chamber. Much of his opening speech comprised a review and defence of the government's policies since taking office in the previous December. Particular achievements were recounted in some detail, but for the most part the Protector spoke in general terms of the order and stability created by the new regime. It had rescued the people from an inheritance of 'division and distractions', from conflict, chaos, poverty and untold evils, leading them out of Egypt, through the wilderness, towards the promised land; the ship of state had been steered from the tempest into calm waters. One further effort would 'put the top-stone to this work' and for that Cromwell turned to parliament. He made few specific requests: MPs were to continue the process of law reform, develop the continental alliances and help settle Ireland. Subsequent events indicate that he looked to members to grant money and to signify approval of his regime, to the extent at least of confirming the conciliar ordinances, senior appointments and other measures taken since December 1653; on 4 September he may also have invited the House to consider and approve the Instrument of Government.[43] In the main, however,

---

[43] It is not clear whether Cromwell's speech included such an invitation. There is nothing on these lines in the printed version of the speech which appeared in mid-September 1654, and is reprinted in Abbott, *Writings and Speeches of Oliver Cromwell*, and elsewhere. However, other contemporary sources, including *A Representation*, p. 6, and a despatch in *Thurloe State Papers*, II, p. 606, claim that the speech had closed with a specific invitation to members to examine the constitu-

Cromwell avoided specific proposals and again spoke in general terms about general requirements. No great initiatives were requested or desired, for the existing policies would continue to bring rich rewards. Parliament should simply maintain the course already set and followed by Protector and Council and confirm and continue the sagacious policies pursued since December 1653. In this way the regime would be strengthened and secured, the nation healed and settled and the people delivered to the promised land.[44]

Despite occasional conflict and ultimate failure, members went a long way towards fulfilling these requirements and, by accident or design, most of the issues raised in Cromwell's speech were considered at some point during the session. Parliament had instituted a wide-ranging examination of abuses in the legal system and the courts and reforming legislation was well advanced by the end of the session. In late September a committee was appointed with instructions to consider all existing legislation relating to Ireland, together with any other matters relating to that country felt to be in need of reform. The Bill for uniting Ireland with England, introduced and given its first reading a week before the dissolution, presumably made detailed provision for the government and administration of Ireland.[45] Parliament instituted a very thorough review of national income and expenditure, with a sub-committee to examine the accounts and personnel of all the financial offices of state, from the Treasury Commissioners downwards, followed by long debates in the House based upon the committee's final report; the results included not only the financial clauses of the new constitution but also an Assessment Bill which lowered the monthly rates by a third, a reduction accepted and implemented by Cromwell and his Council in their own assessment order issued shortly after the dissolution.[46] Cromwell's appointees to senior

---

tion. Gardiner, *Commonwealth and Protectorate*, III, p. 181 n. 1, speculates that the request was indeed made on 4 September but was omitted from the printed version of the speech ten days later because by then constitutional revision had led to chaos and purging.

[44] Abbott, *Writings and Speeches of Oliver Cromwell*, III, pp. 434–43.

[45] *CJ*, VII, pp. 371, 415.

[46] *Burton's Diary*, ed. Rutt, I, lxxvi–lxxix, lxxxiv–lxxxix, cvii, cxx–cxxii; *CJ*, VII, pp. 385, 387, 392–5, 405; *Severall Proceedings of Parliament*, 2–9, 9–16, 16–23 November 1654; copies of the report of the revenue sub-committee are at Bodl., Carte MSS 103 f. 567; BL Add. MSS 28, 854, ff. 1–10, and Stowe MSS 322, f. 76; a mass of notes made on or for the financial debates are at Bodl., Carte MSS 74; *An Order and Declaration for an Assessment of threescore thousand pounds by the moneth, for six moneths, for the maintenance of the Armies and Navies of this Commonwealth*, ([8 February] 1655).

offices of state were approved without a murmur, the preparation of
the western expedition was respectfully left to Protector and Council and the House rarely interfered with the executive's handling of
foreign policy, diplomacy and other matters.[47] Committees and
delegations of MPs attended the Protector to seek his assent to
declarations and to confer with him over religion and the reduction
of the army and demolition of garrisons.[48] Consensus and co-
operation seemed to be bringing positive results.

Nor was constitutional reform anathema to the Protector. By
autumn 1654 Cromwell was probably aware of certain defects in
the Instrument of Government and in his opening speech he may
have asked members to examine the document. Eight days later he
explicitly invited constitutional revision,[49] and thereafter his agents
in the House made no attempt to rush through acceptance of the
Instrument *in toto*. As long as certain fundamental tenets were
retained, Cromwell seems to have been quite willing for members
to rewrite the Instrument, accepting large-scale revision as the
price of obtaining a constitutional platform for his goverment
approved and endorsed by the people in parliament. Much of the
resulting Government Bill was quite unexceptionable, a schedule of
sane and sensible provisions very similar to those of the Instrument
of Government and Humble Petition and Advice, both of which
Cromwell had willingly accepted, albeit after initial hesitation. In
short, MPs made no major break with the past and after 12
September launched no sweeping attacks on the whole Protectoral
system or its work in the period preceding the parliament. By
maintaining many existing policies and by responding construc-
tively to a wide range of problems and grievances, parliament was
presumably fulfilling the principal requirement of the session as
outlined in Cromwell's speech, that of promoting healing and
settling, and of steering the ship of state towards the safe haven.

It would, however, be patently absurd to project parliament and
Protector in this light alone. There was undoubtedly a disruptive
and turbulent side to this parliament, a side which provoked the
pre-session exclusion and in-session purging of MPs, several very
heated exchanges in the Chamber indicative of deep divisions and

---

[47] *Burton's Diary*, ed. Rutt, I, xl–xli, lvii; *CJ*, VII, pp. 369, 374, 378; Bodl.,
Tanner MSS 52 ff. 130, 133, 138.

[48] *Burton's Diary*, ed. Rutt, I, lx, lxxvii–lxxx, xci–xciii; *CJ*, VII, pp. 368, 370, 373,
385, 388.

[49] Abbott, *Writings and Speeches of Oliver Cromwell*, III, pp. 458–63.

distrust, and rumours of further military intervention or a premature and unconstitutional dissolution. Above all, there was clearly
something seriously amiss with a parliament dissolved at the
earliest opportunity, before any of its legislation had reached the
Statute Book and which was dismissed with a very bitter and
condemnatory speech from the head of state. Cromwell attacked
parliament for squandering the trust and opportunity which had
been delivered to it. He had looked to parliament to bring about
'peace and settlement . . . mercy and truth . . . righteousness and
peace . . . reconciling the honest people of these nations, and
settling the woeful distempers that are amongst us'. Instead the
session had brought forth 'weeds and nettles, briers and thorns'
and fomented 'dissettlement and division, discontent and dissaf-
fection, together with real dangers to the whole'. It was, he
concluded, 'not for the profit of these nations, nor for [the] common
and public good' for the session to continue any longer.[50]
    On 4 September the Protector assured assembled MPs that he
had summoned 'a free Parliament . . . I say a free parliament'.[51]
But as members soon discovered there was a distinct limit to
Cromwell's brand of freedom. His favourite term for it was 'reciprocation'. 'I said you were a free Parliament. And so you are, whilst
you own the government and authority that called you hither. For
certainly that word implied a reciprocation, or it implied nothing at
all . . . I think your actions and carriages ought to be suitable.'[52] In
other words, parliament had to respect the system of government
under which it met and could not undo the foundations of the
existing constitution. The crucial tenets of the constitution, the
so-called 'fundamentals', were inviolable and beyond negotiation
or reformation. It was the election of a number of implacable
opponents of the whole edifice of Protectoral government, constitutional fundamentals included, which provoked serious disruption
at the opening of the session. Although a dozen former royalists and
other undesirables were excluded from the outset, the Council
initially admitted a larger group of outspoken opponents, usually
labelled 'republicans'. Under the leadership of Hesilrig, Bradshaw
and Scott, they proceeded during the first week of the session to
launch a full-scale assault upon the foundations of the Protectorate.

---

[50] Ibid., pp. 579–93.
[51] Ibid., p. 440.
[52] Ibid., pp. 451–2.

In response, Cromwell had the military temporarily close the House on 12 September and imposed a written test upon Members, a pledge of loyalty to the constitution. Somewhere between seventy and ninety forthright opponents of the regime felt unable to sign the Recognition and in consequence were barred for the remainder of the session.

Four and a half months later, Cromwell referred to the imposition of the Recognition as an 'abatement of my hopes, though not a total frustration', for members had had 'another opportunity renewed unto you to have made this nation . . . happy'.[53] By January 1655, however, he was certain that the hopes and opportunities had been irreparably shattered and that the session should be ended. His dissolution speech was a rather vague and rambling affair, with accusations of parliament's misdeeds interspersed with long accounts of plots against the government and repeated expositions of divine support and sanction for the regime. Cromwell condemned the parliament in a judgement which, though both unfair and inaccurate, has become the standard verdict: that the parliament had squandered its peaceful and hopeful inheritance by devoting itself solely to 'destructive and violent' constitutional reform, to the exclusion of all other business, thus neglecting its principal duty of making 'those good and wholesome laws which the people expected from you, and might have answered the grievances . . . proper to you as a Parliament.' Healing and settling had given way to briars and thorns.

Cromwell heaped praise upon the Instrument of Government and, although he again expressed a willingness to consider constitutional amendments, he condemned the Government Bill as unacceptable on several counts. The religious clauses, together with other parliamentary actions, seemed to herald a narrowing of toleration, replacing the broad religious freedom under which 'all species of Protestants' could 'worship God according to their own light and consciences', with intolerance and persecution, encouraging people to 'put their fingers upon their brethren's consciences, to pinch them there'. The other unpalatable aspects of the Government Bill were not reviewed with such clarity or detail. Cromwell made a brief and passing reference to command of the armed forces, stressing the necessity of the Single Person retaining permanent joint control and implying that no reductions in the size or

[53] Ibid., p. 580.

costs of the standing forces were possible under the existing conditions of war and disorder. The speech closed with a longer and very
bitter attack upon parliament's failure to make adequate financial
provision for the army, thereby provoking serious danger and
unrest in military circles.[54] Despite the often vague and inconclusive nature of Cromwell's accusations, it is quite clear that parliament and its Government Bill foundered upon the twin rocks of
finance and the army.

There had been heated exchanges during the session over certain
aspects of the new constitution, including the extent of the Protector's veto, his power to make peace and war, the elective or
hereditary nature of the Protectorship and the source of that
election; the vaguely worded religious clauses and parliament's
harsh treatment of certain religious enthusiasts together resur-
rected the spectre of intolerance and persecution; and kingship
briefly raised its disruptive head. But it was when MPs set about
reducing the size and cost of the standing forces and rashly
attempted to gain future control over the military that the whole
edifice collapsed. Parliament called for an army of 30,000 men, all
but halving the existing forces, and set a military budget barely
adequate to support that number. Moreover, although Cromwell
was given joint command of the standing forces for life, members
voted that after his death sole control was to pass to parliament,
which would then dispose of military command as it 'shall think
fit'. Even Cromwell's lifetime joint control was effectively under-
mined, for the annual military budget was to extend only until
December 1659, after which Cromwell, if still alive, would have to
apply to parliament for a renewed grant. Frantic and repeated
attempts by Cromwell's supporters to have the military budget
reconsidered and to add amendments assuring the present and
future Protectors' permanent joint control over the standing forces
and local militias were to no avail. Instead the situation worsened;
on 18 January the House appointed a committee to prepare to pay
off and disband all supernumerary troops over and above the
30,000 and on the 20th a proviso was added to the constitution
giving parliament permanent and sole control over the local militias. Within forty-eight hours the session was at an end.[55]

Finally, what of the tale of party conflict and mismanagement

---

[54] Ibid., pp. 579–93.
[55] Gardiner, *Constitutional Documents*, pp. 444–7; *CJ*, VII, pp. 418–21.

recounted by Trevor-Roper and others?[56] Certainly, factions of
sorts could appear within the Chamber. When crucial issues, such
as the 'fundamentals' and other vital provisions of the new constitution came before the House, the interests of Cromwell and of
the existing Protectoral government were represented and defended
by a particular body of MPs. Identified and occasionally described
by Goddard and others, the 'courtiers' or 'court party' comprised a
coalition of Councillors, civilian and military office-holders and
friends and kinsmen of the Protector.[57] Equally, parliament contained many opponents of the Protectoral system, both the so-
called republicans who attempted to destroy the entire regime
during the first week of the session, and other more moderate critics
of certain aspects of the Instrument – chiefly the powers of the
executive and the size, cost and command of the armed forces –
who came to the fore thereafter. From the meagre evidence that
survives – usually little more than the names of tellers in formal
divisions – it is possible tentatively to identify those who were
prominent or conspicuous on each side: for the existing constitution, Lord Broghill, Philip Jones and Sir Charles Wolseley;[58] for
wholesale destruction of the regime, John Bradshaw, Sir Arthur
Hesilrig and Thomas Scott; for more moderate, though often
extensive, amendment to the constitution, John Birch, John Bulkeley, Sir Ralph Hare and Sir Richard Onslow.

It seems most unlikely, however, that these people led consistent
or coherent parties of any sort. Both personnel and policies were
constantly shifting and alliances surfaced only briefly and uncer-
tainly amid the ebb and flow of interests and the kaleidoscope of
issues. The government had neither a comprehensive programme
of legislative or constitutional reform to introduce, nor a permanent
party within the House to manage the session and to guide it along
a predetermined path. Although the courtiers could work together,
from time to time they found themselves divided and counting for
different sides, even when quite important provisions of the constitution were at stake. Similarly, although many aspects of the

[56] Trevor-Roper, 'Cromwell and his parliaments', pp. 31–5.

[57] *Burton's Diary*, ed. Rutt, I, passim; *A Representation*, passim; *The Protector (So
Called) In Part Unvailed* ([24 October] 1656), p. 21.

[58] This list differs from the account of government 'champions' given by
Trevor-Roper in 'Cromwell and his parliaments', pp. 33–5. In particular, I can
find no firm evidence to support the portrayal of Ashley Cooper as either a leading
government supporter or chief mediator in the House.

regime suffered frequent and vociferous attack, there was no united or long-standing opposition party or grouping. The names of tellers make clear that loyalties were often shallow and shortlived, with members who worked together in one division opposing each other in the next. Ashley Cooper's evolution from loyal Protectoral Councillor, to critic of the constitution in 1654–5, to excludee in 1656, was merely the most dramatic and visible example of a vacillation common to many Protectoral politicians. In such circumstances, the term 'courtier' should be employed with great caution, and 'country', 'Independent' and 'Presbyterian' are better avoided altogether as labels for the political alignments of individual members or groups of MPs. Above all, for much of the session parliament was handling business which produced few serious divisions and which did little to disturb the relative harmony common after 12 September. The discussion of petitions and privileges and the deliberation of public and private legislation provoked many sharp words or heated exchanges, but only occasionally gave rise to major or long-lasting conflicts of interest or to bitter power struggles for control of the House. In a Chamber of fleeting divisions and constantly shifting issues and in which something approaching harmony was the norm, well-organized and antagonistic parties, high-level political management and bitter scrambling for the front benches were naturally absent.

'If a history shall be written of these times and of transactions, it will be said (it will not be denied,) but that these things that I have spoken are true.'[59] Historians have indeed endorsed and restated Cromwell's scathing condemnation of the parliament delivered in his dissolution speech: that it had passed a wasteful and futile session devoted solely to destructive and divisive constitutional reform and had thereby ignored the needs of the people and the nation and failed in its principal duty of making 'good and wholesome laws'. It is easy to understand why the Protector presented such distortions in January 1655 – it was far safer to condemn the entire session in the sweeping and vague tones of half truth than to detail the precise grounds for his discontent, since that would involve describing and defending several dubious elements of the existing regime, namely the origins of the Instrument, the extensive Protectoral powers and, above all, the ominous presence of a very large and expensive standing army. Not so explicable is the willing-

[59] Abbott, *Writings and Speeches of Oliver Cromwell*, III, p. 580.

ness of generations of historians to accept and unreservedly repeat this bleak and inaccurate assessment – some, like Carlyle, adding colourful and excessive embellishments of their own, others, like Trevor-Roper, converting Cromwell's theme of incessant conflict into an account of party struggle and mismanagement. Whilst all these images contain an element of truth, they ignore, exaggerate and misinterpret to such a degree that the final picture is an unacceptable travesty of the whole. Certainly, much of the session was given over to constitutional reform, a process which provoked several bitter debates and deep divisions and which ended with a document unacceptable to Cromwell and an abrupt and angry dissolution. But members handled a mass of other business, from the highest affairs of state to issues of local or private concern, they heard grievances, examined a wide range of subjects and promoted a broad and extensive programme of public and private legislation, thus meeting not only the needs of the people and nation but also many of the requirements stated or implied in the Protector's opening speech. Moreover, much of this work, constitutional reform included, was undertaken and advanced in a spirit of co-operation and consensus. Against the image of constitutional conflict, chaos and rootlessness should be placed one of a parliament peacefully conducting the customary business of an early modern assembly in the customary ways. A parliament hardly worth naming, and to be forgotten by all creatures? The First Protectorate Parliament deserves far better.

Oliver Cromwell and the Localities: the Problem of Consent

ANTHONY FLETCHER

Historians have long recognized that the regime of Oliver Cromwell involved a particular kind of minority rule. Some have labelled it the rule 'of the saints' or 'of the godly'.[1] What matters in such a case, G. E. Aylmer remarked in his introduction to a set of essays on the Interregnum published in 1972, was 'not the size of the minority, but its morale and coherence and the degree of acceptance accorded it by the rest of the population'.[2] Surprisingly little work has appeared since Aylmer's essays on the nature and impact of the Cromwellian regime. There have been two PhD theses on the army and Cromwellian politics and administration and there is work in progress on the well-documented 1656 elections.[3] But the full studies we need of the enforcement of Cromwellian government and of the acceptability of the Protector's rule in the provinces remain to be written. All that will be attempted in this essay is a brief reassessment, as a pointer to the larger problem of consent, of one aspect of Cromwell's rule: the experiment of sending out the major-generals.[4]

It is worth emphasizing at the start how short-lived the major-generals scheme turned out to be. They went down into the

[1] For example, A. Woolrych in *The English Civil War and After* ed. R. Parry (London, 1970), pp. 59–77.

[2] G. E. Aylmer (ed.), *The Interregnum: The quest for Settlement, 1646–60* (London, 1972), pp. 27–8.

[3] D. P. Massarella, 'The politics of the army, 1647–60', University of York PhD thesis, 1977; H. M. Reece, 'The military presence in England 1649–60', University of Oxford DPhil thesis, 1981.

[4] For previous account of the scheme see I. Roots, 'Swordsmen and decimators' in Parry, *English Civil War and After*, pp. 78–92, and D. W. Rannie, 'Cromwell's major-generals', *English Historical Review*, X (1895).

counties in October 1655 and gave sustained attention to their duties for about six months.[5] Thereafter their engagement seems to have been generally more erratic. They were all in London on 21 May 1656 following a summons from the Protector to gather there, ostensibly for a review of their work. The meetings that were held developed into a wrangle over the financial crisis of the regime from which the major-generals emerged triumphant, persuading Cromwell to call a parliament to obtain money. The major-generals returned to their districts to manage the elections in late June or July,[6] but they were back in London for the parliament in September. It is difficult to be certain how far the major-generals were actively concerning themselves in local government during the spring and summer of 1656. It should not be assumed that, because their spate of letters to John Thurloe slackens after a series of reports on the Lent assizes in March, those who no longer wrote were relaxing their efforts. Some at least were still indefatigable. James Berry reported on 26 April that he was 'going his circuit once more'; Charles Worsley told Thurloe, in a letter of 29 April, that he had held meetings at Preston the previous week from Tuesday till Saturday.[7] The Cheshire gentleman,Thomas Mainwaring, noted in his diary that he attended a meeting of the commissioners there, sitting under Worsley's chairmanship, in the second week of every month from November 1655 until June 1656.[8] Unfortunately this kind of specific evidence about meetings is exceptional. But the very real practical difficulties that the major-generals were encountering by the spring of 1656 in keeping their troops in harness must certainly have distracted them from day-to-day matters. William Goffe, forced to dismiss Colonel Busbridge's troop in Sussex in March for lack of funds, found himself involved in angry exchanges with Busbridge and his men.[9] Berry and Worsley were others who were having to deal with reductions in their militia troops around that time.[10] So far as the autumn of 1656 is concerned, the fact that the decimation tax was still then being levied in a number of counties and that major-generals were

---

[5] *Thurloe State Papers*, IV, passim.

[6] Massarella, 'Politics of the army', pp. 435–6.

[7] *Thurloe State Papers*, IV, pp. 742, 746.

[8] J. S. Morrill, *Cheshire 1630–60* (Oxford, 1974), p. 284.

[9] A. J. Fletcher, *A County Community in Peace and War: Sussex 1600–60* (London, 1975), p. 306.

[10] *Thurloe State Papers*, IV, p. 742; Morrill, *Cheshire*, p. 278.

signing warrants for arrears of pay does not of course mean that their oversight of the provinces remained an effective reality.[11] The scheme had clearly collapsed in most areas several months before the vote on 29 January 1657 which, by rejecting the decimation tax, deprived the major-generals of the financial basis of their administration.[12]

'We have at last settled the major-generals all over England,' wrote Thurloe to Henry Cromwell in Ireland on 16 October 1655, 'the greatest creation of honours his highness hath made since his access to the government'. Listing the appointments, he went on to summarize the long and detailed instructions with which the chosen men had been sent out in a succinct statement: 'these are to command the forces within their several precincts and to see to the good government thereof.'[13] So what advantages and disadvantages did the major-generals take with them as they rode down into the shires? Their biggest handicap undoubtedly was that they were outsiders, not in the sense of birth, for most of them hailed from the areas to which they were directed, but in the sense that they did not have a purchase upon power in the districts it was intended they should rule. How far they came from mean social backgrounds can be disputed. If Thomas Kelsey is said to have been a button-maker and James Berry had served as a clerk in a Shropshire ironworks, William Boteler was educated at Oundle and Hezekiah Haynes came of an Essex family of minor gentry.[14] What mattered was that these men's names were not names that counted in the circles of those who by tradition and prescriptive right saw it as their responsibility to govern in the counties concerned. Their qualification was service, not status. They were military careerists who had risen to prominence by their vigour and commitment to the parliamentarian cause. Only William Boteler had never commanded a regiment of his own, but he could offer valuable civilian experience as a JP and government agent during the early 1650s in Northamptonshire and Bristol. Several others – Thomas Kelsey, William Goffe, John Barkstead and Charles Worsley – had been active in army administration. Berry, it was alleged, helped John Lambert

---

[11] For example, A. Everitt, *The Community of Kent and the Great Rebellion* (Leicester, 1966), pp. 293–4; Fletcher, *A County Community*, p. 306.

[12] C. H. Firth, *The Last Years of the Protectorate* (London, 1909), I, p. 125.

[13] *Thurloe State Papers*, IV, p. 88.

[14] Parry, *English Civil War and After*, pp. 83, 91; W. L. F. Nuttall, 'Hezekiah Haynes', *Transactions of the Essex Archaeological Society*, 1 (1964), p. 196.

draw up the Instrument of Government.[15] Above all, these men were Cromwell's men. That is, they identified themselves with him, trusted him, leaned upon him. 'The Lord give me a heart to answer his goodness towards me and make me able to answer the expectations of his highness and council,' wrote Kelsey on 20 November 1655. A few days later Berry asked Thurloe to tell the Protector that though his business was 'toilsome and tedious to me, and indeed somewhat chargeable', yet he would 'go on with comfort and confidence, hoping for the assistance of God and his highness acceptation'.[16]

The major-generals' sense of urgency, based on the knowledge that they were serving a demanding and expectant master, was reinforced by their intense faith. They shared Cromwell's zeal, his belief in God's mission for England as a protestant nation, his conviction that providence led the godly on.[17] There is perhaps no better insight into their mentality than Berry's account of his conciliatory talk with the Welsh Fifth Monarchist Vavasour Powell:

I told him with what confidence I came forth in this work, as sent of God: and that my heart had been towards those poor people in Wales, and particularly I did expect help and encouragement from him and his people and did not doubt that we should come to a right understanding of each other and I should prove useful to them for the obtaining of much good.[18]

Yet for all this general unanimity of purpose, the major-generals were a heterogeneous collection of men, differing in their politics and temperaments. Ivan Roots has noted how strikingly this appears from the record of their contributions to the parliamentary debates on the punishment of the Quaker James Nayler.[19] Out in the provinces, faced with the tangles and thickets of local politics, some proved of stronger mettle than others. Nothing daunted Charles Worsley or Edward Whalley, but William Goffe at times

[15] Massarella, 'Politics of the army', pp. 427–9; P. H. Hardacre, William Boteler: a Cromwellian oligarch', *Huntington Library Quarterly*, 1 (1947), p. 4.

[16] *Thurloe State Papers*, IV, pp. 225, 237.

[17] A. J. Fletcher, 'The religious motivation of Cromwell's major-generals', in *Religious Motivation: Biographical and sociological problems for the church historian*, ed. D. Baker, Studies in Church History, XV (1978).

[18] *Thurloe State Papers*, IV, p. 228.

[19] Parry (ed.), *English Civil War and After*, p. 83.

became pathetic. He was too weak for 'this difficult affair'; he was a 'poor and inconsiderable creature'; he was 'in many respects unworthy of the employment'. The unnerving aspect of a major-general's task, the testing of men's reactions with which the work had to begin, comes into clear focus with Goffe's heartfelt comment from Chichester on 13 November: 'I do not know the hearts of men but I thank God I have not wanted the civil respects of all sorts of persons with whom yet I have had to do'.[20]

There must have been a good deal of trepidation, both in London and in the minds of the major-generals themselves, as they arranged their first meetings to call in royalist or allegedly royalist gentry in order to receive particulars of their estates as a basis for imposing the decimation tax. This, after all, was a fiscal expedient of a designedly political nature which was bound to seem provocative to enemies of the Cromwellian regime. It could be expected to open old wounds in local society. Several of the major-generals seem to have found considerable encouragement in the first stage of their work in the deference and quietness with which cavaliers submitted to their demands. 'Our business goes on very well,' declared Edward Whalley on 14 November, after a busy session with Lincolnshire royalists. Goffe was evidently pleasantly surprised that Sir William Morley, who insisted that he took it very much to heart that he should be still reckoned malignant 'having long been satisfied of the justness of our cause', had nevertheless consented to be taxed for an estate of £1,500 per annum. Haynes was delighted how smoothly things had gone in Norfolk:

such acceptance had this affair in the hearts of all that it carried its conviction with it, honest men encouraging one another in the action and the delinquent not one word to say why ought should be remitted him: that every tongue must confess it was of the Lord, who is a righteous God in the execution of his judgements and when his hand is lifted up he shall not only make them (though most unwilling) to see but also make them ashamed for their envy to his people.[21]

Another constant refrain in the first reports to London was the encouragement the major-generals found in the energy and enthu-

---

[20] *Thurloe State Papers*, IV, pp. 151, 190, 752; V, p. 151; Fletcher, *A County Community*, p. 307.

[21] *Thurloe State Papers*, IV, pp. 197, 208, 216. For the political career of Sir William Morley see Fletcher, *A County Community*, pp. 240, 258, 266, 278.

siasm of their commissioners and militia officers. Worsley was
perhaps the most ecstatic, writing as follows from Manchester on 3
November: 'truly I find a spirit extraordinarily bent to the work
and plainly discern the finger of God going along with it.' Haynes
found the Norfolk commissioners 'exceeding real and forward'
about the Protector's policies. William Boteler, arriving at Bedford,
was met by 'no less than a jury of them at my alighting from my
horse' who at once expressed and quickly showed readiness in
getting down to work.[22] Berry found the Worcestershire commissioners equally energetic. Kelsey reported an attendance of almost
twenty commissioners at Maidstone, 'all unanimously very hearty
and cordial to the work'. Robert Lilborne attained an even larger
attendance at York on 14 December, when the commissioners 'put
things into as ready a method as could be'.[23] It is evident that
almost everywhere there were small groups of militant Puritans
ready to undertake the Cromwellian programme. These, in the
major-generals' terminology, were the 'good people', 'the best of
the people', the 'people of God'.[24]

When, as in some cases they did, the commissioners themselves
wrote to Thurloe or even Cromwell himself about their task they
revealed themselves in their full colours. The Norfolk commissioners were happy to:

promote so good and just a work as the making of a discrimination betwixt
the innocent and the guilty, thereby also to provide a necessary revenue
for the securing, under God, the cause of God and the good people of this
commonwealth in the peaceable enjoyment of their dear and dearly
bought liberties so much envied at by that generation of men.

Sir Thomas Barnardiston, Haynes related, penned the letter from
the Suffolk commissioners which is redolent of the same parti-
sanship. It came well from the son of the great Puritan patriarch of
the county, Sir Nathaniel Barnardiston of Kedington. Nothing was
more equal, it asserted, than that those 'who by their restless
turbulency do create new troubles and disquiet to the commonwealth' should bear the charge themselves: 'we do pray that as the
Lord hath been able to make use of your highness as the instrument
of our deliverance from that implacable generation of men, so that

[22] *Thurloe State Papers*, IV, pp. 149, 171, 207.
[23] Ibid., IV, pp. 215, 224, 321.
[24] Ibid., IV, pp. 179, 187, 324.

he will be pleased to use your highness as the instrument of our preservation and further reformation'.[25] The Essex commissioners approved the new measures for 'restraining the power of that irreconcilable interest'. The Gloucestershire ones spoke bitterly of the 'inveterate and implacable malice of the late King's party', who sought 'upon all occasions to involve the nation in a continuous deluge of blood'. They gave their blessing to a work to secure the well-affected, 'whom God hath owned and stood by the day of their distress'.[26] The ideological conflict at the heart of Cromwellian politics is inescapable in these missives.

It seems likely that the instructions with regard to administrative and moral reform owed much to Cromwell himself. The major-generals were to 'inform themselves of all such idle and loose people that are within their counties who have no visible way of livelihood, nor calling or employment' and see them set to work; to ensure that the genuinely needy were provided for; to 'encourage and promote godliness and virtue and discourage and discountenance all pro-faneness and ungodliness' by seeing to the execution of the laws against 'drunkenness, blaspheming and taking the name of God in vain, by swearing and cursing, plays and interludes and profaning the Lord's Day and such like wickedness and abominations'; and to regulate alehouses, suppressing all of them except those that were 'necessary and convenient to travellers'.[27] Leaving aside the other major topics in the programme – security and decimation – these demands in themselves amounted to a massive task. Suddenly and decisively Cromwell's agents were expected to shake the processes of local government into life, not in one county at a time, which in itself would be difficult enough, but simultaneously in two, three or more shires. They knew what was expected of them. So, from the moment they left London and started writing in to Thurloe, there was the danger that those who read their letters at Cromwell's court would cherish a false view of how much was being achieved. For the major-generals were bound to want to please, to relay their little victories, to leave aside the question of what happened to their new brooms when they left town, as they always did very quickly because they were men constantly on the move. John Thurloe's huge correspondence, now preserved in the Bodleian Library and

[25] Ibid., IV, pp. 131, 225, 227; for Sir Nathaniel Barnardiston see P. Collinson, *The Religion of Protestants* (Oxford, 1982), pp. 164, 181, 273.

[26] *Thurloe State Papers*, IV, pp. 317, 354.

[27] J. P. Kenyon, *The Stuart Constitution* (Cambridge, 1966), pp. 349–50.

largely available in print, is a marvellously rich source of information about the major-generals experiment but every sentence in it
has to be interpreted with care if it is to be made to yield a balanced
assessment of their achievement.

Cromwell's speech to the mayor and corporation of the City of
London on 5 March 1656 shows how determined he was about
reforming local government. There were many and good laws, he
announced, 'yet we have lived rather under the name and notion of
law than under the thing, so that 'tis resolved to regulate the same
(God assisting) oppose who will'. He returned to this theme in
September 1656 when he opened the new parliament, naming the
lax execution and administration of the law as the 'general grievance in the nation'. He did so once more in a speech to a
committee of MPs on 20 April 1657, when he urged them to
consider how the good laws on the statute books against 'the
common country disorders that are everywhere' might be properly
implemented. This was the occasion when he revealed the full
extent of his scepticism about the vigour of the magistracy: 'really a
justice of peace shall from the most be wondered at as an owl if he
go but one step out of the ordinary course of his fellow justices in
the reformation of these things'. So much did Cromwell care about
the 'reformation of manners' that he could not help taking an
optimistic view of the progress of the major-generals in this respect.
Their letters fed his enthusiasm, leading him into something of a
fool's paradise. Hence his dramatized picture, in the March 1656
speech, of the major-generals driving all those who were idle and
vagrant from the shires towards London. The City was a place
known to give 'shelter to many such idle, loose persons', he
reminded the aldermen, but Major-General Skippon and those
commissioned with him were ready to deal as severely with them in
the capital as his colleagues had done in the localities. Hence also
his exaggerated claim in September 1656 that the experiment had
been 'more effectual towards the discountenancing of vice and
settling religion than anything done these fifty years'.

How exaggerated was that claim? What did the major-generals
actually do during their brief interventions in the shires they
commanded to reform government, to improve the enforcement of
the poor laws and the moral code on the statute book? One way of

---

[28] W. C. Abbott (ed.), *The Writings and Speeches of Oliver Cromwell* (4 vols,
Cambridge, Mass., 1937–47), IV, pp. 112, 274, 494.

approaching this question, although we have noted its difficulties, is to consider what they themselves boasted about or harped upon. The overall impression left by the letters to Secretary Thurloe is that much more time was devoted to extracting the decimation tax from royalist gentry and to security in all its aspects than to mundane aspects of government. Yet it quickly becomes obvious, once the record offered by individual major-generals about their performance in particular counties is compared, that will and interest led each man in his own direction. Goffe, preoccupied with attempting to establish working relationships with local gentry and to check disaffection, made no mention at all of administrative matters in more than twenty letters from Sussex.[29] Worsley, by contrast, writing less often, hardly ever omitted them from his Cheshire reports. One of his first actions was to insist upon proclamations in the market towns against drunkenness and pro-faneness, accompanied by searches of the streets at night by the constables. In January 1656 he was able to announce that alehouse regulation was in hand: within a month nearly 200 alehouses had been closed in the county. He and his commissioners also gave attention to brewers and maltsters, ensuring that they gave sureties not to sell to unlicensed persons. They imprisoned a number of people who had been living together after a church wedding but without having gone through the civil marriage procedure estab-lished in 1653. They also sent to the house of correction 'many suspicious idle and loose persons, some whereof to continue till they give very good sureties for their good bearing for the time to come'.[30] This much can be gleaned from *Thurloe State Papers* alone. When we also bring the Quarter Sessions papers into play, as John Morrill has done in his study of Cheshire, the contrast between Worsley's attention to government there and Goffe's total neglect of it in Sussex becomes even more striking. The Cheshire files are full of pitiful appeals from men deprived of their livelihood by the selling of ale. One in particular from Robert Bulkeley, whose neighbours supported his plea that he had kept an alehouse with-out every being accused of allowing disorder for twenty years, confirms the harshness of the 1656 purge. More interesting than this, because it received no mention in the letters to Thurloe, are the scraps of information about Worsley's scheme to check vagrancy

[29] Fletcher, *A County Community*, pp. 302–10.
[30] *Thurloe State Papers*, IV, pp. 247–8, 473, 522–3.

at the county borders by penalizing townships there which let
wanderers enter the shire. The constables of Warburton, for example, found themselves being ordered to pay twelve pence a head for
certain vagrants who, it was alleged, had crossed the boundary into
their parish.[31]

Something then could be achieved, at least temporarily, as
Worsley's performance shows, through the co-operation of a
zealous group of commissioners. But what was really critical, in
order to impose a general reinvigoration of local government, was
personal attendance at sessions and a satisfactory working relationship with the county bench. Patchy survival of sessions records
makes it impossible to determine how many of the major-generals
ever did attend sessions in at least one of their counties. At
Epiphany or Easter 1656 they had the chance to do so, but of
course they could not be in several places at the same time. Not
that it was easy for any of them to make a sudden impact if and
when they did sit. The magistracy was generally slow to be moved:
campaigns and policy changes arose from a gradually emerging
consensus or from changing contingencies rather than from readiness to respond to the intervention of a government inspector. John
Desborough sat regularly on the Devon bench for much of the
1650s but his role in magisterial policy-making there appears to
have been slight.[32] John Barkstead was one of the most active and
conscientious of the Middlesex justices from 1652 until 1658 but his
impact at Midsummer 1656 was hardly impressive, although one
would suppose this to be the height of a reform campaign if one was
initiated by the major-generals. The number of recognizances for
moral offences taken for this Middlesex sessions was certainly a
good deal higher than at the same sessions in 1652. Barkstead took
some of them himself. The sin and vice of the Long Acre and
Covent Garden district was under attack: seventy-five persons were
ordered to appear for drunkenness, swearing, profanation of the
sabbath, prostitution, keeping disorderly alehouses, keeping
brothels, unlawful games, bigamy and fornication. But Barkstead's
role in all this must be put into perspective. Over nine per cent of
recognizances taken at the Midsummer sessions in 1642 had been
for moral offences, and eleven per cent had come into this category

[31] Morrill, *Cheshire*, p. 283.
[32] S. K. Roberts, *Recovery and Restoration in an English County: Devon local administration, 1646-70* (Exeter, 1985), pp. 49-51, 82-7.

in 1652. Eleven per cent would do so again in 1661. The struggle against sin in the Middlesex jurisdiction was endemic. It owed little to Major-General Barkstead. Moreover there were other counties, like Staffordshire and Sussex, where full documentation reveals conclusively that there was no reform campaign at all in 1655 or 1656.[33]

There were occasions when a major-general's chivvying had a material effect at sessions or assizes. General orders about alehouse licensing issued in Hertfordshire and Norfolk can be related to the presence of Tobias Bridge and Hezekiah Haynes respectively. In both cases there was an insistence that the man licensed should be 'well affected to the present government' as well as, more conventionally, 'of an honest life'.[34] Edward Whalley was deeply involved in the management of the grand jury presentments of the 1656 Lent assizes in all the counties of his charge. He settled an enclosure dispute in Leicestershire at the assizes there on terms which, he told Thurloe, he hoped meant that 'God will not be provoked, the poor not wronged, depopulation prevented and the state not damnified'.[35]

By and large, though, there was probably a better chance of achieving higher standards of government on a lasting basis through appointments and procedural reforms than through direct personal initiatives with regard to policy. The crucial issues were the quality of justices, juries and constables. Worsley was quick to notice the inadequacy of the Cheshire, Lancashire and Staffordshire magistracies. 'Upon my observation of the condition of these counties', he wrote on 3 December 1655, he was struck by 'the want of good justices of the peace . . . both as to the condition of some already in and also for the number of them which was very small'. He promised to send up nominations but then twice in the following weeks apologized for his failure to do so. It did not prove easy finding suitable men. But Worsley had put his finger on the necessity of doing so in a letter of 14 December. Moral reform depended upon a firm and reliable lead from the top of county society. He found several constables, he explained, 'that are honest who are doubtful of what power they have and how far they may proceed of themselves in punishing sin'. 'The law is very dark in

[33] J. Mather, 'The moral code of the English Civil War and Interregnum', *The Historian*, 64 (1982), pp. 222–5.

[34] G. E. Aylmer, *The State's Servants* (London, 1973), pp. 313–14.

[35] *Thurloe State Papers*, IV, p. 686.

that,' he declared: these constables had informed him how difficult it was to find justices that 'will encourage them in that work'. Whalley faced the same problem in Coventry and Lincoln where, his allies told him, 'wicked magistrates, by reason of their number, overpower the godly magistrates'. Alehouses were no sooner suppressed than a more lenient justice set them up again. Berry was similarly balked in Wales: 'reformation', he sighed in a letter from Wrexham on 21 December 1655, 'hath many enemies and indeed here wants matter.'[36] The situation in the 1650s was no different from what it had been in the 1580s or 1620s: the godly had always been and were still a minority among the country gentry.[37] In this sense, even if they had been given longer to achieve their aims, the major-generals were fighting a losing battle. Those, like Desborough and Goffe, who did make a number of nominations to the bench, were not necessarily reinforcing the campaign for moral reform. Goffe certainly was shamelessly lobbied by men who wanted to sit on the bench for much more traditional reasons than creating the New Jerusalem.[38]

Jury reform was a problem which had received periodic attention from the Council and judges over the previous fifty years.[39] Cromwell took the matter up after an initiative by a group of Devon justices in April 1655. They planned to make jury service the duty of a reduced body of freeholders, chosen and supervised by the JPs rather than the sheriff. The scheme did not get off the ground in Devon until the following summer when the twelve men on the Midsummer sessions trial jury were newcomers who, unusually, came from a wide area rather than from the hundreds nearest to Exeter. The JPs on this occasion had obviously gone to a good deal of trouble to ensure a jury of approved men.[40] But the major-general in the west, John Desborough, had no part in their proceedings. Indeed he was sceptical, in a letter to Thurloe of 4 February 1656, about the practicability of any kind of jury reform.[41] The Protector, pressed to do so it seems from Devon, was at that time attempting to extend the Devon scheme to the nation as a whole. In

[36] Ibid., IV, pp. 273, 277–8, 315, 334, 473, 485.
[37] Collinson, *Religion of Protestants*, pp. 141–88; J. T. Cliffe, *The Puritan Gentry* (London, 1984), pp. 43–62.
[38] *Thurloe State Papers*, IV, pp. 353, 520; Fletcher, *A County Community*, p. 308.
[39] A. J. Fletcher, *Reform in the Provinces* (London, 1986), pp. 117–20.
[40] S. K. Roberts, 'Initiative and control: the Devon Quarter Sessions Grand Jury 1649–70', *Bulletin of the Institute of Historical Research*, 57 (1984), pp. 169–71.
[41] *Thurloe State Papers*, IV, p. 501.

a letter to all the major-generals of 29 January, he had instructed them to ensure that JPs selected men of 'clearest integrity and prudence, of honest and blameless conversation' from the freeholders books for jury service at the forthcoming assizes.[42] This instruction received a mixed reception. Whalley on the one hand doubted, by the time he had contacted the justices of his counties in early February, whether it was practical to rectify the juries before the sheriffs acted 'in the old way and course'. Worsley, on the other, reported that his commissioners in Cheshire, Lancashire and Staffordshire welcomed the plan and had agreed lists of 'honest judicious freeholders for this year'.[43] The Devon initiative for reform evidently had some impetus because it was pursued on and off until 1664. Elsewhere revision of the freeholders books in the 1650s probably proved as short-lived as it had previously been.

The key officers in the day-to-day conduct of local government were the high constables, who co-ordinated business in each hundred, and the petty constables, who were responsible for reporting village defaults. Their efficiency, or their lack of it, in the last resort determined the tempo of government: they were men who needed to be constantly watched, instructed and chivvied. Several of the major-generals grasped this point but none of them perhaps did so as fully as Charles Worsley who, copying widespread magisterial practice earlier in the century, issued articles to the Cheshire constables.[44] A list of specific questions about their duties which had to be answered one by one was the only effective way to preclude the constable's resort to the customary *omnia bene*.[45] There is evidence that the Cheshire bench was particularly eager to enhance the role of high constables in the 1650s, giving them fresh duties and a new freedom of action.[46] This may explain the readiness that Worsley found there to replace unsuitable constables with 'honest, faithful and judicious men'. It was his sabbatarian zeal which first alerted his interest in the quality of local officers. For he discovered soon after he set to work that in a number of the towns of his district the weekly market was held on Saturday or Monday. The result was that either men spent the sabbath suffering the effects of a long night in the alehouse or they had to travel

[42] Abbott, *Writings and Speeches of Oliver Cromwell*, IV, pp. 87–8.
[43] *Thurloe State Papers*, IV, pp. 511, 534.
[44] Morrill, *Cheshire*, p. 285.
[45] Fletcher, *Reform in the Provinces*, p. 137–42.
[46] Morrill, *Cheshire*, pp. 238–9.

on Sunday to get to market the next day. In many cases, Worsley found, the parish constables, far from setting an example, were themselves the worst offenders, being 'the meanest sort of men' who served the office by rota from house to house along the village street.[47]

Taken as a whole the major-generals' achievement in reforming local government appears to have been minimal. This conclusion is the more convincing when their efforts in any particular sphere are seen in the perspective of the Interregnum decades or of the whole century. Reform in the seventeenth century was always an erratic process, a matter of stabs at problems pursued with varying degrees of energy according to the inclinations of one group of magistrates or another. Cromwell in 1655 and 1656 was no more able than Charles I had been with his *Book of Orders* in 1631 to obviate the independence of the country gentry.[48] Not that he and they were at odds about the basic desiderata for order. It is important to stress that there was a considerable degree of moral consensus among the magistracy and between the magistracy and the central government. Where the Protector differed from many of the provincial JPs was in his sense of urgency. Richard Baxter touched the heart of the problem of enforcement in a letter of advice about the new parliament of 1656 to Sir Edward Harley. 'It will never be well', he wrote, 'till we have either more zealous justices than most are or else there be greater penalties on magistrates and constables for neglect of their duty'.[49]

The hazards of reading more into the major-generals' reports than is warrantable are well illustrated by the case of Robert Beake, the mayor of Coventry in the year that Edward Whalley was active in Warwickshire. Spending a few days in the city in late November 1655, Whalley got to know Beake quite well. After an initial misunderstanding about the mayor's stance, his assessment was that Beake was 'zealous for the present government', the constitutional basis of which, Beake had assured him, he had carefully studied. 'There is none here', he wrote 'I am confident will be more faithful to his highness, none I am sure so able to serve him in these parts, having a very great interest with the godly'.[50] Beake, as it

---

[47] *Thurloe State Papers*, IV, pp. 278, 473, 522.

[48] Fletcher, *Reform in the Provinces*, pp. 56–61.

[49] R. Schlatter, *Richard Baxter and Puritan Politics* (New Brunswick, NJ, 1957), pp. 55–6.

[50] *Thurloe State Papers*, IV, pp. 272–3.

happens, kept a diary in which he noted his day-to-day activities as mayor of Coventry. This shows that he was indeed a militant reformer and a very conscientious governor of the city. But it is evident that he did not become so at Whalley's prompting nor did his talks with him bring new vigour, for the diary indicates that he was just as busy seeking morality and order during the fortnight before Whalley's visit as during the few months after it. On 14 November, for example, Beake sent two servants to gaol for fornication, on the 17th he walked 'to observe what order the streets were in and gave a special charge to remove muckhills', on the 18th and 19th he had people caught travelling on the sabbath set in the stocks and cage; on the 23rd he summoned some alehouse-keepers before him to give an account of misbehaviour in their establishments.[51] Here certainly were Cromwell's 'common county disorders' being scrupulously checked and regulated. The reformation of manners could only be achieved in so far as individuals like Beake gave it their sustained and personal attention. In this sense the major-generals scheme, seen as an administrative experiment, did contain a problem of consent. For there were not enough men like Robert Beake.

If what has been said so far in this chapter is accepted, it follows that the administrative work of the major-generals is largely irrelevant to an assessment of the political response of the country gentry to the scheme. What the gentry felt, in their pockets, or in the pockets of friends and neighbours who were unfortunate enough to be tainted with royalism, was the decimation tax. This rankled exceedingly, as did the insistence in many parts of England on men under suspicion giving security for themselves and their servants. The correspondence of the Verney family between the autumn of 1655 and the spring of 1657 is full of discussion and rumour about the decimation and the taking of bonds.[52] H. M. Reece has argued persuasively that it was the tax, not the military nature of the scheme, which caused fierce opposition.[53] The cry 'no soldier, decimator or man that hath salary' which Goffe reported was heard at the Sussex election for parliament in August 1656, can be regarded as an expression of generalized localism

[51] 'Diary of Robert Beake, mayor of Coventry 1655–6', in R. Bearman, *Miscellany*, I, Dugdale Society, XXXI (1977), pp. 114–37.
[52] M. M. Verney, *Memoirs of the Verney Family* (4 vols, London, 1970), IV, pp. 254–92.
[53] Reece, 'Military presence in England', pp. 203–5.

rather than of specific anti-militarism. Kelsey found the same mood in Kent, where the people were 'generally bitter against swords-men, decimators, courtiers etc.'[54] When John Desborough brought in his bill for the continuation of the decimation tax in December 1656, it was debated in its own terms, not simply as the adjunct of a system of military rule. The diarist Thomas Burton records only one instance of the kind of anti-army rhetoric we might expect. This was Sir John Trevor's declaration that the scheme involved 'a new militia raised with a tendency to divide this commonwealth into provinces, a power too great to be bound within any law.' Trevor spelt out the constitutional implications of the experiment in this speech on 7 January with a clarity no one else had yet achieved. The major-generals, given permanence, would 'cantonise the nation and prostitute our laws and civil peace.' But we should note that this rousing passage came at the end of an argument against the bill which concentrated on the injustice of the decima-tion tax itself. Trevor believed this violated the public faith of the nation set out in the Act of Oblivion. His condemnation of the bill for its divisiveness was probably the point that struck the deepest chord in many of his hearers:

I am not ashamed to plead for my enemies . . . What do we by this but incorporate them against us and put such a character of distinction upon them that they will never be reconciled . . . You provoke and unite your enemies and divide yourselves and necessitate new arms and charges and raise new dangers . . . I like not this middle way of policy neither to oblige nor destroy. It leaves things doubtful and puts men into a constant danger to be undone. To forgive our enemies is God's rule and it is the only way to make them our friends.[55]

From the 1660s until the 1890s there was a current myth about the major-generals: that they were satraps and kill-joy Puritans who successfully imposed some kind of military despotism on rural England. D. W. Rannie's article in the *English Historical Review* and S. R. Gardiner's *History* then showed that this view was untenable. Yet there has still, ninety years later, been no major study made of the scheme as a whole. G. E. Aylmer's suggestion that the major-generals 'represented an infusion of central authority into the

[54] Fletcher, *A County Community*, p. 310; Everitt, *Community of Kent*, p. 295.
[55] The debates on the tax can be followed in *Diary of Thomas Burton*, ed. J. T. Rutt, reprint edn (London, 1974), I, pp. 228–43, 310–19, 364–6, 368–9.

localities which was not to be exceeded until the two world wars of this century' deserves to be fully tested.[56] H. M. Reece by contrast has emphasized the continuity of military involvement in local government from 1649 to 1660. He sees the decisions of 1655 as 'a formalisation of the army's existing role in administration, a difference in degree rather than kind.'[57] Certain tentative conclusions can be offered on the basis of this brief reassessment of aspects of the major-generals' work. It is inappropriate to describe the administrative experiment we have been discussing as the 'rule of the major-generals'. They never did rule. There was not, as has been suggested, an 'interruption' of the accustomed authority of the JPs.[58] In fact in many counties there were still numerous active JPs who broadly represented the leading county families. It can be argued that weakness at the centre in the 1650s gave the rural justices an exceptional and fortuitous chance to consolidate their hold on the processes of government. The confirmation of their autonomy that occurred after 1660 was the predictable outcome.[59] The major-generals did not achieve any appreciable degree of centralization. The whole episode instead reveals the limitations of government at this time. The letters to Thurloe are full of pleas for practical and propagandist support that was not forthcoming. The decimation tax was persistently sabotaged by the skilful manoeuvres of royalist gentry who obtained assistance in escaping it from the Protector himself. As Stephen Roberts has put it, 'the government was trying to operate on the frontiers of procedural possibility and it is difficult to see how it could have fared better.'[60]

This revisionism of course can be taken too far. Nothing much about the scheme, except possibly the administrative emphasis on the traditional tasks of magistracy, conduced to settlement. The presence of the major-generals in the localities, with their troops of horse and their comings and goings, was bound to reinforce an atmosphere of political insecurity. This is what Sir John Trevor fastened upon so perceptively in his speech at Westminster. The

[56] Aylmer, *The State's Servants*, p. 48.
[57] Reece, 'Military presence in England', p. 202.
[58] D. E. Underdown, 'Settlement in the counties 1653–8', in Aylmer, *The Interregnum*, p. 176.
[59] Fletcher, *Reform in the Provinces*, pp. 357–8.
[60] S. K. Roberts, 'Local government reform in England and Wales during the Interregnum: a survey', in *'Into Another Mould'*, ed. I. Roots, Exeter Studies in History, 3 (1981), p. 38.

very notion of sending out men with the powers that Cromwell gave
to the major-generals ran counter to the gentry's main aims of
reconciliation and the reassertion of class solidarity at the apex of
county politics and government. A single vignette will illustrate the
divisive impact of the scheme. One night early in 1657 John Pellet
and Colonel Culpepper shared a room for the night at the Bull Inn
at Lewes in Sussex. When the time came to settle the bill the next
morning, Culpepper refused to pay his share, bitterly inveighing
against the Cromwellian government for decimating him. Pellet
was overheard justifying the policies of the Protector and his
Council in reply by Henry Woodcock, who happened to be at the
inn at the time. Woodcock took Pellet on more ferociously and a
furious quarrel developed. He declared that 'if he had as many lives
as he had hairs, taking himself by a lock of hair, he would spend
them all against such traitors and rebels as were against the
cavaliers.' 'We have always beaten you,' mocked Pellet. But who,
Woodcock replied, did he mean by saying we? 'He meant the
Protector and those that took part with the late parliament . . . who
had conquered the cavalier party at Marston Moor, at Naseby,
Cheriton, Oxford and all places else, where God had given signal
testimonies of his power against the late King's party.'[61] Here is the
bedrock of 1650s politics in a country inn. If Oliver Cromwell's rule
of the godly was defeated by inertia, it also dissolved into recrimination and rancour.

[61] *Thurloe State Papers*, V, pp. 779–80.

The Suffolk Elections to the
Protectorate Parliaments

PAUL PINCKNEY

The discovery of Suffolk poll figures for 1640, 1654, 1656 and 1659 raises more questions than can be answered in a relatively short chapter, but many of the questions can at least be mentioned and one or two considered at some length. What bearing do the figures have on the controversial question of the nature of the county franchise under the Instrument of Government? How does one account for the large number of votes and candidates in 1654 and 1656? Why is the total number of votes in 1656 so much larger than in 1654? How can the almost complete reversal in electoral fortune of the long-time rivals Sir Thomas Barnardiston and Henry North between 1654 and 1656 be explained? This Barnardiston–North rivalry appears to be the common theme running through all these contests, with North losing in all the elections except 1656 when he took first place. An attempt to explain the dramatic success of North in the year of the major-generals will take up most of the second part of this chapter.

Let us first examine the franchise question, starting with a look at the election figures recorded by the noted Suffolk genealogist and armorialist William Blois (or Bloys) of Grundisburgh, MP for the county in 1654 and 1656.[1]

For various forms of assistance concerning manuscripts used at Ipswich and Bury St Edmunds, I am grateful to P. Woodgate, D. H. Allen, Margaret Statham and Joye Rowe.

[1] His papers are now in the Ipswich branch of the Suffolk RO, and the polls appear at the back of a manuscript volume entitled 'Genealogies of all ye ancient families in Suffolk', present reference GC 17: 755. I have rearranged the names in numerical order and supplied several first names. There is an account of Blois and his manuscripts (with no mention of the poll figures) in Edmund Farrer, 'The Blois MSS', *Proceedings of the Suffolk Institute of Archaeology*, 14 (1912), pp. 147–226.

*Table 11.1   Suffolk election results, 1640–1658/9, according to
William Blois*

19 October 1640 – at Ipswich	
Sir Philip Parker	2293
Sir Nathaniel Barnardiston	2186
[Lost] Henry North	1422

12 July 1654 – at Ipswich	
Sir Thomas Barnardiston	1150
Sir William Spring, bart.	1134
Sir Thomas Bedingfield	1098
William Blois	1059
John Gurdon	976
Alderman William Gibbs	955
John Brandling	947 or 942 [*sic*]
Alexander Bence	852
John Sicklemore	837
Thomas Bacon	836
[Lost] Henry North	774
Joseph Brand	639
Francis Brewster	569 or 557 [*sic*]
Robert Gurdon	530
Humphrew Brewster	510
Major Robert Sparrow	356
Captain Anthony Barry	328
Colonel James Harvey	[200?] 'Col. Harvey refused to deliver in his books'

20 August 1656 – at Stowmarket	
Henry North	1943
Edmund Harvey	1824
Edward Wenyeve	1485
John Sicklemore	1443
William Blois	1393
Alderman William Gibbs	1373
Daniel Wall	1363
Sir Henry Felton, bart.	1362
Robert Brewster	1274
Sir Thomas Barnardiston	1176

[Lost]	Thomas Bedingfield	1088
	Thomas Bacon	1079
	Henry Parker	1054
	Joseph Brand	1043
	John Brandling	954
	Major Hezekiah Haynes	809
	Humphrey Moseley	793
	Governor Benjamin Gifford	712
	Daniel Clench	516
	Robert Gurdon	493
	Barnaby Bowtell	487
	James Calthorp	190

17 January 1658/9 – at Ipswich

	Sir Henry Felton, bart.	1388
	Sir Thomas Barnardiston	1030
[Lost]	Henry North	838
	Alderman William Gibbs	600

Can we use these figures to determine what the framers of the Instrument of Government in 1653 intended concerning the expansion or restriction of the county franchise with their provision that voters should have a real or personal estate of £200? Perhaps, if we do not expect absolute proof or certainty and are willing to accept provisional reconstructions. I would not have dared to make some of the suggestions and extrapolations which follow without having read hundreds of the pamphlets of the period which appear by their title to have a political content. Such a survey of the pamphlet literature, a review of the various reform plans of the late 1640s, and the Suffolk poll figures have led to the tentative conclusion that the Instrument intended an increase in the county electorate of the order of fifty per cent, compared to a seventy-five to one hundred per cent increase in the Leveller plans.[2] The drastic reduction in

[2] Among the pamphlets which suggest a moderate increase are: Marchamont Needham, *The True State of the Case of the Commonwealth* (London, 1654); [Anon.], *A Memento for the People, about their Elections of Members for the approaching Parliament* (London, 1654); and *An Admirable Speech made by the Maior of Reading upon the occasion of the late choice of a Burgess for that Town, June 28, 1654* (London, 1654). The literature on the Leveller franchise is vast; for a sample see Keith Thomas, 'The Levellers and the franchise', in *The Interregnum: the quest for Settlement, 1646–60* ed. G. E. Aylmer (London, 1972). For suggesting an increase in my article 'The Cheshire election of 1656', *Bulletin of the John Rylands Library*, 49 (1967), I have been

the Suffolk figures for the 1659 election which reverted to the old
franchise would appear to be conclusive evidence for a significant
increase in 1654 and 1656. We should emphasize, however, that
summary figures for those years by themselves will never give us
the size of the electorate.

In the election to the Long Parliament, we know both from the
Blois figures and the accounts of the sheriff Sir Simonds D'Ewes the
number of votes. From Sir Simonds's manuscripts relating to the
election it is possible to estimate that a total of around 5,900 votes
translated into about 4,000 voters.[3] In 1640 there were only three
candidates, and many electors used only one of their two votes,
supporting the court candidate, Henry North, whose success in
1656 we hope to explain. It seems likely that when instead of three
candidates for two seats there were eighteen (as in 1654) or
twenty-two (as in 1656) for ten seats, most voters would have used
both their votes. This allows us to divide the 1654 total of 13,735 by
two, arriving at 6,868. This is more than a fifty per cent increase
from the 4,000 figure for 1640. However, three of the Suffolk
parliamentary boroughs of 1640 (Aldeburgh, Eye, and Orford) had
been disenfranchised by the Instrument, and the idea comes to
mind that the usual voters in the disestablished boroughs, plus the
£200 townsmen franchised by the Instrument who for some reason
could not vote in the other boroughs (especially Bury St Edmunds
and Dunwich where the franchise appears to have been quite
restricted), would probably have attended the county election. We
know for certain that many men voted both in the Ipswich borough
election and in the county election.[4] There is, of course, no way of
estimating accurately the total of such groups, but 1,000 does not

criticized by John Cannon in *Parliamentary Reform, 1640–1832* (Cambridge, 1973),
pp. 18–19. I have been encouraged by Austin Woolrych's emphasis on the
continuity in army thinking between the Heads of the Proposals of 1647 and the
Instrument of Government in *Commonwealth to Protectorate* (Oxford, 1982), pp. 23,
395.

[3] BL Harley MSS 158, ff. 293–5; 165, ff. 5–8; 286, f. 318b; 384, ff. 65–6. Thomas
Carlyle constructed a witty essay (1844) from them in 'An Election to the Long
Parliament', to be found in his *Critical and Miscellaneous Essays*, IV (London, n.d.),
pp. 322–47. J. H. Plumb, 'The growth of the electorate in England from 1600 to
1715', *Past and Present*, no. 45 (1969), p. 111, says 'approximately 3,000'. Derek
Hirst, *The Representative of the People?* (Cambridge, 1975), p. 225, estimated
'3,500+'. Hirst and I agree that the number lies somewhere between 3,500 and
4,000.

[4] *Thurloe State Papers*, p. 297. For a discussion of this double franchise, see Hirst,
Representative of the People?, p. 40.

seem out of line considering the population and franchise of these towns. On these assumptions, it appears that the 1654 result was actually close to a fifty per cent increase.

However, what if the Suffolk electors had ten votes to parallel the ten places, using the same logic as the traditional arrangement of two votes for two county seats? We know that this method was used by several sheriffs in 1656, with the Derbyshire electors having four votes for four places,[5] the Lincolnshire voters ten for ten,[6] and the Somerset men eleven for eleven;[7] but sheriffs in these years used a variety of traditional and innovative polling methods, and we should remember the sentence Blois inserted at the end of the 1654 figures: 'Col. Harvey refused to deliver in his books.'[8] This sounds like the old system described in the D'Ewes papers in which candidates set up tables before which the electors lined up to give their names to clerks keeping the books. This was troublesome enough in 1640 when electors had two votes but only three candidates, and it is difficult if not impossible to imagine a sheriff asking voters to have their names enrolled in ten separate books. In the Lincolnshire and Somerset cases of 1656, the sheriffs collected the voting papers (slips giving ten or eleven names which were usually, one suspects, the canvassing lists the voters had brought with them) and then tabulated the results. In such a case an individual candidate would not have books which he could refuse to 'deliver in'.

If we divide the 13,735 Suffolk votes in 1654 by ten, we get a figure for the electorate which is so small compared to 1640 or even 1659 that contemporary complaints would probably have survived

[5] Derbyshire RO, 60/20 and 28 (Chandos–Pole–Gell MSS), an incomplete poll book for 1656. Copies were kindly loaned to me by Hayden Schilling of the College of Wooster.

[6] Lincolnshire Archives Office, Massingberd–Mundy VI/10/5–6, voting papers and tally sheets. I am grateful to Gerald Aylmer for bringing these to my attention many years ago and to Clive Holmes for a vigorous discussion about them. Holmes gives a brief summary of the election in *Seventeenth-Century Lincolnshire* (Lincoln, 1980), pp. 214–15.

[7] 'Memorandum Book of Robert Hunt, Sheriff of Somerset 1654–6', App. II of *Somerset Assize Orders, 1640–59*, ed. J. S. Cockburn, Somerset Record Society, 71 (Frome, 1971), pp. 76–7. I am grateful to David Underdown for telling me about this in advance of publication. He gives a brief summary of the 1656 election in *Somerset in the Civil War and Interregnum* (Newton Abbot, 1973), pp. 182–3.

[8] Blois first wrote 'these refused to deliver in their books', referring also to Sparrow and probably Barry, and then crossed out and added words to arrive at the present sentence.

at least in part; but the only complaints I have found in national sources imply a larger electorate, such as Richard Baxter's remarks about 'the confusion that is now at elections' and 'so great a multitude'.[9]

The 23,854 votes cast in Suffolk in 1656 also appear to make a ten-vote arrangement for 1654 improbable. If the electors had the same number of votes in both years, why were 10,000 more votes cast in 1656? The argument here is for an expansion of the electorate in both Instrument years, not for an increase of more than seventy per cent between 1654 and 1656. Admittedly the 1656 election was one of the most hotly fought of the whole century, with possibly a contest in every constituency. Moreover, it is likely that more candidates almost always means more voters, that prosperity added to the £200 ranks, that newly enfranchised men from the towns appeared in large numbers to vote generally for opponents of the greater gentry,[10] and that confiscated land sales were beginning to have an impact.[11] But would all these factors have produced seventy per cent more voters?

Dividing the 1654 totals by two produced a credible if controversial estimate of the electorate. Such a procedure for 1656, producing 11,972 county voters, staggers even the most fertile imagination. Clearly something was different about the 1656 election, and we know that Francis Drake sent Sir Ralph Verney the results of a very similar Norfolk poll of that year 'for the strangeness of it'.[12] A more complete but corroborating version of the Norfolk poll also survives,[13] and in the latter the total for seventeen candidates was 29,712, again an improbable figure if we assume that each voter could only record his name two times. If Drake thought the Norfolk poll 'strange', perhaps it was because in 1656 the sheriffs of Suffolk and Norfolk for their own purposes allowed the electors to vote for more than two candidates. While it is possible that the electors of these two counties were allowed ten votes in 1656 as in Lincolnshire, there is some evidence against it. The reports in the *Thurloe*

[9] *A Holy Commonwealth, or Political Aphorisms, opening the true Principles of Government* (London, 1659), p. 256.

[10] This assertion is in line, I think, with Gardiner's explanation of why the gentry-dominated Parliament of 1654 restored the traditional franchise in its abortive constitutional bill. S. R. Gardiner, *History of the Commonwealth and Protectorate* (4 vols, London, 1903), III, pp. 234–5.

[11] I owe this last suggestion to Paul Hardacre.

[12] 10 September 1656 in the Verney papers from Claydon; the microfilm of this important collection was kindly loaned to me by Dartmouth College.

State Papers concerning the Norfolk election (in which the highly important General Charles Fleetwood, Cromwell's son-in-law, managed only with great difficulty to be elected at all) suggest a very heated contest in which candidates stood for particular places.[14] This was not the case in Lincolnshire or Somerset where voting papers containing entire slates were collected by the sheriffs. Norfolk does not, of course, prove anything about Suffolk, although these counties do show a similar increase in votes between 1654 and 1656.[15]

There are, moreover, several bits of evidence implying an extended and traditional-style election in Suffolk. William Blois recorded in his account book the payment of six shillings to Thomas Brooke, 'Clerk at Stow-market' on 23 August.[16] 'Clerk' indicates the taking of names in books as in 1640 and 1654, and '23 August' points to a contest which lasted three or four days. A comment by Thurloe supports this. Six days after the 1656 election, he wrote 'nor doe I heare certeinlye who is for Suffolk'.[17] If a multiple ballot arrangement had been used, why could not the Suffolk sheriff have duplicated the Somerset sheriff's feat of tabulating the slips in an afternoon?

The 1656 figures for Suffolk are thus very difficult to interpret given the available evidence. It is possible, of course, to make the figures correspond to the hypothesis of a fifty per cent increase. One could assume that the sheriff, working in alliance with the conservative gentry coalition which dominated the election, decided on four votes rather than two and conveniently forgot to tell the more 'Puritan' opposition of the proposed change. Assuming that the electorate was used to voting only twice and that only the sheriff's friends were prepared to vote four times, a combination of two, three, and four votes for the approximately 7,000 voters of 1654 could be made to agree with the recorded total. This suggestion

---

[13] Norfolk and Norwich RO, Rye MS 9, vol II, published with only slight errors by Hudson Gurney in *Norfolk Archaeology*, 1 (1847), p. 67.

[14] *Thurloe State Papers*, V, pp. 328, 370. Berkshire, Hampshire and Kent, among others, used the 'place' procedure. In Kent, Major-General Thomas Kelsey stood for the last of eleven places and lost: PRO SP 18/144.

[15] Clive Holmes kindly sent me a transcript of the 1654 poll figures (totalling 22,731) from the De Gray papers at Merton which I later could not find in the collection's new home in Norwich.

[16] Ipswich Branch of the Suffolk RO, HA 30/787, f. 159b.

[17] *Thurloe State Papers*, V, p. 349.

which may seem fanciful at present, will be further examined later in this chapter.

Let us turn now to the Barnardiston–North rivalry which does not bristle with so many difficulties and which involves real people rather than imaginary numbers. Beginning with 1640, we know from the D'Ewes papers that Sir Philip Parker and Sir Nathaniel Barnardiston, successful as the 'popular' or 'Puritan' candidates for the Short Parliament, faced in October fierce resistance from the Norths, cousins of the more famous noble line of the family in Cambridgeshire. Henry North's father, Sir Roger, is more or less the villain of the story, behaving outrageously and vocally abusing the sheriff on several occasions. Henry was the court candidate and appears to have been supported by the majority of the 'knights and gentlemen', and it is clear that the sailors around Ipswich voted for the Puritans, much to the annoyance of some young gentlemen supporting North, who called them 'water-dogges'. Barnardiston with an annual income of possibly £4,000 represented immense wealth, one of the oldest families in the county, and the popular religion of most of the cloth and port towns in the southern and eastern part of the county.[18] What appears to be Barnardiston's genuine paternalism comes out in a letter to D'Ewes later in the month when he asked the sheriff not to let 'Mr North have any coppyes of your powell bookes, for that may prove hurtful to the country people and give occasion of oppression to some'.[19]

National issues were cetainly present in 1640, as they would be for the next twenty or so years, but it would be misleading not to mention the family relationships among the advanced Puritan group in the county which contested power with Henry North in all the different elections tabulated here. Sir Nathaniel Barnardiston was Parker's uncle. His daughter in 1648 married Nathaniel Bacon, an old friend of Cromwell from the Civil War days when Bacon was chairman of the Eastern Association committee at Cambridge. Nathaniel and his younger brother Francis Bacon, who were always returned together from Puritan Ipswich in these years, would become Masters of Requests to Cromwell in 1657. A sister of the Bacons married Phillip Bedingfield, 1654 MP for Norfolk and brother of the Sir Thomas Bedingfield on our lists.

---

[18] On the predominant influence of the Barnardistons in county affairs, see Alan Everitt (ed.), *Suffolk and the Great Rebellion, 1640–60*, Suffolk Records Society, III, n.p. (1961), pp. 16–20.
[19] BL Harley MS 384, f. 66.

John Gurdon, the 1654 MP and strong Puritan, married the sister of Sir Philip Parker and thus was the brother-in-law of Sir Philip's young brother Henry, one of the unsuccessful candidates of 1656. The Barnardistons were further related to the Bacons by the marriage of Sir Nathaniel's second son to the sister of the Bacons' cousin Thomas Bacon of Friston, the 1654 MP who lost in 1656.[20]

Now although Henry North probably never forgot the blow to his family's prestige that he received at Ipswich in 1640, his father Sir Roger, as MP for Eye, took great pains to smooth over his differences at Westminster with Sir Simonds D'Ewes, the sheriff who somewhat awkwardly had to forward his own return for Sudbury. Sir Roger sat in the Long Parliament with little enthusiasm off and on until 1653, while his son Henry, after a brief flirtation with royalism, became a solid member of the county committee.[21] Alan Everitt has argued that 'the principal county families continued to dominate the Suffolk committee until the Protectorate or even the Restoration', and that the 'control of the Barnardistons in all matters of county government was never relaxed.'[22] This would have been all the more galling to Henry North because the Barnardistons exerted their influence in the county without even taking the trouble to attend the committee meetings, where North was very active. The same pattern emerges from the Justice of the Peace minute books for Suffolk for the 1650s. Henry North was almost always present, Sir Thomas Barnardiston not at all until 1655. On several occasions in 1655 and 1656 it is obvious that Henry North had taken the chair only to relinquish it when Sir Thomas Barnardiston came in late.[23]

The Recruiter elections of the late 1640s brought in from our lists Sir Thomas Barnardiston and D'Ewes's cousin Sir William Spring

[20] Such a list of relationships could go on forever – for these see D. Brunton and D. H. Pennington, *Members of the Long Parliament* (Manchester, 1954), pp. 69–70, 89–90; Pink MSS in the John Rylands Library, Manchester; W. A. Copinger, *The Manors of Suffolk* (7 vols, London, 1905–11), II, pp. 56–7, IV, p. 125, V, p. 131, VI, pp. 18, 37, 125, VII, p. 232; Copinger at III, pp. 86–92, suggests that Sir Henry Felton, bart., the MP of 1656, 1658–9, 1660, and 1661, was a cousin of the Bacons.
[21] *The Autobiography and Correspondence of Sir Simonds D'Ewes, bart.*, ed. James Orchard Halliwell (2 vols, London, 1845), II, p. 255; Brunton and Pennington, *Members of the Long Parliament*, pp. 92–5; Mary Frear Keeler, *The Long Parliament, 1640–1* (Philadelphia, 1954), pp. 286–7; David Underdown, *Pride's Purge* (London, 1971), p. 265.
[22] Everitt, *Suffolk and the Great Rebellion*, pp. 16, 27.
[23] Ipswich branch of the Suffolk RO, B 105/2/3–4, JP Minute Books, 1652–6, 1656–60.

for Bury St Edmunds, Robert Brewster for Dunwich, Francis Bacon for Ipswich and Brampton Gurdon for Sudbury. This is a very Puritan-looking group – there was evidently still no room at Westminster for Henry North. The more 'left-wing' or energetic Puritans, mostly townsmen of Ipswich and Bury, dominated the Barebones selections of 1653, with Francis Brewster, younger brother of the recruited Dunwich MP, probably coming closest to representing the established gentry.[24] Barnardiston and North would both be religiously and politically to the right of the 1653 group, Sir Thomas probably trying along with the Bacon brothers to bring 'Presbyterians' and 'Independents' together, and North probably preferring a moderate Episcopacy which could comprehend most of the 'Presbyterians'. By 1654 their fathers had both died, and the rivalry of the families could enter a new phase. Looking at the 1654 polls, we can see that Barnardiston's friends and relatives won most of the places, again reducing North to the lot of the losers.

The success at long last of Henry North came in 1656, when he embarrassed the Barnardistons by achieving first place in the poll and relegating Sir Thomas to the last of the successful candidates. How are we to account for this amazing turnabout from 1654 when North could not even gain last place? One factor was the introduction in the autumn of 1655 of the regime of the major-generals, represented in Suffolk by Major Hezekiah Haynes. The system of the major-generals involved a new tax on, and the brief imprisonment of, some old royalists and introduction of 'commissioners to secure the peace', both slaps at gentry efforts at reconciliation in these years and their dominance of the county through the traditional Justice of the Peace bench. Another factor was the appointment of a sheriff, Martyn Salter, in sympathy with the more conservative gentry. Of great importance also was the choice of Stowmarket as the place of election. Finally, Sir Thomas Barnardiston allied himself too closely with the distrusted military aspects of the Protectorate and worked harder as a new commissioner than as a JP.

Haynes, although technically a deputy to General Fleetwood, was thought of as a major-general in his own right, for the easy-going Fleetwood, busy at the Council of State in London, left

---

[24] On all matters relating to 1653 and the members of the Barebones Parliament see Woolrych, *Commonwealth to Protectorate*; for Brewster, see esp. p. 412 and n. 3.

provincial affairs entirely to his deputies. Haynes had become a major in Fleetwood's regiment in 1649 and seems to have shared the firm Puritan and East Anglian background of the regiment, itself usually stationed in the area.[25] Major-General Haynes made his headquarters at Bury St Edmunds, the centre of his large East Anglian district, and in 1656 was to be elected in Essex and easily defeated in Suffolk *in absentia*, while choosing to attend the Norfolk poll in person where his influence with the sheriff probably kept Fleetwood from being defeated in that year of gentry reaction to the regime of the major-generals.[26]

Almost all of the major-generals can be fitted into a pattern of what might loosely be called 'military Puritanism' and Haynes was certainly on the energetic wing of this official trend. Just before the election in 1656, he was very apprehensive because there did not seem to him to have been any official help for his sort of Puritan. On 19 July he wrote:

I would be glad I might have but one hint, that some care will be taken as to the encouragement of honest men in their choice of parliament men before and after the election. I now begin to fear Suffolk finding so malignant a grand jury, who will have a great advantage to possess the country, and all occasioned by a malignant simple high sheriff; which was ill advised at such a juncture of time and I suppose his highness may thank Mr. Bacon for it; yet still honest men do their utmost, as they assure me; but as the case stands will be compelled to take in with the Presbyterian to keep out the malignant. . . . If our troops had been put into a condition of service, they would greatly have swayed the choice by their interest, but now it's too late.[27]

Here Haynes shows himself to belong to the Puritan group somewhere to the left of what he calls 'Presbyterian', fearing the strength of the conservative gentry working together and wishing that the new militia could be used to influence the elections, which was out of the question now because they had never been paid. Haynes also points to Cromwell's acquiescence in the advice given him by his civilian-lawyer friends in the government: Haynes

[25] Charles Firth and Godfrey Davies, *The Regimental History of Cromwell's Army* (2 vols, Oxford, 1940), I, pp. 94–7, 101. Haynes was the son of John Haynes who left a good estate in Essex to become the third governor of Massachusetts and the first governor of Connecticut.

[26] *Thurloe State Papers*, V, p. 370.

[27] Ibid., V, p. 230.

blamed 'Mr. Bacon' for nominating the 'malignant simple high sheriff', Martyn Salter, an undoubted reference to Nathaniel Bacon, mentioned above as part of the Puritan kinship group, and perhaps the most important legal person in Suffolk, serving as Recorder for both of the major towns Ipswich and Bury St Edmunds, but now with his brother Francis in daily contact with Cromwell in London. These Cromwellian moderates will be further discussed at the end of this chapter.

In wading through the seven huge volumes of Copinger's *Manors of Suffolk*,[28] plotting the seats of the gentry on a map, it became apparent that the sheriff's estate at Battisford and one of Henry North's three main estates, that of Great Finborough, were within a few miles of each other. Great Finborough moreover, lies next to Stowmarket, almost exactly in the middle of the county but removed from the Puritan influence of the large trading town of Ipswich. The sheriff would have picked the grand jury, and the grand jury, as Haynes's letter suggested, would probably have agreed on a list of candidates, as happened in many other counties. When Haynes called Salter a 'malignant simple' sheriff, he meant that he was a conservative and possibly malleable or dependent friend of many conservative gentry people, including some with royalist pasts or possibly only royalist cousins. It seems quite probable that North and the sheriff worked together not only in arranging the place of the election but in deciding on how best to organize the votes of the electors.

Could North and the sheriff have devised a voting plan similar to the 'fanciful' arrangement suggested above? William Blois was possibly telling us something when instead of the numerical order employed in 1654 he wrote down the names of candidates for 1656 and 1659 in a particular way, using parallel columns on the manuscript page thus:

[1656]		[1659]	
Sir H. Felton	1362	Sir H. Felton	1388
Sir T. Barnardiston	1176	Sir T. Barnardiston	1030
Mr. Henry North	1943	H. North, Esq.	838
Alderman Gibs	1373	Ald. Gibs	600
[etc.]			

One suspects that Blois was hinting at alliances in 1656, perhaps contemplating the strange fact that approximately the same

[28] Copinger, *The Manors of Suffolk*.

number of votes which gave Felton and Barnardiston first and second places in 1659 put them eighth and tenth in 1656, and possibly remarking in graphic style the vast reduction between 1656 and 1659 in the votes cast for North and Gibbs. Extending the comparison to 1654 and 1656 we find that North and Gibbs in 1654 together garnered 1,729 votes; in 1656 their total was 3,316. What is the simplest way to account for this almost one hundred per cent increase? The other side of the argument is the lack of change in Barnardiston's votes between 1654 and 1656, when the overall total went from 13,735 to 23,854 but his personal total rose only from 1,150 to 1,176. It is tempting to explain this consistency on the grounds of North's group being in on the four-vote arrangement and Barnardiston's having to work alone or possibly with Felton, his colleague in 1659. We know from the D'Ewes papers of 1640 that North had on that occasion been somewhat outmanoeuvred by Parker and the elder Barnardiston when he only took votes for himself at his table compared to the sharing of the two successful Puritan candidates. It would have been sweet revenge indeed for North in 1656 to use organizational planning with the sheriff to make things come out his way for a change.

Another factor in the difference between 1654 and 1656 was the death in late 1654 of Sir William Spring of the rich ramily of Lavenham and Pakenham, who came in second in 1654. It appears from some of the North papers in the Bodleian Library that the Spring heir, under age in the 1650s, but as the second baronet to represent the county in the Exclusion Parliaments, was closely attached in these years to Henry North's cousin Dudley North, later fourth Baron North, often an MP for Cambridgeshire but living in Suffolk in the 1640s and 1650s. For instance, Sir William Spring's will of 1654 is included in the collection of Dudley North papers at Oxford. This arrangement might have originated in the early 1660s when North's daughter married young Spring; but since North's estate at Tostock and young Spring's estate at Pakenham were close to each other, and since there are so many papers about the Spring estates, jointures and the like for the revolutionary period, I suspect that the association was already there in the 1650s. Thus there is a likelihood that the North family in 1656 controlled the great power of the Spring family through the young heir.[29]

---

[29] Bodl. North MSS b 12 and 26, c 5 and 30.

Yet another event affecting the 1656 election was the return to Suffolk affairs of the very controversial Colonel Edmund Harvey. His estates at Wickham Skeith and Stoke Ash were only seven or eight miles north of Stowmarket, but his landed income of only £300 or £400 could not account for his taking second place in the poll. He had served on the major county committees early in the 1640s, had done well for himself both as a silk merchant in London and as an army commander in the Civil War, and from his gains in the war had bought Fulham Palace, the episcopal seat in London. He became a very influential customs commissioner in 1649 but in 1655 came under grave suspicion of having embezzled funds, and was actually imprisoned in the Tower for several months from November 1655. However, in the summer of 1656 he was free if still under an official cloud, and if he chose to come home to Suffolk since the government had embarrassed him, it could well be that the conservative gentry thought that by electing Harvey they could embarrass the government. (Harvey did have wide influence in the London area, having been returned for Middlesex in 1654.)[30] It seems more likely, though, that his coming in second in Suffolk in 1656 was the result of a conservative coalition which must have included many neutralists and even slightly royalist gentry. Although Edmund Harvey spelled his name Harvey, and the neutralist and royalist Herveys of Ickworth who long dominated the election returns for Bury St Edmunds spelled their name Hervey, it is quite clear that they were descendants from the same Bedfordshire family, and the Herveys of Ickworth acknowledged this in manuscript genealogies dating from these years.[31] It might well be that the Ickworth Herveys wanted to get back at Major-General Haynes for making Bury St Edmunds his town instead of theirs. But the initiative might well have come from Edmund

[30] On Harvey see the *DNB*; Brunton and Pennington, *Members of the Long Parliament*, p. 65; Underdown, *Pride's Purge*, pp. 138, 187, 241; Everitt, *Suffolk and the Great Rebellion*, pp. 27, 43, 52, 59–60, 67, 74, 76; G. E. Aylmer, *The State's Servants* (London, 1973), pp. 161–2; BL Add. MS 19,134, f. 256; John Rylands Library, Pink MS 303. There is probably a connection between Edmund Harvey and Henry North through the Poleys who sold Harvey part of his Stoke Ash estate. For this and a possible Harvey connection with Sir Butte Bacon, ejected with Harvey from the justice bench early in 1656, see Copinger, *Manors of Suffolk*, III, pp. 303, 334–5. Butte Bacon was the uncle of the Bacon of Gillingham who was technically lord of the manor of Wickham Skeith, Harvey's main estate: BL Add. MSS 19,116, ff. 5–6.

[31] Bury St Edmunds Branch of the Suffolk RO, 941 (80), 'Genealogical Notes on the Hervey Family'.

Harvey himself, who doubtless thought that as an MP he would be more secure from harassment or imprisonment and in a better position to influence the government to clear his accounts, which was finally accomplished in June 1657, when he was allowed to take his seat. His brother James, the Colonel Harvey of 1654 hidden poll book fame, was probably also urging him to restore the family's honour.

The return of another native son about this time can be more definitely linked to Henry North's electoral victory in 1656. This was the rich merchant and former lord mayor and sheriff of London, Thomas Cullum, whose account books have been used by many economic historians.[32] Cullum bought the large Hawstead estate near Bury in 1656 for around £18,000. It is interesting to note that Cullum's son and Henry North's daughter married around 1656, their son Dudley Cullum being born in 1657, and that Cullum and North were the first two baronets created in Suffolk by Charles II after the Restoration. Cullum had amassed a huge fortune as a merchant in London and had served as an excise commissioner from 1643 to 1651. We know something of his political attitudes since as sheriff of London in 1647 he had been rather kindly disposed to Charles I and had been committed to the Tower. Dudley Cullum, who was born at Henry North's estate at Wickhambrook, about six miles from Hawstead, in 1657, was later to be Sir Dudley Cullum third Baronet, high sheriff in 1690 and MP for the county in 1702. That the Cullum alliance was a help to North in 1656 can be asserted with some confidence.[33]

Part of the anger or concern of the conservative gentry of 1656 doubtless had to do with the removal of representatives of old families from the justice bench early in 1656, people like Sir Butte Bacon, bart., and Thomas Tirrell, esq. Sir Butte Bacon, younger son of England's first baronet and one of the most active JPs in the years from 1652 to 1655, had connections both with the royalist family of Jermyn of Rushbrooke and with Mildenhall, part of the North estates. The Tirrells of Gipping were major landowners in

---

[32] Bury St Edmunds Branch of the Suffolk RO, E2/29/1.1–2. They were used, for example, by Alan Simpson in 'Thomas Cullum, draper, 1587–1664', *Economic History Review*, 2nd ser., 11 (1958), pp. 19–34.

[33] Simpson gives a biography and implies a North–Cullum tie even before 1656. Cullum provided London real estate for his son worth £9,300 to match North's marriage portion of £2,000: ibid., pp. 28, 32; BL Add. MSS 19,172, ff. 61, 70; *Proceedings of the Suffolk Institute of Archaelogy*, 2, pp. 23–8.

the Stowmarket area. Thomas Tirrell was also the son-in-law of Sir
William Hervey of Ickworth, mentioned above as a distant cousin
of Edmund Harvey with a possible grievance against the major-
general concerning Bury. Tirrell's younger brother William, the
'Lord of the Town' of Bury as they said in those days, was taken off
the JP list in July 1656. The tension between Major-General
Haynes and the gentry's traditional attitudes about the JP bench
and the town of Bury is probably shown in two facts recorded on
the same day in the JP Minute Books. Haynes attended only one JP
meeting in Suffolk during his entire tenure in office, in Bury on 21
July 1656. Henry North on that day was placed last on the list of
those attending instead of the usual first or second. Some of the
suggestions put forth above concerning malice and planning begin
to seem more realistic as we plunge deeper into the records and
relationships involved.[34]

Stowmarket is important not only for being away from the
Puritan electoral strength of Ipswich, but also as the location of
important estates of probably disaffected gentry. We have mentioned the Tirrells, who controlled an aisle in Stowmarket church;
Henry North, whose large estate at nearby Great Finborough sold
later in the year for over £10,000; and the sheriff with his estate at
Battisford. Other important wealthy people around Stowmarket
included the Poleys of Stowupland and Stowmarket, friends of
Henry North, and Sir William Hervey of Ickworth, whose estate at
Little Stoneham was owned by right of his wife Lady Penelope,
widow of Sir John Gage, bart. We know from the Ickworth letter
books that Sir William and Henry North moved in the same social
circles. Also connecting the revulsion against the major-generals
with Stowmarket is the imprisonment in October 1655 of Sir
William Pooley, whose estate at Radley adjoined Stowmarket. The
selection of Stowmarket could therefore be all-important, being
close to the estates of influential people who could work together
against the Puritan group.[35]

[34] Additions to and omissions from the commission of the peace are recorded in
PRO C231/6. BL Add. MSS 19,189, f. 168. Many statements in this paper
concerning the seats, relationships, and incomes of the gentry are taken from a
very revealing manuscript in the BL Add. MSS 15,520, extensive notes made
primarily in 1655-7 by Matthew Candler, the vicar of Coddenham. This MS is a
copy of the original, now Society of Antiquaries MS 667. I am grateful to John
Hopkins for allowing me to investigate the original when the Society's library was
technically closed.
[35] BL Add. MSS 15,520; Copinger, *Manors of Suffolk*, IV, pp. 173-9; Arthur

Some miscellaneous deeds in the Bury Record Office show Henry North and Edward Wenyeve, the third successful person on the 1656 list, working together in various land and mortgage deals in the 1640s and 1650s; and a very interesting document connects Lady Penelope Gage, wife of Sir William Hervey, with Henry North and Wenyeve. It looks as if these two were involved in very complicated land arrangements in these years, protecting their royalist friends and relatives,[36] as happened in many counties, with similar gentry persons serving as fronts for former royalists who could not appear publicly but who could use their friends and influence indirectly.

One of the major reasons for the reversal in Henry North's and Sir Thomas Barnardiston's electoral fortunes between 1654 and 1656 has to do with Barnardiston's serving as a new 'commissioner for securing the peace', a separate list of people from the traditional justice bench whom we might call enthusiastic Puritans working under the major-generals. In this capacity he was willing to impose the hated decimation tax on his fellow gentry, such as Sir William Hervey, a neutralist with a royalist son and recusant wife who had been so far rehabilitated as to serve as sheriff in 1651 but who now under this new, and as it turned out brief, phase of 'military Puritanism' was to be taxed at a level of £200 a year.[37] And we know from the energetic Major-General Haynes's letters to Secretary Thurloe that Barnardiston was intimately involved in the work of this new commission. In a letter of 20 November 1655 Haynes said: 'Sir Thomas Barnardiston and a considerable number of the gentlemen are come to town the last night. This day their affections will be tryed.' They certainly were tried, and Barnardiston turned out to be quite eager – a very revealing letter sent by the Suffolk commissioners to Cromwell on that day was written by Barnardiston himself. This is one of the few occasions where we know what

---

Hervey, 'Ickworth Manor House', *Proceedings of the Suffolk Institute of Archaeology*, 1, pp. 29–32; *Letter-Books of John Hervey, First Earl of Bristol . . . 1651–1750*, 'Suffolk Green Books' (3 vols, Wells, 1894), I, p. 28; *Calendar of State Papers, Domestic, 1655*, p. 368; cf. *Calendar of the Committee for Compounding*, p. 1475. Why did North sell the Great Finborough estate in November 1656? Candler thought it reduced his income from around £2,000 to between £1,400 and £1,500. BL Add. MSS 15,520, f. 71v. He needed the dowry money for the Cullum match, but is it possible that he had spent lavishly during the election.

[36] Bury St Edmunds Branch of the Suffolk RO, 326/43–6.

[37] Sir William's first wife was a daughter of the royalist house of Jermyn of Rushbrooke; BL Add. MSS 19,189, f. 168; Copinger, *Manors of Suffolk*, I, p. 417.

an important gentry person was thinking, a person whose family
had dominated county affairs for decades but who now was supporting a continuing Puritan reformation through the major-
generals, the decimation tax, and all the other activities that would
be so offensive to the conservative gentry in the 1656 election.
Barnardiston wrote thus:

We are very clear in our opinions, that this undertaking [the tax on
royalists] is not only honorable in itself, but also the most probable and
likely means to secure the peace and happiness of this commonwealth,
nothing being more equal in our judgments than that those, who by the
restless turbulency of their spirits do create new troubles and disquiet to
the commonwealth, should bear the necessitated charge thereof themselves, without bringing a further burden upon the good and peaceable
people of this nation who have a long time born the heat of the day. We
acknowledge ourselves bound to bless God, who hath moved your highness and council's heart to be thus careful of the security and ease of the
good people of this commonwealth, and of those their dear liberties
purchased with the price of so much precious blood and vast expense of
treasure. We do pray, that as the Lord hath pleased to make use of your
highness as the instrument of our deliverance from the implacable generation of men, so that he will be pleased further to use your highness as the
instrument of our preservation and further reformation, which shall be the
daily request of [and then all the commissioners sign their names headed
by Thomas Barnardiston and including many of the candidates in the
1656 election who were swamped by the conservative gentry].[38]

Less than two months before the 1656 election Barnardiston was
still very active among the commissioners. Haynes wrote to Thurloe on 27 June about a meeting in which Sir Thomas and others
had proceeded against one of the JPs, Robert Lane, as a 'desperate
malignant enemy to good men'.[39] Now the conservative gentry
were trying to smooth over all these old feelings and to reunite the
county along more traditional lines. They would not at all appreciate another gentry person, possibly the richest, considering any of
them desperate malignants or enemies to good men – that was
certainly not their image of themselves. And so Sir Thomas Barnardiston in this phase of the revolution was much too close in spirit to
those advisers around Cromwell who were still pushing the increasingly unpopular programme of 'Godly Reformation'.

[38] *Thurloe State Papers*, IV, p. 225. The printed list of commissioners leaves out
two and garbles three. The original is Bodl. MS Rawlinson A32, f. 691.
[39] *Thurloe State Papers*, IV, p. 302.

With his attitudes and activities, Barnardiston's election was not objected to by Haynes, militia captains, religious tolerationists, or any of the other losers in the 1656 election. However, the seven candidates with the most votes from Suffolk in that year were all among the hundred or so MPs excluded by the Council of State. Often these MPs have been described simply as opponents of the 'government'. But it is clear that the Suffolk gentry blamed this insult on the major-generals, not on Cromwell or the government as a whole. One contemporary report, for example, said that Edmund Harvey 'was chosen into the parliament by the county of Suffolk in 1656 but not suffered by the Major Generals to sit because he had stoutly stood up, in the cause of the County, in opposing some things which they favoured'.[40] Contemporaries could distinguish between the different groups of people advising Cromwell and so should we. The influence of Nathaniel Bacon in choosing a conservative sheriff has already been demonstrated. His brother Francis, a civilian adviser favouring a Cromwellian monarchy who was related to almost every gentry family in Suffolk, undoubtedly worked in coalition with William Blois, elected in both 1654 and 1656, who was Bacon's brother-in-law and neighbour in Ipswich. John Sicklemore, also an MP in 1654 and 1656 and also excluded with Blois in the latter year, was another wealthy lawyer from Ipswich who was probably part of this Bacon–Blois connection.[41] A like-minded MP who was also excluded was William Gibbs, a former London alderman, sheriff and warden of the Goldsmith's Company who had retired from politics between the execution of the king and his election in 1654 for Suffolk, where he had set himself up as a well-to-do country gentleman. What did Gibbs think of Cromwell? When he was allowed to sit in January 1658, he said that Cromwell was 'a conscientious person, and we may bless God we have such an one. Long may he live to keep us in settlement, and I am confident he will do all he can in order to safety and settlement.'[42] Many other MPs excluded for Suffolk in 1656 would have concurred.

[40] BL Add. MSS 15,520, f. 76v. The copyist made a rare mistake and wrote 'proposing' for 'opposing'.
[41] Ibid., f. 12. Bacon and Blois had married daughters of the ancient house of Wingfield of Letheringham, and Bacon had bought his house in Ipswich and other property from Blois. Sicklemore married Bacon's niece in 1657.
[42] Diary of Thomas Burton, Esq, repr. edn (4 vols, New York and London, 1974), II, p. 427.

The 1656 election in Suffolk was thus dominated by a conservative but not anti-Cromwellian coalition. Groups of civilian Crom-
wellians, neutralists, ex-royalists and wealthy gentry from the
county committee days of the early 1640, a time before any one had
thought of killing the king or a social revolution, came together to
combat the reforming purpose and outside interference of upstart
major-generals, the religious zeal of some old Puritans and many
new sectarians, and the rising county ambitions of many lesser
gentry and wealthy townsmen.[43]

This theme of returning to the safer days of the early 1640s when
county affairs were in the hands of the traditional gentry is the
main point of the election sermon preached in Stowmarket by
William Gurnall, installed at Lavenham by Sir Simonds D'Ewes in
1644. Gurnall emphasized experience, wisdom, property, and religious moderation in describing the ideal MP, and tried to unite the
broad middle ground of the English political-religious spectrum in
support of the Protectorate while favouring the conservative wing.
He was obviously worried about a huge crowd of voters who were
either 'profane' or eager to vote for those 'of the Hectick Feaver'.
He hoped that God would 'make them vote for those they little
thought on'. Otherwise, 'I should wonder how a faithful, godly
parliament-man could be chosen in England, where the heap
carries it.' Gurnall's conservative attitudes were shown clearly in
his nostalgic text from Isaiah, i.26: 'and I will restore thy judges as
at first, and thy counsellors as at the beginning.'[44]

---

[43] Including army men who had become 'new gentry', e.g. Barnaby Bowtell,
1653 MP for Lincolnshire, who purchased Parham from Lord Willoughby of
Parham. Candler said that he 'rose from a meane degree . . . he hath now a faire
Estate'. BL Add. MSS 15,520, ff. 121v–122; Woolrych, *Commonwealth to Protectorate*,
pp. 269, 412–13.

[44] *The Magistrate's Pourtraiture drawn from the Word, and preached in a sermon at Stowe
Market in Suffolk upon August the 20, 1656, before the election of Parliament men for the same
county* (London, 1656).

12

Godliness and Government in Glamorgan, 1647–1660

STEPHEN ROBERTS

The Act for the Better Propagating and Preaching of the Gospel in Wales, passed by the Rump Parliament on 22 February 1650,[1] was in force for little over three years, and yet its provisions and implications dogged parliamentary perceptions of Welsh affairs for the rest of the Interregnum and for the first four years of the Restoration. 'Propagation' involved the state seizure of church livings, whether held by bishops, deans and chapters or by lay delinquent royalists, and the use of those assets by a secular commission to fund a 'preaching ministry' in what, as Christopher Hill reminds us, the Puritans considered 'dark corners of the land'. The lay commission charged with administering the act became the power-house of government in Wales in its heyday, but even during its life it acquired a notoriety which persisted after its demise. A clause of the Act of Indemnity and Oblivion of 1660 was a direct response to continuing petitions from within Wales that church and public revenues had been misappropriated by the propagators for private gain.[2] Modern historians, too, have given the commission and the issues it tackled a good airing and have continued to reassess its significance. For a Welsh-speaking *littérateur* like Thomas Richards, it was the English and military character of the commission which was striking; for A. H. Dodd, writing about 'the power of the Committee',[3] the propagators were the crack

[1] *A & O*, pp. 342–88; Thomas Richards, *A History of the Puritan Movement in Wales* (London, 1920), reproduces the text and offers the fullest discussion.
[2] *Statutes of the Realm*, vol V, pp. 226–34; Sir R. Baker, *Chronicle of the Kings of England* (London, 1679 edn), p. 721; A. G. Veysey, 'Colonel Philip Jones, 1618–74', *Transactions of the Honourable Society of Cymmrodorion* (1966), pp. 316–40. I hope to deal with the question of corruption separately.
[3] A. H. Dodd, *Studies in Stuart Wales*, 2nd edn (Cardiff, 1971), ch. 4.

troops of the government in Wales in general. Christopher Hill
vindicates the commissioners and their subordinates of corruption
and attributes the notoriety of the experiment to fears among the
English ruling class that it was a prototype being tested for use in
England.[4] Anthony Johnson has considered the secular work of the
commissioners, in particular their role as an indemnity committee,
while the most recent treatment of the commission is set in the
context of the fortunes of the Glamorgan gentry over a century and
a half.[5] Much has been written on the religious and political
context of the propagation era and on its administrative affinity
with what occurred east of Offa's Dyke; less has been said about the
substructure of the commission and the impact it had on social and
economic life in the Principality. What, if anything, did propagating the Gospel mean for the Welsh people? This chapter will
consider the implications of the scheme in Glamorgan and attempt
to unravel the complexities of day-to-day administration. It is
hoped to present evidence that propagation involved a shift in the
balance of lay power in Glamorgan during the 1650s and that it
was aimed at and depended on the Welsh 'middling sort' for such
success as it enjoyed; and to show that the commission offered most
to parish elites and could have been seen in some quarters as an
attack on the local hegemony of the gentry.

Behind the Puritans' vocation of propagating the Gospel was, as
we shall see, the business management of parochial livings, glebe
and tithes, so it is necessary to describe the topography and
farming pattern upon which the pre-revolutionary clergy had depended for their income. Every writer on Glamorgan has begun
with the striking, indeed visually breathtaking, division of the
county into *Y Fro*, the Vale of Glamorgan, and *Y Blaenau*, the hill
country to the north of the coastal plateau, 'Glamorgan's glove-
shaped valleys' (see Map 1).[6] This is much more than a topog-

[4] C. Hill, *Change and Continuity in Seventeenth-Century England* (London, 1974),
ch. 1.

[5] A. M. Johnson, 'Wales during the Commonwealth and Protectorate', in *Puritans and Revolutionaries: Essays in seventeenth-century history presented to Christopher Hill*,
ed. D. H. Pennington and K. Thomas (Oxford, 1978), pp. 233–56; idem, 'Politics
and religion in Glamorgan during the Interregnum, 1649–60', in *Glamorgan County
History*, IV, ed. G. Williams (Cardiff, 1974), pp. 279–309; P. Jenkins, *The Making of
a Ruling Class: The Glamorgan gentry, 1640–1790* (Cambridge, 1983).

[6] The phrase is, I believe, that of the Anglo–Welsh poet, John Tripp. For what
follows: Rice Merrick, *A Booke of Glamorganshire Antiquities*, ed. J. A. Corbett
(London, 1887); H. J. Randall, *The Vale of Glamorgan: Studies in landscape and history*

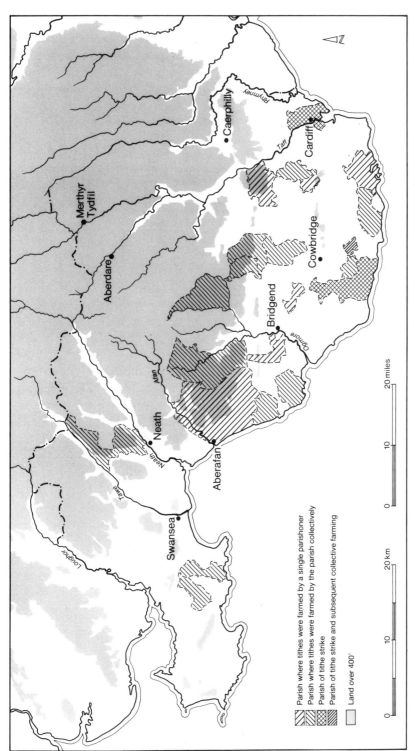

Map 1   Tithe-farming in Glamorgan, 1647–1660

raphical description, of course. The so-called 'Vale' is in some places spectacularly hilly; to stand on Crack Hill near Colwinston and look towards Mynydd-Y-Gaer is to look from one summit to another, even though the former place is in the Vale and the latter in *Y Blaenau*. This apparent quirk of geography gives a clue to the real identity of vale and hill country; they are not simply topographical realities but historical ones too. The Vale comprised the manors created by the Conquest, organized under Norman lords much as manors in England and thus known as the Englishry, while the upland areas, where Norman rule had not penetrated, were known as the Welshry and continued to foster Welsh customs. Place-names in the Englishry were more likely to consist of English elements even though Welsh ones were there in plenty; English names were rare in the Welshry. Surnames in the Vale of Glamorgan were more likely to be English; even as late as the mid-seventeenth century, names in probate wills and inventories and records of taxation suggest that in the Welshry surnames had not even yet settled finally and that patronymic forms were nearly universal. Inheritance customs were different too; gavelkind or partible inheritance prevailed in the Welshry, though oddly enough the custom in the Vale had been Borough English, inheritance by the younger son. Even settlement patterns differed between Vale and uplands; in the English areas villages were likely to be compact and in the hills settlements were usually scattered and parishes huge. There were anomalies, of course; there was the 'Border Vale' or Welshry of the topographical Vale, and beyond Swansea lay the Gower peninsula, largely English except in the mountains between the rivers Loughor and Tawe where large common pastures provided the livings of the freeholders and tenants of the Welshry there.

The partial conquest of Glamorgan by the Norman *advenae* had thus contributed profoundly to the manorial and social structure of

---

(Newport, 1961); *Wales: a physical, historical and regional geography*, ed. E. G. Bowen (London, 1957), ch. 16; *Glamorgan County History* III, ed. T. B. Pugh (Cardiff, 1971); D. J. Francis, *The Border Vale of Glamorgan* (Barry, 1976); G. T. Clark, 'Manorial particulars of the County of Glamorgan', *Archaeologia Cambrensis*, 4th ser., 32 (1877), pp. 249–69; 33 (1878), pp. 1–21, 114–34; M. Davies, 'Field systems of South Wales', in *Studies of the Field Systems of the British Isles*, ed. A. R. H. Baker and R. A. Butlin (Cambridge, 1973), pp. 480–529; probate wills and inventories in NLW, hearth tax and assessment records at PRO E 179/264/47, E 179/221/294.

the county, but by 1640 political control of the area was nominally concentrated in the hands of absentees. The manors of Glamorgan were largely the property of the two factions of the Herbert family: the royalist Marquis of Worcester and the parliamentarian earls of Pembroke.[7] Pembroke influence was concentrated in the Vale, while the Marquis of Worcester held Gower. Neither branch of the Herbert dynasty controlled their manors particularly vigorously and lax manorial administration encouraged freeholder and customary tenant independence.[8] In the Vale, old Norman families ruled unchallenged. Freehold was in any case the dominant form of land tenure in the Welsh areas[9] and a consequent propensity for independence was further developed by agricultural enclosure and the development of industry. Encroachments and enclosures by those engaged in husbandry were always a natural temptation in a county in which common lands and waste abounded then as now. 'Industry in the countryside' played a part in West Glamorgan and along the outcrop of the coalfield in the Border Vale. Coalmining was developing, particularly in the Neath area, replacing the Tudor ironworks, established in the county by entrepreneurs from the Sussex Weald, who had been driven there in the quest for supplies of timber for charcoal.[10] We know little about the industrialists before 1680 and less about the workforce, but the work of Buchanan Sharp and others has shown how elsewhere industry brought with it its social disorder and at the very least created in its investors and workers a spirit of independence from the landed gentry.[11]

[7] Jenkins, *Making of a Ruling Class*, pp. 5–7; *Glamorgan County History, IV*, pp. 161–4.

[8] D. Howell, 'Landlords and estate management in Wales', in *The Agrarian History of England and Wales, V, 1640–1750: Agrarian Change*, ed. J. Thirsk (2 vols, Cambridge, 1985), p. 270.

[9] Ibid., p. 289; F. V. Emery, 'West Glamorgan farming 1580–1620', *National Library of Wales Journal*, 9 (1956), pp. 392–400; 10 (1957), pp. 17–32.

[10] W. Rees, *Industry Before the Industrial Revolution* (2 vols, Cardiff, 1968); NLW, Penrice and Margam MSS, e.g. 5758, 7019; Jenkins, *Making of a Ruling Class*, pp. 57–60, esp. sources at n. 76; J. Thirsk, 'Industries in the countryside', in *Essays in the Economic and Social History of Tudor and Stuart England*, ed. F. J. Fisher (Cambridge, 1961); S. K. Roberts, 'Juries and the middling sort: recruitment and performance at Devon quarter sessions, 1649–70' in *The English Criminal Trial Jury*, ed. J. S. Cockburn and T. A. Green (forthcoming).

[11] B. Sharp, *In Contempt of All Authority: Rural artisans and riot in the West of England, 1586–1660* (Berkeley, 1980); R. W. Malcolmson, ' "A set of Ungovernable People": The Kingswood colliers in the eighteenth century', in *An Ungovernable People: the English and their law in the seventeenth and eighteenth centuries*, ed. J. Brewer and J. Styles (London, 1980), pp. 85–127.

Much common land and waste lay in the uplands and was of poor quality, but in the Vale there were tracts of unenclosed downland overlying carboniferous limestone and offering sweet grazing for flocks of sheep. In the Gower manor of Kittle (Pennard), three-quarters of the customary acreage was under arable (including land on the limestone), but the graziers relied heavily on open commons in a district in which open-field farming persisted well into the sixteenth century. F. V. Emery presents evidence that on English manors of the Gower, we could expect to have found that half to three-quarters of the acreage was given over to arable farming. Further inland in West Glamorgan, on the Welsh manors, the numerous freeholders were busily encroaching and enclosing the commons; Emery suggests that over 3,000 acres were taken from the waste in the second half of the sixteenth century. Here the dominant mode of agrarian production – over half the acreage in one Welsh manor in West Glamorgan – lay in sheep-rearing, a pattern encountered further east in the county in the lowlands, particularly in downland parishes. The 'limestone' parishes of the Vale lie along the portway from Cardiff westwards (now the A48) and are particularly extensive in the St Bride's Major and Newton Nottage districts, drained by the Ogmore, Ewenny, Alun and Kenfig rivers. These were the best sheep districts; elsewhere in the county, cattle and arable farming prevailed. In the Vale, crops were more likely to outweigh cattle husbandry; in the hills the reverse was true, although the principal source for the most recent detailed study of agriculture in Glamorgan, probate inventories, has to be treated with some caution if we are to derive parish-by-parish surveys of seventeenth-century husbandry.[12]

Many freeholders, much common land and enclosing, a variety of property customs, a weak manorial structure, the presence of industry – these would seem to be preconditions for political instability, and it is true that the course of the latter part of the Civil War in the county was marked by localist unrest and disturbance. Glamorgan was a Clubman county: that is to say that by mid-1645 a force or 'peaceable army' had emerged voicing resentment at parliamentarian intrusions and the hint of a new order.[13]

[12] Emery, 'West Glamorgan farming'; B. Osborne: 'Glamorgan agriculture in the seventeenth and eighteenth centuries', *National Library of Wales Journal*, 20 (1977), pp. 387–405.
[13] C. M. Thomas in *Glamorgan County History*, vol IV, pp. 268–76.

As the parliamentary war machine and its supporting civilian committees pushed into Glamorgan, the club movement became a reaction to a new class of committeemen and soldiers. Discontent spilled over into open rebellion in February 1646 and June 1647, but if the rebels were sturdy independent freeholders on the march, they were led by gentry Vale families of eminence, making a last stand to defend old values. As Rowland Laugharne (later Cromwell's adversary at the battle of St Fagan's but in the summer of 1647 still a confidant of Sir Thomas Fairfax) wrote, the principals in the peaceable army were 'ancient malignants of a deep stain', Bassetts, Stradlings, Gwyns, Meyricks and Edward Carne, their leader, and were fighting for a lost world of hospitality, patronage and honour.[14] They were suspicious of newcomers, particularly of those of inferior status, and feared that the Anglican ritual was to be swept away. Their petitions pleaded for the Prayer Book.[15] What of the men they led – several thousands, if the sources may be trusted? The Clubmen came together at musters called publicly by high constables; they were not simply the tenantry of Vale grandees peremptorily called out in sympathy. We need to question the docility implied in the description of Wales as 'the nursery of the king's infantry'. The people of Glamorgan were not necessarily willing to be led by the nose.

The Second Civil War in Wales, culminating at St Fagan's in May 1648, was in some respects simply an irrelevant distraction and a further opportunity for the new parliamentary rulers of Glamorgan to dig themselves in further. The first regular committee for Glamorgan had been appointed in June 1647[16] to oversee assessments, and comprised the lesser men and poorer cousins of the greater houses; it might have been a response to the complaints of the Clubmen. Bassetts, Stradlings and Herberts were there – but they were overshadowed by the new men led by Colonel Philip

---

[14] J. R. Phillips, *Memoirs of the Civil War in Wales and the Marches* (2 vols, London, 1874), pp. 335–8; *HMC*, 13th Report, App. 1, Portland MSS (London, 1891), pp. 348–50.

[15] J. S. Morrill, *The Revolt of the Provinces* (London, 1976), pp. 128–9, 201–2.

[16] *A & O*, I, p. 999. For genealogy and economic status of both committeemen and royalists, see G. T. Clark, *Limbus Patrum Morganiae et Glamorganiae* (London, 1886); Richards, *Puritan Movement*, and idem, *Religious Developments in Wales 1654–62* (London, 1923); *Dictionary of Welsh Biography* (London, 1959); Veysey, 'Colonel Philip Jones'; PRO E179/264/47; SP 29/398/283–4; R. Symonds, *Diary of the marches of the Royal Army*, ed. C. E. Long (London, 1859).

Jones, a Llangyfelach freeholder of '£20 per annum',[17] and Rowland Dawkins of Cilfriw, West Glamorgan, military governor of Tenby and Carmarthen, and like Jones a patron of religious radicalism. After the débâcle of the Second Civil War, this cadre of radicals was strengthened by the appearance on important committees of allies and kinsmen of Jones and Dawkins: for example, Henry Bowen, of a large Gower family, John Price of Gellihir, another West Glamorgan man, and Bussy Mansel, a turncoat scion of the Penrice and Margam family.[18] There was a remarkable shift in the territorial basis of power in the county during the Civil Wars, from the Vale of Glamorgan with its Norman families, arable economy and English socio-economic structure, to a Welsh, freeholding and West Glamorgan faction, made coherent by commitment to new religion and a new career.

When the Act for the Better Propagation and Preaching of the Gospel in Wales and Redress of Some Grievances passed the Rump Parliament on 22 February 1650 it was imposed on a Principality whose social order had been profoundly disturbed, and no county had been more destabilized than Glamorgan. Economic and social differences between the new committeemen and the defeated royalist class were heavily underscored by a territorial gulf and possibly a cultural rift, for the new men could not trace their ancestry to the Norman *advenae*; their surnames belied their pretensions to armigerous status.

As Christopher Hill has shown, the Propagation Act was 'the culmination of two or three generations of Puritan aspiration and effort'.[19] It was the fruits of the labours and lobbying of ministers like Vavasour Powell and Walter Cradock, observed and approved by lay commentators and millenarian soldiers like Hugh Peter and Major-General Thomas Harrison. 'The impressions of the pious soldier, the analysis of the secular Puritan and the expert advice of the Welsh minister'[20] were the crucial influences on the Commonwealth government in its decision to introduce propaga-

---

[17] *A Second Narrative of the Late Parliament* (1658), in *A Selection from the Harleian Miscellany* (London, 1793), p. 421. Llangyfelach was the poorest hundred in the county: PRO SP 28/251.

[18] A. M. Johnson, 'Bussy Mansell (1623–99): political survivalist', *Morgannwg*, 20 (1976), pp. 9–36. J. R. S. Phillips, *Justices of the Peace in Wales and Monmouthshire, 1514–1689* (Cardiff, 1975), can be used to trace the infiltration of Jones and his clique.

[19] Hill, *Change and Continuity*, p. 35.

[20] Richards, *Puritan Movement*, p. 80.

tion measures to Wales and subsequently to the northern counties of England. In its methods the scheme responded to the problem of many church livings to be filled and not enough ministers to fill them. At the disposal of parliament were livings formerly held by bishops, deans and chapters of cathedrals, by the crown and by royalist delinquents. From many of these, inadequate or hostile clergy had already been ejected. The Propagation Act nominated seventy-one lay commissioners and a further twenty-five ministers to examine ministers and schoolmasters. Resources were to be pooled, and the profits and rents of the sequestered livings were to produce a salary of a maximum of £100 for each minister approved and placed in a parish. Ejections proceeded apace as soon as the act was passed; 151 men in South Wales lost their livings, of whom twenty were Glamorgan ministers.[21] The difficulties faced by the commissioners trying to reconstruct a godly ministry were how to reconcile doctrinal variety and disagreements, how to compensate the ejected clergy, whose grievances kept John Walker in plentiful material for his post-Restoration *Sufferings of the Clergy*, and how to overcome an inadequate supply of well-qualified ministers. Itinerant ministers had to be appointed; they were academically unimpressive and were not well received in the parishes. The commission was not organized on a county basis, but was a compilation of support where it was available; Glamorgan did well, providing one-third of the South Wales lay commissioners.

The Welsh-speaking historian of the propagation period, Thomas Richards, spoke of the 'thoroughly English atmosphere' of the commission, and A. H. Dodd described the commission as providing 'the real government of Wales' from 1650 to 1653. Christopher Hill considers that Richards spoke 'perhaps a trifle strongly' about the Englishness of the body.[22] It is true that the first and most eminent name on the list of the commissioners was that of Major-General Thomas Harrison, of no Welsh ancestry and simply a military governor with an interest in hastening the kingdom of Jesus Christ, but in other respects the case of the Englishness of the regime calls for further comment. Harrison turned out to be a pure figurehead; as Anthony Johnson has shown, he had nothing to do with the implementation of the scheme.[23] The undoubted leaders in

[21] Johnson, 'Politics and religion in Glamorgan', pp. 284–5.
[22] Richards, *Puritan Movement*, p. 93; Dodd, *Studies in Stuart Wales*, p. 148; Hill, *Change and Continuity*, p. 33.
[23] Johnson, 'Wales during the Commonwealth and Protectorate', p. 236.

Glamorgan were the group of radical small squires from the west, led by Philip Jones. As individuals they were as Welsh as any, and by ancestry were more Welsh than many of the Vale gentry they had eclipsed. They were of course in the employ of a regime which had ridden roughshod over the local sensibilities of Carne's peaceable army, but the case for or against the Commonwealth as a centralizing government should be judged on performance, not simply on participation.

Dodd's view that the propagation commission provided the effective government of the Principality is supported by Anthony Johnson's findings that the commissioners acted as an indemnity committee and judged disputes between parliamentary soldiers and civilians on the one hand, and disaffected critics and suitors on the other. This side of the commissioners' business was 'very onerous', and appeals from their decisions were heard by the Indemnity Committee in London.[24] Ann Hughes has shown how in England these indemnity disputes contributed substantively to definitions of politics and helped shape the responsibilities and sphere of influence of the state; furthermore, they 'reveal the processes by which provincial people, often of relatively humble social status, made sense of or worked out the implications of their war-time experiences'.[25] In its indemnity provisions, therefore, the propagation commission had to deal with ordinary lay Welsh people, and was not simply a kind of Gabbitas-Thring for clergy seeking posts, however highly charged that quest may have been. In its day-to-day deliberations and administration, the commissioners and their subordinates were nearer to the daily lives of the Welsh laity than most commentators have acknowledged, and in the rest of this chapter this proximity will be further explored.

The essence of the commissioners' work was the management and redirection of the money from parochial livings, and at the heart of these were tithes.[26] Milton's outburst against the 'huckster-

---

[24] Idem, 'Politics and religion', p. 288.

[25] A. Hughes, 'Parliamentary tyranny? Indemnity proceedings and the impact of the Civil War: a case study from Warwickshire', *Midland History* (forthcoming). I am grateful to Dr Hughes for letting me see this in draft.

[26] For tithes, see C. Hill, *Economic Problems of the Church* (Oxford, 1955), esp. ch. 5; D. M. Barratt, 'The condition of the English parish clergy from the reformation to 1660, with special reference to the dioceses of Oxford, Gloucester and Worcester', unpublished University of Oxford DPhil thesis (1949); *Ecclesiastical Terriers of Warwickshire Parishes*, ed. D. M. Barratt (2 vols, Oxford, 1955), I, intro.; M. James, 'The political importance of the tithes controversy in the English Revolution,

age of piddling tithes' was born of exasperation, but the problems of church finance were real and politically fraught. Religious separatists were demanding the abolition of any state-funded church and the elevation of voluntaryism to universal application. By the 1650s a formidable body of opinion, from John Milton and leading army republican officers like Edmund Ludlow to Levellers, Baptists and Independents, was calling for the abolition of tithes completely.[27] Against them were ranged not only Presbyterians and the scattered adherents of Anglicanism (perhaps greater in number than was once thought, if J. S. Morrill is correct),[28] but also a very considerable section of wealthy gentry opinion, used to the benefit of the lay impropriation of tithes. Oliver Cromwell's personal commitments on the issue of tithes may be taken as a useful barometer of changing opinion. After the battle of Dunbar, he was reported to be in favour of abolishing tithes; by 1656 he was telling the Second Protectorate Parliament: 'I should think I were very treacherous if I took away tithes, till I see the legislative power settle maintenance to ministers another way.'[29] The 'other way' was elusive, and had dogged debate in the Barebones Parliament, and among the suggestions for an alternative was the notion that they should be replaced by a parochial rate. As Austin Woolrych points out, there was a 'reformist' group, Cromwell perhaps among them, who were prepared to recognize the problems of conscience presented to those of genuine religious scruples, but who neverthe-less believed that the state had a part to play in ensuring that the gospel was preached across the country.

Many of those who served the propagation venture as lay commissioners or as clergy later became pure voluntaryists, but the management of tithes was a very substantial part of the propaga-tors' responsibilities. As D. M. Barratt and Christopher Hill have shown, earlier historians have tended to predate the commutation

1640–60', *History*, 26 (1941), pp. 1–18; E. Evans, *The Contentious Tithe* (London, 1976); idem, 'Tithes', in *Agrarian History of England and Wales*, V, 2, pp. 389–405; R. J. P. Kain and H. Prince, *The Tithe Surveys of England and Wales* (Cambridge, 1985).

[27] Austin Woolrych, *Commonwealth and Protectorate* (Oxford, 1982); B. Worden, *The Rump Parliament* (Cambridge, 1974).

[28] J. S. Morrill, 'The church in England, 1642–9', in *Reactions to the English Civil War, 1642–9*, ed. Morrill (London, 1982), pp. 89–114.

[29] *The Writings and Speeches of Oliver Cromwell*, ed. W. C. Abbott (4 vols, Cambridge, Mass., 1937–47), IV, p. 272; Woolrych, *Commonwealth to Protectorate*, pp. 235–50; Evans, 'Tithes', p. 394.

of tithes to money payments.[30] The tithes paid in mid-seventeenth-
century Glamorgan were usually paid in kind. The rector, lay or
clerical, was entitled to collect sheaves of corn on the field or to
expect delivery of fleeces after shearing. When Thomas Hilliard,
rector of Newton Nottage, took on his parishioners in the Exchequer over their neglect or refusal to pay tithes for 1657, he accused
one of the local farmers of failing to deliver tithe wool on a hundred
sheep (valued at twenty shillings), two lambs worth 3s 6d each, and
the tenth of the produce of six acres of wheat, six acres of barley and
six of oats and peas.[31] To the tithe-payer this was at best a
perennial irritation and at worst a disincentive to agrarian progress
and a moral iniquity. In areas of agricultural change, the application of the right to tithe could be hotly contested. A tithe-owner
would wish to arrive at a *modus decimandi*, an agreement about
tithes, with parishioners, which might or might not involve commutation to a money payment, but which would certainly include
an agreement about the value of tithes collected. Such a *modus* had
been reached at St Fagan's, for example, before the incumbent,
Edmund Ellis, sued Morgan Gibbon. Tithes there were worth 10s
per acre on wheatfields, 8s an acre on oats, and sums on wool and
for lambs were suggested which were comparable with those being
disputed in Newton Nottage, even though the latter was a pastoral
parish and St Fagan's was predominantly arable.[32] There is nothing in the existence of a *modus* which in itself implies commutation, however, and of course the reason the disputes reached the
Exchequer was precisely because the *modus* itself was no longer
acceptable to parishioners. In a county like Glamorgan, the St
Fagan's dispute was typical: among the valuations at issue was the
tithe payable on agistment, taking in someone else's cattle for
pasture at a profit, a common practice here and elsewhere in the
highland zone, where large tracts of common, heath or downland
were available. In a limestone parish, agistment could wreck the
tithe-owner's calculations, but his attempt to recover the tithes on
it would be seen as an attempt to throttle what was never a
particularly easy way of earning a living.[33]

[30] Hill, *Economic Problems*, p. 95.
[31] PRO E 112/352/Glam.13.
[32] Hill, *Economic Problems*, p. 93 et seq.; E 112/352 Glam.14.
[33] Hill, *Economic Problems*, p. 81; Osborne, 'Glamorgan agriculture', pp. 395–7;
Agrarian History of England and Wales, IV, ed. J. Thirsk (Cambridge, 1967),
pp. 76–7.

The propagation commissioners therefore found themselves embroiled in a world of perpetual negotiation, mutual suspicion and grudging consent. Whatever the importance of the Llanfaches congregation of 1639 in founding the Welsh Puritanism of the temper of the 1640s,[34] it could not be said that all Wales would welcome a new dispensation based on tithes. How did the commissioners set about their work in such inauspicious circumstances? From the first, the commissioners were forced to submit to the logic of geography. There had to be separate commissions for the north and south, in effect, and, as Thomas Richards noted, they worked in different ways. The North Wales body always met as one group, while in South Wales the commission conformed to the patterns of committee government and divided informally on a county basis.[35] In each county, the commissioners were served by agents who carried out the administration of the programme. In 1650, John Bowen of Swansea was treasurer for the Glamorgan parishes managed by the commission, but the following year the county was divided into its eastern hundreds, under the management of Jenkin Williams, a client of committeeman John Herbert of Cardiff, and its western hundreds, for which John Price of Park, one of the Philip Jones clique, was responsible.[36] The sequestration committee established in Glamorgan to deal with the royalist delinquents after the Second Civil War was a useful training school for the agents and their deputies. Jenkin Williams earned his post-1660 reputation for 'every villainy and barbarity' by his service as an agent to the sequestration committee in 1649, and John Griffith, James Dennis, Edward Richards, John Howell and Thomas Walker were all drafted in from the work of punishing the Lord's enemies to help establish His kingdom.[37] I have identified some fifteen to twenty men who helped the commissioners in managing Glamorgan livings, and the overlap between personnel in different jurisdictions is striking.[38] The propagation sub-structure derived from the local county committee and later moved on to support the

[34] Richards, *Puritan Movement*, pp. 25, 26, 28.

[35] Ibid., ch. 16, passim.

[36] Bodl. MS J. Walker c.13, ff. 16–32. As ever in identifying Welsh people, we must distinguish him from John Price of Gellihir and from John Price of Parke, Montgomeryshire. Biographical details from Dodd, *Studies in Stuart Wales*.

[37] PRO E 113/1/1 (old ref.), answers of William Owen, John Stephens.

[38] Much of what follows is based on PRO E 113. This class has been renumbered since the Harvester Press microfilm edn (1977, ed. M. J. Hawkins). Old refs. E 113/1/1; new refs. E 113/2,3. Old refs. have been retained here.

commission for ejecting scandalous ministers during the Protectorate; along the way its members did what they could to help the general cause of government in the county as undersheriffs and commissioners for assessments.[39]

Administrative costs amounted to twelve and a half per cent of the budget of the commission in Glamorgan during the first year of its life.[40] Administrative costs in other places in central and local government were around ten per cent,[41] so the propagators were unexceptional. The officials were drawing fairly hefty salaries; John Bowen of Swansea, alderman and son of a fishmonger,[42] was the first Glamorgan treasurer, and like his successor, John Price of Gellihir, drew £200 per annum. A solicitor and clerk each got £40, while the two agents, Williams and John Price of Park, made £60 apiece. Both men who served as salaried treasurer were named commissioners, one of a number of features of the experiment which built up to provide Philip Jones's political opponents with a battery of evidence of corruption.[43]

Seventy out of 120 – nearly sixty per cent – of the parishes in Glamorgan came under the auspices of the commissioners: all those in the gift of the bishops, deans and chapters of Llandaff and St David's and of other episcopal authorities (Llancarfan parish was a rectory of the dean and chapter of Gloucester, for example), all those in the hands of sequestered royalists (this was where the experience of the former sequestrators was so valuable) and those where clergy had already been ejected because of inadequacy or implacable hostility to the rule of parliament.[44] All parts of the county were affected, although the Vale of Glamorgan harboured

---

[39] PRO E 113/1/1; *A & O*, passim.; T. Nicholas, *The History and Antiquities of Glamorgan and its Families* (London, 1874), for under-sheriffs.

[40] Bodl. MS J. Walker c.13, ff. 16–32.

[41] S. K. Roberts, *Recovery and Restoration in an English County: Devon local administration, 1646–70* (Exeter, 1985), pp. 51, 124, 126–8, 144–5, 178–9, 181; G. E. Aylmer, *The State's Servants* (London, 1973), pp. 29, 40.

[42] W. S. K. Thomas, 'The history of Swansea from the accession of the Tudors to the Restoration settlement', unpublished University of Wales PhD thesis (1958), II, pp. 161, 332.

[43] Bodl. MS J. Walker c.13, ff. 16–32.

[44] Bodl. MS Clarendon 75, ff. 411–42; MS J. Walker e. 7, ff. 208v–229r; MS J. Walker c.4; BL Harley 595, ff. 1–8; J. Bacon, *Liber Thesaurus rerum Ecclesiasticarum* (London, 1786); G. B. Tatham, *Dr John Walker and the Sufferings of the Clergy* (Cambridge, 1911).

the most egregious royalists and the wealthiest parishes.[45] Even for a well-paid body of officials, the work of handling the revenues of these livings and of providing sufficient clergy to replace those ejected was a daunting task. The latter responsibility was at least partly met by the expedient of developing a system of itinerant ministers. John Powell was placed at St Nicholas and at St Lythans from 1652 to 1655, then left St Nicholas but hung on to St Lythans while preaching at St George's. Henry Nicholls started at Llandow in 1644, presented by the Bishop of Llandaff, and in 1646 the Puritan-inclined Philip Herbert, Earl of Pembroke and Montgomery, settled him at Bedwas and Rudry. The propagators restricted the holding of pluralities, so Nicholls took up their offer of the rectory of Coychurch in 1650, having given up Bedwas and Rudry. He still kept Llandow, and went back there after only a year. In 1652 he finally renounced Llandow and went back to Coychurch for the rest of the Interregnum. The ubiquitous Nicholls was called 'the bishop' of the Vale. As Johnson and Richards make clear, only three itinerants could be described as full-time Glamorgan preachers; another fifteen covered Glamorgan and Carmarthenshire. Of the approvers named in the Propagation Act, only two or three worked in Glamorgan.[46]

The administrative problem was how to pool the resources of the seized livings into a central fund to pay for the itinerants and the newly-settled ministers and to augment the livings of the well-affected clergy already in post. It was achieved by letting the livings. For the officials given the task, propagating the Gospel was really a tax-collecting enterprise but one in which not just the sum but the whole principle of collection was different in every parish. In the first year the rent set on all the Glamorgan parishes in the scheme was £2,560 11s 6d, and disbursements came to £2,833 8s 10d. The shortfall was the cumulative deficit owing to uncollected arrears of rents and deductions which had to be made from rents for paying the monthly assessments imposed by the Rump Parliament, and for 'fifths', the allowance of one-fifth of the revenues of a living to the dependents of a sequestered minister, under the provisions of an ordinance of 1643. The accounts of the

---

[45] *Calendar of the Committee for Compounding with Delinquents*, ed. M. A. E. Green (3 vols, London, 1888).

[46] PRO E 113/1/1, depositions of Powell and Nicholls; Richards, *Puritan Movement*; Johnson, 'Politics and religion in Glamorgan', p. 286, where Nicholls is 'Nicholas'.

South Wales commissioners, audited at Neath in 1655, show how hard it was to balance the books; arrears sometimes reached twenty per cent of the sum expected to be raised by letting.[47]

'Letting the living' involved the farming out of parochial glebe-lands and of scattered barns and fields formerly owned by non-parochial church bodies and lay impropriators, but the single biggest source of revenue was the farming out of tithes. There was nothing new about tithe-farming. It was prevalent in the Church of England generally before 1640, as Hill has demonstrated.[48] Despite the disapproval of bishops and archbishops, leasing, sometimes for very long periods, offered the parochial clergy and lay tithe-owners a regular income and ready relief from the burdensome uncertainties of collecting tithes. The farming of tithes can be compared to the farming of taxes by governments of the early modern period; both arose from the inadequacies of administration. For the lessor there was ready cash and freedom from further trouble, and for the lessee there was the excitement of speculation and the prospect of profit. All a tithe-farmer needed was enough cash up front to pay an annual rent. Under the propagators, at least one lesson was learnt from the experiences of earlier bishops and rectors; the tithes were leased only for a year, so as to prevent any one lessee from making a killing and so as to be able to adjust the rent up or down according to how the commissioners read the market. In some cases this meant reducing the rent, as in the case of Ilston, Gower, where the 1650 rent of £60 was reduced for the rest of the propagators' rule to £55; in other places it meant a rent increase. At Newton Nottage it went from a 1650 level of £60 in stages to a 1652 level of £75. In some parishes rents rose then fell again. It was these individual negotiations which made almost impossible demands on the hard-pressed agents.[49]

It is perhaps surprising to find that after 1653 and the demise of the commission, tithe-farming continued as before. The depositions of the tithe-farmers, taken after the Restoration, are full of references to farms under the commission for ejecting scandalous ministers of August 1654, on which twelve Glamorgan men sat, eight of whom were ex-propagators.[50] The agents continued in office, and remarkably, the local tithe-farmers seem not to have distinguished

[47] Bodl. MS J. Walker c.13, ff. 16–32.
[48] Hill, *Economic Problems*, pp. 98, 114–17.
[49] Bodl. MS J. Walker c.13, ff. 16–32.
[50] *A & O*, II, p. 976; PRO E 113/1/1.

very clearly between the old regime and the new. The farmers of Merthyr Dyfan tithes referred in 1662 to John Price as agent to the Propagation commissioners in 1658. William Owen, who farmed the tithes there in 1657, spoke of John Stephens as agent of the propagators 'or commissioners for the ejectioners'. In 1659 the Baptist committeeman and army captain, Thomas Evans, contracted on behalf of the parishioners of Cilybebyll for their tithes with John Price, 'who was or then pretended to be an agent or to have some authority from some of the commissioners for the Propagation of the Gospell in Wales'.[51] This was six years after the commission expired. It is impossible to distinguish administrative practice before and after 1653; like the Exchequer commissioners who took depositions from them in the accounting drive after 1660,[52] modern historians have to consider the Interregnum tithe-farmers as one body.

Who were the tithe-farmers? The results of Restoration investigations into the management of church revenues during the 1650s are a rich source for the details of farming of tithes by Glamorgan men. Most of them were locals. Later in the Interregnum we find the names of outsiders – but still Welshmen – like Richard Gwyn of Cardigan who farmed a tithe barn at Canton near Cardiff and the tithes of Merthyr Mawr parish. Gwyn was exceptional.[53] Nearly all the other farmers came from parishes at least within an easy ride of their tithes. There was an identifiable group of farmers who specialized in this kind of investment.[54] Watkin Richard farmed the tithes of St Mary Church, Llanhari and Llanblethian in 1650 for £100. From 1651 to 1652 he turned his attention from these Vale and Border Vale parishes to the upland and very extensive parish of Llandyfodwg, whose glebe he farmed. He subsequently took on the whole tithes of Llandyfodwg vicarage in negotiations with sub-agent Griffith John. Christopher Jenkin contracted for the tithe and glebe of Flemingston, paying £33 in 1650 and 1651, and £11 in 1652 and 1653. In 1650 he farmed the tithes and glebe of Llancarfan for £33 and in 1655, with John Corrock, he took on the tithes of the

[51] PRO E 113/1/1: answers of Edward Adam, John Love, William Owen, Thomas Evans.

[52] S. K. Roberts, 'Public or private? Revenge and recovery at the Restoration of Charles II', *Bulletin of the Institute of Historical Research* (forthcoming), for full details.

[53] Lambeth Palace Library, Comm XIc./12.59.

[54] For what follows, see PRO E 113/1/1 under name of farmer, and Lambeth Palace Library, Comm. XII b./1.

parish of Eglwys Brewis for £4; all of them lush Vale parishes. Just as there were 'contractors' who specialized in the traffic in confiscated crown, church and royalist lands, so in Wales during the Interregnum there was a comparatively humble group of speculators who stepped into the breach between governmental aspiration and performance.

Another group of tithe-farmers were those who contracted for the tithes of their own home parishes. This was allowed, usually for a year or two at a time, as the commissioners for propagation and later for scandalous ministers seem to have been always uneasy about permitting long leases. There do not seem to have been any cases of tithes being farmed by individuals in particular parishes for many years successively. In 1658 Edward Adam and John Love farmed the tithes and the glebe of Merthyr Dyfan for a rent of £19. They took the profits, and £19 10s was divided between two local ministers with 10s left over to pay tenths due on the living. In 1655 George Matthew and John Ever of Barry farmed the tithes of that parish for £5. William Lewis of Afan took the tithes there for £10 in 1655. On this evidence it would seem that 'corruption', in the sense of an easy surrender to habitual profiteering never developed. The common tendency for lessees to contract for the tithes of several parishes at the same time may even suggest a paucity of would-be farmers.

In his detailed, perceptive but sadly undervalued study of the propagation years, Dr Thomas Richards long ago noticed that the tithes of some Welsh parishes were offered directly to the parishioners as a body, without the mediation of a middleman farmer. The accounts of the propagation commissioners in South Wales, audited at Neath in 1655, show that in Brecknockshire there were 5 such cases in 1650, 22 in 1651 and 22 in 1652. In Monmouthshire there were 28, 36 and 47 in the same years.[55] By studying these declared accounts alone, Richards undoubtedly underestimated the extent of this expedient and also may have mistaken an administrative convention for common practice. The later depositions of the tithe-farmers strongly suggest that tithes were taken on by parishioners where there was a local will to do so and that in places where there was not, individual farmers and even outsiders were allowed to move in. In John Price's accounts for the parishes for 1651 and 1652, only Ilston and Bishopston parishes are de-

[55] Richards, *Puritan Movement*, pp. 238–9; Bodl. MS J. Walker c.13.

scribed as farmed by the parishioners. The farmers' depositions make it clear that parish farming was much more extensive: it did not always appear in audited accounts because parishes frequently nominated individuals to deal with the commissioners on their behalf, and it was their names which appeared in the accounts.

In Glamorgan the tithes of the following parishes were farmed by the parishioners by collective assent at various points during the Interregnum: Kenfig, Cadoxton-juxta-Neath, Cilybebyll, Llandyfodwg, Llanmaes, St Mary Church, St Fagan's, Penmark, Llangynwyd, Ilston, Newton Nottage, Llanilid, Llanhari, Llansannor, Bishopston, Llantrithyd.[56] There may easily have been more and very probably were, as the Exchequer commissioners after 1660 could not hope to round up every farmer or make him give a detailed affidavit. In these parishes there was a strategy for dealing with the propagators. At St Fagan's in 1651, Thomas Lewis, Matthew Rees and William Howard, all residents, farmed the tithes there for £100 at the behest of Morgan Williams, Thomas David and the rest of the parishioners. Christopher Richard swore that the parishioners of Llanmaes farmed the tithes there in 1651 for their own use. William Punter and Edward Thomas collected the money to give to the agent. At Kenfig, Lewis Aylward and Evan Lyddon took the farm from agent Griffith John for one year for £10 'at the request of all or most of the parishioners'. Howell Gwyn of Ystradgynlais was asked 'by all or most of the parishioners' to farm the tithes there for £45. Initiatives were taken by parishes; they were not passively manipulated by the propagators. Parochial initiatives outlived the propagation commission, which fizzled out in 1653. The Ystradgynlais tithes were farmed by the parish in 1656, Llanmaes tithes remained in the hands of inhabitants there down to 1660; Newton Nottage tithes were taken by the parish in 1655.

What incentive did a parish have to negotiate collectively? Certainly not the prospect of avoiding paying anything. The experience at Llanmaes is typical. William Punter, one of the parishioners delegated to deal with Jenkin Williams, the agent, declared later that:

The said defendant and the rest of the parishioners of the said parish enjoyed each man his own particular tythes for the said year 1651, for

[56] PRO E 113/1/1; Bodl. MS J. Walker c.13, ff. 16–32; Lambeth Palace Library Comm. XII b./1.

which every of them the said parishioners paid his ratable proportion towards the raysing of the said summe [of £45].[57]

So there was in these parishes a system of commutation, which at least replaced the uncertainties, inequalities and indignities of tithe with a fixed money payment. This was a new *modus*, and in effect prefigured the Tithe Commutation Act of 1836. The difference between these parochial initiatives and simple farming was that in the former no-one made a profit. The propagators set a sum on the parish and villagers were left to sort it out for themselves. In some parishes the delegated contractor was an individual with enough money to pay the rent; in others, as in Llangynwyd, a group of five parishioners rented the tithes on behalf of their neighbours.[58] In all these parishes, however, there must have been collective debate and collective action.

Why did some parishes and not others farm the tithes in this collective way? Was there anything which may have predisposed some parishes to farm? Map 1 shows those places in which the farming was undertaken either by an inhabitant for profit, or by the tithe-payers collectively. It is important to note that this does not include those parishes, many in number, in which farming by people from outside the parish occurred. This is really a map of parochial initiatives, and it suggests that parishes in the north and the hilliest country were less likely to respond positively to this challenge from outside. Settlements were scattered, and parish meetings may have been few. There was more interest in the Vale, but the parishes where farming was taken up most frequently lay in the Border Vale, the 'Welshry of the Vale', and in the limestone parishes along the portway and in the moorland and coastal region between Neath and Bridgend, the sheep-farming areas.

Sheep- and cattle-farmers making their livings on this kind of land may have welcomed particularly the prospect of regularizing their tithe dues. Districts where there was much common and waste bordering on lusher enclosures lent themselves to agistment, pasturing other people's stock. Disputes about tithe on agistment were a regular part of agrarian life, partly because the practice was difficult for a tithe-payer to monitor and partly because it was a *casus difficultatis*; should the stockowner or the person on whose land

[57] PRO E 113/1/1: William Punter.
[58] PRO E 113/1/1: Jenkin Edwards, Llewellyn Morgan.

his beasts were tacked be liable to pay tithes? It was even argued in some quarters that animals grazed on common land were not titheable at all.[59] In places like Penmark in the Vale, where convertible husbandry – alternating tillage and pasture – had developed, there were other, new problems: how should tithing custom change to meet altered practice?[60] Surely the option of farming the tithes would naturally commend itself to the husbandmen and yeomen of these places?

There were influences other than those of geography and economics. The St Mary Church parish farm was preceded in 1651 by a tithe strike, most tithe-payers simply refusing to pay. At Llantwit Major in 1651, the parishioners considered the rent set by the commissioners too high, and refused to pay more than £30 of the £85 set on them.[61] Sometimes the minister could himself contribute to a display of parochial independence. Jacob Christopher took the living of Newton Nottage – a limestone parish, and 'a little museum of ancient tenures' – in 1653. He 'was not of the opinion to take tithes', and they were left uncollected. When he moved on, his parishioners agreed to pay the treasurer for the commission for scandalous ministers £30, and naturally objected when their new minister, Nicholas Hilliard, started to claim his tithes in kind again. The subsequent lawsuit ended up in the Court of Exchequer.[62]

The tithe-farmers were yeomen, husbandmen and rural tradesmen. Some of them left behind probate wills and inventories, and their names were listed in tax records. Edward Adams, who farmed the tithes of Merthyr Dyfan for his own profit in 1658, was a yeoman who farmed at least twenty-five acres when he died. His house contained a hall, a chamber upstairs, a loft and a dairy. His neighbours reckoned his goods to be worth £131. John Greenwood of St George's, a limestone parish, was a tanner who lived in a one-hearthed house. In 1652 he rented a couple of acres of glebe from William Howell, a fellow parishioner who had got the farm from Jenkin Williams. William Howard was described as a gentle-

[59] Osborne, 'Glamorgan agriculture', p. 397.

[60] M. Griffiths, *Penmark and Porthkerry Families and Farms in the Seventeenth-Century Vale of Glamorgan* (Cardiff, 1979), passim; PRO E 112/352/Glam. 20; E 113/1/1: Sir Thomas Lewis, Pierce Jay, Thomas Love; Glamorgan RO D/DF/E/61.

[61] PRO E 113/1/1: Evan Thomas, William Davids, William Thomas, William Owen.

[62] Ibid.: William Nicholas, William Jones; E 112/352/Glam. 13; Randall, *Vale of Glamorgan*, p. 65.

man when he died in 1673, although his house was modest enough with only one hearth. He left two bushels of barley to the poor in his will, and was one of the men who spoke for the parish when they all took the tithes in 1651. Pierce Jay of Penmark occupied a two-hearthed house there with five rooms in it and died in 1671, leaving goods valued at £78 16s 8d.[63]

Jay was one of the Penmark parishioners who in 1651 decided to take the tithes on behalf of their fellows, specifically because they had heard that someone from outside was about to step in on Jenkin Williams's instructions. The other leaders were Thomas Love and Arthur Spencer, yeomen of substance, and Sir Thomas Lewis. Sir Thomas was exceptional among tithe-farmers in his status: he was a former MP and deputy-lieutenant, and sat on all the assessment commissions from 1649 to 1660. Lewis and Love were two of fourteen families in Penmark who occupied houses each with three hearths or more. It was a wealthy place, and people there were neglecting – or refusing – to pay tithes from 1649.[64]

Tithe-farmers were people with a material stake in seventeenth-century society, and they participated in its public life. We have noted already that the agents and sub-agents of the propagation commission were also sequestrators and committeemen. Tithe-farmers involved themselves in government too, but in an older, more recognized tradition. They frequently served as parish constables and overseers of the poor and of highways, and one can assume they would have sat on juries.[65] They were, in short, part of the parish elites of their districts, and they were working with the government in order to secure their own interests.[66]

Propagating the Gospel thus came to have material benefits when it was put into practice. It could make a man some money, or at least it could enable a parish to ease its tax-load. It contributed to the capacity of the middling sort (surely the best description of

---

[63] Probate wills and inventories in NLW; PRO E 179/221/294.

[64] 'GTC', 'ROJ': 'Some Account of Penmark Parish', *Archaeologia Cambrensis*, 3rd ser., 7 (1861), pp. 11–15; Griffiths, *Penmark*, pp. 18, 21, 26, 27.

[65] PRO E 113/1/1; E 179/221/294, E 179/221/286; Glamorgan RO, Llangyn-wyd parish register contains lists of constables. Other parish records are thin and quarter sessions records do not survive. Corroborative evidence comes from my published work on Devon; see *Recovery and Restoration in an English County: Devon Local Administration 1646–70* (Exeter, 1985), and work cited therein.

[66] C. Hill, 'Parliament and people in seventeenth-century England', *Past and Present*, no. 92 (1981), pp. 119–20; K. Wrightson and D. Levine, *Poverty and Piety in an English Village* (New York, 1979).

these people) to run their own affairs in a period when the power of
the great landowners was temporarily broken. However, one can
take this materialist argument too far: should we see the religious
history of Wales in this period as simply a matter of hard-headed
sheep-farmers cashing in on the wild-eyed dreams of Trevor-
Roper's 'Tammany Hall demagogues'?[67] What was the *religious*
significance of propagation?

In the heyday of neutralism in the county from 1646 to 1648,
there were demands that the Prayer Book be read in churches and
calls for an adequate translation of the Prayer Book into Welsh.
There were also tithe strikes, and J. S. Morrill has argued that a
high proportion of refusals to pay tithes before the advent of the
Quaker movement were really royalist and Anglican refusals to
support ministers intruded by parliament.[68] Given the royalist and
Clubman rhetoric in Glamorgan, the county should provide some
good local examples to support this theory. At Cardiff in 1647, John
Hengott and John Griffith, two sequestration agents, could get no
tithes at all from the inhabitants, who 'utterly refused' to pay; but
by 1648 Hengott was managing to raise small sums there. The
money went to support the intruded minister, Richard Ivey. At St
Mary Church, the strike was the prelude to the parishioners taking
the farm themselves during the propagation years. In June 1658,
William Thomas, settled in Llantrithyd rectory, received an order
from the commissioners for the approbation of public preachers to
take the profits of St Mary Church tithes, but again most parishioners refused to pay. At Llantwit Major, where a schoolmaster was
settled by the commissioners in 1651, and where the Triers of
ministers actually held their meetings, only £30 of the £85 could be
collected by the sub-agent. The people there refused to pay any
more.[69]

So there was at least in some places a revulsion from the methods
and the policies of the propagators and their successors. None of
this can be said to be a defence of Anglicanism, however; the
petitions of the Vale gentry in their Clubman period seem not to
have been echoed by the tithe-strikers, who like small farmers

[67] H. R. Trevor-Roper, 'Oliver Cromwell and his parliaments' in *Essays Presented to Sir Lewis Namier*, ed. R. Pares and A. J. P. Taylor (London, 1956), p. 21.

[68] Morrill, 'The church in England', pp. 103, 110–11.

[69] PRO E 113/1/1: John Hengott, Evan Thomas, William Davids, William Thomas, William Owen; Bodl. MS J. Walker c.13; Richards, *Puritan Movement*, p. 235.

everywhere, seem to have been united only by a dislike of change and dislike of taxes.

There is much more evidence that propagating the Gospel encouraged grass-roots Puritanism. One of the parishes in which the inhabitants collectively took the farm was Kenfig, a decayed borough of coastal dunes and limestone pasture. The principals speaking for the parish were Lewis Aylward and Evan Lyddon. Aylward was described as 'Mr' in tax returns in which he was recorded as occupying a three-hearthed house. He was an Independent, and his house was licensed to hold nonconformist meetings in the 1672 Indulgence. Later, he was arrested in the aftermath of Monmouth's Rising.[70] One of the farmers of Afan tithes (whether for profit or for the parish is not clear) was Robert Thomas of Baglan, under-sheriff in 1652 and a licensee under the Indulgence for Independent services. The farmer at St Bride's Major in 1656 was Thomas Williams; a widow Williams was a 1672 Baptist licensee.[71] Rees Powell farmed the tithes of Laleston in 1649; he was a committeeman, a lawyer, sheriff of the county in 1653 and a leading Presbyterian.[72] Two trends emerge. First, individual farmers were likely to be involved in government in other ways and were likely to have Puritan leanings. Second, those parishes which had asked to farm their own tithes tended later to be nonconformist in sympathy. The list of twenty-two parishes in which meeting-houses were licensed during the Indulgence includes six places where tithes were farmed collectively and another half-dozen where someone farmed the tithes for profit. In the following century, the tradition of Old Dissent still survived in places like Cadoxton-juxta-Neath, Llandyfodwg, Llangynwyd, Llanharan, Newton Nottage and Llantrisant, whose tithes had been farmed during the 1650s. New Dissent – Calvinistic Methodism – sprang up in unexpected places, including those where tithes had been farmed a century earlier: Llanblethian, right in the heart of the Tory Vale, harboured 'Methodists of all trades and denominations – tinkers,

[70] Randall, *Vale of Glamorgan*; PRO E 113/1/1: E 179/221/294; *Glamorgan County History* VI, pp. 476, 498; T. Richards, *Wales under the Penal Code* (London, 1925), p. 92; idem, *Wales under the Indulgence, 1672–75* (London, 1928), p. 158.

[71] PRO E 113/1/1: Nicholas, *History and Antiquities*; Richards, *Wales under the Indulgence*, p. 158; *Glamorgan County History*, IV, pp. 498–9.

[72] *Glamorgan County History*, IV (many refs. to Powell of Llwydarth family); Richards, *Religious Developments*, p. 150; *A List of the Names and Residences of the High Sheriffs of Glamorgan from 1541 to 1966*, ed. G. Williams (printed privately, 1966); *A & O*, passim; PRO E 113/1/1.

thatchers, weavers and other vermin', in the charitable words of the vicar there.[73]

Barry Reay has recently analysed the vociferous opposition of Quakers to the principle of tithes.[74] Not only did Friends refuse to pay tithes, they organized petitions against them and during the later 1650s lobbied MPs and army officers with the aim of getting them abolished. They formed the spearhead of the voluntary principle. It seems remarkable then to find that Quakers were among those who dealt in tithes in Glamorgan. William David farmed the St Fagan's tithes in 1650. In 1663 he refused to swear to his deposition, saying that he was a Quaker. John Gawler of St Fagan's, brother of the better-known Quaker, Francis Gawler, a Cardiff feltmaker, rented a tithe barn in Whitchurch near Cardiff in 1648 and glebe land in 1652, and later could not swear to it, 'by reason of his tender conscience'.[75] William Williams farmed the tithes of St Nicholas Barry and Porthkerry in 1651 and was later recorded in the Exchequer depositions by commission as a Quaker. It is immediately noticeable that all three farmed church property before the Quaker movement was established; the first contacts between George Fox and the leader of the Welsh Independents, Morgan Llwyd, took place in July 1653.[76] The subsequent involvement in Quakerism of the tithe-farmers, after the collapse of the propagation experiment, could perhaps be taken as a measure of their disillusionment with the concept of the godly magistrate. On the other hand, Gawler was sufficiently acceptable to the Protectorate to be nominated from 1655 as a justice of the peace, and from 1657 as an assessment commissioner,[77] though whether or not he served is not known. But the evidence would suggest that Quaker propaganda needs to be reassessed: religious radicalism and material profit were not incompatible.

[73] *Glamorgan County History*, IV, ch. 9 passim; NLW MS Church in Wales LL/QA/1.

[74] B. Reay, *The Quakers and the English Revolution* (London, 1985); idem, 'Quaker opposition to tithes, 1652–60', *Past and Present*, no. 86 (1980), pp. 98–120, where Reay discusses Quaker collusion in tithe payment from the late seventeenth century; Richards, *Religious Developments*, p. 255.

[75] PRO E 113/1/1; Richards, *Religious Developments*, p. 248; F. Williams; 'Glamorgan Quakers, 1654–1900', *Morgannwg*, 5 (1961), pp. 49–75; Glamorgan RO D/DF/ L/8; PRO E 179/221/294.

[76] Richards, *Religious Developments*, pp. 242–5; G. F. Nuttall, *The Welsh Saints, 1640–60* (Cardiff, 1957), ch. 4.

[77] PRO C 231/6; C 193/13/6. He was also named as a militia commissioner in July 1659 and March 1660; *A & O*, II, pp. 1086, 1328, 1448.

Finally, how typical was Glamorgan? Work on tithe-farming in the other counties of Wales has yet to be undertaken, although Thomas Richard's evidence would suggest that parish farms were common elsewhere in the Principality. The Exchequer commissioners uncovered evidence of tithe-farming in England when they took depositions by commission in the provinces during the early 1660s. There, though, the pattern was for pre-war lay lessees of rectories to hold on through the Civil Wars and Interregnum. In the early years of the Restoration they produced leases from deans and chapters to vindicate their tenure. Most of these impropriators were gentry; even if they had been royalist they were left alone to enjoy quietly their long leases. On terms laid down by the gentry impropriators, the middling sort were sometimes allowed to benefit as sub-contractors. To take a few examples from Devon: seven Stoke Canon yeoman were by 1662 the beneficiaries of a dean and chapter of Exeter lease of the tithes there to Edward Holwell, gentleman. Bernard Luxton had been granted the tithes of Winkleigh in 1629; by the Restoration three men, two relations of his, were profiting from them.[78] I have yet to uncover an example of tithe-farming by a parish in the collective way of the propagation experiment.

An attempt has been made here to argue that the Commission for the Propagation of the Gospel in Wales was essentially an appeal to the middling sort. It offered less material benefit to the gentry, who were as likely to be tithe-owners as tithe-payers, than to practising farmers, the yeomen and husbandmen. The new arrangements about tithes would have appealed to any agriculturalist, and particularly to those who farmed in geographical areas where disputes were likely to arise. This is not to deny or to undermine the role that ideology played in motivating the lay commissioners, the approving ministers and some of the agents and sub-agents; nor is it to suggest that those Puritan parishioners who led initiatives to farm tithes were somehow 'really' moved by material self-interest alone, thinly veneered by piety. What is suggested is that godliness and good government coincided in the propagation years, and that the experiment was a progressive one because – perhaps by accident – it offered something to the ordinary parishioner, and especially to the godly one. The Rump failed to continue the scheme, but in

[78] PRO E 113/3/1, depositions of William Warren and Francis Cole (Stoke Canon), Scipio Luxton et al. (Winkleigh).

a real sense it appears to have continued anyway. Tithe-farming carried on, some parishes continued to treat collectively with the agents of the commission for the ejection of scandalous ministers, and some people continued to refer to these men as being in the employ of the Commissioners for the Propagation of the Gospel. The refusal of the Rump Parliament to renew was a refusal to recognize any value in the commission. A historian of Puritan proselytization has commented on fears that the scheme would be extended to England,[79] and the general reluctance of Interregnum parliaments to alter tithe arrangements is well known. Gentry and MPs could be lay impropriators; they could sustain no enthusiasm for a government agency that offered more to the middling sort than to them.

'The Leveller dream of political and judicial decentralisation could have no place in the thoughts of the Propagators, operating from on top and dependent on support from London. The local backing that they won necessarily remained restricted.'[80] Christopher Hill's verdict on the commission remains valid as a comment on the thought processes of Philip Jones and other leading laymen. Some of them were formidable careerists and for them the future lay in continued army service or civilian office at the court of the Protector. Yet how different things could look in Llanmaes, Llangynwyd or Penmark. Surely this was decentralization: surely this was a stimulus to local initiative and to community self-regulation? In the context of the development of early modern British government, the Commission for the Propagation of the Gospel in Wales exemplifies the potentialities of the English Revolution, not simply in its ethos but in its management structure. And in the thread which I believe runs from propagation to Methodism and eventually to the rebirth of Wales as a nation in the nineteenth century, the history of Glamorgan well illustrates one of the important consequences of the 'Late Troubles in England'.[81]

---

[79] Hill, *Change and Continuity*, p. 35.
[80] Ibid., p. 39.
[81] Ivan Roots has atoned for the title of his 1969 inaugural lecture by writing more recently about 'Union and disunion in the British Isles', in *'Into Another Mould': Aspects of the Interregnum 1642–60*, Exeter Studies in History no. 3, ed. I. Roots (Exeter, 1981).

13

Scandalous and Malignant Priests in Essex: the Impact of Grassroots Puritanism

JIM SHARPE

I

Amidst the fog of controversy which shrouds the origins, progress and significance of events in England between 1640 and 1660 two themes, it seems safe to claim, are universally recognized as being of central importance. The first of these was already distressingly familiar when the pikes and muskets were first levelled in the summer of 1642: that religion was one of the first things being contended for. The second has emerged as a result of the labours of historians, Ivan Roots among them, over the last twenty years or so: that a grasp of contemporary local tensions and local pre-occupations, especially among the 'county communities' of the gentry, is a vital aid to understanding what happened in the two troubled decades in question.[1] Recently, however, important de-velopments, most of them made independently of the labours of students of the Civil Wars and their immediate aftermath, have occurred both in the study of the history of early modern religion and in approaches to English regional and local history. Religion, and especially that most elusive of entities, Puritanism, has been subjected to some new questions and to reformulations of old ones.[2]

[1] For a summing up of this approach, written by one of its pioneers, see A. M. Everitt, *The Local Community and the Great Rebellion*, Historical Association, General Pamphlet Series, 70 (1969). Ivan Roots's first contribution lies in his work on *The Committee at Stafford 1643–5: the Order Book of the Staffordshire County Committee*, ed. D. H. Pennington and I. Roots (Manchester, 1957).

[2] This recent work is exemplified by Patrick Collinson, *The Religion of Protestants: the church in English society 1559–1625* (Oxford, 1982). Two recent articles which are

Similarly, the history of the locality has shifted its focus from the world of the gentry county community to that of the pre-industrial village.[3] English historians now feel able to explore, along with other aspects of what the *Annales* school has termed *mentalités*, the religious attitudes not only of clergymen and gentry, but also of poor townsmen and villagers.[4] Popular reactions to the Civil Wars, despite some fascinating work,[5] have not yet been fully investigated, and there is room for considerably more research into a number of issues, popular Puritanism being among them. The object here is to investigate this phenomenon and, in particular, popular ideas about what constituted an effective clergyman, through the medium of the evidence given against twenty-seven allegedly scandalous and malignant Essex clergymen during a parliamentarian purge in 1644.[6]

Three days after the opening of the Long Parliament the House of Commons established a Committee of the Whole House 'for Religion', an action which provided a focus for the flood of petitions against ineffective or Laudian ministers which was already

---

representative of the most recent thinking on the significance of religion in the Civil War period are J. S. Morrill, 'The church in England, 1642–9', in Morrill (ed.), *Reactions to the English Civil War 1642–9* (London, 1982); and idem, 'The religious context of the English Civil War', *TRHS*, 5th ser., 34 (1984). See too the wider perspectives of J. Bossy, *Christianity in the West, 1400–1700* (Oxford, 1985).

[3] For a discussion of approaches to this subject and of the relevant source materials see Alan Macfarlane, Sarah Harrison and Charles Jardine, *Reconstructing Historical Communities* (Cambridge, 1977). A very relevant village study is Keith Wrightson and David Levine, *Poverty and Piety in an English Village: Terling 1525–1700* (New York, San Francisco and London, 1979).

[4] For a detailed case study, see Margaret Spufford, *Contrasting Communities: English villagers in the sixteenth and seventeenth centuries* (Cambridge, 1974). Barry Reay, 'Popular religion', in *Popular Culture in Seventeenth-Century England*, ed. Reay (London, 1985), is an excellent general introduction to the subject.

[5] See, for example, Brian Manning, *The English People and the English Revolution* (London, 1976).

[6] My interest in this type of material was aroused by reading *The Suffolk Committees for Scandalous Ministers 1644–6*, ed. Clive Holmes, Suffolk Records Society, 13 (1970), whose account of the genesis of the Eastern Association Committees is followed closely here. For another body of interesting comparative material, see J. W. F. Hill, *The Royalist Clergy of Lincolnshire* (n.p., 1938). These materials should be read in conjunction with John White, *The First Century of Scandalous, Malignant Priests, made and admitted into Benefices by the Prelates, in whose hands the Ordination of Ministers and Government hath been* (London, 1643). See also Alfred Kingston, *East Anglia and the Great Civil War: the Rising of Cromwell's Ironsides in the Associated Counties of Cambridge, Huntingdon, Lincoln, Norfolk, Suffolk, Essex and Hertford* (London, 1897), pp. 316–32.

reaching Westminster. Improving the standard of the clergy had been a major theme in that groundswell of heightened expectations that led to the European Reformation, and it remained a constant preoccupation in the English church after 1558. The activities of Laudian priests in the 1630s had added an edge and a new dimension to this well-established concern, and in the early 1640s many felt that a unique opportunity had presented itself for the installation of a doctrinally sound and able ministry. Accordingly, the Commons set up a sub-committee 'for Preaching Ministers', among whose duties was the investigation of 'scandalous ministers' as an essential first step towards their replacement with more suitable clergymen. This sub-committee led an irregular existence, its exact responsibilities being unclear and its role being in any case overtaken by events when war broke out in 1642. Late in that year, however, the responsibility for investigating and purging malignant and scandalous ministers fell to the newly formed Committee for Plundered Ministers. The powers of this committee grew through-out 1643, but were largely limited to the south-east. In July of that year the Commons, anxious to extend the replacement of unreliable clergy, voted that an ordinance should be brought in enabling county committees to sequester and replace scandalous ministers.

Scattered evidence suggests that some county committees acted on these instructions, but the system was not fully implemented until the passing of a series of ordinances early in 1644. These tightened up the procedures by which either the local county committee or military commander could hear evidence against allegedly unreliable ministers, and eject them where necessary. One such ordinance was passed on 22 January 1644, specifically for 'Regulating the University of Cambridge, and for removing the Scandalous Ministers in the seven Associated Counties' of the Eastern Association: Essex, Norfolk, Suffolk, Hertford, Cambridge, Huntingdon and Lincoln. The importance of the ordinance went far beyond purely religious matters and, as Clive Holmes's work has demonstrated, must be understood in the political and military context of early 1644.[7] In particular, this legislation enabling the Association's military commander, the Earl of Manchester, to purge the clergy coincided with attempts to improve both the

---

[7] Clive Holmes, *The Eastern Association in the English Civil War* (Cambridge, 1974), ch. 9, 'The politics of the Earl of Manchester's command, February–August 1644'. For the text of the ordinance, see *A & O*, I, pp. 371–2.

administration and the financing of the military machine in the
seven counties. Ideological purity was desirable in the pulpits of
those counties, not least because hostile comments from those
pulpits might deter parishioners from supporting parliament's
cause with either money or recruits.

Between 24 February and 15 March 1644 Manchester, as empowered by the ordinance, commissioned committees for the investigation of suspect clergy in the various counties of the Association.
Essex, in common with Norfolk and Suffolk, had two committees,
one covering the centre and south of the county, the other the
north. Instructions on how to run investigations were laid down by
Manchester.[8] Committees were to encourage the bringing of complaints by parishioners and, in case local villagers lacked the
necessary enthusiasm, they could also ask for information against
scandalous ministers from the well-affected of various hundreds.
On receiving a complaint, the committee would issue warrants
summoning the hostile witnesses, who would then give evidence,
which was noted down, on oath. The accused minister would then
make his response to these written depositions and, on completion
of their investigations, the committee would send both the depositions and the clergyman's responses to Manchester's chaplains,
Simeon Ashe and William Good. If the charges were deemed
proven, a warrant was issued ejecting the minister, his successor to
be chosen by the parishioners in question, subject to the approval
of the Westminster Assembly of Divines. The system remained the
standard method of dealing with suspect priests in the Association
until Manchester's fall from power in the summer of 1645.

The vicissitudes of time have wrought havoc with many historical
documents, those relating to the examination of scandalous and
malignant ministers in the Eastern Association among them. Those
relating to northern Essex have come to us in the form of a copy of
the originals made in 1757 by the noted scholar and antiquarian
William Cole, then vicar of Bletchley in Buckinghamshire. The
original documents had been given to Cole by Stephen Soame, a
Suffolk gentleman, who had himself received them in 1752 from a
representative of one of the most powerful East Anglian gentry

---

[8] The names of the members of these committees are given in Harold Smith, *The
Ecclesiastical History of Essex under the Long Parliament and Commonwealth* (Colchester,
1933), p. 116. The instructions are reproduced in Hill, *Royalist Clergy of Lincolnshire*,
pp. 85–7.

clans, 'my Lady Barnardiston of Kedington' in Essex.[9] The transcription is contained in a volume full of jumbled antiquarian notes,
and it is not impossible that Cole, despite the manifest care with
which he went about his task, might have made a few errors. The
transcript is also, as befits the work of a scholar of the Age of
Reason looking back on an earlier, more enthusiastic, period,
larded with appropriate interpolations: at one point Cole found the
materials he was copying 'enough to make one sick of the hypocrisy
of those sanctified tymes & . . . to bless one's self that we have not
to do with such sanctified villains'.[10] Nevertheless, the transcript
provides a most useful guide to those forms of conduct and practice
which the Puritan 'well-affected' thought inappropriate in a clergyman.

II

As we have noted, depositions gainst a total of twenty-seven north
Essex clergy survive in Cole's transcription,[11] and some idea of the
accusations brought against them can be derived from table 13.1.
The accusations were obviously wide-ranging, and the comprehen-
siveness of the charges brought against some of these ministers is at
times suspicious. Complaints of misconduct brought against
Elizabethan and early Stuart clergymen, as recorded in ecclesiastical court records, were often of similar breadth, and it is tempting
to see the complaints of 1644 as resting firmly in that tradition.

---

[9] BL Add. MSS 5829, ff. 2–74; quotation from f. 2. Details of Cole's life are given
in the *DNB*.

[10] BL Add. MSS 5829, f. 62. It is ironic to note that in 1767 Cole left Bletchley to
go into semi-retirement at Waterbeach, near Cambridge, which, according to the
DNB, was 'a parish which abounded with fanatics of almost all denominations'.

[11] Joseph Bird of Otten Belchamp; John Chamberlain of Little Maplestead;
Timothy Clay of Wickham St Paul; Samuel Cock of St Giles, Colchester; George
Crackenthorpe of Bradwell by Coggeshall; John Crosse of Gosfield; William Evett
of Great Yeldham; Daniel Faulkner of Aldham; Robert Fisher of Belchamp St
Paul; William Frost of Middleton; Robert Guyon of White Colne; William Hall of
Ulting; George Holland of West Bergholt; Gabriel Honifold of St Mary Magdalen,
Colchester; John (or James) Jarvis of Greensted; William Jegon of Sible Heding-
ham; William Jones of Ashdon; John Lake of Great Saling; John Mowe of Great
Bardfield; Stephen Nettles of Lexden; Thomas Newcomen of Holy Trinity,
Colchester; Christopher Newstead of Stisted; Edward Shepherd of Great Maples-
tead; John Simpson of Mount Bures; Roland Steward of Alphamstone; Edward
Strutt of Faulkbourne; Thomas Wilson of Debden.

Table 13.1   Accusations against scandalous and malignant priests in north Essex, 1644

	Unsound doctrine	Malignancy etc.	General negligence and unfitness	Swearing	Drunkenness	Sexual immorality	Allowing games on the sabbath	Supporting the Book of Sports	Sabbath-breaking
Joseph Bird		X	X	X	X				
John Chamberlain	X	X	X		X				
Timothy Clay	X	X		X	X				
Samuel Cock	X	X	X						
George Crackenthorpe	X	X		X	X				
John Crosse	X	X	X				X	X	X
William Evett		X							
Daniel Faulkner	X	X	X	X	X			X	
Robert Fisher	X	X		X					
William Frost	X	X			X	X		X	
Robert Guyon	X		X						X
William Hall		X	X	X					
George Holland	X	X		X	X			X	
Gabriel Honiford			X	X			X		
John Jarvis		X	X	X	X				
William Jegon	X	X		X	X				X
William Jones		X	X					X	
John Lake	X		X	X	X	X			
John Mowe	X	X	X		X				
Stephen Nettles		X	X	X	X	X	X		
Thomas Newcomen	X	X	X						
Christopher Newstead	X	X	X						
Edward Shepherd	X	X	X						
John Simpson	X	X	X	X			X		
Roland Steward	X	X	X	X	X	X			
Edward Strutt	X	X	X	X					
Thomas Wilson	X		X						

Source: BL Add. MSS 5829, ff. 2–74.

Certainly, some of the accusations have an almost timeless ring, in particular those involving allegations of negligence or general inability, often linked with charges of pluralism or insufficient learning. Such complaints were doubtless given an additional impetus by the higher expectations of clerical standards engendered by the Reformation, but they were already familiar by the late Middle Ages.[14] To them might be added the charges of immoral conduct, notably swearing, drunkenness, and sexual misbehaviour. Twenty of the clergy in our sample in table 13.1 were accused of general negligence, inefficiency or unsuitability, and although only 4 of the group were accused of sexual immorality, 15 were allegedly swearers and blasphemers and 14 drunkards. Less traditional, however, were the numerous accusations of doctrinal unsoundness or malignancy towards parliament, most of the former and all of the latter being essentially a product of the circumstances of the times. Only three of the clergy in question escaped from such charges, and all of these were accused of that more general unsuitability which so often comprehended allegations of guilt in these more specific matters. These charges of doctrinal unsoundness and malignancy should now be examined.

Some of the sentiments attributed to the malignant clergy were simply blimpish reiterations of conservative sentiments which had probably been common since the 1530s, but which it is nevertheless interesting to find a century after that decade: 'it was pitty the bible was ever translated into English'; 'it was never merry world since there was so much preaching, for now all hospitality & good fellowship was laid a bed'; 'now every woman & beggarly fellow thinke themselves able to dispute with reverend divines'; 'it was not fit for farmers or tradesmen to know the mistery of their salvation, but only for himself, & such as he was.'[13] Such sentiments, however, shaded into more focused hostility towards notions and practices dear to God-fearing protestant English men and women. A number of the clergy complained against to the committee were already known anti-Puritans. Roland Steward of Alphamstone had attended Laud's visitation at Kelvedon in 1631, and sat on a committee investigating divines suspect to that regime.[14] Stephen Nettles of Lexden had published a book refuting Puritan ideas on

[12] See, for example, Peter Heath, *The English Parish Clergy on the Eve of the Reformation* (London, 1969), ch. 7, 'Clerical discipline'.

[13] BL Add. MSS 5829, ff. 10, 12, 21–2, 65.

[14] Smith, *Ecclesiastical History*, p. 45.

tithes, in which at one point he went so far as to refer to 'the divine right of tithes'.[15] Christopher Newstead of Stisted's reputation as a supporter of suspect doctrine had followed him from his previous living at Abingdon, and his arrival in the Essex parish in May 1643 was greeted by a riot in which he was denied entry to the church and rectory,[16] while Thomas Newcomen and Gabriel Honifold, both incumbents of parishes in Colchester, were mobbed during the breakdown of authority in the weaving areas in the summer of 1642.[17] Others were accused of words or actions likely to offend the godly. William Jegon of Sible Hedingham, apparently a notorious drunkard, in his sermons reproved officers attempting to suppress alehouses, John Crosse of Gosfield jeered at godly divines while they preached, and John Mowe of Great Bardfield declared that many of those who 'would runn three miles to a sermon', if examined, would be found to have 'no more religion in them than a dogg'.[18]

The most consistent doctrinal charge was, of course, adherence to Arminian innovations. As I. M. Green has noted, the most frequent specific complaint in Essex was that communion had been administered at the newly erected altar rails,[19] and this most visible symbol of the Laudian regime does seem to have aroused especial hostility in the county. Altar rails were smashed and burnt in rioting in the county in the summer of 1640, while three years earlier one of the ministers complained against before Manchester's committee had been indicted by his parishioners for insisting that communicants came up to the rail, and refusing to administer the

[15] Stephen Nettles, *An Answer to the Jewish Part of Mr. Selden's History of Tithes* (Oxford, 1625), p. 172.

[16] Ursula Simmon, *Small Beer: an Essex village from Elizabeth I to Elizabeth II* (Stisted, n.d.), pp. 9–10. Stisted at that time was a very troubled community: J. A. Sharpe, *Crime in Seventeenth-Century England: a county study* (Cambridge, 1983), p. 75. Newstead's career is recounted in the *DNB*.

[17] *Mercurius Rusticus: or, the Countries Complaint of the Barbarous Out-Rages committed by the Sectaries of this late flourishing Kingdom* (Oxford, 1646), pp. 2, 12.

[18] BL Add. MSS 5829, ff. 10, 30, 60.

[19] I. M. Green, 'The persecution of "scandalous" and "malignant" parish clergy during the English Civil War', *English Historical Review*, 94 (1979), p. 511. Green's analysis owes much to two earlier works which were essential points of reference in the writing of the present essay: John Walker, *An Attempt towards Recovering an Account of the Numbers and Sufferings of the Clergy of the Church of England, Heads of Colleges, Fellows, Scholars &c. in the late Times of the Grand Rebellion* (London, 1714); and A. G. Matthews, *Walker Revised: being a Revision of John Walker's Sufferings of the Clergy during the Grand Rebellion* (Oxford, 1948).

sacrament to those who objected. It is, therefore, hardly surprising that complaints should be made against Thomas Wilson of Debden, described as 'so notorious an innovator, as yf he set up the railes at his owne chardge, & that a yeare or 2 before any Injunction'.[20]

Equally alarming to Puritan sensibilities were expressions of doctrinal sentiments which helped confirm fears that the innovations encouraged by Archbishop Laud were the thin end of a popish wedge. William Jegon was reported to have said that 'he saw little or no difference betweene the papists & us in matters of religion', while Christopher Newstead preached that the sin of ignorance was a small sin, and that the papist was as likely to be saved as a Puritan, although 'a papist must go a little further about.' Newstead had, it was declared, encouraged some very dubious practices in his previous living at Abingdon. He had 'buried many dead corpses with crosses on their brests' there, and in the church had 'caused to be raced out [i.e. erased] some scriptures which were upon the wall', whose purpose was to show the unlawfulness of 'the pictures of God the Father, & of Purgatory' which apparently still survived there. Purgatory, it seems, formed a theme in a sermon by Edward Shepherd of Great Maplestead, who preached that some went to heaven, some to hell, '& some to a middle place from which they might be resolved by prayer'. Christopher Newstead, quite apart from preaching universal salvation, held that 'God had spareing mercies for the damned in hell', while George Crackenthorpe of Bradwell by Coggeshall caused equal outrage by declaring from the pulpit that 'almes purge away sin & good workes deliver from death.'[21]

Such sentiments doubtless helped produce the protestant backlash which was so powerful a force in 1640, and it is easy to see why they should be offensive to those who had been reared in traditional English protestanism. Dealing with the malignant, or anti-parliamentarian, comments which came after 1642 is rather more difficult. Some of the ministers appear to have been deliberately provocative: John Lake of Great Saling, for example, gave the sacrament to 'a wandring pedlar that railed against roundheads', while John Crosse read royalist proclamations from the pulpit.[22]

[20] Sharpe, *County Study*, pp. 84–5; Smith, *Ecclesiastical History*, p. 66, BL Add. MSS 5829, f. 70.

[21] Ibid., ff. 10, 18, 13, 20, 14.

[22] Ibid., ff. 15, 29.

Others seem simply to have expressed conservative views. John
Lake opined that 'he was sure God had made a king, but not a
parliament', while John Mowe echoed this sentiment by declaring
that parliaments 'were not ordeyned by the word of God as Kings
were, but were meerely by the favour of the king to his subjects'.
Mowe was also reputed to have said that even if Charles I 'were not
a religious king we ought not to take upp armes, for the weapons of
the church were prayers & teares.'[23]

Other depositions reveal a more complex situation. I. M. Green
has argued that many of the clergy accused of malignancy had not
so much expressed anti-parliamentarian sentiments, as been a little
late in expressing their wholehearted support for parliament's
cause.[24] This is not so evident from the Essex depositions, which
do, however, demonstrate a perplexity about the issues involved
and the disillusion of moderates. Edward Strutt of Faulkbourne, for
example, was being far too pointed when he said that he thought
the Houses of Parliament were as guilty of treason as the Earl of
Strafford, since 'he sought to bring the land into arbitrary government, & so doth the parliament', while Edward Shepherd probably
expressed a widespread doubt when he averred that 'he knew not
whether they [i.e. parliament] or the king were for the truth.'[25]
Similarly, some of the adverse comments about the expenditure of
blood and treasure in parliament's cause seem understandable.
Sometimes the attack on the activities of the county authorities was
all too overt: Daniel Faulkner of Aldham, to take a very pertinent
instance, informed his parishioners that if normal times returned he
would 'try a suite' with any of their number who had helped assess
or collect parliamentarian taxes, 'by which meanes some persons
have beene much discouraged in the service to the parliament'.
Conversely, one can feel considerable sympathy with Roland Steward of Alphamstone, who was reported for 'his blaming one of his
neighbours for letting his sonne goe a voluntier; and when some of
them were killed, he said to one of his neighbours, I told you what
would come of it.'[26] It is, therefore, no surprise that two of the
clerics complained against, Edward Strutt and John Fisher of
Belcham St Paul, should be active supporters of what C. Holmes
has described as 'the last collective demonstration of opposition to

[23] Ibid., ff. 18, 62, 56.
[24] Green, 'Persecution', p. 514.
[25] BL Add. MSS 5829, ff. 38, 22.
[26] Ibid., ff. 46, 11.

the policies of Pym's group in the course of the first civil war', the petition for peace of early 1643.[27]

By June 1643, the Vow and Covenant, instituted by parliamentary ordinance in the wake of Waller's Plot,[28] provided the parliamentary authorities with a handy test of loyalty. At least five of the Essex ministers under consideration were hostile or equivocal in their attitude to this document. Thus Edward Shepherd, after initially simply reading the Vow and Covenant without taking it, later took it on a weekday while expressing his reservations about the business. Stephen Nettles showed his contempt by not only attempting to dissuade his parishioners from taking the Vow and Covenant, but also by giving it 'to boyes that came out of the streets from play'.[29] Details from other parishes, however, provide insights into splits in the community as the neutral and war-weary confronted the more militant. At Faulkborne, Edward Strutt persuaded an influential local gentleman, Sir Edward Bullock, not to subscribe to the document, which must have dissuaded a number of other parishioners, while at Middleton William Frost dissuaded his parishioners from subscribing 'until Mr. Wall, one of the parish, did persuade us thereunto'. At Great Bardfield, so witnesses reported, John Mowe refused to take the Vow and Covenant until some of his parishioners pressured him into it.[30]

Arminian, even neo-papist, doctrines and lack of enthusiasm for the cause of parliament were, therefore, charges which were frequently levelled against our sample of priests. Another body of complaint, as we have noted, arose from more general concern over proper priestly standards, and these echoed complaints made routinely against the clergy since the Middle Ages. Others were very trivial. As we have seen, fifteen of the twenty-seven ministers in the sample were alleged to have sworn or blasphemed, but the oaths they used were almost invariably 'by faith' or 'by troth'. Only one, William Jegon, was alleged to have profaned the sabbath by pursuing his worldly business on it, although he did threaten to cudgel his more godly manservant 'because he argued to the unlawfulness of it'. A number of the ministers were alleged to have taken an easy attitude to their parishioners' activities on the

---

[27] Holmes, *Eastern Association*, p. 47; BL Add. MSS 5829, ff. 37, 58.

[28] For the text of this document, see *A & O*, I, pp. 175–6; for remarks on its implementation, *Suffolk Committees for Scandalous Ministers*, ed. Holmes, p. 21.

[29] BL Add. MSS 5829, ff. 13, 49.

[30] Ibid., ff. 39, 43, 57.

sabbath, like John Simpson, who allowed the young of the parish to play football on the Lord's Day, or Stephen Nettles, who 'suffred bowling and football in his own yard on the fasting day'. A number of deponents noted that their minister had given general support to such activities by praising the Book of Sports, while some had even indulged in them. Rowland Steward played 'cat & trap' with the boys of the parish, 'and a constant looker on them, that played thereat, teaching his children therein that day.' More prosaically, Gabriel Honifold was accused of playing 'cards & tables' on the sabbath.[31]

Allegations of drunkenness were more numerous, and perhaps more worthy of serious concern. Heavy drinking was commonplace among all social groups in this period,[32] but it was a practice unworthy of the priest, not least in the eyes of Puritans. The conduct of several of the ministers under consideration, if accurately reported, can have done little to enhance the reputation of the clergy. George Crackenthorpe, it was reported, was a regular heavy drinker who on one occasion could not make his way home 'without reeling into the hedges & this is usuall with him'. William Frost was at one time 'so distempered with drink, yt he could not speake plaine nor goe right in the streets'. John Lake of Great Saling, in company with another priest who had since gone to join the king in Oxford, indulged in a drinking session during which they 'kept a noted whore with them sometimes in private the most part of 2 daies & 2 nights'. On another occasion, Lake drank solidly for seven or eight days, 'till he was distempered to distraction, that Mr. Ady (his Phisitian) sent him word, that if he did not leave his drinking sack, he would be starke mad'.[33] Such behaviour, or that of John Chamberlain of Little Maplestead, who had an altercation with parish officers who reproved him for his drinking, or of Crackenthorpe, who reduced one witness's apprentice to laughter

---

[31] Ibid., ff. 9, 15, 50, 11, 67.

[32] For some general comments, see Keith Thomas, *Religion and the Decline of Magic: Studies in popular beliefs in sixteenth- and seventeenth-century England* (London, 1971), pp. 17–19. It is instructive that the author of a standard handbook for clergymen should describe drunkenness as 'the most popular vice' and warn his readers against it: George Herbert, *A Priest to the Temple: or the Country Parson, his Character and Rule of Holy Life*, 2nd edn (London, 1671), p. 6.

[33] BL Add. MSS 5829, ff. 13, 31, 17. 'Mr. Ady' was presumably Thomas Ady, author of a sceptical tract on witchcraft published in 1656: see Alan Macfarlane, *Witchcraft in Tudor and Stuart England: A regional and comparative study* (London, 1970), pp. 184, 185 n. 38.

because he 'so misbehaved himselfe in his speeches' while drunk, was bad enough.[34] Even worse were those times when clergymen attempted to carry out their priestly functions while drunk. Daniel Faulkner, to take one example, allegedly disrupted a baptism he was conducting because 'he had drunke so much as he ran his head against the wall and there shamefully vomitted'.[35]

Other deponents gave details of that most constant source of medieval complaints against the clergy, sexual immorality.[36] Roland Steward, it was claimed, 'hath brag'd, he had had the use of divers women besides his wife. And this he hath spoken before his wife', while John Lake was described as 'notoriously vile in attempting the chastity of divers mayds, by often allurements, & sometimes by violences, not forbearing the Lord's Day', this latter claim being attested to by four female witnesses.[37] The most alarming charges, however, were levelled against William Frost and Stephen Nettles. Frost, quite apart from offering 'to forgive a woman divers debts . . . if she would give him a kiss', had also 'offered to put his hand under a woman's clothes, in an obscene & uncivill manner', kept a whore in his house for several years, and had been charged with sexual immorality some years before at the Court of High Commission.[38] The accusations against Nettles give us, by implication, a number of insights into what was regarded as normal behaviour: one witness, for example, told how 'in his kissing of women he putteth his tongue into their mouthes, as he hath offerd to doe to this deponent more than once'. More seriously, he had attempted to seduce a young but childless married woman, saying 'I wonder such a lusty young woman as thou hast no children . . . didst ever use the meanes of trying any other man besides they husband?' She said she had not, 'for she thought God should not pardon it', to which the clergyman replied, 'God forbidd but that we should thinke God able to pardon such a sinne', and went on to ask here 'whether she would doe it for love, or if not, for money'.[39] Such conduct was obviously very far from that thought proper to a priest, but it should be remembered that only five of our sample were accused of sexual immorality, a small number given the ease

---

[34] BL Add. MSS 5829, ff. 26, 28.
[35] Ibid., f. 47.
[36] Heath, *English Parish Clergy*, p. 104.
[37] BL Add. MSS 5829, ff. 12, 16.
[38] Ibid., f. 32; Smith, *Ecclesiastical History*, p. 48.
[39] BL Add. MSS 5829, f. 51.

with which the suspicions which so often underlay gossip of this type might arise from a clergyman's confidential dealings with his female parishioners.[40] It is, moreover, remarkable that no such allegations were made against Edward Shepherd, whose peculiar sexual practices came to light after he attempted to prosecute his maid for theft,[41] and comforting that none were made against Christopher Newstead, author of a tract in defence of the female sex.[42]

Quite apart from charges of immorality and drunkenness, most of our twenty-seven clergy were regarded as being generally below the standard which the godly now expected of their clergy, the model 'able godly preaching minister' with which at least one parish managed to replace their scandalous and malignant priest.[43] Edward Shepherd was described as 'a man not fitted for the ministry, having a very bad utterance, &, as they conceive, a weake memory.' Faulkner was described as 'an ungifted & unfitt man for the ministry', Steward as a man who 'hath bin alwaies negligent in his function.'[44] Some of the complaints centred on the traditional grievances, pluralism and absenteeism. Shepherd was complained against as an absentee, so that 'the parish hath bin wholly destitute of any meanes for their soules, except what they procured by their private uses', while Honifold, Jarvis and Wilson were also accused of pluralism and absenteeism, a witness against this last minister remarking sourly that he never came to Debden 'for the most part but to receive money or compound for his tithes'.[45] Against such traditional complaints must be set some new ones, the most frequent of these being that the clergyman in question was a poor preacher: John Crosse of Gosfield might claim that 'preaching is but man's invention',[46] but the godly obviously regarded it as an

---

[40] A point noted by Herbert, *A Priest to the Temple*, p. 27, who recommended marriage as an antidote to suspicion. Cf. the comments of Heath, *English Parish Clergy*, p. 106, for a period when this option was not open to the clergy.

[41] Sharpe, *County Study*, pp. 66–7. For another Essex clergyman's comments on this incident, see *The Diary of Ralph Josselin 1616–83*, ed. Alan Macfarlane, Records of Social and Economic History, new ser., 3 (1976), p. 40.

[42] Christopher Newstead, *An Apology for Women: or, Women's Defence* (London, 1620). The tract is entirely conventional, and reads very much like a literary exercise.

[43] Smith, *Ecclesiastical History*, p. 298, a contemporary description of William Smith, Roland Steward's successor at Alphamstone.

[44] BL Add. MSS 5829, ff. 12, 47, 11.

[45] Ibid., ff. 23, 66, 74, 69.

[46] Ibid., f. 29.

essential one. Thus it was deposed against Honifold that 'he preached seldome & that unprofitably', and against Shepherd that 'his people delighted not to heare him, because he made no application of his doctrine, & did not reprove sin'. John Simpson, we are told, was so lazy in his function 'that for many yeares he preached the same sermons over & over againe', while not only was the matter of John Jarvis's sermons 'very weake & unprofitable', but his delivery left much to be desired: he was not 'able to deliver any thing his sermons more than he reads out of his booke, pointing with his finger, for the most part, to every line he reades.' Such a performance was not likely to meet the expectations of Puritan parishioners.

Some of the clergymen deposed against in 1644 were clearly either inefficient or perhaps entering their dotage. Robert Guyon of White Colne, for example, was thought to be distempered in his brain, and demonstrated this by saying some very peculiar things in the pulpit and making such mistakes as reading part of the marriage service while carrying out a baptism, or saying the wrong prayers on Easter day.[48] Stephen Nettles of Lexden was also probably mentally ill by 1644: Ralph Josselin recorded how, in the August of that year, he was 'caryed through towne in a coach deprived of his sense, and very mad as they reported.'[49] More often, however, we must conclude that complaints, when they were not concerned with such traditional clerical failings as pluralism, drunkenness, or sexual immorality, arose from those heightened expectations concerning clerical conduct to which we have already referred. Insufficient abilities when preaching were, as we have seen, a common cause of complaint: two other sets of depositions, however, demonstrate more specific points. Daniel Faulkner, so some of his parishioners at Aldham complained, was a man who 'bestowes much of his tyme about worldly imployments as dressing corne' and other agricultural concerns. This, his parishioners averred, was especially serious because he often did so late on a Saturday night, 'when it were better he were in his Studdy'. A similarly Puritan line was taken by William Jegon's flock at Sible Hedingham, who noted that 'he did very seldome pray in his

[47] Ibid., ff. 66, 22, 14, 74.
[48] Ibid., f. 24.
[49] Diary of Ralph Josselin, ed. Macfarlane, p. 17. This was a sad fate for a man who had earlier been regarded as 'a smart and learned person': Walker, Sufferings, p. 318.

familie, or reade the scriptures to them'.[50] The criticisms made of these Essex clergymen came firmly from the attitudes engendered by mainstream, respectable godly protestantism of a type which had been fostered between 1558 and the advent of Arminianism. The deponents of 1644 were not radicals: they were, indeed, ready to refer doubtful cases to what they considered the proper authorities. They asked that Jarvis might be examined by 'the earle of Manchester's chaplains, or some other able minister in these parts', or that Robert Fisher 'may preach before my Lord's chaplains, upon triall', or that Samuel Cock 'may be tried by some judicious divines'.[51] The spectacle of a body of clergymen being subjected to detailed and articulate criticism by their more enthusiastic parishioners was remarkable enough: but Manchester and his fellow Presbyterians could still be confident that the forces being unleashed in the parishes of the Eastern Association could be contained.

III

Understanding these forces presents the historian with a number of problems. Perhaps the greatest of these, especially given that the responses of the ministers and depositions on their behalf do not survive, lies in the credibility of the allegations made by these ostensibly godly villagers. Obviously, the full story of what lay behind these allegations will never be known, although detailed village reconstruction would doubtlessly expose a pattern of parish tensions, litigation, and of factional divisions within the village playing themselves out against the background of civil strife. Clive Holmes has claimed that 'the accusers may not have been motivated entirely by considerations of abstract justice',[52] and detailed work on the village communities in question might help demonstrate this point. The Essex accusations do give occasional insights into tensions between incumbent and parishioners which were outside doctrinal issues. William Jones of Ashdon was not only an absentee, but chose 'a notorious convicted drunkard' as his tenant in the parsonage 'as we conceive, to vex the parish'. John Lake of Great Saling had been involved in a dispute with one of his

[50] BL Add. MSS 5829, ff. 46, 10.
[51] Ibid., ff. 74, 37, 72.
[52] *Suffolk Committees for Scandalous Ministers*, ed. Holmes, p. 23.

parishioners, Thomas Porter, about his dog. William Jegon predicted that the outcome of the Civil Wars would be a return of
traditional church government with episcopacy even more powerful than before, in which case 'he would plague his parishioners
more than ever'. John Mowe, it was deposed, had been involved in
what must have been the most common source of friction between a
minister and his flock, a dispute over tithes.[53] Other tensions had
arisen when parishioners went to hear other ministers whom they
felt to be more 'profitable' than the man in their own parish. Daniel
Faulkner visited a very godly man who was experiencing a period
of illness, and informed him that it was God's punishment for him
'for going from his ministry', and refused to bury another of his
flock who went 'to hear the word of God at other places'. John
Mowe refused poor relief to two old women in his parish who went
elsewhere to hear sermons. One of them, the widow Carder,
claimed 'she went to other churches to heare good ministers, she
being an old poore woman, and . . . could not understand him.'[54]

As this last instance reminds us, the deponents of 1644 represented a very broad cross-section of contemporary society. Taking
a much larger sample, Dr Green has calculated that only a very
small proportion of deponents were gentry (two of the 250 or so
Essex deponents) and that a fair number were servants.[55] William
Cole was anxious to write off those complaining against the clergy
as 'all sorts of people, & those of the lowest & basest sort in each
parish',[56] but even a preliminary investigation of those deposing in
Essex provides a more complex picture. Doubtless every parish
could tell its own story, and these stories will remain elusive until
the interplay of conflicting personalities and factions in each village, as well as the interaction between these local tensions and the
instructions coming down from the county authorities, have been
fully delineated. Nevertheless, it is clear that a fair proportion of
those deposing against scandalous and malignant priests were
drawn from that stratum of richer villagers whose support for
godliness has been identified as being of crucial importance in the
spread of Puritan ideas at the grass roots.[57] Taxation returns, for

[53] BL Add. MSS 5829, ff. 28, 55, 10, 59.
[54] Ibid., ff. 47, 61.
[55] Green, 'Persecution', p. 518.
[56] BL Add. MSS 5829, f. 2.
[57] Wrightson and Levine, *Poverty and Piety*, pp. 155–72; Keith Wrightson, 'Two
concepts of order: justices, constables and jurymen in seventeenth-century Eng-

example the Ship Money listings for Sible Hedingham or White
Colne,[58] sometimes reveal that leading witnesses were also among
those rated highest in taxable wealth. Other witnesses held or were
to hold parish office, as constable or surveyor of the highways for
example.[59] Yet others, among them Robert White of Wickham St
Paul or Thomas Dier of Belchamp St Paul, were later to appear as
elders in the Presbyterian churches established in the wake of the
ejection of scandalous ministers.[60] Female participation in the
attack on unsatisfactory or suspect priests should not be forgotten:
perhaps the most striking example came at Great Maplestead,
where '16 women of his parish, some of the good sort, came to the
committee to desire a godly minister, affirming Mr. Shepard
altogether unfit to be a minister.'[61] The witnesses of 1644, whatever
their sex, were evidently in large measure drawn from that 'good
sort' who had formed the backbone of the godly, and who were
perfectly capable of formulating and voicing complaints against
what they considered unsuitable clergymen.

As we have seen, however, the allegations levelled at these
clergymen contained a number of complaints which would have
been found in lay criticisms of the clergy at almost any point in the
late medieval or early modern periods. As C. Holmes has noted, the
parliamentarian attack on scandalous ministers in the early 1640s
was part of a much longer-term disquiet at pluralist, non-resident,
immoral or incompetent clerics,[62] and the pre-Reformation clergy
afforded many examples similar to those turned up by Manchester's commissioners. This, perhaps, raises an important issue:
historians have, perhaps for fairly obvious reasons, long been most
interested in Puritanism as an agent of social, economic or political
change, and hence with what has been regarded, either implicitly
or explicitly, as its intrinsic novelty. It might be instructive, especially when dealing with the phenomenon on a popular level, to

---

land', in *An Ungovernable People: The English and their law in the seventeenth and
eighteenth centuries*, ed. John Brewer and John Styles (London, 1980), pp. 41–6.

[58] Essex RO, T/A 42, ff. 128–9, 220.

[59] Essex RO, Quarter Sessions Rolls, Q/SR 360/18 (Robert Wood of Stisted);
Ibid., 343/47 (William Cowell of White Colne).

[60] *The Division of the County of Essex into Severall Classes: together with the Names of the
Ministers and Others to be fit of each Classis* (London, 1648), pp. 16, 15.

[61] BL Add. MSS 5829, f. 23. Increased female participation in local religious
affairs was a feature of the 1640s and 1650s: see Keith Thomas 'Women and the
Civil War sects', *Past and Present*, no. 13 (1958).

[62] *Suffolk Committees for Scandalous Ministers*, ed. Holmes, p. 9.

examine it in the light of continuities stretching between the late medieval period and the eighteenth century. Even so, it would be otiose to write off the depositions of 1644 simply as a replication of pre-Reformation complaints. However selectively, a more active and demanding Christianity had made its impact upon and been internalized by Essex villagers: the higher expectations of clerical standards implicit in the complaints against these scandalous and malignant ministers were an important consequence of these processes.

The complaints also help illustrate something of importance on the stage of national politics, the extent and depth of disquiet at what were regarded as the neo-popish innovations of the 1630s. Debate continued over the exact meaning and impact of Arminianism in the two decades before 1640.[63] Revisionist historians of the period, having discredited the socio-economic causes of the Civil Wars and dismantled all but the shortest term of their political causes, are now denying its religious causes, and arguing that 'it is difficult to discern any doctrinal high road to civil war'.[64] From the perspective of theological debate among the educated elite, such a difficulty is, without doubt, a genuine one: but once we leave 'top person's history'[65] the issue becomes much clearer. Our godly Essex villagers had a very precise idea of what they did and did not want in matters religious, and the 'innovations' of the 1630s, however undeserving of the label 'Arminian', and however far from the reality of the popish practices they so feared, were categorically among the things they did not want. It was, perhaps, inevitable that dislike should focus on the visible and concrete target provided by altar rails: but, as we have seen, objections to the innovations also comprehended doctrinal matters, notably what was considered as a dilution of predestinarian doctrine. Those seeking to construct arguments refuting the importance of Arminianism, or fear of that entity, as a cause of the English Civil War would do well to turn from the abstractions of theological debate, important and fascinat-

[63] The key to recent reworking of this subject was provided by Nicholas Tyacke, 'Puritanism, Arminianism and counter revolution', in *The Origins of the English Civil War*, ed. Conrad Russell (London, 1973). For the debate currently surrounding the subject, see Peter White, 'The rise of Arminianism reconsidered', *Past and Present*, no. 101 (1983), pp. 34–54; and William Lamont's 'Comment' on this piece, *Past and Present*, no. 107 (1985), pp. 227–31.

[64] White, 'Rise of Arminianism', p. 54.

[65] Lamont, 'Comment', p. 227.

ing though these are, and spend a few days working through local government records for the late 1630s and early 1640s.[66] Many God-fearing English men and women, however ill-equipped they may have been to argue points of theology with Laud, Neile, or their bishops, were convinced that their religion was being subverted from above, and they were anxious to do something about this when the opportunity was given to them.

Yet, as many conservatives had already grasped by 1644, encouraging even well-affected villagers to assess and criticize their minister was assisting the release of a number of genii from their bottles, genii that were unlikely to be decanted peacefully into the shattering vessel of hard-line Presbyterianism. Manchester's instructions of early 1644 were insistent that in replacing scandalous ministers commissioners should 'take a special care that no anabaptist or antinomian be nominated; but only such as are very orthodox in their opinions, & such that the Assembly of Divines now assembled at Westminster will accept of'.[67] However, within four years Ralph Josselin was expressing disquiet at the prospect of meeting Leveller soldiers, and within five, Presbyterian disquiet at the drift to the left was being noted in an Essex parish register.[68] Even before that date, sectarianism had arisen in the eastern counties, and Laurence Clarkson, the future Ranter, had wandered through Essex, sleeping rough in church porches as he went.[69] A few years later James Parnell the Quaker was dead as a consequence of a hunger strike in Colchester gaol, where he had been incarcerated after insulting the county government, and his follow-

---

[66] To take one very pertinent illustration of this point, a Nicholas Sworder of Faulkbourne and his wife, of the parish of the strongly anti-parliamentarian Edward Strutt, were presented before the local archdeacon in 1640 for refusing to take communion kneeling at the rails, but 'according to the peace of his owne conscience': Essex RO, Archdeaconry of Colchester Act Books, D/ACA 54, f. 140v.

[67] BL Add. MSS 5829, f. 8.

[68] *Diary of Ralph Josselin*, ed. Macfarlane, pp. 94–5; Smith, *Ecclesiastical History*, pp. 100–2.

[69] A. L. Morton, *The World of the Ranters: Religious radicalism in the English Revolution* (London, 1970), p. 131.

ers were waiting in eager anticipation of his resurrection.[70] Some members of the lower orders had adopted religious positions far more radical, or at least far more exotic, than those of the deponents of 1644, who were merely angered by Laudian innovations or drunken and lascivious priests. Yet the ideas and aspirations of this popular Puritanism demands as much attention as those of the religious radicals upon whom so much research has been done, not least because this moderate popular Puritanism was as likely to be offended by the Ranter as by the Laudian innovator. Further investigation along these lines might well throw some light on the limitations of popular radicalism in the Interregnum.

[70] *Diary of Ralph Josselin*, ed. Macfarlane, pp. 366–7, 397; PRO King's Bench Ancient Indictments, K.B.9, 874/177; Barry Reay, *The Quakers and the English Revolution* (London, 1985), p. 36.

14

The 'French Cromwell'?
The Cardinal de Retz and
the English Revolution

COLIN JONES

The Coadjutor has always spoken with veneration of Cromwell as a man sent by God to England, saying that he would bring forth others in other countries; and once in respectable company . . . he said, so as to restore the courage of the Duke of Beaufort: If Monsieur de Beaufort is Fairfax, I am Cromwell.

This second-hand piece of tittle-tattle according to which Jean-François-Paul de Gondi, the 'mitred Frondeur', coadjutor to the archbishop of Paris and the future Cardinal de Retz, compared himself to 'God's Englishman', came from the pen of Cardinal Mazarin in April 1651, as from temporary exile at the height of the Fronde he struggled to retain the affection and trust of the Queen Regent, Anne of Austria, mother of the infant Louis XIV.[1] The remark could doubtless be dismissed as springing from that febrile paranoia familiar to hounded statesmen – though paranoia may be too unkind a word, given the almost universal loathing which the political nation displayed for most of the Fronde towards Richelieu's successor as 'cardinal minister'. The fact that Henrietta Maria had been installed in the Louvre since her escape from England via Exeter in 1644 doubtless made the English comparison

I would like to thank David Bond, Anne Duffin and Sarah Jones, post-graduates working at Exeter under the supervision of Ivan Roots, for their encouragement and help in writing this chapter.

[1] *Lettres du Cardinal Mazarin à la reine, à la princesse palatine . . . écrites pendant sa retraite hors de France en 1651 et 1652*, ed. J. Ravenel (Paris, 1836), p. 5. The phrase 'Frondeur mitré' is used of Retz in a contemporary pamphlet, *Les Frondeurs champêtres. Eclogue allégorique sur les affaires du temps* ([Paris], 1651).

seem apposite: just as Mazarin and the court began to get jumpy about the intentions of the Frondeurs, there the English queen would be, ululating doomfully and rattling her rosary beads. Retz haunted Mazarin down to his death-bed – '[his] name alone was more capable than entire armies of making Mazarin tremble', one contemporary recorded[2] – and the English prism through which the cardinal minister viewed his rival only accentuated his dread: he warned Anne that she should consider Retz a republican; he blamed him for having translated a work at the outbreak of the Fronde describing the background to England's Civil War; and he reproached him for (allegedly) commissioning one of his retainers of Scottish extraction to write a history of England which would encourage speculation on the execution of kings.[3] It seems in fact that the charges of republicanism and regicidal intentions were far from the mark, though Mazarin's suspicions may have been stimulated by knowledge of an approach made to Retz by Cromwell in 1651 through Sir Henry Vane (which the coadjutor, if we are to believe his account, cold-shouldered).[4]

The yoking together of the names of Retz and Cromwell, and the political situations of England and France, is a helpful reminder of the international range of political reference which statesmen could evoke in this period which historians are still prone to view as an age of 'General Crisis'.[5] If the latter term has won wide acceptance,

[2] Godefroy Hermant, *Mémoires*, cited in R. Golden, *The Godly Rebellion. Parisian Curés and the Religious Fronde. 1652–62* (Chapel Hill, 1982), p. 18.

[3] *Lettres du Cardinal Mazarin*, pp. 5, 6, 9. Cf. Mazarin's private note-books, excerpts of which are to be found in vol IX, pp. 436–60, of Retz's *Oeuvres*, Grands Ecrivains de France ser., ed. A. Feillet, J. Gourdault and R. Chantelauze (10 vols, Paris, 1870–96). The work of Retz's retainer in question was R. Mentet de Salmonet's *Histoire des troubles de la Grand' Bretagne* (Paris, 1649) – in point of fact a staunchly royalist tract.

[4] Cardinal de Retz, *Oeuvres*, Pléiade edn, ed. M. T. Hipp and M. Pernot (Paris, 1984). This recent edition of Retz's works is a fine addition to literary scholarship and places the cardinal more in the context of recent historical studies than other editions. No historian will, however, want to be without the ten volumes of the Works in the Grands Ecrivains de France series, for they contain a great deal of fascinating historical documentation.

[5] As useful an introduction as any to the 'General Crisis' literature are the early essay collection, T. Aston (ed.), *Crisis in Europe 1560–1660* (London, 1965), and the more recent collection, G. Parker and L. M. Smith (eds), *The General Crisis of the Seventeenth Century* (London, 1978). For Anglo–French relations, see the erudite overview of P. A. Knachel, *England and the Fronde. The Impact of the English Civil War and Revolution on France* (New York, 1967). There is still much to be gleaned, too, from R. Ascoli, *La Grande-Bretagne devant l'opinion française au XVIIe siècle* (2 vols, Paris, 1930).

there has been surprisingly little research done on the perceptions of participants in revolts and rebellions in these decades of those involved in similar exploits elsewhere in Europe. Evidently the rebellions of the 'General Crisis' did not share a common ideological frame of reference – as was to be the case, for example, with the international phenomenon of jacobinism in the 1790s – but even if we view the revolts and rebellions of these years as sharing little in common but their contemporaneity, this modest comparative approach does seem worth attempting. The aim of the present study will be to investigate how England and the main dramatis personae of the 'Great Rebellion' were perceived by the Cardinal de Retz, arch-conspirator, leading Frondeur, one of the most intelligent analysts of the dynamics of rebellion of the early modern era and a keen student of comparative politics, who was well aware that the period in which he was living was 'infamous for the great and strange revolutions which have therein occurred'.[6]

Scion of a family which since leaving Italy in modest circumstances in the early sixteenth century had raised itself to a position of considerable eminence within the French aristocracy, the young Retz had from early manhood been fascinated by rebellion – theory and practice, French and non-French, past and present. At first, this might have been ascribed to youthful swashbuckling of a piece with the duelling escapades and erotic adventures which he was to describe with such relish in his *Mémoires*. It was soon apparent, however, that it was more than that. In 1639, he drafted a study of the Fieschi rebellion in Genoa in 1547 (it would eventually be published in 1665 as *La conjuration de Jean-Louis de Fiesque*) which constitutes a straightforward apologia for revolt.[7] Hero-worship of the eponymous rebel leader, Gian-Luigi de' Fiesqui, bespeaks the most patent wish-fulfilment, while the allegorical nature of the essay must have made the ears of the Cardinal Richelieu burn as he read from an early manuscript which fell into his hands of the evil doings of the tyrannical Gianettino Doria. Richelieu is said to have marked out the young Retz as 'un petit audacieux' with a gallows look about him, and blocked his promotion within the church

[6] The quotation is taken from the preface to the work by Salmonet de Mentet, cited above, which was dedicated to Retz. There are a number of biographies of Retz, the most recent of which is J. H. M. Salmon, *Cardinal de Retz. Anatomy of a Conspirator* (London, 1969).

[7] For the *Conjuration de Fiesque*, besides the Pléiade edition of the *Oeuvres*, pp. 1055–87, see also D. Watts's edition (Oxford, 1967).

which – very much against his will and in spite of his being by his own admission 'perhaps the least ecclesiastical soul ever to exist in all the universe' – his father had forced him to enter.[8] In 1641, he entered into an aristocratic conspiracy directed by the Count of Soissons to overthrow Richelieu. In the event, the revolt aborted: the count, who was to have given the signal for revolt in Paris on defeating a royal army under Châtillon at the battle of La Marfée, was thoughtless enough, as he toured the battlefield surveying his victory, to attempt to raise his visor with a loaded pistol and succeeded only in blowing his brains out. (Aristocratic para-cretinism is a factor in the failure of noble revolts which historians have tended to neglect, but of which Retz – witness his portrayal of the witless Duke of Beaufort in the *Mémoires* – was only too well aware.)

With Richelieu dead (in 1642), the way seemed clearer for Retz's advancement within the church which he saw as his destiny and his birthright. The Gondi family had held the see of Paris as its fief since 1568, so the young Retz's preferment in 1643 to the post of coadjutor to his uncle, the dissolute Jean-François de Gondi, archbishop of Paris, came as no surprise. To buttress his standing in the church he was in the same year appointed archbishop of Corinth *in partibus infidelium*. Only then did he take holy orders, also receiving spiritual instruction from Vincent de Paul. Given the long absences of his uncle from Paris, the new coadjutor virtually ran the diocese. By patient administration, liberal charities and elo-quent sermons – which he had publicized in the *Gazette de France* – he built up a popularity among the diocesan clergy and among his flock which would stand him in good stead during the Fronde. He continued to nurture his conspiratorial designs, however, and the Fronde broke out at an ideal stage in his career for him to engage in political activity: 'I allowed my senses to be tickled', he recorded of his activities in 1648, 'by the title of leader of faction that I had always honoured in Plutarch's *Lives*.' (Pléiade, p. 227.)

Retz received pretty rough handling from his contemporaries for the role which he played during the Fronde. Where Cromwell had to await the Restoration for the influential frontal assaults of a James Heath and a Slingsby Bethel, Retz was assailed even in the

[8] For Richelieu and Retz, see the Pléiade edition of the *Oeuvres*, pp. 135–9. The 'ecclesiastical soul' quotation will be found in Pléiade, p. 129. Henceforth quota-tions are given with indications in the text as to their page-numbers in the same edition. Translations are my own.

course of the Fronde in the most vicious and distorting way (though it must be admitted that in the clutch of *mazarinades* which he penned Retz gave quite as good as he got).[9] Moreover, although Retz and Cromwell were accused of similar nefarious characteristics – both were said to be frenetically ambitious, wildly hypocritical, past-masters at using religion as a façade for their fell designs and tyrannical behaviour – the mud has been more difficult to wipe from the character of the Frenchman, to the extent that his name is still often viewed in standard works on the Fronde as a byword for duplicity and ambition. His dubious reputation has long besmirched the value of his memoirs, and it is only in relatively recent years that, in a veritable renaissance of Retzian scholarship, the sincerity of their author has been upheld and their utility highlighted in offering a priceless *aperçu* of the ambiance of revolt in early seventeenth-century France.[10]

Perhaps the most critical distorting factor in Retz's memoirs is the fact that they were the product of an acknowledged political failure, and the temptation to transmute recorded recollection into a compensating device is often very strong. Retz was effectively 'bought off' from amidst the ranks of the Frondeurs in 1651 with the promise from the court of a cardinal's hat – a circumstance about which, more than any other, he is coy and guarded in the memoirs.[11] But he was only in his thirties when the Fronde finished – Mazarin was fifty – and a full political career still beckoned. In the event, he was to be arrested and imprisoned by Mazarin in 1652. Although in 1654, in a cloak-and-dagger style which doubtless delighted Alexandre Dumas, he escaped from captivity – he had kept rabbits in prison, but soon became bored – and in the

[9] See Pléiade, pp. 53–124, for *mazarinades* ascribed to Retz; and for a sampler of pamphlets attacking him, see C. Jones, *Contre Retz. Sept pamphlets du temps de la Fronde* (Exeter, 1981).

[10] The key works in the renaissance of Retzian studies are A. Bertière, *Le Cardinal de Retz mémorialiste* (Paris, 1977); D. Watts, *Cardinal de Retz. The Ambiguities of a Seventeenth-Century Mind* (Oxford, 1980); and the Pléiade edition of the *Oeuvres*. See also the wider perspectives offered in M. T. Hipp, *Mythes et réalités. Enquête sur le roman et les mémoires (1660–1700)* (Paris, 1976). Other historical revaluations include H. Carrier, 'Sincérité et création littéraire dans les Mémoires du cardinal de Retz', *XVIIe siècle*, nos. 94–5 (1971); M. Pernot, 'L'Apport des mémoires du cardinal de Retz à la connaissance historique du XVIIe siècle', *Bulletin de la Société d'histoire moderne*, 1980; and C. Jones, 'The organisation of conspiracy and revolt in the *Mémoires* of the Cardinal de Retz', *European Studies Review*, 11 (1981).

[11] For the incriminating evidence, cf. R. Chantelauze, *Le Cardinal de Retz et l'affaire du chapeau* (2 vols, Paris, 1878).

same year succeeded his deceased uncle as archbishop of Paris, he was to spend most of the ensuing decade in enforced political exile trudging remorselessly round Europe before finally agreeing in 1661 to resign the archbishopric of Paris, and to live in retirement away from that city. Retz's attempts to involve himself in French politics while in exile had not been successful. He had from 1654 nurtured the so-called Religious Fronde whose origins lay in his own equivocal status as archbishop and exile. He played the role of prelate-in-exile with considerable flair. Comparisons with Cromwell now made little sense, and if he looked for English parallels with his predicament, it was Thomas Becket, 'the famous defender of ecclesiastical freedom', whose name he evoked.[12] By the late 1650s, moreover, the Religious Fronde had developed into a wrangle over the power and perquisites of the Parisian clergy and the position of the archbishop was in danger of being forgotten. Back in France from 1661, with Mazarin dead, but with Louis XIV firmly in the saddle, and with his old power-base in Paris gone, Retz had little room for manoeuvre. He performed the occasional diplomatic mission for Louis XIV, though the monarch always maintained an icy demeanour towards him which kept him firmly in place. Penned up in his estates at Commercy in Lorraine – he shunned society for fear of appearing, he explained to Madame de Sévigné, 'a fairground hermit'[13] – he became more interested in spiritual matters and underwent something of a conversion from his louche old ways. The roué and the rebel turned hermit now at least had the time to write his memoirs (scholars now date their composition to between 1675 and 1677),[14] having retained his old lucidity, imbued with a more stoic serenity and a pretty fair remembrance of things past. He could make of his recollections not only the history of his life but a thoughtful distillation – tinctured on occasion, it is true, by the might-have-been – of a lifetime of meditation and practice on the theme of rebellion.

In everything regarding rebellion, Retz thought comparatively as well as analytically. Even the etymology of the epithet, the 'Fronde', as well as its political exploitation, was inflected by foreign experience of revolt:

[12] For the Becket comparisons, see the Grands Ecrivains de France edition of the *Oeuvres*, VI, pp. 31–2, 205, 361–2, etc. Cf. *Thurloe State Papers* V, p. 390, for confirmation on this point from an unexpected source. For the Religious Fronde generally, see Golden, *The Godly Rebellion*.

[13] Cited Pléiade, p. 1341.

[14] Cf. Bertière, *Retz mémorialiste*, pp. 104–20.

Bachaumont said in passing one day that the Parlement was acting like schoolboys who play catapult [*fronde*] in the Paris ditches, who run off as soon as they see a police official and who regroup as soon as he leaves. This comparison, which people found rather funny, was commemorated in song . . . We gave some encouragement to it, because we noticed that this distinction by names stimulated people's spirits. The President Bellièvre remarked to me that the First President was using this little gibe against us, but I showed him a manuscript of Saint-Aldegonde, one of the founders of the Dutch Republic. Here it was remarked that when Brederede reacted angrily to the fact that they were called *Beggars*, the Prince of Orange wrote to him saying that he did not understand his true interest, and that they should not fail to put on their cloaks little embroidered tramping bags as a badge. That evening we determined to wear hat-bands which had some sort of catapult or sling . . . The effect this trifle had was unbelievable. Everything was in the 'fronde' fashion – bread, hats, garters, gloves, sleeves, fans, costume lace – and we were ourselves in the fashion more by this bauble than by the essential. (Pléiade, pp. 428–9.)[15]

When analysing the dynamics of rebellion, Retz did, it is true, tend to prefer to look to French history for his examples: 'Why seek foreign examples', he exclaims at one point, 'when we have so many domestic ones?' (Pléiade, p. 195.) He does, however, have a wide range of historical reference at his command (examples abound from biblical history, Antiquity, Swiss, Italian, even Turkish history) yet seems oddly reticent about the English experience of revolution in the 1640s. The execution of Charles I in 1649 had had a dramatic effect on European opinion.[16] *Mazarinades* and memoirs in their very different ways attest to the traumatizing effect of the event in a France in the throes of the Fronde. If the occasional pamphleteer flippantly evoked the English hurling kings' heads around as if they were tennis-balls,[17] the general response was far from light-hearted. There seemed something irrefrangibly base about the act of killing a monarch which made rational analysis of causes a difficult procedure, so that it was easiest to ascribe the 'Revolution' to the native propensity of the

---

[15] The existence of such a manuscript seems dubious, though the point about the 'Sea Beggars' is clearly close enough to the truth. Bachaumont and Pomponne de Bellièvre were allies of Retz in the Parlement of Paris; while the 'First President' was senior parlementarian Mathieu Molé, who was closer to the king's party at the time of the citation.

[16] Knachel, *England and the Fronde*, pp. 53 ff., is especially good on this.

[17] Ascoli, *La Grande-Bretagne*, p. 79.

English to lunacy. Opponents of the Regency government had
henceforth the taint of crypto-republicanism to live down, especially since, as Retz and other memoir-writers record, the occasional
republican slogan was shouted at high spots during the Fronde,
and also in the light of the republican fling associated with the
Ormée in Bordeaux in 1652–3.[18] The wish to deny republican aims
and sympathies was doubtless as real when Retz composed his
memoirs under the stifling cultural atmosphere of the Sun King as
during the Fronde itself, and this, together with the seemingly
irrational aspect of Charles I's execution, may well be a factor in
explaining his reserve in analysing the causes of the 'Great Rebellion'.

Another factor in this was Retz's personal acquaintance with
several of the protagonists of the English Revolution. Even in the
1650s this was having its effect on Retz's attitudes. Trade war
between Cromwell's England and Mazarin's France had been
ended in 1655 in the Treaty of Westminster, which also stated that
neither power would in future harbour the domestic enemies of the
other. In practice, the latter clause, which was kept secret, meant
that any chance of Bourbon help in a Stuart restoration had passed
and that Charles II would not be permitted to reside in France. A
further treaty in May 1657 stipulated that, in return for the help of
6,000 soldiers plus naval assistance in the war against Spain, the
French would hand over to the English the ports of Dunkirk,
Gravelines and Mardyke, the former in perpetuity once it had been
captured from Spain. This treaty enraged Retz and stung him into
a reproachful critique from his exile which enjoyed a limited
success in Europe, the *Très Humble et Très Importante Remonstrance au
Roi sur la remise des places maritimes de Flandres entre les mains des Anglais.*
(Pléiade, pp. 103–24.) Historians have tended to view this polemic
as a renewal of Retz's combat against Mazarin, who is here accused
of leading the king astray with putatively 'machiavellian' policies
which constituted 'an infraction of all the ancient laws of [the]
kingdom' (Pléiade, p. 103.) – a familiar Retzian theme as we shall
see – and, in the guise of seeking an end to the war, only making a
general peace more difficult to achieve.

[18] For republican strains in the Paris Fronde, cf. Pléiade, pp. 386, 1392, etc. The
standard work on the republican Ormée movement – with which Retz had no
connection whatever – is now S. Westrich, *The Ormée of Bordeaux. A Revolution during
the Fronde* (Baltimore and London, 1972).

Although the anti-Mazarinian theme in the *Très Humble Remonstrance* is strong, the pamphlet is equally, however, an attack on Oliver Cromwell. The English, who had scarcely consoled themselves for the loss of Calais in 1558, would be delighted to have a military foothold on the continent from which even Paris would no longer feel secure, all the more in that republican England posed a greater threat to European peace than England under a monarchy. Not only had Mazarin sealed an alliance with an old, unforgiving and powerful enemy, that enemy was also represented by a usurper, 'a soldier [*sic*] who has no other throne but the scaffold on which he bore the son-in-law of the Great Henry'. (Pléiade, p. 106.) This usurper was, moreover, a heretic. Retz painted a lurid picture of the rights of the catholic inhabitants of the three port towns being trampled under foot by Cromwell (though in fact, unbeknown to Retz, clauses in the treaty of 1657 had guaranteed that the inhabitants would be permitted to practice catholicism unmolested). Cromwell, this 'false prophet who looks down from the Tower of London', was on the *qui-vive* for any opportunity which would make 'the Protector of England protector of the protestants of France'. (Pléiade, pp. 110, 108.) Thus the concession to England would be opening up the Pandora's Box of confessional strife which had bedevilled France throughout the sixteenth century. Cromwell would rub his hands, Retz suggested, at the prospect of 'two or three thousand clods' (*goujats*) from England being sufficient motive for the co-religionists of France and Spain to slaughter each other in their thousands. It would stimulate his appetite for expansion, an appetite which other powers, even protestant ones like Holland, 'the sagest republic to exist in all the universe', feared. (Pléiade, pp. 110, 115.) 'The fruit of our prostitution' in signing the Anglo–French accord was thus 'to confound us with the declared enemies of all crowns and of all kingdoms'. Mazarin had supped with the devil himself – this 'demon of ambition', this 'modern Attila', the 'parricide of royalty', this 'tyrant, the murderer of [the] uncle [of Louis XIV]' (Pléiade, pp. 110, 115, 117, 106 . . .) – but not with a long enough spoon.

The vehement string of injurious epithets with which Retz assails Cromwell in the *Très Humble Remonstrance* of 1657 raises the suspicion that the cardinal, aware of his reputation in Mazarinian propaganda as a 'French Cromwell', did protest too much. Although his religious rhetoric is in a way very much par for the course, coming as it does from a cardinal of the catholic church, there is little sign of Retz having an inkling of the possible religious motivation of the English statesman: the robust religious bellicosity of that Puritanism whose impact in the English Revolution historians are still debating, might have come from another planet from the world of shady political dealing and artfully pious sophistry inhabited by Retz.

The element of crude polemic in the pamphlet does however seem to have established Retz's credentials as an opponent of Cromwell, and indeed in the following year he was approached by the entourage of Charles II to act as a go-between in negotiations with the pope.[19] Charles wished to get Retz to intercede in secret with the pope to build up diplomatic pressure on German and Italian princes in favour of his restoration. The negotiations failed, but not before they had allowed Retz a chance to imagine for himself a new revolutionary career in England as the protector of English catholics. He described himself in October 1658 as being 'unimaginably impatient' to serve Charles, and petitioned him that if the latter 'thought that because of my rank I can do something among the catholics of England, I would hold myself the happiest man in the world to be not altogether useless to him, and would journey to London with more joy than ever I would take the road to Paris.'[20] Charles poured cold water on this outlandish idea – Retz could not even speak English – and their relationship blossomed very little more after this. Retz's attempts to get Charles to intercede for him after the Restoration were not crowned with success, the new king of England preferring to give him money. By 1661, anxious to foster Anglo–French entente, Charles was pooh-poohing to Mazarin the very idea of any friendship or obligation on his part to the still-itinerant Retz.[21]

Although relations between Charles II and Retz had cooled by the time the latter wrote his memoirs, the memory of his friendship with Charles doubtless coloured his view of Cromwell on a personal level. But Retz's pamphlet also struck a more ideological note. It is instructive that Retz should at one stage in the pamphlet characterize Cromwell as a 'soldier'. (Pléiade, p. 106.) This touches on a leitmotiv apparent throughout Retz's political thinking, namely the

[19] F. J. Routledge, 'The negotiations between Charles II and the Cardinal de Retz, 1658–9', *TRHS*, 5th ser., 6, 1956.
[20] T. Carte, *A Collection of Original Letters and Papers concerning the Affairs of England from the Year 1641–60* (London, 1739), p. 143.
[21] *Clarendon State Papers*, III, Supplement, pp. iii, iv, v, ix.

severe limitations in public affairs of violence, as represented by the soldier, when unrestrained and unfettered by the force of law. The resort to violence at the expense of law was a development which he associated with the ideas of Machiavelli – a name which was used as an ideological projectile throughout the period of the Fronde – and the historical phenomenon of the growth in the power of the state.[22]

Retz was no warrior, even if he would have liked to have been. The basis of his power and influence in the Fronde lay above all in his political skills, in the 'science [of faction]'. (Pléiade, p. 822.) He never controlled a faction which had a reliable force of fighting men in tow. At the time of the siege of Paris in 1649, Retz had levied a small force to help in the defence of the city, though the 'regiment of Corinth' (as it was dubbed in reference to Retz's archiepiscopal status) was routed in farcical manner when confronted by royal troops.[23] Similarly the following which he cultivated among the Parisian bourgeois militia was useful for keeping control of the streets and for crowd manipulation, but it clearly would not stand the heat of pitched battle.[24] Of course the great nobles with whom he allied had their retinues of retainers and followers, and Retz himself on occasion called up men from his estates to act in his defence, and took on other troops as needed – he mentions several hundred Scots who helped protect him in his palace in 1651 – but these composed a large personal bodyguard rather than a private army.[25] On the occasion during the Fronde in 1649 when Retz came close to winning over a royal army, headed by Turenne, to the cause of the Frondeurs, he had been frustrated by Mazarin buying off Turenne's army before their general could act. In the negotiations concerning this army which he conducted with Turenne's brother, the Duke of Bouillon, Retz portrays himself in the *Mémoires* as using all his variegated political skills to rein in the aggressive instincts of the battle-hardened *condottieri*. Bouillon and his ilk would cheerfully have relied totally on naked coercion to

---

[22] Excellent background in E. Thuau, *Raison d'état et pensée politique à l'époque de Richelieu* (Paris, 1966); and N. Keohane, *Philosophy and the State in France: the Renaissance to the Enlightment* (Princeton, 1980). Cf. too H. Carrier, 'Machiavel dans les pamphlets de la Fronde', in *L'Italianisme en France au XVIIe siècle. Actes du VIIIe Congrès de la Société française de littérature comparée* (Turin, 1968).

[23] Cf. Salmon, *Cardinal de Retz*, pp. 113, 118, 120.

[24] Pléiade, pp. 228–9, 592–4, 607–8, etc.

[25] For example, Pléiade, pp. 612, 785.

achieve the aims of the Frondeurs. However viable this might seem in the short term, however, Retz was convinced that in the long term it would be suicidal. Any revolt, in his eyes, needed the legitimation of law, and for this reason the support of the Parlement of Paris. 'It's my old song,' he has himself say to Bouillon in the course of one of their debates, 'everything with the Parlement, nothing without it.' (Pléiade, p. 358.)

Retz's political position was a brand of that 'aristocratic constitutionalism'[26] also to be found in the early seventeenth century in England where, however, the scale of constitutional innovation against which it protested was far less extreme than in France. Accordingly, Retz placed great stress upon the Parlement, which extended a degree of legitimate sanction to revolt which any government would only ignore at its peril. The trend towards absolutism, which minimized the constitutional role of the parlements, he regarded as wholly regrettable. The kings he admired were monarchs like Saint Louis, Charles V, Louis XII and Henri IV, who had respected the Parlement and had allowed it to act as a 'wise link . . . between the licence of kings and the libertinage of peoples', checking the pretensions of the former and, as supreme legal body within the state, maintaining law and order among the people at large. (Pléiade, pp. 195, 256.) Stable monarchical rule, he held, was characterized by:

. . . the conjunction of arms and laws . . . [T]his conjunction is so necessary that [the monarchy] cannot be maintained except with them both. Laws without arms fall into contempt; arms which are not moderated by laws soon fall into anarchy. (Pléiade, p. 195.)

To attempt to overthrow this equilibrium between force and law is ultimately unwise because it sets in motion forces which threaten the state's long-term existence. Infringement of the rights of the law, he states, is a procedure 'which always pleases unenlightened princes, because they imagine that it will mean the extension of their authority . . . but which in consequence serves as pretext for the great and as motive for the people to rise in revolt.' (Pléiade, p. 195.) The genesis of revolt thus lay, for Retz, in the abuse of

---

[26] J. H. Elliott borrows this phrase, originally used by Michael Roberts in a Swedish context, for a wider European referent in his essay 'England and Europe: a common malady?', in *The Origins of the English Civil War*, ed. C. Russell (Old Woking, 1981 edn), p. 255.

executive power and, in the French case, in the long-term trend towards absolutism embodied most strikingly in the policies of Richelieu, who 'formed in the most legitimate of monarchies the most scandalous and the most dangerous tyranny'. (Pléiade, p. 194.) By pursuing absolutist policies, Richelieu had reduced France to a state of torpor and lethargy which he and his successor, Mazarin, mistook for resignation and acceptance. In fact, by preferring coercion to consent they were incubating revolt. In the *Conjuration de Fiesque*, Retz has one of the rebels say on the eve of revolt, 'the state in which . . . our Republic lies has something about it of the nature of those great illnesses which in spite of the stricken condition they cause excite in the mind of the sick violent desires for cure.' (Pléiade, p. 22.) In the *Mémoires*, he follows the same line of analysis. On the eve of the revolt of the Swiss cantons in the fourteenth century, the Swiss had seemed 'stifled by their chains'. In the sixteenth century, in the Dutch Revolt, 'the Dutch believed themselves to be subjugated by the Duke of Alba.' Just as in all these cases, apparent 'lethargy' had been followed by 'convulsions', this would be the way that the Fronde broke out, in the resistance of the Parlement of Paris to the constitutional innovations of the cardinal minister. (Pléiade, pp. 200–1.)

Historians who have compared the English Revolution and the Fronde have often tended to draw attention to the political weakness of the French Parlement in contrast with the English Parliament. Certainly the representative claims of the former and its part in the legislative process were of an inferior order to those of the latter. The Paris Parlement was in essence a high court of law, staffed by about two hundred magistrates, none of whom was elected, all of whom had purchased their office and all of whom – for the going rate was rather high – were drawn from the Parisian elite of wealth. The English Parliament had a national basis which the Paris Parlement, whose jurisdictional area did not even cover the whole of France, could not match. The Parlement did have representative claims, however, and these derived from its role as constitutional watchdog. All royal decrees had to be registered in the Parlement before they enjoyed the force of law. The Parlement had the right to refuse to register a law either on technical grounds or because it infringed the 'fundamental laws of the kingdom' – a woolly way of referring to an even woollier corpus of tacit agreements and unwritten conventions which made up the French constitution. If he chose, the monarch could ignore the 'remonstr-

ances' of the Parlement and forcibly register a law in a special
ceremony known as a *lit de justice*. The constitutional functions of
the Parlement were in a critical state in the 1640s. Because the
national representative body, the Estates General, had not met
since 1614, many constitutional thinkers argued, first of all, that the
representative function of the Estates was held in commission by
the Parlement until their next convocation. Second the aggressive
foreign policies of Richelieu and Mazarin had necessitated innovatory policies – higher taxes, the introduction of the system of
Intendants, the breaking down of municipal and provincial privileges – which caused a good deal of discontent and upset the
customary constitutional balances. Third, the king was still a
minor (he had been born in 1638) and it was possible to cite
historical precedent to the effect that it was invalid to push through
major legislation, as had become the habit of the Regency government in the 1640s, by *lit de justice*. Thus although the representative
status of the Parlement was weak, the legalistic umbrella it erected
against state innovations made its constitutional position rather
strong, a point of which Retz was well aware.[27]

Historians are wont to make less of the constitutional opinions of
individual Frondeurs than of their personal ambitions and animosi-
ties. New light has recently been thrown on this important area by
the researches of Daniel Dessert.[28] The French state required
massive funding for its ambitious war policies from the 1630s
onwards. Though usually channelled through those financiers who
were to be the convenient scapegoat of French society, this money
tended to come, in the final analysis, from those in French society
with the most wealth, namely the great aristocracy. The latter lent
money to the state, using – for money-lending was even more taboo
in the aristocratic code of ethics than in canon law – a variety of
subtle stratagems (front-men, secret cartels, etc.), thus hiding their
tracks as effectively from contemporaries as, later, from historians.
These individuals would, one imagines, be relatively content so
long as the state honoured its financial engagements. In the fren-

[27] A. L. Moote, *The Revolt of the Judges: the Parlement of Paris and the Fronde, 1643–52*
(Princeton, 1971), which contains an admirable survey of the 'administrative
revolution' achieved by Richelieu and Mazarin, argues this point very cogently.
Moote has, however, been criticized for under-rating the specific contribution to
the Fronde of the non-Parlementarian nobility: cf. R. Bonney, 'The French Civil
War, 1649–53', *European Studies Review*, 8 (1978).
[28] D. Dessert, *Argent, pouvoir et société au grand siècle* (Paris, 1984).

zied financial atmosphere of the late 1630s and 1640s, however, this was not the case: the king's council had to engage in all manner of devaluations and revaluations, depreciations of state bonds and annuities, and the like, just to keep afloat. In order to protect themselves against adventitious losses caused by the irrationality of the state's financial policies, the aristocracy became more demanding of lucrative offices and other perquisites which were always, however, in relatively short supply. In the extreme case, as during the Fronde, a take-over of the king's council and the assassination or exile of the principal minister might be envisaged.

The Frondeurs were clearly out, then, for all they could get. An additional strength of Dessert's work is to demonstrate that so was everybody else. The conventional distinctions which underpin much of the writing on the Fronde between the 'modern', disinterested state bureaucracy virtuously trying to hold the line against large numbers of 'archaic', 'feudal', selfish Frondeurs is exploded for the myth it is. All noses were in the trough, or wanted to be. Although Mazarin, for example, lost his entire fortune in the Fronde, he was to die less than ten years later the wealthiest private individual in the entire history of the Ancien Régime, a status he achieved through corruption and peculation on a truly epic scale.[29] So great was the amount of money passing through the hands of the state's servants – income from higher taxes, from the now nationalized system of venal office-holding, from massive loans and so on – and so great were the financial benefits which would accrue to anyone with inside knowledge of the state's financial policy, that it took superhuman efforts for money not to stick to the hands. 'Taking a percentage' was a staple part of the political morality espoused by the servants of the state.

In the light of Daniel Dessert's researches, we may be tempted into thinking that the Fronde looks less like the Alamo and more like the St Valentine's Day Massacre, less the gallant stand than the bloody episode in a gangland war. Personal avarice did not necessarily rule out, however, broad ideological consensus on a range of issues by those opposed to the government (nor indeed by figures in government). Noble conspiracies and revolts were legion in the middle decades of the seventeenth century – Richard Bonney

[29] Idem, 'Pouvoir et finance au XVIIe siècle: la fortune du cardinal Mazarin', *Revue d'histoire moderne et contemporaine*, 23 (1976). Joseph Bergin, *Cardinal Richelieu: power and the pursuit of wealth* (New Haven, 1985) appeared after this article was completed.

has counted a score between 1620 and 1670[30] – and it would be absurdly simplistic to ascribe all of these to the politics of personal interest. In fact there were common threads running through enough of them to suggest a broad measure of ideological coherence. Most notably, the high nobles were opposed to the war strategy followed by Richelieu and Mazarin and the innovatory administrative policies which flowed from it. Representative of the high nobility of which he formed part in wanting power for its own sake, if possible through control of the king's council, Retz shared the disquiet at the policies of the cardinal ministers and based his political strategy on yoking the discontent and the ambitions of *les grands* to the constitutional chariot of the Parlement. Private interest, that 'honorable emulation and high-minded ambition' he had detected vicariously in the sixteenth-century Genoan rebel Gian-Luigi de' Fieschi, did not rule out awareness of and commitment to the general weal, that 'public interest' which was one of the rallying cries of the Frondeurs.[11]

Retz contended that it was by a combination of force with legal sanction that a revolt was constitutionally well-founded and primed for success, and he supported this position with a parallel drawn from the French Wars of Religion. He showed a considerable admiration for the Duke of Maine, one of the key figures in the Catholic League. On a number of occasions in the *Mémoires*, Retz depicts himself using the example of Maine as a parable to keep his aristocratic allies in line. (Pléiade, pp. 321, 326 . . .) The Duke of Maine had, he explained to the Duke of Orléans on one occasion, a political organization far better developed than that of the Fronde, yet he had brought about the demise of his party by allowing his supporters in Paris to purge the Parlement of elements within it recalcitrant to the League's policy. Legal sanction for his revolt suffered at once, and as middle-class support drained away, the duke was forced to rely over-heavily on plebeian support and on the aid of the Spanish army, which even further compromised his efforts. Retz saw the events of the Fronde in 1652 in very much the same light. The Frondeur faction represented by the Prince of Condé (which was by then at daggers drawn with the Retzian faction) had cut its moorings from the forces of law and order,

---

[30] In his *Political Change in France under Richelieu and Mazarin, 1624–60* (Oxford, 1978), p. 283.
[31] Keohane, *Philosophy and the State*, pp. 227 ff., for an interesting discussion of 'public interest' and its intersection with private interests during the Fronde.

snubbed the Parlement and allowed a mob to start a fire in the Paris town hall which killed a number of city councillors. The extent to which Retz in his memoirs would condemn Condé is limited – after all, by the 1670s, the prince had been reconciled with the court and was widely viewed as the greatest soldier and one of the most outstanding figures of the age. Yet it must be noted that in turning his back on legal legitimation for his revolt and in attacking the Parlement, Condé was acting the part of the warrior rather than the statesman; he was rather uncomfortably close, in other words, to the 'soldier' Cromwell, scourge and purger of parliaments.

For Retz, movements of this sort were unlikely to prevail, since in any legitimate and successful revolution support was essential from the middle-class members of society who had an unthinking reflex of respect for the established order. It was the kind of middle-class people who invested in government bonds and annuities, 'an infinite number of families of the middling sort', who were, Retz affirmed, 'always the most redoubtable in revolutions'. (Pléiade, p. 450.) Condé, like Maine, had become 'tribune of the people', the puppet of demotic will like the Gracchi. Once Condé had alienated middle-class opinion by the town hall fire of July 1652, he remained a demagogue only 'as long as it pleases the most lunatic riffraff'. (Pléiade, p. 870.) Retz made a careful distinction between the statesman who was a demagogic 'tribune of the people' and an individual like himself who could claim to be 'master of the people'.[32] Doubtless this is the kind of distinction which is made rather more easily in old age sitting by the fireside than in the heat of political action, but it is clear that even during the Fronde he regarded himself as an expert in maintaining the popularity and support of the people of Paris, without relying largely on the poorer, less respectable elements of Parisian society, without sacrificing his basic constitutional position, and without losing support in the Parlement.

There were a number of ways in which Retz endeavoured to command a popular base which would not compromise his position or tie his hands. Alliance with the Parlement ensured Retz's much solid middle-class support, but there were other ways too in which Retz sought to nurture the allegiance of respectable society. One of

[32] C. Jones, 'Organisation of conspiracy and revolt', passim, for this critical distinction and for a discussion of the means by which Retz cultivated popular support in Paris.

the most important ways in which he did this was through discreet
use of his ecclesiastical position. H. G. Koenigsberger has pointed
out the extent to which religious belief in the Wars of Religion in
the sixteenth century had fulfilled many of the functions later to
be ascribed to party discipline, while the English Revolution is
replete with examples of the subtle interplay of politics and
religion.[33] Although there seems little concrete evidence in support
of the view, widely held at the time, that Retz was using the
Jansenists as a kind of 'proto-party', it certainly is true that –
keenly aware that 'the vices of an archbishop may be in an infinity
of conjunctions the virtues of a faction-leader' (Pléiade, p. 227.) – he
brazenly used the episcopal control which he enjoyed as coadjutor
over the parish clergy of Paris as a party weapon, in intelligence-
gathering about the state of public opinion, for example, and in
spreading 'rumours' about his conduct or defending his position.[34]
He also supplemented his robust and anonymous political
pamphleteering with use of the sermon and private charities for
political ends. In the 1640s and 1650s, Paris was at the height of the
religious revival associated with the Catholic Reformation, and the
elevated status which the religious reform accorded those exercising episcopal functions must have benefited Retz, while the long
family association and friendship of the Gondis with the saintly
Vincent de Paul can have done no harm either.[35] Although there
was a strong tradition of political quietism among the catholic
reformers, many religious militants were attracted to the *dévot* view
which, very much the mirror-image of the Puritan foreign policy
outlook cited above by Barry Coward, stressed the congruence of
religious and political morality, distrusted international alliances
which ran athwart of religious bonds and gave priority to the
combat against protestantism. The foreign policy dimension of the
dévot position was regret that France was engaged in war against
another catholic power (Spain – and before 1648 Austria as well),
and a wish to bring an end to the war so that the anti-protestant
campaign could be waged with more vigour at home and abroad.
This view overlapped, therefore, with the constitutionalist position

[33] H. G. Koenigsberger, 'The organisation of revolutionary parties in France
and the Netherlands during the sixteenth century', in his *Estates and Revolutions.
Essays in Early Modern European History* (Ithaca, 1971).
[34] R. Chantelauze, 'Le Cardinal de Retz et les jansénistes', in Sainte-Beuve,
Port-Royal (Pléiade edn, Paris, 1955). Cf. Golden, *The Godly Rebellion*, passim.
[35] R. Chantelauze, *Vincent de Paul et les Gondi* (Paris, 1882).

adopted by Retz. Although the latter played the *dévot* card only sparingly during the Fronde – the most blatant example of its deployment at his hands was in fact the *Très Humble Remonstrance* of 1657 – the harangue with which he had closed the Assembly of the Clergy in 1646 calling for a renewal of the anti-protestant crusade had established his credentials in *dévot* circles.[36] And throughout the period of the Fronde he does seem to have been sensitive to the extent to which the slogan of a general peace would elicit support among catholic activists.

Grounded in religious morality, popular rather than (like a Cromwell) populist, legitimate because orientated around the historic claims of the Parlement, Retz's conception of revolt also distanced itself from any English parallel in the psychological motivation behind it. Retz saw himself above all as an aristocrat, with a code of values whose high-mindedness a Huntingdon squire and 'false prophet' could scarcely begin to encompass. Retz viewed himself in revolt as a *généreux* – an individual who operated less from attachment to personal advantage than from a disinterested devotion to an ideal.[37] It was standard practice for Mazarinian propaganda throughout the Fronde to highlight the personal aims of the rebels rather than the ideological or constitutional basis to their actions; and Retz was in fact pilloried unmercifully for acting egotistically and with overweening ambition.[38] In Retz's insistence on his altruistic adherence to constitutional orthodoxy and political morality there is doubtless the kind of wish to set the record straight which occurs in – and distorts – most political memoirs. Nevertheless, he does seem to have had a point.

I do not wish to dwell here on the manifestations or incidence of the *générosité* of Retz's behaviour during the Fronde, but rather to assess how it influenced his attitudes towards England and its revolution. One important initial point is that *générosité* was above all an aristocratic virtue, a gentleman's prerogative. When *les grands* revolted against the dynastic drift towards ministerial tyranny, in Retz's view, they were motivated by an altruism which no other rebellious group could approach. The common people revolted

---

[36] The speech is given *in extenso* in the Grands Ecrivains de France edition of the *Oeuvres*, IX, pp. 22–42.

[37] Bertière, *Retz mémorialiste*, and Watts, *Cardinal de Retz*, are excellent on this point.

[38] R. Bonney, 'The Cardinal Mazarin and his critics', *Journal of European Studies*, 1980.

because they have an intrinsic predisposition to rebellion – the people is normally *frondeur*, he commented on one occasion (Pléiade, p. 524.) – and indeed one of the critical functions of public-spirited rebels like Retz was to rein in their propensity to anarchy and to canalize their rough energies in directions which did not undermine the state.[39] The middle classes tended to be involved in rebellion because their pockets were hit and behaved in a mercenary manner at the antipodes of aristocratic *générosité*. Even the Parlement – and in Retz's view we can see the French aristocracy's age-old 'cascade de mépris' – tended to act in ways which placed them among the people rather than with individuals like himself: 'Nothing is more *peuple*', he commented in one exasperated aside, than the Parlement. (Pléiade, p. 769.) Only *les grands*, then, could hope to have the public-spiritedness and altruism to rise above considerations of private advantage. And only a shrewd member of the aristocratic caste could hope to build up a power base which, while eschewing naked coercion, could effect substantial political change. (While we may smile at the vainglorious and self-regarding aspect of the latter view, it is worth pointing out that recent analyses of the Fronde have highlighted the Frondeurs' lack of political alliances and their lack of capable leadership by *les grands* as key factors in the revolt's failure.)[40]

When he looked across the Channel, Retz could see precious few signs of that *générosité* which he regarded as the key element in legitimate revolt. What he could see, especially with hindsight, was a 'soldier' (and a heretic to boot) who had led an attack on Parliament after first provoking the senseless murder of a peer of the king of France. Cromwell thus stood condemned in Retz's eyes not merely because he was a protestant and a soldier but also because he exhibited singular baseness: the baseness of spirit which went with the ambition of a social climber. This attitude comes across well in a passage – which has, it is true, a slightly apocryphal ring to it – where Retz records a conversation he had with his ally Bellièvre, who had met Cromwell in England. The Protector had apparently said to him that:

---

[39] C. Jones, 'Organisation of conspiracy and revolt', for further references on this important point.

[40] R. Bonney, 'The English and French Civil Wars', *History*, 65 (1980), pp. 369, 371, etc.

. . . one never rises so high as when one does not know where one is going. You know, I said to M. de Bellièvre, that I detest Cromwell; but however great a man we are told he is, I add scorn to my hatred if this is his feeling, for it seems to me the opinion of a madman. M. de Bellièvre in . . . returning home, where there was a numerous company awaiting him, told them of this remark . . . . [This] was reported to the Protector who sourly recalled it and said to M. de Bordeaux, the French ambassador in England, 'I know of only one man in the world who looks down on me, and that is the cardinal de Rais.' (Pléiade, p. 722.)

Retz felt less in common with Cromwell, in fact, than with someone like Montrose. For Retz the latter, 'head of the house of Grem' (sic), was:

the only man in the world who gave me the idea of certain heroes that one meets with only in Plutarch's Lives. He had supported the party of the king in his own country with a greatness unparalleled in this century; he beat the Parliamentarians though the latter were victorious everywhere else and he only disarmed after the king his master had thrown himself into the hands of his enemies. (Pléiade, p. 488.)

Retz had treated the Scottish earl well when he passed through Paris, which won Montrose, Retz slyly recalls, Mazarin's undying hostility.

The nobility of spirit which Retz detected among disinterested aristocrats he also saw in the person of the French monarchs who had resisted the secular trend towards absolutism. Chief among these is Henri IV, and it is symptomatic of Retz's approach that in the *Très Humble Remonstrance* of 1657 he accused Cromwell of being the 'murderer of the son-in-law of the Great Henri'. The obverse of this particular coin is an attachment to, or perhaps indulgence for, the descendants of Henry IV from across the Channel, Queen Henrietta Maria and Charles II.

Retz scores points heavily off Mazarin for neglecting Henrietta Maria's fortunes. Visiting her in January 1649 in her apartments at the Louvre, he found the 'poor Queen' cold and miserable, with her daughter still in bed to keep warm. Retz records how he valiantly prevailed upon the Parlement to agree to pay the queen a pension in lieu of the funds that Mazarin was failing to make available to her; not however before reflecting that: 'Posterity will find it hard to believe that a daughter of England, grand-daughter of the Great Henri [sic] could have wanted for a stick of firewood to warm

herself one January in the Louvre.' (Pléiade, pp. 294–5.)[41] Retz
glows with a special inward satisfaction when he can display his
wonted generosity on behalf of deserving royalty. The same applies
for the grandson of Henri IV, Charles II. In 1651 Retz records:

The king of England who had just lost the battle of Vorcester arrived in
Paris with milord Taf, who served him as chamberlain, valet of the
bedchamber, high butler and master of the goblet. The equipage was
worthy of the court: he had not changed his shirt since leaving England.
Milord Germain gave him one of his on arrival; but the queen his mother
did not have enough money to give him to buy one for the next day I
was ashamed for him, I was ashamed for myself; I borrowed 1,500 livres
from M. de Morangis . . . and I brought the sum to milord Taf, for the
king his master. (Pléiade, pp. 520–1.)[42]

The lofty ethic of the open-handed and open-hearted aristocrat –
an attitude of mind which calls into question whether the Corneil-
lian cult of the hero which literary critics have detected in Retz's
writings was less a concept of fiction than of *mentalité*, less a decorative
façade than an authentic structure of sensibility – thus bound
together the exiled English king-in-exile and the French arch-rebel.
If Mazarin and other supporters of strong central power tended to
view the politics of rebellion through an English prism, and thus to
make of Retz a 'Cromwell', it was equally evident that Retz and
many Frondeurs like him viewed politics through the supra-
national prism of aristocratic hauteur, blood-dues and *fidélité*. The
Retz who found so alluring the high birth and noble demeanour of
the cavalier king, grandson of Henri IV, could feel little in common
with the professional soldier, heretic, base social climber and
demagogue that was, in his eyes, Oliver Cromwell. Retz's very
different attitudes towards these two key figures of the 'Great
Rebellion' provides a striking example of the psychological gulf
which separated English revolutionary from French Frondeur; and
they highlight the paradox that, in this age of 'General Crisis',
revolutions were not yet for export.

[41] Cf. a related remark in the *Très Humble Remonstrance* pamphlet of 1658:
Pléiade, p. 105.
[42] Note Retz's gallicization of Vicount Taaffe and Henry Jermyn. Morangis was
a high official in the state's financial bureaucracy.

Select Bibliography of the Writings of Ivan Roots, 1957–1986

Ivan Roots's activities in journalism and book-reviewing are far too extensive to be included in what must inevitably be only a select bibliography of his work to date.

1957 With D. H. Pennington, *The Committee at Stafford 1643–5: the Order Book of the Staffordshire County Committee* (edited with an introduction) Staffordshire Record Society (Manchester University Press), lxxxii + 389 pp.

1958 With S. B. Chrimes, *Select Bibliography of English Constitutional History* (Historical Association, London), 39 pp.

1962 'Gentlemen and others', *History*, 47, pp. 233–8.

1965 'Die Englische Revolution', in G. Mann and A. Nitschke (eds), *Propylaen–Weltgeschichte*, vol VII (Propylaen Verlag, Berlin).

1966 *The Great Rebellion 1642–60* (Batsford, London), x + 326 pp.

1967 *Conflicts in Tudor and Stuart History* (ed.) (Oliver and Boyd, Edinburgh and London), vi + 128 pp.

1968 *The Great Rebellion 1642–60* 2nd edn (Batsford, London), x + 326 pp.
'The central government and the local community', in E. W. Ives (ed.), *The English Revolution 1600–60* (Edward Arnold, London, repr. 1971), pp. 34–47.

1969 *The Late Troubles in England,* inaugural lecture, University of Exeter (Exeter), 24 pp.
'La revoluzione Inglese', in G. Mann and A. Nitschke (eds), *I propilei Grande Storia Universale,* vol VII (Mondadori, Milan).
'The sixteenth century' and 'European history 1660–1713/21', in *Annual Bulletin of Historical Literature,* 53 (Historical Association, London)

1970 'Swordsmen and decimators: Cromwell's major-generals' and 'Interest – public, private and communal', in R. H. Parry (ed.), *The English Civil War and After 1642–58* (Macmillan, London), pp. 78–92, 111–21.
'The seventeenth century', in *Annual Bulletin of Historical Literature,* 54 (Historical Association, London), pp. 28–51.

1971 With M. M. Goldsmith (eds), John Lilburne, *Come out of her my people* (1639) (The Rota, Exeter; 2nd edn 1984).
With M. M. Goldsmith (eds), John Trenchard, *An argument, shewing that a standing army is inconsistent with a free government* (1697) (The Rota, Exeter).

1972 *The Great Rebellion 1642–60,* 3rd edn (Batsford, London), x + 326 pp.
'Cromwell's Day 1971', address given at the Annual Commemoration Service at the Houses of Parliament, 3 September 1971, *Cromwelliana* (1972), pp. 6–7.
'Cromwell's ordinances: the early legislation of the Protectorate', in G. E. Aylmer (ed.), *The Interregnum: The quest for Settlement 1646–60* (Macmillan, London; 2nd edn, 1974), pp. 143–64.
With M. M. Goldsmith (eds), Slingsby Bethel, *The World's Mistake in Oliver Cromwell* (1668) (The Rota, Exeter; repr. 1981).
With M. M. Goldsmith (eds), *London's Liberties or a Learned Argument of Law and Reason* (1651) (The Rota, Exeter; repr. 1982).

1973 *Cromwell: a Profile* (ed.), (Hill and Wang, New York, and Macmillan, London), xviii + 238 pp.
With D. H. Pennington, 'The General Crisis of the seventeenth century' and 'The Thirty Years War', tape recording (Audio Learning, London).
With M. M. Goldsmith (eds), Abiezer Coppe, *A Fiery Flying Roll* (1650) (The Rota, Exeter).
With M. M. Goldsmith (eds), *Hic Mulier: or, the Man–Woman* and *Haec Vir: or the Womanish-Man* (1620) (The Rota, Exeter).
With M. M. Goldsmith (eds), John Stearne, *A Confirmation and Discovery of Witchcraft* (1648) (The Rota, Exeter; repr. 1982).

1974 'Lawmaking in the Second Protectorate Parliament', in H. Hearder and H. R. Loyn (eds), *British Government and Administration: Essays presented to S. B. Chrimes* (University of Wales Press, Cardiff).

Introduction to and additional material in *The Diary of Thomas Burton Esq., member in the parliaments of Oliver and Richard Cromwell from 1656 to 1659*, reprint edn (4 vols, Johnson Reprint Corporation, New York and London).

'The seventeenth century, 1603–1713: British history', in *The Annual Bulletin of Historical Literature*, 57 (Historical Association, London), pp. 46–54.

With M. M. Goldsmith (eds), Laurence Clarkson, *The Lost Sheep Found* (1660) (The Rota, Exeter).

With M. M. Goldsmith (eds), R. G., *A Copy of a Letter from an Officer in the Army in Ireland* (1656) (The Rota, Exeter).

With M. M. Goldsmith (eds), Henry Sacheverell, *The Perils of False Brethren* (1709) (The Rota, Exeter).

With M. M. Goldsmith (eds), John Lord Somers, *A Letter Ballancing the Necessity of keeping a Land Force in Times of Peace* (1697) (The Rota, Exeter).

1975 Preface to A. S. P. Woodhouse, *Puritanism and Liberty: being the Army Debates, 1647–9*, 2nd edn (Dent, London).

With A. H. Woolrych, 'Oliver Cromwell – his rise to greatness' and 'Oliver Cromwell – Lord Protector' tape recording (Audio Learning, London).

With M. M. Goldsmith (eds), Bernard Mandeville, *Wishes to a Godson* (1712) (The Rota, Exeter).

With M. M. Goldsmith (eds), Sir John Spelman, *The Case of our Affaires in Law, Religion and other circumstances* (1643) (The Rota, Exeter).

1976 'De Engelse Revolutie', in G. Mann and A. Nitschke (eds), *Universele Wereld Geschiednis*, vol VII (Uitgeverij Scheltens & Giltay, The Hague).

With M. M. Goldsmith (eds), Sir Robert Filmer, *An Advertisement to Jury-Men on England, Touching Witches* (1653) (The Rota, Exeter).

With M. M. Goldsmith (eds), Richard Overton, *An Arrow Against All Tyrants* (1646) (The Rota, Exeter).

With M. M. Goldsmith (eds), John Evelyn, *Fumifugium, or the Inconvenience of the Aer and Smoak of London* (1661) (The Rota, Exeter).

1977 With M. M. Goldsmith (eds), John Garfield, *The Wandring Whore: A Dialogue* (1660–1) (The Rota, Exeter).

With M. M. Goldsmith (eds), Benjamin Spenser, *Vox Civitatis or London's Complaint against her Children in the Countrey* (1625) (The Rota, Exeter).

With M. M. Goldsmith (eds), Thomas Edwards, *Gangraena: Or a Catalogue and Discovery of Many of the Errours, Heresies, Blasphemies and Pernicious Practices of the Sectaries of this Time* (The Rota and University of Exeter, Exeter).

1978 'The tactics of the Commonwealthsmen in Richard Cromwell's parliament', in D. H. Pennington and K. Thomas (eds), *Puritans and Revolutionaries: Essays in Seventeenth-Century History presented to Christopher Hill* (Clarendon Press, Oxford), pp. 284–309.

'The Mirror of Princes: Crown and Commonwealth under the Tudors and Stuarts', in *The Monarchy: Silver Jubilee Lectures 1977*, (Exeter University and Devon Library Services, Exeter), pp. 11–18.

With M. M. Goldsmith (eds), Marchamont Nedham, *A True State of the Case of the Commonwealth* (1654) (The Rota, Exeter).

With M. M. Goldsmith (eds), Lady Eleanor Davies, *The Restitution of Prophecy* (1651) (The Rota, Exeter).

With M. M. Goldsmith (eds), *A Book of Fruits and Flowers* (1653) (The Rota, Exeter).

1979 *Tracts and Pamphlets: An aspect of the impact of printing in its first two centuries* (Wynkyn de Worde Society, London), 18 pp.

'Die Englische Revolution', in G. Mann and A. Nitschke, *Weltgeschichte–Eine Universalgeschichte*, vol VII (Prisma Verlag, Gutersloh), pp. 231–74.

The Great Rebellion 1642–60, 4th edn (Batsford, London), x + 326 pp.

With M. M. Goldsmith (eds), John Dury, *Considerations Concerning the Present Engagement* (1649) (The Rota, Exeter).

'The Humanity of Oliver Cromwell', address given on Cromwell's Green, Westminster, 2 September 1978, *Cromwelliana* (1979), pp. 1–3.

With M. M. Goldsmith (eds), William Sherlock, *The Case of the Allegiance due to Soveraign Powers* (1691) (The Rota, Exeter).

With M. M. Goldsmith (eds), *The Life of Mr Thomas Hobbes of Malmesbury written by himself* (1680) (The Rota, Exeter).

1980 'The short and troublesome reign of Richard IV', *History Today*, 30 (March 1980), pp. 11–15.

Introduction to T. P. S. Woods, *Prelude to Civil War 1642: Mr Justice Malet and the Kentish Petitions* (Michael Russell, Salisbury), pp. ix–xi.

Preface to T. A. Reuter (ed.), *The Greatest Englishman: Essays on St Boniface and the church at Crediton* (Paternoster Press, Exeter).

1981 'The speeches of Oliver Cromwell', *Cromwelliana* (1980–1), pp. 35–41.
'Into Another Mould': Aspects of the Interregnum (ed.), Exeter Studies in History No. 3 (University of Exeter, Exeter): 'Introduction: the Interregnum', pp. 1–4, and 'Union and disunion in the British Isles 1637–60', pp. 5–23.

1982 'Oliver Cromwell: man and movie', *Cromwelliana* (1981–2), pp. 25–9.
'Oliver Cromwell 1599–1658', and 'Richard Cromwell 1626–1712', in R. L. Greaves and R. Zaller (eds), *Biographical Dictionary of British Radicals in the Seventeenth Century* (Harvester Press, Brighton), vol I, pp. 196–9 and 200–1.

1983 *The Great Rebellion 1642–60*, 5th edn (Batsford, London), x + 326 pp.
'Reading history: 1649–60, the Interregnum', *History Today*, 33 (May 1983), pp. 47–50.
'John Lambert', in R. L. Greaves and R. Zaller (eds), *Biographical Dictionary of British Radicals in the Seventeenth Century* (Harvester Press, Brighton), vol II, pp. 167–70.

1984 'John Thurloe', in R. L. Greaves and R. Zaller (eds), *Biographical Dictionary of British Radicals in the Seventeenth Century* (Harvester Press, Brighton), vol III, pp. 237–8.
'Sir William Waller', in R. L. Greaves and R. Zaller (eds), *Biographical Dictionary of British Radicals in the Seventeenth Century* (Harvester Press, Brighton), vol III, pp. 281–2.
With M. M. Goldsmith (eds), Thomas Gainsford, *Vox Spiritus or Sir Walter Rawleigh's Ghost* (1621) (The Rota, Exeter 1984).

1986 Preface to A. S. P. Woodhouse, *Puritanism and Liberty: being the Army Debates, 1647–9*, 3rd edn (Dent, London).
'The Debate on the "Other House" in Richard Cromwell's Parliament', in R. Ollard and P. Tudor-Craig (eds), *For Veronica Wedgwood These* (Collins, London), pp. 188–203.
The Monmouth Rising: Aspects of the 1685 Rebellion in The West Country (ed.), (Devon Books, Exeter). Introduction.

Notes on Contributors

ROBERT ASHTON has been Professor of English History at the University of East Anglia since 1963. He is a former pupil of R. H. Tawney and the author of *The Crown and the Money Market 1603–40* (1960), *James I by his Contemporaries* (1969), *The English Civil War: Conservatism and Revolution 1603–49* (1978), *The City and the Court 1603–43* (1979) and *Reformation and Revolution 1558–1660* (1984).

BARRY COWARD is Lecturer in History at Birkbeck College, London and author of *The Stuart Age* (1980) and *The Stanleys, Lords Stanley and Earls of Derby* (1983).

ANTHONY FLETCHER is Reader in History at Sheffield University, and the author of *Tudor Rebellions* (1968), *A County Community in Peace and War* (1975), *The Outbreak of the English Civil War* (1981) and editor with John Stevenson of *Order and Disorder in Early Modern England* (1985).

PETER GAUNT's research was supervised by Ivan Roots and he received his doctorate at Exeter in 1983. In 1984 he was postdoctoral fellow in the Department of History at the Victoria University of Wellington, New Zealand. He is currently working on a number of projects within the field of central government during the Protectorate.

MAURICE GOLDSMITH taught at Columbia University and has been Professor of Political Theory at the University of Exeter since 1969. He collaborated with Ivan Roots in establishing *The Rota* to reprint British tracts of the Stuart era. He has written a number of articles on seventeenth- and eighteenth-century political thought, as well as *Hobbes's Science of Politics* (1966) and *Private Vices, Public Benefits: Bernard Mandeville's Social and Political Thought* (1985).

CHRISTOPHER HILL was formerly Master of Balliol College, Oxford. His books include *Puritanism and Revolution* (1958), *Century of Revolution* (1961), *Reformation to Industrial Revolution* (1967), *God's Englishman* (1970), *The World Turned Upside Down* (1972) and *Change and Continuity in Seventeenth-century England* (1974).

COLIN JONES is Lecturer in History at Exeter University. He has published on a wide variety of aspects of French social history between the seventeenth and nineteenth centuries. He has edited *Contre Retz. Sept pamphlets du temps de la Fronde* (1981) and is author of *Charity and 'bienfaiss-ance'. The treatment of the poor in the Montpellier region 1740–1815* (1982). He is General Editor of the Exeter Studies in History.

DEREK MASSARELLA is Associate Professor in the Faculty of Economics, Chuo University, Tokyo, and Editor of *Transactions of the Asiatic Society of Japan*. He was an undergraduate at Exeter University before going on to do a DPhil at York on army politics 1647–60, and an article based on this work was published in Ivan Roots's *'Into Another Mould'* in 1981. He is currently working on Euro–Japanese relations in the early modern period.

P. R. NEWMAN has published *Royalist Officers in England and Wales 1642–60* (1981), *Marston Moor* (1981) and *An Atlas of the English Civil War* (1985).

DONALD PENNINGTON was formerly Fellow of Balliol College, Oxford. He is the author of *Members of the Long Parliament* (1954), with D. Brunton; *The Committee of Stafford* (1957), with Ivan Roots; *Seventeenth Century Europe* (1970); and editor with K. Thomas of *Puritans and Revolutionaries* (1978).

PAUL PINCKNEY is Associate Professor of History at the University of Tennessee, Knoxville, and worked with Ivan Roots on the Burton Diary project. He has published several articles on the 1650s and has just completed the manuscript of a book on 'Cromwellian Politics and the Major Generals'.

STEPHEN ROBERTS was a postgraduate student under Ivan Roots and was awarded his doctorate in 1980. Formerly tutor in the Department of History and Archaeology at Exeter University, he is currently tutor/organizer for the West Midlands District of the WEA. He is the author of *Recovery and Restoration in an English County: Devon local administration, 1646–70* (1985), and a number of articles on seventeenth-century British local administration.

JIM SHARPE was tutor in the Department of History at Exeter University in 1972 and is now Lecturer in History at York University. His main interests are in early modern social history, especially the history of crime, on which subject he has published *Defamation and Sexual Slander* (1980), *Crime in Seventeenth-Century England* (1983), and *Crime in Early Modern England* (1984).

AUSTIN WOOLRYCH was Professor of History at Lancaster University from its foundation in 1964 until 1985, and Visiting Fellow of All Souls 1981–2. His publications include *Battles of the English Civil War* (1961), *Complete Prose Works of John Milton*, vol 7 (1980), *Commonwealth to Protectorate* (1982) and *England without a King (1983)*. A Study of the General Council of the Army entitled *Soldiers and Statesmen* is in the press.

Index